INSIGHT GUIDES

BARCELONA

HOW TO USE THIS BOOK

This book is carefully structured both to convey an understanding of the city and its culture and to guide readers through its attractions and activities:

◆ The Best Of section at the front of the book helps you to prioritize. The first spread contains all the Top Sights, while the Editor's Choice details unique experiences, the best buys or other recommendations.

◆ To understand Barcelona, you need to know something of its past. The city's history and culture are described in authoritative essays written by specialists in their fields who have lived in and documented the city for many years.

◆ The Places section details all the attractions worth seeing. The main places of interest are coordinated by number with the maps.

◆ Each chapter includes lists of recommended shops, Restaurants, Bars and Cafés.

◆ Photographs throughout the book are chosen not only to illustrate geography and buildings, but also to convey the moods of the city and the life of its people.

◆ The Travel Tips section includes all the practical information you will need, divided into five key sections: Transport, Accommodation, Activities (including festivals, nightlife and sports), an A–Z of practical tips and Language.

◆ A detailed street atlas is included at the back of the book, with all hotels, Restaurants, Bars and Cafes plotted for your convenience.

PLACES AND SIGHTS

Chapters are **colour-coded** for ease of use. Each neighbourhood has a designated colour corresponding to the orientation map on the inside front cover.

A locator map pinpoints the specific area covered in each chapter.

A four-colour map shows the area covered in the chapter, with the main sights and attractions coordinated by number with the text.

Margin tips provide extra snippets of information, whether it's a practical tip, a whimsical quote, an historical fact or advice on shopping and eating.

PHOTO FEATURES

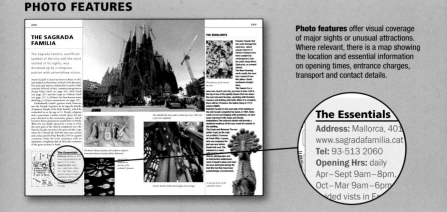

Photo features offer visual coverage of major sights or unusual attractions. Where relevant, there is a map showing the location and essential information on opening times, entrance charges, transport and contact details.

The Essentials

Address: Mallorca, 401
www.sagradafamilia.cat
Tel: 93-513 2060
Opening Hrs: daily
Apr–Sept 9am–8pm,
Oct–Mar 9am–6pm
~~ided vists in E~~

SHOPPING AND RESTAURANT LISTINGS

Shopping listings provide details of the best shops in each area. **Restaurant listings** give the establishment's contact details, opening times and price category, followed by a useful review. Bars and cafés are also covered here. The coloured dot and grid reference refers to the atlas section at the back of the book.

Gran Bodega Saltó
Blesa, 36
http://bodegasalto.net
[🔵 p284, D3]
This wonderful old *bodega* has become an essential stop in Poble Sec's increasingly trendy scene. Like an unofficial cultural centre, its quirky decoration, Sunday lunchtime *vermut* and live music attract a colourful crowd.
Sirvent

TRAVEL TIPS

From the Airport

Barcelona is only 12km (7 m~~iles~~)
from El Prat airport and is ea~~sily~~
~~re~~ached by train, bus or taxi
~~?~~ Trains to Sants and Pa~~sseig~~
~~de Gràcia~~ depart every 30
~~minutes~~

Travel Tips provide all the practical knowledge you'll need before and during your trip: how to get there, getting around, where to stay and what to do. The A–Z section is a handy summary of practical information, arranged alphabetically.

Contents

THE BEST OF BARCELONA: TOP ATTRACTIONS

At a glance, everything you can't afford to miss in Barcelona, from Gaudí's Sagrada Família and Casa Milà to the Miró Foundation and the beaches.

▷ **Palau de la Música Catalana.** A World Heritage site, the Palau is a modernista dream. See page 125.

△ **La Boqueria.** This covered market on La Rambla selling wonderful fresh produce is one of Europe's most attractive markets. See page 97.

▷ **Sagrada Família.** Gaudí's glorious, unfinished cathedral. See page 204.

△ **La Rambla.** Barcelona's famous tree-lined avenue is a good starting point for any visit. See page 93.

◁ **Museu Picasso.** One of the most popular attractions in Barcelona, the city where the artist grew up. See page 128.

▷ **Beaches.** Barcelona's waterfront has become the city's playground. See page 170.

▽ **Fundació Joan Miró.** A luminous space that displays Miró's works to their best advantage. See page 184.

▷ **Park Güell.** Colourful ceramics in the park Gaudí designed to be a garden suburb. See page 220.

▽ **Santa Maria del Mar.** The city's most beautiful church. See page 129.

▽ **La Pedrera.** The 'witch-scarer' chimneys of Casa Milà, known as La Pedrera. See page 197.

THE BEST OF BARCELONA: EDITOR'S CHOICE

Breathtaking views and fantastic food, top museums and shops, family outings and money-saving tips personally selected by our editor.

BEST VIEWS

Barcelona Bus Turístic. Worth every cent to see the city from the open top deck of the Tourist Bus. See page 246.

Torre de Collserola. The lookout platform on the 10th floor of this communications tower gives you a 360 degree view of Catalonia, including, on a good day, the Pyrenees. See page 213.

Transbordador Aeri. Get the city into perspective by gliding over the port in the cable car from Montjuïc, the Torre de Jaume I or the Torre Sant Sebastià. See pages 159 and 186.

Eclipse Bar, W Hotel. Slip into this slick bar on the 26th floor for panoramic views of the waterfront and city, best at sunset. See page 160.

La Pedrera. Glimpse the Sagrada Família and other Eixample monuments from a new angle from the roof. See page 197.

La Pedrera.

BEST BUILDINGS

CaixaForum. An award-winning *modernista* textile factory converted into a cultural centre. See page 177.

Palau de la Música Catalana. Laden with Catalan symbolism and ornamental detail, Domènech i Montaner's extraordinary concert hall is the paragon of *modernisme*. See page 125.

La Pedrera. If you see no other Gaudí building, don't miss this 1910 apartment block. It gives an insight into the brilliance of the city's most famous architect. See page 197.

Torre de Martí I. A medieval watchtower in the Plaça del Rei, in the Barri Gòtic. See page 119.

Pavelló Mies van der Rohe. Less is more in this seminal building of the Modern Movement, designed as the German Pavilion for the 1929 International Exposition. See page 176.

Torre Agbar. The headquarters of a water company at Plaça de les Glòries, this sleek tower is a 21st-century addition to the Barcelona skyline. See page 191.

Santa Maria del Mar. A beautiful Catalan Gothic church, with stunning stained-glass windows, that will make your spirit soar. See page 129.

Torre Agbar.

BARCELONA FOR FAMILIES

Out and about. Barcelona is child-friendly in true Latin tradition. Locals, shops and restaurants welcome children, street performers abound and the many traffic-free areas in the Old Town are good for bikes and skateboards.
Aquàrium. One of the largest aquariums in Europe. See page 156.
Beaches. Somorrostro and Nova Icària beaches are sheltered

At the Aquàrium.

by the Port Olímpic and have climbing frames. See page 163.
Ciutadella. Park with rowing boats, ducks, picnic areas, play areas and a great zoo. See page 132.
Club Nataciò Atlètic Barceloneta. Swimming club with an outdoor pool shallow enough for children. Plaça del Mar, 1. See page 159.
Granja Viader. A magnificent milk bar. Good for thick hot chocolate and the nutty drink *orxata* in summer. Xuclà, 4. See page 107.
Tibidabo. A 100-year-old funfair overlooking the city. See page 215.
Concerts and theatre. The Auditori concert hall, the CaixaForum, Fundació Miró and the Liceu opera house run regular family programmes.

In the Fundació Miró shop.

BEST MUSEUMS

CCCB. Technically a cultural centre, this wonderful space stages intriguing exhibitions as well as diverse festivals – film, music and performance. See page 143.
CosmoCaixa. The born-again science museum has hands-on exhibits for all ages, plus a re-creation of the Amazon. See page 217.
Fundació Miró. Flooded with Mediterranean light, this purpose-built museum has

one of the largest collections of Miró's work. See page 184.
Museu Nacional d'Art de Catalunya. The National Museum houses a millennium of Catalan art, from its famed Romanesque collection to 20th-century photography. See page 179.
Museu Picasso. Comprehensive display of Picasso's startling early work and some later pieces, in five medieval palaces. See page 128.

TOP SQUARES

Plaça del Rei. The essence of medieval Barcelona. Best early in the morning or on summer nights, when it is sometimes a concert venue. See page 118.
Plaça Reial. Daytime bustle, petty crime and night-time partying don't detract from this handsome 19th-century square. See page 100.
Plaça Sant Felip Neri. The very heart of the Gothic Quarter. To feel

its peace, wait for the children in the adjacent school to return to class. See page 113.
Plaça del Sol. One of several fine squares in the district of Gràcia, it is a meeting place for young and old. See page 209.
Plaça Vicenç Martorell. Just off La Rambla in El Raval and popular for its terrace cafés and playground. See page 141.

In Plaça Reial.

Revellers at Correfoc festival.

FLAVOURS OF BARCELONA

La Boqueria. All the food markets are a trip for the senses, but this one takes first prize for its colours, tropical flavours, Mediterranean aromas and overwhelming vitality. Also includes several good restaurant-bars. See page 97.

La Seu. An indulgent range of farmhouse cheeses from all over Spain, kept to perfection. Tastings take place on Saturday mornings. Also offers excellent olive oils. See page 120.

J. Múrria. A traditional small grocer's shop in the Eixample with its original painted glass facade and a mouthwatering array of goods, from the finest hams and cheeses to the most expensive wines. Roger de Llúria, 85. See page 200.

Pa amb tomàquet. When the bread is fresh, the tomatoes hand-picked and the olive oil cold-pressed, this traditional accompaniment is a meal in itself and cannot be bettered.

BEST BARCELONAN TRADITIONS

Correfoc. Part of the La Mercè festivities, this is the wildest of celebrations, when fire-spitting dragons and their accompanying devils threaten to engulf in flames anyone fool enough to taunt them.

Dancing. Barcelonans of all ages love to dance the *sardana*, the Catalan national dance.

Fiestas. Whether it's buying red roses on the day of Sant Jordi, the patron saint, or roasting chestnuts in the autumn, the people of Barcelona continue their traditions with enthusiasm.

Going out for breakfast. Sitting up at a classic steel bar with your favourite daily newspaper, fresh crusty sandwich and piping hot coffee is a cherished part of life.

Paella. Meeting up with friends or family for a paella on the beach or in the woods is possible even on sunny winter days, and always a treat. This is a dish often cooked by the man of the house.

Sunday lunches. Not a Sunday goes by without Catalan families reuniting for a big family meal, usually in the grandparents' house. Someone will bring a dessert, fresh from the pastry shop and wrapped up with paper and ribbon.

Weekend escapes. Catalans work hard all week, but weekends are sacrosanct. They escape to the ski slopes in winter and the beaches in summer.

Jamon for sale at La Boqueria.

BEST BUYS

Leatherwear. Spain is still a good place to buy shoes and bags. The best areas are Portal de l'Angel, Rambla de Catalunya, Passeig de Gràcia and Diagonal.

Fashion. Apart from the ubiquitous Zara and Desigual, more upmarket Spanish designers include Adolfo Domínguez and Antonio Miró. Independent boutiques are mostly in the Old Town.

Bric-à-brac and an- tiques. Visit Els Encants flea market in Glòries, the antiques market in the Cathedral Square and the art market in Plaça Sant Josep Oriol.

Interior design. From Vinçon in Passeig de Gracia to Cosas de Casa in Plaça Sant Josep Oriol, the city is full of design ideas.

Wine and edibles. From cava to handmade chocolates. For more information, see page 66.

In a branch of Desigual.

La Font Màgica.

FREE BARCELONA

La Font Màgica. Designed for the 1929 exhibition, the Magic Fountain offers free *son et lumière* displays most of the year. See page 176.

Open-air museum. The side streets off Passeig de Gràcia and Rambla de Catalunya are like a museum of *modernisme*: buildings, balconies, stained-glass windows and carved doors can all be appreciated as you wander around the neighbourhood. See pages 193 and 195.

Neighbourhood fiestas. Hardly a month goes by without a fiesta with giants, parades and *castells* (human pyramids).

Street performers. Musicians, tango dancers, opera singers – the streets of the Old Town are full of free entertainment – although they all appreciate a donation in the hat.

MONEY-SAVING TIPS

Articket The ticket that gets you into six art centres for around €30 is good value. It includes CCCB, MACBA, Museu Picasso, Fundació Joan Miró, Fundació Tàpies and the Museu Nacional d'Art de Catalunya. Purchase online for a discount (www.barcelonaturisme.com) or at a tourist office.

Menú del dia Most restaurants offer a set menu at lunchtime, with three courses and a drink at a price well below the sum of its parts. It's a good idea to eat your main meal at lunchtime and snack in the evening, although the cost of tapas can add up.

Museum entrance Some museums (Picasso, History of Catalonia, Museu d'Història de Barcelona (MUHBA), CosmoCaixa, DHUB, Museu Nacional) can be visited free on the first Sunday of the month, and all municipal museums (Disseny Hub, Picasso, MUHBA) are free on Sunday afternoons. Others have a reduced rate on certain days, e.g. the MACBA on a Wednesday. The CaixaForum now charges a small fee and the Catalunya Caixa exhibition space in La Pedrera is free.

T10 card A card of 10 journeys for use on metro, bus, train or tram for just under €10. If you transfer from metro to bus, tram, funicular or inner-city stations of the FGC (the Generalitat-run suburban train) within an hour and a quarter of leaving the metro (or vice versa) it is considered part of the same journey, and the ticket is not repunched when it is passed through the machine.

You can also travel from one bus line to another, and to train lines as far as stations within Zone 1, like the airport, and Castelldefels beach in the south. Excellent value.

Sunbathing on Barceloneta beach.

Plaça Reial at night.

AN IRREPRESSIBLE CITY

A potent mix of traditional architecture and
contemporary design, long days of sunshine and
never-ending nightlife has turned this spirited
city into one of the world's top destinations.

Barcelona shot to international fame in 1992, having designed and successfully managed one of the most spectacular Olympic Games of modern history. For years before, though, it had been regarded as Spain's most cosmopolitan city and in medieval times had been the hub of a huge Mediterranean domain. The canny Catalans seized the opportunity of the Games to bring the city up to speed after years of suppression under the Franco regime. The momentum of its success launched the city towards the 21st century with efficient new services, cutting-edge architecture, a born-again waterfront and, above all, a redeveloped urban environment with public art for its citizens to enjoy.

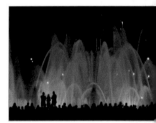

Font Magica de Montjuic.

As the grey veil of the dictatorship lifted, the city's treasures came into the limelight, from the huge stones and watchtowers of its Roman past through its glorious medieval palaces to its extraordinary modernista architecture by Gaudí and colleagues, which has given Barcelona such a distinctive stamp. Wandering through the narrow lanes of the Gothic Quarter or pacing up the elegant Passeig de Gràcia, lined with exclusive shops and some of the jewels of the modernista period, the energy that shaped this city is palpable. An endemic Catalan spirit has coursed through its turbulent history, resisting oppression and proudly standing out of line. That the Catalan bourgeoisie accepted the revolutionary and dream-like designs of Gaudí showed some daring. The same driving force is behind the current bid for independence from Spain as the nationalist flags adorning the middle-class balconies of the Eixample testify.

Lichtenstein's El Cap de Barcelona.

Today's visitor can enjoy Barcelona on many levels, soaking in its history while having a coffee in a quiet square in the Old Town or poring over exhibits in one of the many museums. See the works of leading 20th-century artists linked to the city, like Miró, Picasso or Tàpies, then shop in indie boutiques in El Born or taste the gourmet tapas of award-winning chefs. If you coincide with one of the city's many festes, you can run with devils and fire-spitting dragons or indulge in festive food. When the mix becomes too heady, take time out on one of Barcelona's nine golden beaches and sip a cocktail as the sun goes down.

THE BARCELONANS

Life in Barcelona is characterised by dynamic commercial activity and a vibrant social scene – seasoned with a dash of cosmopolitanism thanks to the many outsiders who come here to work and play.

Catalans in general, and Barcelonans in particular, are famed for their business acumen, passion for work and economic ability. The laid-back *mañana* attitude of the old Spanish stereotype scarcely exists in Barcelona. But then, as Catalans never tire of telling you, Catalonia and its capital are *not* Spain. In Barcelona, 10 o'clock means 10 o'clock, not 11.30. '*Anem per feina*' is a common expression, once pressed into service as a Catalan national-ist election slogan: 'Let's go to work.'

Market trading

Like England, Catalonia has been dubbed a nation of shopkeepers, and indeed, Barcelona has a staggering number of shops. This is not so surprising when you consider its mercantile background, going back to the Phoenicians. This bourgeois city was built up through fam-ily enterprise, and has now become one of *the* places to shop. The slogan once sported by car-rier bags of the famous Vinçon design store puts it in a nutshell: 'I shop, therefore I am.'

Barcelona exudes an air of prosperity, and is no longer a particularly cheap city. The stand-ard of living is high, but it has to be paid for, and the work ethic is especially noticeable if you come here from elsewhere in Spain. You can see it in the comparatively early closing

Fresh produce at La Boqueria market.

(by Spanish standards) of bars and restaurants. Efficiency, punctuality and reliability are of the essence. Barcelona works *very* hard.

In Andalucía they have a saying: 'The Andalucian works to live, the Catalan lives to work.' But it is not as straightforward as this. For how do we square this view of Catalans with the wild celebrations of La Mercè, the week of festivities around 24 September, the day of Barcelona's patroness, when giants and fan-tastical creatures parade around on stilts, free concerts are put on with no regard for cost, and fiery dragons career through the crowds in the hair-raising *correfoc* or 'fire-running'?

> Stylish young executives cut a dash as they speed around the city on mopeds, screeching to a halt on pavements as they race into meetings or business lunches.

Young Barcelonans by the beach.

Prudence versus impulse

The Catalans call these apparently contradictory facets of their character *el seny* and *la rauxa*. The former is a combination of prudence, profound common sense and good judgement, the latter a fit, impulse or emotional outburst: a kind of attack of wildness.

You can see both sides of the Catalan character in the way they drive. Unlike in other flamboyant cities, the traffic in Barcelona is orderly. Drivers stop on red, and go on green. But if you hesitate a split second, or worse still, stall, you'll be deafened by furious honking. When traffic gets really snarled up, *rauxa* takes over. Patience is no longer a virtue: you must get going, be on the mark, have your wits about you.

Barcelonans may work until they're blue in the face, but they're still a Mediterranean people: creative, fun-loving, noisy and gregarious. As Barcelona's celebrated Olympic Games of

THE CATALAN LANGUAGE

First lesson to visitors: Catalan is not a historical relic, surviving only in the countryside. It is spoken by some 6 million people in Catalonia, Valencia, the Balearics, Andorra, the Roussillon region of France and the town of Alghero in Sardinia, and Catalan-speakers form by far the largest linguistic community in Europe without their own state.

Catalan is a Romance language, like Castilian Spanish, French and Italian, but with a sharp, staccato quality that gives it a very distinctive sound. It was used in public life very early on, but absorption into the Spanish monarchy led to a downgrading of the language. Nevertheless, industrialisation and the rise of a native middle class in the 19th century provided a backdrop for Catalonia's cultural *Renaixença* or 'rebirth'. Literature, music and the Catalan press all flourished. This made the total shutdown after Franco's victory in 1939 all the harder to bear. Catalan was banned from public use, with penalties even for

speaking it on the street. A generation grew up unable to read or write in the language they spoke at home.

Catalans are intensely attached to their language, and whenever the pressure upon it has relaxed, Catalan has revived. So it was after Franco's death in 1975. Catalan and Castilian are now both official languages, but in practice Catalan is the primary language. The 'linguistic normalisation' undertaken by the Catalan government since 1980 has been a remarkable success, but also controversial, and the many ramifications of linguistic politics remain a constant local topic. All state schools teach exclusively in Catalan.

Barcelona itself remains a linguistic soup, since half or more of its population are Castilian-speakers. There are determined Catalan-only speakers, as well as their opposites; most people, though, want to get along, and readily hop back and forth.

In a fashionable La Ribera café.

1992 set out to show the world, Mediterranean high spirits and street life do not have to be synonymous with sloth and inefficiency, and Barcelonans are capable of first-class technology and efficiency without relinquishing any of their vibrancy and zest.

A clash of cultures

Barcelonans work hard all week, then sit in traffic jams every Friday afternoon so they can enjoy weekends by the sea or in the mountains. They have little time for the wishy-washy: theirs are the strong, bright primary colours of Miró. They are adventurous travellers, visiting the most remote corners of the world. They value initiative and pioneering enterprise. Barcelona is intensely involved internationally in science, education, ecology and other fields.

But they do come over as reserved and serious beside the many citizens originally from other parts of Spain, the migrants who flooded

> The key to the Barcelonans' unique exuberance is the 'passionate energy' noted by George Orwell in 1936 as he watched Barcelonan men, women and children build barricades in the war-torn city.

FOOTBALL CRAZY

Barcelona Football Club – Barça – was founded in 1899 by Hans Gamper, a Swiss living in Barcelona. One of its slogans is that it is més que un club – more than a club – but one of its special features is that it really is a club: its 105,000+ paid-up fans are members who vote for the board, not 'season-ticket holders'. This huge fan base comes from the whole of Catalonia, not just the city. Barça is a symbol of Catalonia, even when its stars are from Brazil, Argentina or Mali.

The club gained its curious political role as a champion of Catalan freedom during times when Catalan identity was blocked everywhere else, under Primo de Rivera in the 1920s and, far more intensely, under Franco. Stadium crowds are hard to censor, and the blue-and-maroon *(blaugrana)* flag of Barça became a substitute for the Catalan colours. Catalan emotions came to a head in meetings with Real Madrid, a symbol of the regime and right-wing Spain.

After the return of democracy, this kind of football politics did seem to fade for a while, and it even seemed possible that football could just be a game, but it has revived with vigour. Currently Barcelona has one of the best teams in the world, universally admired and flying higher than ever (see page 265).

in during the 1950s and 1960s in search of work. Coexistence has sometimes been a thorny matter, with ethnic, class and cultural differences all intertwined: the Catalan middle classes often take a dim view of the ebullient non-Catalan working class, and vice versa. Sometimes still referred to by the derogatory label *xarnegos* (the original meaning of which is a child of a Catalan and a non-Catalan), some of these 'other Barcelonans' form distinct communities, mostly in the outer neighbourhoods. Barcelona's *Feria de Abril* (April Fair), held in Parc del Fòrum near the beach, is no longer a pale, homesick imitation of the Andalucian original, but a big event in its own right that attracts nearly a million visitors. And, of course, the second and third generations of so-called *xarnegos* are Barcelona born and bred.

Barcelona Football Club is more than the city's main football team, it is one of Catalonia's flagship institutions (see box, page 21). It is also a force for local unity. Barcelonans and Catalans of all ages, classes, genders, shapes, sizes and even ethnic origins now happily unite to dance in the streets when Barça beats

Enjoying some Mediterranean sun.

A local enjoys a liqueur at a La Boqueria marketside bar.

Madrid or wins any kind of trophy. The red and gold of the Catalan flag combine with Barça's *blaugrana* in a swirling mass down La Rambla. Corks pop and cava sprays far into the night.

Peaceful coexistence, solidarity, citizen participation – these are just a few of the buzzwords

> Barcelonans love dashing around, being busy and generally having lots of irons in the fire. Ask them how they are and they'll say 'vaig de bòlit!' – 'I'm speeding!'

bandied about by Barcelona's policy-makers, and personified by the volunteers who give free Catalan classes to the ever-increasing immigrant community, determined to integrate them as new Catalans.

Barcelonans' identity

Like all good Mediterraneans, Barcelonans are a street people. All it takes is a few tables squeezed onto a postage stamp of pavement, and they'll sit for hours over their drinks and olives, apparently oblivious to the fumes and

Barcelona is home to many students.

filled with young foreigners who had come to defend democracy. In the 1960s, as the Spanish-language publishing capital, the city was home to intellectuals such as Gabriel García Márquez and Mario Vargas Llosa.

This foreign presence has grown massively since the 1990s. Irish pubs, Japanese restaurants and Pakistani groceries abound. Barcelona's popularity as a venue for international trade fairs and meetings makes for an exciting cosmopolitan buzz. As technology makes physical location less relevant, more foreigners are choosing Barcelona as a place in which to live, attracted by its climate and lifestyle.

Independence and tolerance

Catalan tradition places a high value on independence, both collective and personal. Their climate allows Barcelonans to live life outside. They are masters of sociability when out in the streets and squares, bars and restaurants; they engage fully in the community life of offices and shops, parks and sports fields. However, they are fiercely protective of their homes, their safe haven. This translates into a great respect

traffic noise. When it rains, the milling throngs leap into cars and taxis, causing the traffic to 'collapse', as they put it, in a cacophony of blasting horns.

One of the highest accolades a Barcelonan can receive is that he or she is *espavilat* or *espavilada*, which can be translated as awake or alert. This proactive zooming around encompasses not only work, but a host of other activities – from culture, shopping and social life to voluntary work, chauffeuring children, sports... you name it, Barcelonans do it with gusto.

Barcelonans are devoted to their traditions, as anyone witnessing them dancing the *sardana*, Catalonia's intricate dance, can testify (see box, page 25). Yet at the same time they are open to innovation. Creativity is part of the Catalan identity. Its traditions are bound up with Catalonia's defence of its identity as a nation – a cultured and tolerant nation that is open to new ideas and influences.

Seductive city

Barcelona has worked magic on foreigners as well. In his *Homage to Catalonia*, George Orwell chronicled the Barcelona of 1936,

Shooting hoops outside the university in El Raval.

Street musician.

Strolling down the Rambla at night.

for individual privacy – the Infanta Cristina of Spain (daughter of the King of Spain) lived in the Sarrià district for years, with no intrusive interest from locals.

Barcelona is also one of the most tolerant places in Spain. Gay and feminist movements were largely pioneered here, and alternative medicine, self-help and New Age culture thrive. The respect for creativity extends to eccentrics. Look at Gaudí: far from being the archetypal misunderstood artist, he was positively sought out and encouraged in his creative flights.

Above all, good humour rules. Walk through any Barcelona market. The stallholders have been up since dawn, buying stock, loading and unloading, cooking lentils, chickpeas and the like. Yet they're filled with good cheer, cracking jokes and gossiping, their talk peppered with endearments like *rei*, *reina*, *maco*, *maca*. They're shopkeepers to the core, but enjoy themselves.

Putting on a show

This good humour and flair for combining work, fun and creative imagination is the essence of life in Barcelona. On Carnival Thursday, for example, it's business as usual at the Boqueria market on La Rambla – but in fancy dress. A cardinal in full regalia blesses shoppers trundling their carts in and out. Ballet dancers, chest hair bristling from pink tutus, cart crates of potatoes. Plumed cavaliers slice chorizo, while Moorish princesses gut fish.

In the old districts of Gràcia and Sants locals work all year to prepare for their *festa*

> Barcelona is a meritocracy, with little regard for petty titles and nobility, but a huge respect for creativity.

major (annual fête) in mid-August. Entire streets are turned into decorative fantasies, with prizes for the best. Each street or square organises its own programme. Kids get puppet shows and hot chocolate parties; live salsa and rock bands play through the night. By day it's still business as usual, except you'll go shopping in *Jurassic Park*, or something out of the *Arabian Nights*.

A day of roses, books and dragons

The epitome of the Barcelona personality is the feast of Sant Jordi (St George), patron saint of Catalonia, on 23 April. This is also the anniversary of the deaths of Shakespeare and Cervantes, and is celebrated by giving gifts of books and roses. Sant Jordi is an inspired blend of culture, moneymaking and fun: it's not actually a public holiday, so everyone is sucked into the *festa* as they go about their business.

Bookshops set up stalls on La Rambla and in streets and squares, and give discounts. TV shows interview authors on La Rambla. It's a field day, too, for florists and hawkers, who sell roses in metro stations. Children in Catalan national dress greet their parents at school gates with paper roses and paintings of expiring dragons. Later, as men hurry home, each one bears a red rose beautifully wrapped and tied with red-and-yellow ribbon, and record book sales figures appear on the late-night news.

IN THE RING: DANCING THE SARDANA

The *sardana* is Catalonia's national dance, one of the region's most recognisable symbols. In its present form it grew out of the 19th-century *Renaixença*, when Catalans rediscovered their cultural identity. No festival is complete without it.

In Barcelona *sardanes* are danced in the cathedral square each Sunday at noon, Saturday at 6.30pm and Wednesday at 7pm, and at weekends there is a *sardana* school for children in Plaça de Catalunya. The band, the *cobla*, is unique to the dance: the leader plays a *flabiol*, a three-holed pipe, and a *tabal*, a small drum strapped to his elbow. Woodwind instruments are also traditional –

especially the *tenora*, the special Catalan clarinet, while the brass section is more conventional. Each tune lasts about 10 minutes, and just as you think it is dying away, it starts up anew.

As the music gets going, a few people in the crowd start to dance, linking hands to form a small circle. Soon others join in, making their own circles or joining existing ones, until the whole square is filled with dancers, solemnly counting the short sedate steps, which suddenly change to longer, bouncy ones. True aficionados wear espadrilles with coloured ribbons, but most people dance in their ordinary shoes, be they Sunday best or trainers.

FIESTA FEVER

The Barcelonans' reputation as sober workaholics is seriously undermined when one of the city's many annual festivals erupts onto the streets and the crowds come out to play.

Hardly a month passes in Barcelona without at least one excuse to party, usually a *festa major*, *celebrating a patron saint of the city or* one of its *neighbourhoods*, which calls for a public holiday, enormous family meals, flowing cava and noisy antics in the streets late into the night. With the return of democracy in the post-Franco era the Catalans have enjoyed resurrecting many customs that were repressed during the dictatorship.

Depending on the *festa*'s status, it will probably entail dancing *gegants* (giants), *dracs* (dragons), *dimonis* (devils) and legendary beasts, plus processions of dignitaries and mounted guards (*guardia urbana*), *castells* (human towers) and *sardanes* (the traditional Catalan dance) in public squares, which are taken over by rock or jazz bands at night. There is nearly always an air raid of fireworks.

There are also more demure festivals, such as the Fira de Sant Ponç (11 May), when medicinal herbs, honey and crystallised fruits are sold all along Carrer Hospital, in the Raval district. At the other extreme are the wild festivals like La Mercè, the *festa major* in September celebrating the city's patroness, which consists of a whole week of uproarious fun culminating in the *correfoc*, a pyromaniac's dream. Santa Eulàlia, affectionately known as Laia, is the other patroness whose party is in February and mostly focused on children remembering the tender age at which the saint was martyred. It is also worth looking out for the numerous cultural festivals, including the Grec, a month-long summer festival of music and the arts, or other music festivals themed on jazz, flamenco or ancient music.

Fire devils at the climax of the correfoc.

Fireworks over the Font Màgica in Montjuïc.

The five-year-old anxeneta crowning a five-storey or more castell is the most breathtaking and unmissable moment of a festa.

OTHER FESTIVAL HIGHLIGHTS

A performance at the Mercè fiesta.

BAM Barcelona Acció Musical is now an established part of the Mercè fiesta in September, providing free music concerts in locations around the city, from Plaça Reial to the Parc del Fòrum.

Castanyada An autumnal festival held around All Saints' Day (1 November) in homes, schools and public squares. Roast chestnuts and sweet potatoes are eaten, followed by *panellets* (small almond-based cakes) with muscatel sweet wine.

Grec For over 35 years the city has held this festival of music and the arts, using locations all over the city. Runs throughout July.

L'Ou com Balla Often missed, this low-key celebration of Corpus Christi is one of the most delightful: an egg dances in the beautifully decorated fountains of the medieval courtyards of the Gothic Quarter.

Sant Jordi celebrates St George, the patron saint of Catalonia, on 23 April. According to legend, the blood of the slain dragon transmutes into a rose. Men and women exchange gifts of books and roses, as this is also the date of Cervantes's anniversary.

La Mercè is the festival to beat all festivals when the city celebrates its patroness, Mercè, for a whole week around 24 September. With fireworks, devils and concerts by night, castells (human pyramids, see left), gegants (giants) and dracs (dragons) by day, there's something for everyone.

Each neighbourhood has its own festa major. One of the most popular is in Gràcia in mid-August, when neighbours get together to decorate their streets elaborately and bands play late into the night.

Books for sale on Sant Jordi.

DECISIVE DATES

A statue remnant from the ruins of Empòrion.

Early History: c.700 BC–AD 415

c.700 BC
The Iberians settle in the fertile area between the Rivers Llobregat and Besòs.

c.600 BC
Greek ships appear off the Catalan coast, and found the city of Empòrion on the Costa Brava.

Roman walls in the Barri Gòtic.

c.300 BC
The Carthaginians occupy parts of Catalonia.

264–200 BC
In the Punic Wars between Rome and Carthage, the Romans capture the area around the future Barcelona in about 200 BC.

c.15 BC
Roman soldiers found Barcelona as a small town on the road between Rome and Tarraco (Tarragona), during the reign of the Emperor Augustus. The colony's full name is Julia Augusta Faventia Paterna Barcino.

c. AD 300
Roman city walls built.

415
The Visigoths enter Spain and capture Barcelona. Their leader Ataülf makes it his capital, but this later moves to Toledo.

The marriage of Count Berenguer and Petronella.

Moors, Franks and the Catalan-Aragonese Monarchy: 711–1469

711
The Moors invade Spain and capture Barcelona in 713.

801
The Franks under Louis the Pious take Barcelona and found the Marca Hispànica (Spanish March) in what would become Catalonia.

c.880
Wilfred the Hairy *(Guifré el Pilós)*, Count of Ripoll, unifies the Catalan counties and establishes the House of Barcelona, a dynasty that lasts 500 years.

985
Al-Mansur, Grand Vizier of the Caliph of Córdoba, sacks Barcelona.

988
Count Borrell II renounces all obligations to the kings of France after receiving no help against Al-Mansur, making Catalonia effectively independent.

1150
Count Berenguer IV of Barcelona marries Petronella, heiress to the throne of Aragón, forming the joint Catalan-Aragonese monarchy.

c.1190
The *Usatges*, the Catalan legal code, is compiled and written in Catalan.

1213
Count-King Pere I is killed at the battle of Muret in Languedoc, and loses lands in southern France.

1229
Jaume I takes Mallorca, first of a series of major conquests that led to dominance in the Mediterranean.

1274
Barcelona's city government, the Consell de Cent, is established.

13th–14th century
The Catalan-Aragonese monarchy extends its power to Sardinia and Sicily. Barcelona's maritime law, the *Llibre del Consolat del Mar*, governs sea trade. Splendid buildings go up in Barcelona's Barri Gòtic.

1347–50
Black Death kills half Barcelona's population.

1359
Les Corts Catalanes or Catalan Parliament is established, with a council, the Generalitat de Catalunya, to administer finances.

The 1714 siege of Barcelona.

1391
Anti-Jewish pogroms in Barcelona and throughout Aragón and Castile.

1462–73
Catalan civil war.

Imperial Spain: 1469–1808

1469
Fernando II of Aragón marries Queen Isabel I of Castile, uniting all the Spanish Christian kingdoms in one inheritance.

1492
Islamic Granada falls, Columbus discovers America, and all Jews are expelled from all the Spanish kingdoms.

1522
Charles V denies Catalans permission to trade directly with the American colonies, insisting they can only do so via Seville.

1640
After the governments of King Felipe IV demand Catalonia contribute more to the Thirty Years War,

Catalans rise in revolt in the War of the Reapers *(Guerra dels Segadors)*, and the Generalitat tries to place the country under the authority of French king Louis XIII. Spanish troops are unable to recapture Barcelona until 1652.

1659
In the Treaty of the Pyrenees, all of Catalonia north of the Pyrenees – Roussillon and Perpignan – is ceded to France.

1702–14
Barcelona sides with the Habsburg Archduke Charles in the War of the Spanish Succession, against the French Bourbon Felipe V. French and Spanish troops take the city after a year-long siege on 11 September 1714.

1715–16
The victorious Felipe V issues his decrees of *Nova Planta*, abolishing the remaining Catalan institutions and establishing Spain as a single, centralised state. In Barcelona half of

A panoramic view of the Barcelona Exposition, 1929.

La Ribera district is destroyed to make space for a fortress, the Ciutadella.

1808–14
Napoleon's troops occupy most of Spain, including Barcelona. Catalans rise up against the French. Experiments are made in democratic government, but when King Fernando VII is restored in 1814 he only seeks to reinstate the absolute monarchy.

The Modern Era
1814 onwards
Barcelona's trade and industry steadily expands, and from the 1830s it has the first steam-driven factories in Spain.

1836–8
Dissolution of most of Barcelona's monasteries, opening up large areas for new building.

1842
Barcelona is bombarded from Montjuïc to suppress a radical revolt.

1848
Spain's first rail line is built from Barcelona to Mataró.

1854–6
The Ciutadella and the medieval city walls are demolished.

1860
The building of the city's grid (Eixample), designed by Ildefons Cerdà, begins.

1868–73
September Revolution, against Queen Isabel II, begins six years of agitation. The first anarchist groups are formed, and in 1873 Spain briefly becomes a republic.

1888
Barcelona hosts its first Universal Exposition.

1901–9
Radicalisation and anarchist influence in the workers' movement are reflected in general strikes, and the *Setmana Tràgica* (Tragic Week) in 1909, when churches are destroyed in riots after the government tries to conscript extra troops for its colonial war in Morocco.

1914
The *Mancomunitat*, a joint administration of the Catalan provinces, is set up. Industry flourishes during World War I.

1919
A general strike begun at La Canadenca electricity company initiates a period of intense social conflict.

1923–30
Military dictatorship of Primo de Rivera suppresses unions and Catalan freedoms.

1929
A second Universal Exposition is held on Montjuïc. The Plaça d'Espanya, Palau Nacional and Poble Espanyol are all built.

1931
Second Spanish Republic proclaimed: Catalonia is given autonomy, with a restored Generalitat under Francesc Macià.

1936–9
Spanish Civil War: right-wing generals revolt against the Republic, but in Barcelona are initially

The Italian air force bombing Barcelona in 1938, in support of General Franco.

An offical poster from the 1992 Barcelona Olympic Games.

defeated by the people in the streets. But, after three years of war, bitter fighting and destruction, Barcelona falls to Franco's troops on 26 January 1939.

1959–60
After years of scarcity, the local economy begins to revive as tourism and foreign investment enter Spain.

1975
Franco dies on 20 November. King Juan Carlos oversees moves towards a restoration of democracy.

1977–8
First democratic general elections since 1936, and first local elections, won in Barcelona by Socialists. Catalan autonomy statute granted and Catalan recognised as official language.

1980
Jordi Pujol is elected first president of restored Catalan Generalitat.

1982
Pasqual Maragall becomes Mayor of Barcelona.

1992
Barcelona Olympic Games.

1997
Maragall resigns and is succeeded by Joan Clos.

2003
Jordi Pujol retires; Pasqual Maragall heads left-wing coalition. Barcelona holds one of the largest demonstrations in Europe against the Iraq War.

2004
Socialists led by José Luis Rodríguez Zapatero take over Spanish central government after Partido Popular is discredited by its response to the 11 March Al-Qaeda bombings in Madrid.

2006
Maragall coalition in Generalitat replaced by one under fellow Socialist Josep Montilla. New Statute for Catalonia passed in Congress.

2008
AVE rail link finally connects Barcelona and Madrid.

2009
Despite world recession, the 22@ business district forges ahead.

2010
The centrist Convergència i Unió (CiU) takes over the Generalitat.

2011
Beleaguered by the economic situation, Socialists suffer defeat nationally. Mariano Rajoy's Partido Popular wins the general election and CiU takes over Barcelona city council.

2012
Generalitat President Artur Mas leads a fervent campaign for Catalan independence, aiming for a referendum in 2014.

2013
In the first quarter of 2013 unemployment figures in Spain reach an all-time high of over 6 million (27 percent of the working population). With 57 percent of young people unemployed, many are seeking work abroad.

People marching in favour of Catalan independence, 2012.

The footballers' union organises aid for Republican refugees during the Civil War.

ELS FUTBOLISTES RECLAME
L'AJUT ALS REFUGIATS

ORGANITZAT PER COMISSIÓ
PRO REFUGIATS U.G.T. S.R.I. i
SINDICAT PROFESSIONALS FUTBOL.

THE MAKING OF MODERN BARCELONA

The city rose to power under Catalonia's medieval count-kings, then fell into decline, only to wake up to find itself under the control of Madrid. The urge to break out of this inertia, and a deep Catalan identity, are at the core of Barcelona's inventive energy.

Barcelona has all the attributes of a great metropolis and the self-consciousness of a capital city, but much of its dynamism has come from it always having had something to prove. In the Middle Ages it was the centre of the greatest Mediterranean empire since Roman times, but never became a sovereign city in its own right, like Venice or Genoa. Until 1716 it was the capital of a Catalan state, but as Catalonia was absorbed into the Spanish monarchy Barcelona fell into the status of disregarded subordinate to its upstart rival Madrid, the source of endless frustrations.

In the 19th century, a once-more economically vibrant Barcelona became the centre of

Barcelona's Roman walls, built around AD 300, made it a valued stronghold for 1,000 years.

A floor mosaic, Museu de Arqueologia de Catalunya.

a resurgent Catalan culture and the groundbreaker for everything modern in Spain. And recently Barcelona has leapt out of its seclusion again to win an image as one of Europe's most fashionable, most inventive, liveliest cities.

Roman beginnings

The Roman colony that grew into Barcelona was founded around 15 BC. It fed well off its 'sea of oysters', and had such amenities as porticoed baths and a forum, but was a small town, covering about 12 hectares (30 acres). Its city walls were dwarfed by those at nearby Tarragona. Roman Barcino was built on top of a small hill, roughly where the cathedral is today.

For half a millennium after the end of Roman rule, Barcelona's history is sparsely documented. Thanks to its walls it remained a coveted stronghold, but most of the surrounding region was a no-man's-land. Of the occupiers of those years – the Visigoths, the Moors, the Franks – only the first seem to have esteemed the city much. In 415 the Visigoth king Ataülf seized Barcino from its last Roman governor, and briefly made it his capital.

The ramshackle Visigothic kingdom fell apart, though, when Muslim armies swept over the Iberian peninsula in 711. For 80 years Barcelona was ruled by a Moorish governor under the caliphs of Córdoba, rulers of Al-Andalús. Its next change of ownership came in 801, when Louis the Pious, son of the Frankish Emperor Charlemagne, seized control of the territory as far south as Barcelona, making it the Marca Hispànica or 'Spanish March' of his father's empire, to protect it from Moorish invasions.

The birth of Catalonia

To guard this new frontier, Frankish aristocrats were left as counts to rule the Pyrenean valleys. Catalonia grew out of these counties, and this is one of the differentiating facts of Catalan history. The Christian kingdoms in western Spain descended from communities who had retreated north before the Muslim advance; Catalonia had its roots north of the Pyrenees. Hence the Catalan language, for example, is closer to French and above all Provençal than it is to Castilian.

The Llibre Verd, as illuminated by Arnau Penna in 1380, listed Barcelona's privileges.

Barcelona itself long remained a remote frontier fortress. Its potential only began to be realised with the emergence of a nascent Catalan state. Wilfred the Hairy – the precise translation of *Guifré el Pilós* – the man acclaimed as the founder of the House of the Counts of Barcelona, actually had little to do with the city. He was a man of the mountains, who from his stronghold in Ripoll managed in the 880s to unite most of the patchwork of Catalan counties under his authority, including Barcelona.

Once incorporated into Wilfred's inheritance, though, the old Roman citadel rapidly gained importance. Around 911, Wilfred II founded the monastery of Sant Pau del Camp outside the city, and chose to be buried there. It was this sort of princely patronage that began to turn the former backwater into a medieval metropolis.

> From the 10th to the 12th century Catalonia was an important centre of Romanesque art and architecture, producing jewels such as the church of Sant Pau del Camp (see page 147).

Moorish threat

In 985 Barcelona was a rich enough target to be sacked by Al-Mansur, the Grand Vizier of the Caliph of Córdoba. Frankish authority over the counts of Barcelona had been ephemeral for a century, but in theory they were still feudal vassals of the Frankish king. Count Borrell II accordingly sent off a request for aid to his lord in this crisis. Nothing came back, so Borrell renounced all obligations to the kings of France, effectively declaring his independence.

Barcelona recovered from its sacking, and the Moorish threat did not survive Al-Mansur's death in 1002. The caliphate was enfeebled by internal intrigue, and in the 1030s dissolved into competing emirates called *taifas*. This allowed the Christian states to make big advances, and the Catalan counts expanded their lands to the south and west. Barcelona enjoyed a bonanza on the proceeds of booty, ransom and trade.

Barcelona's merchants traded throughout the Mediterranean.

Wealth and empire

By 1075, 95 percent of transactions in Barcelona were in gold. For the next 500 years, maritime enterprise supplied the city's wealth and formed its character. In 1060, the Barcelonans were still hiring galleys from Moorish ports. By 1080 the counts had a fleet of their own.

For years, the counts of Barcelona still divided their attention between both sides of the Pyrenees, acquiring lands in the Languedoc as well as towards the Ebro. In 1150, however, Ramón Berenguer IV married Petronella, daughter of the King of Aragón. Their successors would be 'count-kings', rulers of a complex inheritance known as the Crown of Aragón. Since a king was inherently more important than a count, this entity was often known just as Aragón, but its political and economic hub was Barcelona, and for centuries its main language would be Catalan. The title King of Aragón initially served the House of Barcelona mainly to ensure them due respect from other monarchs.

Island invasions

In 1213 the count-kings lost their main lands north of the Pyrenees to France, after Pere I of Aragón died at the battle of Muret. This, however, was only a prelude to the Catalan monarchy's greatest expansion, as it directed all its energies towards an onslaught against the Muslim kingdoms to the south.

Barcelona had to gain access to the Balearic Islands, then under Moorish rule, to become

INTERNATIONAL TRADE

Barcelona's count-kings were often at war with Muslim rulers, but its merchants traded with the entire Mediterranean, in grain, wines, silks and spices. Charters from the counts make clear the scope of this trade: in 1105 Ramón Berenguer III gave a profitable monopoly to four Jews of Barcelona on shipping home ransomed Muslim prisoners. In 1160 the Jewish chronicler and traveller Benjamin of Tudela reported seeing ships from 'Pisa, Genoa, Sicily, Greece, Alexandria and Asia' all lying off the beach at Barcelona waiting to unload.

One of the glories of Catalan Gothic, the rose window of Santa Maria del Mar.

a trade centre rivalling Genoa or Pisa. The seizure of Mallorca in 1229 was celebrated as a great triumph. Conquests of Ibiza (1235), Valencia (1238), Sicily (1282), Menorca (1287) and Sardinia (1324) gave the count-kings control of a network of Mediterranean ports, landmarks of an empire of grain and gold, silver and salt. In governing his new lands,

> *Barcelona's medieval elite were a merchant aristocracy, and their ideal residences were the Gothic palaces of Carrer Montcada (see page 128).*

however, Jaume I kept the complicated legal structures the Catalans had inherited from the Franks. Already sovereign of two entities, Aragón and Catalonia, he did not absorb the new territories into either, but made Valencia and Mallorca two more kingdoms under the crown – a system that would never coalesce into a cohesive state.

GOLDEN AGE

The Middle Ages were the first great period of Catalan literature. Like its neighbour Provençal, Catalan was already used to write poetry and documents in the 12th century, when most of Europe wrote only in Latin, and the Catalan law code or *Usatges* was written down in Catalan in about 1190. The court was unusually literate, and Jaume I (1213–76) and Pere III (1336–87) both wrote memoirs in their own language. In the 1280s, the great scholar Ramon Llull became the first European for centuries to write philosophy in anything other than Latin or Greek. A huge amount of medieval Catalan writing survives, including Tirant lo *Blanc*, written by Joanot Martorell in 1490 – the first true European novel.

Medieval metropolis

Imperial exploits were matched by Barcelona's desire for adornment at home. The Gothic cathedral is the prime monument of the late 13th century, and the decades after its construction began in 1298 were a time of frenzied building. The chapel of Santa Agata, in the count-kings' Palau Reial in Plaça del Rei, was built by Jaume II (1291–1327). The first stone

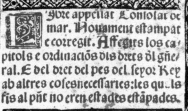

The Catalan Book of the Consulate of the Sea.

of Santa Maria del Pi was laid in 1322, and that of the exquisite Santa Maria del Mar in 1329.

Not even the Black Death – which killed half the city council – crushed the city's confidence. Never was Barcelona so spectacularly embellished as in the reign of Pere III (1336–87); he built the vaulted halls of the Saló de Cent in the Ajuntament (town hall) and the Saló del Tinell in Plaça del Rei, and rebuilt on a vast scale the royal shipyards, the eight great bays of the Drassanes at the foot of the Ramblas (now the Maritime Museum). Private builders filled the Carrer Montcada with ornate town mansions.

The passing of glory

However, as the empire grew, its costs came to exceed its benefits. The ambition to control the western Mediterranean led to wasteful wars with Genoa, and Sardinian resistance to Catalan rule exhausted the conquerors.

The empire that made a metropolis of Barcelona also sucked the rural life-blood out of Catalonia, as the population balance shifted. The countryside could no longer keep armies

supplied with men or the city with food. In 1330 Barcelona had its first serious famine.

In 1410 the line of count-kings descended from Wilfred the Hairy came to an end with Martí I, and the Crown of Aragón passed to a Castilian noble dynasty, the Trastámaras. Over the next century, the influence of Barcelona within the monarchy diminished. Alfons V 'the Magnanimous' (1416–58) mainly governed the Crown of Aragón from as far away as Naples.

In the century after 1360, not a decade went by without a plague or famine in Barcelona. Insecurity led to violent unrest. In 1462, Catalonia exploded in civil war, combining urban discontent with a peasants' revolt. Barcelona rose against Joan II, but the siege that ended the war in 1473 was devastating.

Marriage of power

Barcelona was thus at a low ebb when the political framework around it was transformed. In 1469 Fernando (Ferran, in Catalan) of Aragón married Isabel of Castile, a union that for the first time would bring all the main Christian kingdoms of Spain under the same rulers.

Soldiers of the army of King Jaume I (1208–1276).

Christopher Columbus standing before the King and Queen of Spain, with Indians from the New World, 1493.

Legally, each part kept its institutions for another 200 years – as the different elements already did in the Crown of Aragón – but nevertheless, as the joint monarchy developed, Catalonia became increasingly regarded as an annexe of Castile.

Multinational takeover

In contrast to Catalonia, Castile was on a rising curve of expansion. In 1492 Granada, last

---

THE LOST RENAISSANCE

No visitor to Barcelona can fail to be struck by the relative dearth of great Renaissance and Baroque buildings. Examples of grandeur are few and far between: the Ajuntament (Town Hall) hides its medieval core behind a Renaissance facade. The Carrer Ample was opened as a gesture to Renaissance town planning, but most of what survives from this time reflects private effort, not public wealth or patronage.

This is largely due to the fact that the Habsburg monarchs and ministers were mainly concerned with their empire, its wars and their great seat of power in Castile, Madrid.

Muslim state in the Iberian peninsula, was conquered, and Fernando and Isabel sponsored Columbus's first voyage to America. American conquests would bring unheard-of power and booty, but Barcelona got little share of this or the new Atlantic trade, as Catalans were not allowed to trade directly with the colonies for over 270 years. On Fernando's death in 1516 his Spanish kingdoms went to his grandson Charles V of Habsburg (Carlos I of Spain), who was also ruler of Burgundy, the Netherlands and Austria, and Holy Roman Emperor. Catalonia became a minor part of a global empire. The Habsburg rulers mainly visited Barcelona on their way to somewhere else, and so it progressively lost the courtly status that had been one of the foundations of its fortune.

Differences in Castilian thinking were a worsening source of conflict. In Castile, civic liberties normally rested in a charter from the king, and royal authority could rarely be resisted long – especially after Charles V crushed the revolt of the Castilian *comuneros* in 1521. The identity of Barcelona, however, was bound up with its status in law, and that of

Catalonia and its *Corts* (Parliament) as a partner in the Spanish monarchy. In Catalonia, the Habsburgs had to negotiate a patchwork of traditional assemblies, each determinedly aware of its historic rights. To an aristocracy accustomed to absolute power, this attitude looked like simple disloyalty.

Rebellion and defeat

In the early 17th century the Spanish monarchy began to totter under the effects of overambition and endless wars. In their attempts to stop the rot the ministers of Felipe IV (1621–65)

> The Habsburg monarchs often saw Catalonia's representatives as a gaggle of disloyal, troublemaking lawyers.

made insistent demands for money and manpower from non-Castilian territories of the crown. Catalans feared for their rights.

The cost of the Thirty Years War and war with France brought the monarchy's demands to a peak. Catalonia rose in revolt in 1640, after an attempt to conscript Catalans into the royal armies, and the rebels tried to transfer their allegiance to Louis XIII of France.

However, a controlled rising by Barcelona lawyers exploded into a ferocious peasants' revolt. The war dragged on for years, and the siege of Barcelona in 1652 ended only when the citizens were 'reduced to eating grass'. The victorious Habsburgs were unusually generous, and allowed the Catalan institutions to remain in place.

The end of the Habsburgs

In 1700 the chronically infirm Carlos II, last Spanish Habsburg, died without an heir. Two candidates disputed the throne in the War of the Spanish Succession: one French, Felipe V, grandson of Louis XIV, and one Austrian, the Archduke Charles. After a slow start, the Barcelonans became the most committed opponents of Felipe V, and clung on even after their British and Dutch allies withdrew in 1713. The final siege lasted from August 1713 to 11 September 1714, when the city fell, a date commemorated as the *Diada de Catalunya* – Catalonia's national day.

In 1716 Felipe V finalised his decrees of *Nova Planta*, which, following lines set down by his grandfather in France, finally made Spain a single, centralised state. All the assemblies and rights of Catalonia and other Aragonese territories were abolished, and Castilian was made sole

Barcelona falls to the armies of Felipe V, 11 September 1714.

language of law and government. Barcelona was reduced to a provincial city, and suffered the indignity of an occupying army billeted in a glowering new fortress, the Ciutadella.

Expansion

The city was prostrate and revival slow, but the 18th century was also an era when sustained

> In 1836, the first steamship rolled off a slipway in Barceloneta, gaslight was introduced in 1842, and in 1848 Spain's first railway linked Barcelona to Mataró, 30km (19 miles) north.

economic growth began in Barcelona, thanks to new activities such as direct trade with the Americas – finally open to Catalans in the 1770s – and the beginnings of industrialisation based on American cotton. In the 1780s, the Catalan economy accelerated fast.

War and revival

In 1808, Napoleon seized King Carlos IV and the Spanish royal family and put his brother Joseph on the Spanish throne. He tried to win over Catalonia by offering a separate government, but perhaps surprisingly the Catalans had none of it, and supported the Spanish monarchy throughout the war (1808–14).

This war and its aftermath reduced the Spanish state to chaos. Barcelona's manufacturers, though, were not deflected from their plans, and Catalonia became one of very few areas in southern Europe to join the Industrial Revolution before 1860.

The walls come down

Barcelona was the most insanitary and congested city in Europe. Observers blamed the cholera epidemic of 1854, which took 6,000 lives, on overcrowding. It was still a militarised city, contained by walls and watched over by two hated fortresses, Montjuïc and the Ciutadella. Strict ordinances banned building outside the walls. Inside, every metre was occupied. Barcelona was bursting at the seams.

Permission to tear down the walls and the Ciutadella came in 1854, and ordinary people, eager for fresh air, joined in the demolition. An idealistic engineer, Ildefons Cerdà, drew up a plan for the 'Extension and Reform' of Barcelona.

Cerdà's design for the Eixample (Extension) joined Barcelona to Sants, Gràcia and other

A 1700 map shows Barcelona and the surrounding countryside.

A 19th-century riot on La Rambla.

hinterland towns by means of a giant grid of crisscrossing streets, broken by two great diagonal avenues. It was a utopian dream, but with a scientific basis. Most criticisms of today's Eixample – such as the lack of open space –

> The modernista style combined a strong sense of Catalan tradition with a powerful enthusiasm for the new: intricate, elaborate, but set against the rationality of the machine age.

result from the debasement of Cerdà's plan that has been allowed by successive city councils.

Catalan rebirth

The September Revolution of 1868, which swept Queen Isabel II from the Spanish throne, brought another promise of democratic reform, and another brief time – six years – when repression was cast aside and ideas and movements proliferated in Barcelona. Workers'

unions blossomed, and the first anarchist groups were formed. Barcelona had a flourishing café society, and new ideas – the Catalan *Renaixença* or rebirth, socialism, anarchism – were avidly debated. Radical forces, however – in Catalonia and Spain as a whole – were chronically weak and divided. Spain briefly

EXHIBITION FEVER

As Barcelona's prosperity grew in the 19th century, the city's movers and shakers, ignored by the government in Madrid, felt they needed to do something to bring their city to the world's attention. Their exuberance was ideally expressed by the 1888 Universal Exposition. With less than a year to prepare, Barcelona threw itself into a frenzy of construction: most of the Parc de la Ciutadella (the main exhibition site), the Arc de Triomf, the Columbus Column and more, all date from 1888. The exhibition knocked up huge debts, but Barcelona felt it had been worth it – so much so that it staged another expo' in 1929, which led to the redesign of Montjuïc and Plaça d'Espanya, and these collective memories clearly fed into the huge enthusiasm for the Olympic project in the 1980s.

In early 20th century Barcelona.

became a federal republic in 1873, but this was soon toppled by a military coup, followed by the restoration of the Bourbons under King Alfonso XII.

A new era

The restoration of the monarchy, and the renewed suppression of radical movements, did not halt the expansion of Barcelona. Rather, it allowed it to take off, as the middle classes felt a new burst of confidence. The building of the Eixample went on apace, as the fashionable quarter for the wealthy and professional classes. Its owners competed with each other to commission the most opulent buildings, so it became the great showcase for Gaudí and other Catalan *modernista* architects (see page 54).

By 1900 two forces were most prominent: the new Catalan bourgeoisie, who sought modernisation and economic and political autonomy within the established social order, and the new working class, among whom revolution was the stuff of everyday conversation.

Dissent grew with the loss of Spain's last colonies and their markets in 1898. Anarchism gained strength. There were general strikes in 1901 and 1902, and in 1909 the city suffered the *Setmana Tràgica*, a week of rioting when 70 religious buildings were burnt down.

The 20th-century crisis

The early 1900s were the peak years of the Lliga Regionalista, a conservative Catalan nationalist party that sought to give respectable expression to the sentiments of the *Renaixença*. In 1914 they won from the Madrid government the *Mancomunitat* or confederation of the four Catalan provinces, the first pan-Catalan institution since 1714. Their confident plans, though, would be knocked aside by bitter conflicts within Catalan society.

With World War I Barcelona saw a whole new opulence, generated by supplying the Allies. This also brought massive inflation, which post war triggered a social and economic crisis. Workers flocked to the anarchist union, the CNT.

In 1923 the army commander in Barcelona, Miguel Primo de Rivera, used this chaos as justification for a military coup, taking over the Spanish government as first minister under

A late 19th-century bull fight.

Miliciana on guard above the Plaça de Catalunya, July 1936.

King Alfonso XIII. The Catalanist elite, terrified by unrest, gave him their support, only to be rewarded with the renewed banning of the Catalan flag and public use of the language.

The Second Republic

Primo de Rivera retired to his Andalucian estate in 1930. Alfonso XIII sought to stabilise the situation with local elections in April 1931, but when these were overwhelmingly won by anti-monarchist candidates the king went into exile. Spain's Second Republic was proclaimed. Left-wing nationalists had won the elections in Catalonia, and their popular leader Francesc Macià became provisional president of a restored Catalan Generalitat, or autonomous

BARCELONA IN THE CIVIL WAR

The Spanish Civil War began on 18 July 1936, when the army launched a coup against the left-wing Popular Front government in Madrid and its allies, such as the Catalan Generalitat. In Barcelona, leftist parties and unions fought back, and were victorious by 19 July.

Barcelona then underwent a revolution: normal authorities were suspended, and trams, factories and stores became workers' collectives – a time captured by Orwell in *Homage to Catalonia*. This euphoria, though, had shaky foundations. The Nationalists led by General Franco had been successful in many parts of Spain, and were advancing on Madrid. They were armed by Germany and Italy, while the Republicans, cold-shouldered by Britain and

France, had no other source of arms than the Soviet Union, which gave the Communists disproportionate influence. In Barcelona tension mounted between Communists and Anarchists, coming to a head in street battles in May 1937.

The Republican army, meanwhile, made little headway against Franco's troops, and behind the lines there were acute shortages and hunger. In 1938, Barcelona was heavily bombed by the Italian air force. For months, the Republic struggled to turn the tide at the battle of the Ebro, in southern Catalonia. When this failed it had no strength left, and Franco's army took Barcelona in January 1939. Nearly half a million refugees crossed into France, and 35,000 Republicans were executed by the new regime.

British diver Tracey Miles is captured high over the Sagrada Familia during a pre-1992 Olympics competition.

government. What cellist Pau Casals called a 'veritable cultural renaissance' began. The five years between 1931 and the Civil War are seen by Catalans as another very brief golden age, when Barcelona, in euphoric mood, threw itself into another of its bursts of enthusiasm for new projects and creative ideas.

CREATIVE REGENERATION

In the post-Franco years, long-frustrated creativity was released and Barcelona rediscovered its artistic traditions. The pinch-spirited drabness of Francoism was left behind by a stylish, inventive, clearly Catalan style. Barcelona's Socialist council, under charismatic mayor Pasqual Maragall from 1982, sought to harness this new mood; it enlisted Barcelona's creative community, typified by architect Oriol Bohigas, the city's chief planner, who set in motion a renovation of the whole city. Nor was this just a matter of image and quality of life: by attracting service industries they could compensate for the decline of the city's traditional economic core – textiles, chemicals and engineering.

The Spanish Civil War (see box, page 43) ushered in one of Spain's darkest periods, and under Franco's iron hand Catalan identity, language and culture were subjected to brutal repression for nearly 40 years.

Getting by in the grey years

During the Franco regime, the middle classes worked hard, looked after their businesses and made money, reinforcing Barcelona's status as the manufacturing capital of Spain. Madrid, which held the purse strings, neglected and underfunded 'Spain's factory'. Waves of immigrants from Spain's impoverished south poured in looking for work in the 1950s and 1960s, and cheap, drab housing blocks were thrown up in a ring of badly serviced satellite suburbs.

By the late 1960s, the iron grip Franco had held over Spain was becoming enfeebled. Tourism, the basis for an economic boom, also opened the country to the world. In Barcelona, opposition movements were ever more active.

Autonomy and a new beginning

Legend has it that on 20 November 1975, when Franco died, Barcelona partied so hard the city ran out of cava. A few months later, King Juan Carlos appointed an obscure Francoist official, Adolfo Suárez, as prime minister with the task of returning Spain to democracy.

Spain's first democratic elections since 1936 came in June 1977. In Catalonia the two main winners were the Socialists and the conservative nationalist Convergència party of Jordi Pujol. Suárez saw that a democratic Spain had to admit Catalan aspirations, and an autonomy statute gave Catalonia substantial potential self-government. In every local election since 1978 the Socialists held control of Barcelona council, until 2011, when the Convergència i Unió candidate, Xavier Trias, became mayor.

Radical change

Politics were only one aspect of a drastic change in the whole of Barcelona as the city shook off the repressive years (see box, page 44). A key element in this was hosting the 1992 Olympic Games – as a pretext for attracting international attention and investment to help carry out the plans for a new city. What could beat the Olympics to put the city back on the global map?

Post-Olympic city

Apart from major new infrastructures, the most stunning transformation has been on the waterfront. In the 1980s, Barcelona had a grimy industrial harbour, and a grubby, unloved beach. A key part of the Olympic plan was to

> With its return to the sea, Barcelona seems to have distilled the essence of a Mediterranean city.

open Barcelona to the sea, with the creation of the Olympic Village and port and the opening up of kilometres of clean beach.

It's often unnoticed that many of Barcelona's projects were carried out *after* 1992, like the transformation of the Port Vell into a spectacular leisure area. Barcelona's Ajuntament has been an international benchmark for dynamic city administration, and its love affair with the

world's architects is unending. However, with the retirement of both Jordi Pujol and Pasqual Maragall by 2006 – key leaders in shaping post-Franco Catalonia – the political scene entered a grey period. It was difficult to emulate the large strides that had been made in the 1980s and '90s and the advent of recession slowed down some grand designs, though the latest brainchild, the 22@ business district, is progressing slowly.

Since 2011 people all over Spain, young and old, have attended massive demonstrations about soaring unemployment, inept bankers and corrupt politicians. With recession and austerity measures strangling the country, the Catalans expressed dissatisfaction about their financial deal with Madrid in a historic march on 11 September 2012, the *Diada* or Catalan National Day. This marked the beginning of a new bid for independence headed by Convergència i Unió leader Artur Mas, the President of the Generalitat, in coalition with Esquerra Republicana, the Republican Left. The aim is to hold a referendum on independence for Catalonia in 2014, amid controversy about whether it is constitutional or not.

Modern Torre Agbar.

The interior of Barri Gòtic's Cathedral.

ARCHITECTURE

Barcelona has a rich architectural heritage, from soaring Gothic arches to flamboyant *modernista* mansions. A spate of exciting building projects has rejuvenated the city's image since the return of democracy.

In 1999, the Royal Institute of British Architects awarded their annual gold medal, the most prestigious award for architecture in the world, not to an individual but, for the first time, to a city: Barcelona. The award stated: 'Inspired city leadership, pursuing an ambitious yet pragmatic urban strategy and the highest design standards, has transformed the city's public realm, immensely expanded its amenities and regenerated its economy, providing pride in its inhabitants and delight in its visitors.'

Since the 1980s Barcelona has attracted the attention of architects from all over the world for its bold contemporary architecture, urban design and successful programme of renewal. The effect has been to catapult the city from a dusty European backwater to a shining example of how cities should be managed.

Architecture has always been on any visitor's agenda due to the works of Antoni Gaudí and his *modernista* contemporaries, but their work, extraordinary though it is, comprises only a part of the city's rich architectural heritage.

Understanding the city

Set between the sea and the Collserola mountains, and contained by Montjuïc to the south and the River Besòs to the north, Barcelona is one of the most densely populated cities in Europe. At its heart lies the Casc Antic, the medieval area which, until the middle of the 19th century, contained the entire city within its walls – the oldest of which date back to the Romans.

Catalan Gothic has a distinctive character: dignified but somewhat dour. The interiors are often strikingly large. Some are very fine,

15th-century architecture in the Barri Gòtic.

embodying the secular and religious splendour of the time. Not to be missed are the Saló del Tinell, with its enormous arches, in the Palau Reial Major, the Museu Marítim/Drassanes, where the galleons of the Armada were made, and the Església de Santa Maria del Mar, for its elegance and serenity. The area's dwellings are mixed: dingy flats rub shoulders with splendid merchants' palaces in Montcada, which house the Museu Picasso and other institutions.

Inventive restoration

Restoration of such palaces has been carried out as part of the city's regeneration

programme. Contemporary insertions and details sit proudly beside medieval structures in a style that does not seek to create exact replicas. The purpose has been to complement the existing buildings rather than to imitate past architectural styles.

This attitude is prevalent in all restoration work carried out in the city. A notable example is the 18th-century Casa de la Caritat, in El Raval, which has been transformed into the stunning Centre de Cultura Contemporània de Barcelona (CCCB, (see page 143) by architects Vilaplana and Piñón.

A radical solution

By the 1850s, it was necessary to build an expansion, or 'Eixample', to relieve overcrowding. Engineer Ildefons Cerdà proposed an

Recently some inner patios of Eixample blocks have been restored as gardens with play areas, emulating Cerdà's original plan, like Jardins Jaume Perich (Gran Via 657).

Gaudí's Casa Viçens.

Detailed tile work in Plaza de Toros.

enormous grid that would spread out over the surrounding plain, intersected by avenues lined with trees. The project was radical, proposing a vision of the city that would be full of sunlight, air and open spaces, and well ordered, with integrated public facilities and transport networks.

The existing Eixample, however, is very different. Almost as soon as the grid was laid out, the council allowed plots of land to be bought up, and families made their fortunes building speculative housing. The quality of housing was graded depending on location; the fashionable streets became the sites for some extremely grand *modernista* blocks, with glazed balconies and tiled and carved facades. In the more obscure locations are poorer imitations – badly built, narrow, dark flats, with similar but smaller layouts, sometimes with a touch of *modernista* detailing on the entrance and facade. The internal spaces of each block, originally intended as communal parks, became factories, workshops and, later on, car parks.

Torre Agbar.

Modernisme was considered the epitome of bad taste in the years following its heyday, but the pendulum has swung back again, and modernista buildings are now symbols of the city.

Development has been a continuous process from the early *modernista* housing, through 1960s architecture, to contemporary apartments. Height restrictions and building lines of the strict grid layout have generally been maintained, resulting in a lively but homogeneous design. The population of the Eixample is great enough to sustain the small shops and bars that give it its pulse, and the area has adapted well to changes in transport and lifestyle.

Urban villages

The city has a number of outlying 'villages', such as Gràcia, Sants and Sarrià. Although encroached on by the Eixample, these areas retain a strong and vibrant identity, with their own local history, fiestas and culture. The buildings are generally smaller, with narrower streets, small squares and parks, four- to five-storey blocks of flats and a limited amount of single-occupancy housing. The whole city is ringed by blocks of flats built in the 1960s to house the thousands of immigrant workers from the rest of Spain. These blocks are variable in quality, and some estates have severe social problems.

RADICAL ARCHITECT

The German Pavilion that Ludwig Mies van der Rohe (1886–1969) designed for the 1929 International Exposition on Montjuïc challenged contemporary notions of space, with no windows, doors or walls in the conventional sense; steel columns support the roof, and the space flows seamlessly from interior to exterior rooms. Frameless glass blurs the concept of thresholds, with panels and screens used to create particular spatial effects.

One of the most influential buildings of the 20th century, it still appears extremely modern. A replica, built in 1986 to mark the centenary of the architect's birth, replaces the original, which was demolished after the Exposition.

The Mies van der Rohe Pavilion, Montjuïc.

Architectural regeneration

After the stagnation of Franco's rule (ending with his death in 1975), the new Barcelona City Council was quick to implement plans for regeneration. By the time the Olympic bid was won in 1986, the city was already receiving international attention for its architecture programme. Design was the highest consideration. Each area was subject to a plan based on a study of all aspects of the urban fabric, from the provision of schools and parks to traffic organisation and major infrastructure projects.

International profile

For the high-profile public buildings, and to lend international status to the programme, 'star' architects were invited to contribute: Japanese architect Arata Isozaki built the Palau Sant Jordi (see page 183), a huge steel-and-glass indoor arena with a levitating roof, on Montjuïc hill; English architect Norman Foster built the Torre de Collserola (see page 213), now an icon of the skyline and sometimes known as the Torre Foster; US architect Frank Gehry constructed the huge copper fish glittering on the seafront (see

ARCHITECTURE OF THE VALL D'HEBRON

The Vall d'Hebron Olympic site, located on metro line 3 at Mundet, is home to some of the most interesting, if lesser known, Olympic buildings.

The most impressive is the Velodrome, built by Esteve Bonnell. It is a beautifully simple, modern interpretation of an ancient, essentially Mediterranean, building type, set in a landscape surrounded by cypress trees. It was built in 1984, at a time when postmodernism was prevalent, incorporating a characteristically classical pastiche and superficial decoration, using high-quality materials such as stone, marble, steel and glass. The site also contains the now dilapidated archery range by Enric Miralles and

Carme Piñón. Nearby is a replica of the pavilion of the Spanish Republic, designed by Josep Lluís Sert for the 1937 Paris Exhibition, and used to exhibit Picasso's *Guernica*. Sert established modern architecture in Barcelona in the 1920s and 1930s after coming into contact with other European modernists, most notably Le Corbusier, but was later exiled to the United States.

The pavilion was rebuilt in 1992 using the original cheap materials of thin steel sections and asbestos panels, but it is nevertheless very sophisticated. It currently houses a university and research centre (Av. Cardenal Vidal i Barraquer).

Some excellent architectural guidebooks, many in English, can be obtained from the shop in the Col.legi d'Arquitectes in Plaça Nova (see page 110).

page 162), while another American, Richard Meier, designed and built the contemporary art museum (MACBA, see page 142).

Home-grown talent

The planning authorities also invested trust in many virtually unknown Catalan architects, and the support of the city's inhabitants, plus an appreciation of their cultural and architectural heritage, have enabled them to flourish.

The many buildings constructed or renovated for the Olympic Games in 1992 continue to be fully functional, like the Institut Nacional d'Educació Fisica de Catalunya, a sports university, and the Palau Sant Jordi, which is used for concerts.

Catalan architects have always designed more than just buildings. Street furniture, kiosks, paving slabs, tree grilles and shop fronts are all architect-designed. Such work tends to be craft-based, and the continued existence of

The 2004 Fòrum building designed by Herzog and de Meuron.

Modern houses juxtaposed with old on Passeig de Gràcia.

The sculpture Dona i Ocell was designed by Joan Miró.

small metalworking shops, marble masons and stained-glass ateliers allows buildings to be creatively detailed.

Although in the post-Olympic period building work slowed, the regeneration programme continued. This resulted in more public housing and facilities such as university buildings and projects like Rafael Moneo's Auditori concert hall and Ricardo Bofill's Teatre Nacional, as well as commercial ventures like French architect Jean Nouvel's Torre Agbar, an office block.

The port area of Barcelona was opened up with Maremàgnum, a major shopping and leisure district, and the World Trade Center. Several large new shopping centres have been built, such as L'Illa and Diagonal Mar. Leading national and international architects such as Herzog and de Meuron were brought in for some of the Fòrum 2004 building work (see page 168).

Ongoing projects

The new business district known as 22@ (see page 166), a showground for national and international architects, is work in progress. It should eventually tie in with a major new station for the AVE high-speed train. On a more domestic level, renovation of the city's food markets continues, like the wonderfully colourful Mercat de Santa Caterina, part of an impressive urban regeneration scheme. Despite recession there are still plenty of grandiose projects on the drawing board, such as further development of the port and smaller social and cultural ones, but the question now hovers 'Will they ever come to fruition?'

Barcelona has an ideal climate for fine architecture, the strong light allowing sculptural forms to be read more clearly. The lack of weathering also makes flat facades and the use of rendering and tiling appropriate.

The city has always nurtured its architects, indulged their idiosyncrasies and encouraged them to be forward-thinking and individualistic. Though they understand the history of Barcelona's architecture, and love Gaudí and Domènech i Montaner, they are not intimidated by them, building alongside this legacy in a confident and contemporary style. Their achievements are as good as their predecessors', and have their roots in the same traditions of attention to detail and local craftsmanship.

ME hotel, designed by Dominique Perrault, in 22@ district.

Urban Regeneration

In post-Franco Barcelona far-seeing politicians joined forces with creative architects on schemes to bring light and space into neglected areas of this notoriously dense city.

It all began in 1981, when architect Oriol Bohigas was asked to establish a new department of urban design for Barcelona City Council. Previously, he had been the head of the city's School of Architecture, so he took with him his most able students, who became known as the Golden Pencils. Each architect was allocated an area of Barcelona and asked to develop a plan for its regeneration. There was a desperate shortage of public space and, since buildings were expensive, parks and squares became the main focus. The proposals ranged from small areas of paving to large parks on derelict former industrial land, from the opening up of the Eixample blocks to the renovation of traffic interchanges.

Hard squares

Initially some of these spaces were disparagingly dubbed 'hard squares'. With time, though, they have become part of the urban fabric, appreciated and used to the full by Barcelona's citizens. A symbolic development for Catalans was the creation of the Plaça Fossar de les Moreres, next to Santa Maria del Mar, to commemorate the Catalan Martyrs of 1714.

Parc Creueta del Coll, by architect firm Martorell-Bohigas-Mackay, lies in the site of an old quarry in an outlying area (metro L5 El Coll/Teixonera). An enormous sculpture by Eduardo Chillida is suspended above a public swimming pool. The Parc de l'Escorxador on the site of the old abattoir near Plaça d'Espanya, once a dry and dusty space, has been transformed into a series of rectilinear terraces and walkways, pinpointed by an enormous Miró sculpture. Difficult to categorise, the park has been described as a cross between a formal garden and a wild Mediterranean landscape.

In Gràcia, architects Bach and Mora redesigned eight existing but neglected squares. Plaça del Sol now has lampshades resembling the setting sun, while the design of Plaça del Diamant contains references to the book of the same name by Catalan writer Mercè Rodoreda (1908–83; see page 280). They have become the focal points of Gràcia nightlife.

Ongoing policy

The momentum of these inspired policies has continued. In 2007 the International Urban Landscape Award went to a regeneration project by architects Arriola and Fiol, in a socially conflictive district – the Parc Central de Nou Barris. This sustainable urban space, the second-largest in the city, was praised for its function as a recreational area and its role in integrating the district.

A more recent example is the new Rambla del Raval, which entailed controversial demolition of old housing and relocation of residents. Originally envisaged by 19th-century town planner Cerdà to breathe life into an overcrowded neighbourhood, it was finally achieved in the 21st century. This broad walkway between jacaranda and palm trees is used for community events and as a meeting place in this multicultural district.

Parc Central de Nou Barris.

MODERNISME

The city's defining architectural style looked to Catalonia's glorious medieval past for its principal influences, combining these with the new technologies of the period.

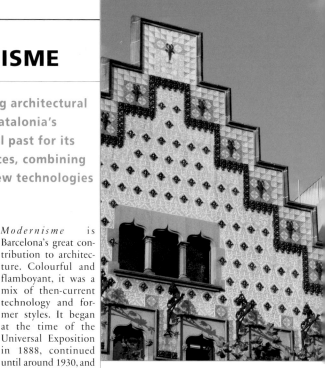

The Hospital Sant Pau, designed by Domènech i Montaner.

Elaborate décor at Casa Amatller.

Modernisme is Barcelona's great contribution to architecture. Colourful and flamboyant, it was a mix of then-current technology and former styles. It began at the time of the Universal Exposition in 1888, continued until around 1930, and corresponded to the Arts and Crafts and Art Nouveau movements in the rest of Europe, with which it shared a preoccupation with sinuous line, organic form and ornament.

Its greatest practitioners were Lluís Domènech i Montaner (1850–1923), a professor at Barcelona University's School of Architecture, and one of his pupils, Josep Puig i Cadafalch (1867–1957). For the Universal Exposition, Domènech designed El Castell dels Tres Dragons, in today's Parc de la Ciutadella, based on Valencia's red-brick Gothic Stock Exchange. It afterwards became a workshop for ceramics, wrought iron and glass-making. Furnishings and details were an essential ingredient in *modernista* buildings.

Modernisme was a part of the Catalan *Renaixença* (renaissance), and it looked to the past, taking on Catalan Gothic with its tradition of ironwork, while acknowledging the styles of Islamic Spain. The 19th-century expansion of the city (the Eixample) gave architects the freedom and space to experiment, and this is where most *modernista* buildings are to be found.

Puig i Cadafalch's Dutch-gabled Casa Amatller and Gaudí's scaly-tiled Casa Batlló jostle for attention on the 'Block of Discord'.

Knights and damsels are a recurring theme: like the Arts and Crafts movement, modernisme harked back to a romantic Golden Age. This ensemble symbolising music is by Miguel Blay and dominates a corner of the Palau de la Música Catalana.

Knuckled columns on the undulating windows of Casa Batlló represent the dragon's victims in the legend of St George.

THE HIGHLIGHTS

Chimney details.

Illa de la Discòrdia The best starting point to understand modernisme is the 'Block of Discord', in Passeig de Gràcia. Within a few metres of each other are Domènech i Montaner's Casa Lleó Morera, Puig i Cadafalch's Casa Amatller and Gaudí's Casa Batlló (see page 193). Gaudí did not regard himself as a modernista, but though there are some differences in style, the discord is not obvious.

Palau de la Música Catalana A Unesco World Heritage Site, this sumptuous building can be visited in a tour or by attending a concert beneath the stained-glass dome that suffuses the auditorium with natural light (see page 125).

Antic Hospital de la Santa Creu Domènech i Montaner's extraordinary hospital was the most advanced in Europe when it was completed in the early 20th century (see page 201).

CaixaForum The Casaramona textile factory built by Puig i Cadafalch at the foot of Montjuïc is now the CaixaForum cultural centre (see page 177).

Palau Güell One of Gaudí's first major commissions, this extravagant town house (1885–90) is crammed with detail, from the stables in the basement to the highest chimney pot (see page 101).

Coloured mosaics and fancy ironwork pervaded commercial premises as well as private houses. This Rambla chocolate shop has been run since 1820 by the Escribà family.

The lustrous floor-to-ceiling and wall-to-wall oak infuses this first-floor room of Gaudí's Casa Batlló with a rich warmth, aided by careful positioning and colouring of windows. Most riveting, perhaps, is the fireplace, a sensual inglenook backed by earthy coloured tiles.

Modernista architects paid great attention to the detail of buildings both inside and out. Stained-glass, wood, stone, marble, iron, brass, ceramics – every available material was considered for embellishment. Doorknobs, hinges and light switches all had to be in keeping. Furniture was important, too, and the decorative arts were often included in an architect's overall scheme. In their time, some of these interiors might have been almost overwhelmed with decoration, as they were in Victorian England. But today, stripped of their furnishings, the lines and intent of the interiors can be fully grasped.

Modernista furniture and decorative art can be seen in the Museu Nacional d'Art de Catalunya on Montjuïc (see page 179), and in the attractive new Museu del Modernisme Català, in a modernista building by Sagnier (Balmes, 48).

A coffee pot from Casa Batlló; no item was left undesigned.

The stained glass of a country scene brightened mealtimes in the dining room of Domènech i Montaner's Casa Lleó Morera.

Stained glass ceiling dome at the Palau de la Música Catalana.

In Vinçon, an interior design store on Passeig de Gracia.

WHERE TO EAT AND SLEEP MODERNISME

Café Vienés in luxury hotel Casa Fuster, where once all of Barcelona society dropped by.

Casa Fuster, Gran de Gràcia, 132. Domènech i Montaner's last work was the city's most expensive private building at the time. Now a five-star hotel, you can try jazz sessions in the ground-floor Café Vienés.

Els Quatre Gats, Montsió, 3. Seminal café by Puig i Cadafalch where Picasso held his first solo exhibition (see page 123).

La Font del Gat, Passeig Santa Madrona, 28. Outdoor restaurant-café near the Miró Foundation on Montjuïc, designed by Puig i Cadafalch (see page 180).

Hotel España, Sant Pau, 9–11. Now a superior-grade hotel, the recent revamp highlights the Domènech i Montaner architectural details and the murals by Ramón Casas in the dining room (see page 253).

Escribà, La Rambla, 83. A coffee and pastry on the terrace of this famous chocolate shop gives you time to study its ornamental exterior (see page 107).

A modernista café sign.

Rebecca Horn's 'L'Estel Ferit' on
Barceloneta beach.

ART AND INSPIRATION

With a legacy left by Picasso, Miró and more recently
Tàpies, and a lively contemporary aesthetic, art in the
city has never been more alive and exciting.

To visit Barcelona is to breathe in a complex and exciting visual art history. The streets map the impressions that have inspired three of Spain's prime movers in the story of modern art: Pablo Picasso, Joan Miró and Antoni Tàpies. Ironically, Picasso only spent a few years here before moving on to Paris; Miró also came and went. Only Tàpies, who died in 2012, made his permanent base here, but the legacy left by these three great artists is clearly appreciable through the work of young contemporary Catalan artists.

Pablo Picasso

Pablo Ruiz Picasso (1881–1973) was born in Málaga, in southern Spain. His family soon moved on to La Coruña in Galicia before arriving in Barcelona in 1895, where his father took up the post of Painting Professor at the city's La Llotja School of Art (see page 128). As a young

Miró paving on La Rambla.

> The Picasso Museum occupies a series of 15th-century palaces. In the same medieval street, Montcada, several more palaces serve as venues for different cultural activities.

man, before leaving the city, first for Madrid then for Paris, he was to encounter Barcelona's artistic circle that met at the now famous Els Quatre Gats (The Four Cats) café. It was here, on 1 February 1900, that Picasso exhibited for the first time.

The many drawings of friends included portraits of Jaume Sabartés, Picasso's lifelong friend and secretary. The Museu Picasso in Barcelona was initially founded largely thanks to Sabartés, who donated his personal collection of the artist's work. Picasso also designed the menu cover for Els Quatre Gats, which was influenced by Henri de Toulouse-Lautrec (1864–1901). This influence was just one stage of many during Picasso's phenomenal development. Picasso entered his melancholy Blue Period (1901–4) after the death of his Catalan friend Casagemas, before emerging into the warmth of the Rose Period (1904–6).

Then came the pioneering breakthrough into Cubism, which he was to develop over the next 20 years. He returned to Catalonia on several

Detail of a Nativity frieze designed by Picasso, on the exterior of the Col.legi d'Arquitectes.

occasions, and donated a considerable number of paintings (almost all his youthful works and the *Las Meninas* series from the 1950s) to the Museu Picasso in Barcelona (see page 128).

City of art

Barcelona is exceptional for the quantity and quality of exhibition venues and is a sheer delight for any visitor interested in art. You will find well-produced catalogues, usually with texts in English, and shows on a par with those in most capital cities. Start at the Palau de la Virreina in La Rambla for information about current shows throughout the city, including its own, or the revamped Arts Santa Mònica at the end of La Rambla, an exciting space with avant-garde and experimental work.

Joan Miró

Outside Terminal 2 at Barcelona airport you will find one of Miró's ceramic murals, a collaboration with his friend Llorens Artigas. Barcelona born and bred, Miró (1893–1983) returned here throughout his life, between periods spent in Paris and Mallorca. While studying at La Llotja School in Barcelona, he joined the arts society Cercle Artístic de Sant Lluc, which still exists.

Miró was already aware of Dada at this time, though Fauvism, Cubism and Paul Cézanne (1839–1906), in particular, were the major influences on his work. Catalan landscapes featured strongly. *The Farm* (bought by Ernest Hemingway and now in Washington), a major painting of his *detalliste* period, portrays the family farm,

MIRÓ AND THE SURREALISTS

An apocryphal story about Miró tells of how, in his desire to be considered a member of the Surrealist group, he went about trying to get himself arrested – the surest way to attain credibility among his peers. Although he was peaceful by nature, Miró summoned up the courage to walk around the streets of Paris shouting: 'Down with the Mediterranean!'

Miró was invoking the Mediterranean in its symbolic role as the cradle of Western civilisation, but his choice of words was ironic given the importance of Mediterranean light and colour in his work. Of course, no one arrested him and the rest of the group scorned his efforts.

Mont-Roig, near Tarragona. It features many of his subsequent motifs: stars, insects and animals, as well as showing a characteristic respect for manual labour. Gradually, realism gave way to suggestion and poetry, a progression aided by his contact with French Surrealism.

Like his friend Picasso, Miró suffered greatly during the Civil War, and he produced (among other things) the 'Aidez L'Espagne' poster to raise funds for the Republic. Miró's works, showing limited use of certain colours, were precisely composed. He also had wide-ranging skills, turning his hand to theatre design, printmaking, tapestry, ceramics and bronze sculptures as well as painting and drawing. The permanent collection at the Fundació Miró (see page 184) on Montjuïc covers all of these areas. This building is testimony to the understanding Miró had with his friend, architect Josep Lluís Sert, who designed both this and Miró's studio in Mallorca. It is a celebration of Miró's work, and showcases a varied programme of exhibitions, as well as other important works such as Alexander Calder's Mercury Fountain.

You will find evidence of Miró all over the city, whether walking over his ceramic pavement in La Rambla, admiring the monumental Woman and Bird sculpture in the Parc Joan Miró (see page 201), or simply noticing the La Caixa bank logo he designed.

Antoni Tàpies

Antoni Tàpies (1923–2012) was probably Spain's best-known living artist of recent times. His work forms an artistic link between Miró's generation and the new work being produced in the Catalan contemporary art world. Tàpies knew Miró and revered his work; the latter's influence is seen in Tàpies's early work, on view at the Fundació Tàpies (see page 195). The museum, which redeploys an important Domènech i Montaner building, has a permanent collection of work by Tàpies as well as high-quality contemporary exhibitions. Tàpies was 'deeply committed to pluralism and diversity' in art. The first thing you see when you arrive at the building is the mass of metal wires on the roof, entitled Cloud and Chair. Tàpies intended it to be an emblem for the building.

'Dona amb barret i coll de pell (Marie-Thérèse Walter)' by Picasso, 1937.

Sculpture on the roof of the Fundació Joan Miró.

A dirty aesthetic

During the repression under Franco, when all Catalan culture was effectively illegal, methods of expression became highly creative. In 1948 the *Dau al Set* (Dice on Seven) group was set up, with members Tàpies, Tharrats, Cuixart, Ponç, Puig and Brossa. The 'visual poems' of Joan Brossa (1919–98), a long-neglected Catalan artist-poet, have been at the forefront of recent Catalan art (see box, page 63).

Catalan artists also employed street graffiti to voice dissent. The use of signs and symbols, already seen in Miró's painting, appeared to different effect in Tàpies's work. In keeping with the international Arte Povera and Art Autre movements, Catalan Informalism combines existentialist ideas with simple materials to produce the so-called 'dirty aesthetic' that still reigns in Barcelona. The Joan Prats Gallery in Rambla de Catalunya displays representative work from contemporary and earlier artists. Or try Consell de Cent, the commercial gallery street one block down from the Fundació Tàpies.

The art scene today

The Informalist legacy is tempered by Catalan Conceptualism nowadays, as represented in the permanent collection of the Museu d'Art Contemporani (MACBA). There is also work from the *Dau al Set* group, and the bed-piece hanging at the entrance is by Tàpies.

Visit the theatre foyer at the Mercat de les Flors (see page 262) and look up at the ceiling to get some idea of Miguel Barceló's vision.

Miguel Barceló is another contemporary Catalan artist with work in the MACBA's collection. This Mallorcan painter now carries the torch for art in Barcelona. His stays in Mali, West Africa, have produced some epic 'relief' paintings.

Pere Jaume's work is great fun, neatly fusing questions of representational art and how to frame it. This theme is on permanent display in his ceiling of the Gran Teatre del Liceu, rebuilt and reopened in October 1999.

Susana Solano, another internationally known Catalan artist, finally gained an ample retrospective of her enigmatic metal constructions here in the late 1990s. Other artists representative of established trends include painters Xavier Grau, Ràfols-Casamada, Hernàndez-Pijuan and Grau Garriga. Artists producing work in multidisciplinary techniques include Carlos Pazos, José Manuel Broto, José María Sevilla and Sergi Aguilar.

The Museu d'Art Contemporani is situated right next door to the Centre de Cultura

'Dona i flors' by Miquel Blay, in MNAC.

Exhibiton at MACBA.

Contemporània de Barcelona (CCCB). This labyrinthine building was set up as a force for social, urban and cultural development, and has a full programme of striking, thought-provoking exhibitions, talks, music, dance and videos.

Preserving the past

On Montjuïc hill, the Museu Nacional d'Art de Catalunya (see page 179) is unmissable. It offers a fabulous opportunity to marvel at Catalonia's wealth of Gothic and Romanesque painting and sculpture, including medieval wall paintings. In a bid to collect 1,000 years of Catalan art under one roof, the pieces from the former Museu d'Art Modern were transferred here in 2004, including important works by Ramón Casas, Santiago Rusiñol and other major *modernista* artists from the late 19th and early 20th centuries.

THE PHENOMENON OF STREET ART

Street art is prevalent in all areas of the city, thanks to the initiatives in the 1990s to create new urban spaces. Eduardo Chillida's heavyweight sculpture *Elogi de l'Aigua* (In Praise of Water), in the Parc Creueta de Coll, is a fine example. Artist-poet Joan Brossa is ever-present in the city: his giant-sized letters are scattered about the Passeig Vall d'Hebron, and his bronze tribute to 'Barcino' is set in front of the cathedral.

In the Passeig Picasso, Tàpies pays homage to his idol with a large glass cube containing planks, a piano and painted blankets. The cube itself was designed by the great-grandson of Lluís Domènech i Montaner.

On the beach at Barceloneta is Rebecca Horn's reminder of the original beach huts and restaurants which were torn down to make way for the new waterfront development. Models of the huts, cast in bronze and lit like beacons from within, lie piled one on top of the other. Nearby is Juan Munoz's typically enigmatic and melancholic piece *A room where it always rains,* which is a caged 'room' filled with his figures that could perhaps roll on their round bases, but for their weight of cast bronze. Also down by the port is Lichtenstein's *Barcelona Head,* in front of the main post office. It uses Gaudí's technique of setting broken pieces of ceramic into cement.

DESIGNER CITY

In Barcelona your whole day can be a designer experience, from breakfast in your boutique hotel to dinner in a stylish restaurant, via shops and museums that have all been given the designer treatment.

Vinçon, high temple of interior design.

Buying the greens in your local market in Barcelona can be a designer experience, as can going to pay your dues in the Town Hall, and, if you have the misfortune to need attention in the Hospital del Mar, console yourself with the fact you are walking into a carefully planned space where sleek seats in the

Innovative design has never been an alien concept in Catalonia, a society that has always striven to represent its individuality to the world.

waiting room offer views over a sculpted promenade and landscaped beaches where even the showers have the stamp of a well-known design name. Exaggeration? Well, no, because this is the city where design forms part of daily life.

Liberation of ideas

The great boom in design that swept through Barcelona in the 1980s following Franco's death is legendary. Fuelled by the challenge of preparing for the Olympics, it forms the basis of contemporary Barcelona. But awareness of design – above all architecture – and an individual approach to it is nothing new here.

Style consciousness

Catalan Gothic already stood out from other European Gothic architecture in the 14th century. As art critic Robert Hughes commented: 'Catalan architects did not want to imitate the organic profusion of detail in northern Gothic. They liked a wall.' Similarly, with *modernisme*, Catalonia had its own take on Art Nouveau. The extraordinary creativity of Gaudí was an extreme case for any society to accept, yet bourgeois industrialists were his patrons and had homes built by him. They had a designer hospital too, Domènech i Montaner's radical Antic Hospital de la Santa Creu, in use until 2009, when it expanded into a new building.

The first 'design bars', among them Nick Havanna and Torres de Avila, dazzled in the 1980s, and architecture magazines began to applaud Barcelona's urban spaces. From there, the design movement gained momentum, eagerly supported by city authorities keen to

A suite at Hotel Omm.

In Barcelona, impersonal chain hotels are snubbed for new boutique hotels, such as Neri, Casa Camper and Omm (see pages 252, 253 and 256).

enhance Barcelona's image and promote local talent. Street furniture is designed by the likes of Oscar Tusquets, and drinking fountains by Santa & Cole. City markets have had multimillion-euro facelifts.

The same is true of the public Hospital del Mar, which has a catchment area that is one of the city's most needy. Visiting the hospital, one is struck by the Mediterranean light filtering through skylights, the space, the sea outlook, and the healthy breezes sweeping through patios where patients stroll.

Altered images

There was a time when visitors were drawn to Barcelona for its heady mix of Mediterranean culture and the kind of decadence associated with a dirty old port. Bars selling absinthe and seedy Barri Xino cabarets were sought out by night, while restaurants with starched table-cloths and grumpy waiters were patronised by day. Nowadays visitors swarm in for a sophisticated blend of culture and commerce. Hand luggage on return flights is a walking advertisement for brands such as Custo and Camper.

Following the trend of the Born with its boutique prettification, the once notorious El Raval neighbourhood has been the most recent subject of the designer makeover. Already home to the MACBA, the CCCB (Centre for Contemporary Culture) and FAD (Foment de les Arts Decoratives, promoting new design and located in a Gothic convent), it is sprouting galleries, shops, restaurants and hotels. It's still to be seen whether the balance will be kept between all these newcomers and old local groceries and cobblers.

The designer city has its attractions, and its pursuit is in the Catalan genes, but the other traits of Barcelona that give it its colour and charm will never be totally eclipsed.

RETAIL THERAPY

Barcelona has earned a reputation as a top shopping destination, with its infinite options ranging from traditional grocery stores to cutting-edge fashion boutiques.

Whether you are after a sharp Antonio Miró suit or a unique outfit by a young Catalan designer hot from the catwalk, handmade rope-soled shoes or trendy Camper sandals, rustic ceramics or oven-roasted nuts, antiques or handicrafts, it's all here. And finding it can be part of the pleasure, with shops located in attractive settings. If you stroll along the elegant central avenues of the Eixample, past some of the greatest examples of modernista architecture, you'll come across top national names in fashion, such as Antonio Miró, Sita Murt, Adolfo Dominguez, Loewe and Purificación Garcia. The major international names all seem to be clamouring now to have their patch on Passeig de Gràcia, from Gucci, Louis Vuitton and Chanel to Stella McCartney. Wander through the medieval lanes of the Born in the Old Town for one-off independent boutiques like Anna Povo or Cortana, and the Gothic quarter is best for traditional crafts and antiques. The food markets are a trip for the senses and provide great ideas for gifts to take home, from organic olive oil to roasted nuts. There's even a shopping centre lapped by the Mediterranean in the harbour, Maremàgnum, and another, Diagonal Mar, right by the beach. Shopping can be punctuated with coffee breaks at terrace cafés or lunchtime *menús* in a local bar, or even a dip into a gallery or museum en route. The streets off Plaça Catalunya, like Portal de l'Angel and Pelai, are best for shoes and the main chain stores, especially for young fashion. See Shopping listings for each neighbourhood under the relevant chapter.

International shoe chain, Camper, started in Barcelona.

Sombreria Obach (Call, 2) is a treasure just off Plaça Sant Jaume, run by the two grandsons of its founder. Gaze at the array of hats in the polished window, from traditional berets to suave panamas, but don't miss its impeccable interior.

Latest on the fashion scene are small boutiques where young designers sell their ultra-creative collections. On Land (Princesa, 25) stocks several Catalan designers, like Miriam Ponsa, Josep Abril, Name and their own label.

ONLY IN BARCELONA

Even chocolates have been given the designer treatment in Xocoa (Vidriera, 4) and other outlets. Expect exotic fillings like green tea.

One of the joys of shopping here is that traditional shops still run by the third or fourth generation of the family manage to hold out among the hip and cool, despite soaring rents. Get off the beaten track and you'll find curious little shops selling everything from the ubiquitous brown earthenware cooking pots to olive oil dispensers. In the central Eixample, Guantes Victoriano (Mallorca, 195) will make gloves to your size. The heady scent of fresh flowers in the sunshine is quintessentially Mediterranean as you wander down La Rambla de les Flors, or find bouquets or balcony-sized olive trees 24/7 at unique florists Navarro (València, 320), which doesn't even close for Christmas. Even chocolates have been given the designer treatment in Xocoa (Princesa, 28) with stylish packaging and exotic flavours like wasabi or green tea, but if you favour a classical approach Fargas (Pí, 16) has barely changed since it opened in 1827. Boutique wine shops have sprung up in most neighbourhoods, but for expert advice on Catalan and Spanish wines go to Vila Viniteca (Agullers, 7). For the ultimate Barça souvenir, head to one of the football club's official shops (including at Jaume I, 18).

Get off the beaten track and you'll find curious little shops selling everything from earthenware pots to perfumes in styles which are hard to resist.

Take a look inside one of the many old chemists' shops, with fixtures and fittings from the height of the modernista period.

Born in Barcelona of Swiss parents, Desigual has grown fast into a brand with a totally Barcelonan identity. True to its name, its clothes are different to most of the high street, with wacky designs, bright colours and a spirit of fun. Stores are located all over the city, in shopping centres, on La Rambla and in Passeig de Gràcia, and are starting to spread around the globe.

MARKETS

Discover enticing markets bursting with local produce from farms, mountains and the sea, as well as tropical fruit from far afield.

The ornate façade of La Boqueria.

There are more than 40 municipal markets in Barcelona. The largest of them – La Boqueria, Sant Antoni (both built on the site of former monasteries) and El Born (now a cultural centre, see page 131) – are impressive late 19th-century iron-and-glass structures. These cathedrals to food are ideal places to display Catalonia's wide variety of produce from the mountains, rich farmlands and the sea, often sold by third- and fourth-generation vendors. In recent years, however, tradition has been giving way to trend, with juice bars and fusion food, and prices, particularly in touristy La Boqueria, have been rising. Santa Caterina and Barceloneta have been dramatically overhauled to become stylish markets with a designer edge. Sant Antoni is next. However, they all still retain a vital Mediterranean energy which is totally intoxicating.

Explore the lesser known markets for the most genuine experience, like La Llibertat in Gràcia, or Poblenou, both dating from the late 19th century. Every neighbourhood has at least one market and they all have bars where you can eat something freshly prepared, and some have stalls on the outer edge selling bargain clothes or kitchen utensils.

Elsewhere, squares and open spaces are put to good use with regular stamp, book, craft, antiques and bric-à-brac markets. The latest is the lively multicultural weekend market in Rambla del Raval. The main flea market, one of the oldest in Europe, is El Encants in Glòries, settling into its new 21st-century space under a dazzling roof, part of the new Glòries complex. Get there early to dig out a bargain.

In Mercat de la Concepció.

Mercat Santa Caterina was recently rebuilt by architects Enric Miralles and Benedetta Tagliabue with a distinctive multi-coloured roof. Building work revealed the ruins of the monastery on which it stands.

Shopping for exotic fruits at La Boqueria.

Bric-à-brac at El Encants flea market in Glòries. Arrive early in the morning for the best buys.

WHERE TO EAT MARKET PRODUCE

A carnivore's dream at Mercat de Barceloneta.

For a visitor, much of the food on offer at the city's markets is merely for looking at, unless you are self-catering. Fresh bread, olives, cheese and charcuterie make for a delicious impromptu picnic, but to really savour the range of produce, visit the market cafés and restaurants, which use the fresh supplies all around them. Many of the established ones are institutions. In La Boqueria, **Pinotxo**, run by the Bayen family, opens at 6am and specialises in oysters and cava. Rub shoulders with the city's high-fliers as you sit at the bar. Foodies gather for breakfast from 8am at **Quim de la Boqueria** towards the back of the market, where Quim Márquez produces innovative dishes. In Mercat Santa Caterina, **Cuines Santa Caterina**, from the Tragaluz group, serves fusion food in a cool, modern space, while **Bar Joan** offers excellent traditional dishes from its economically priced menú del dia. At the revamped Mercat de Barceloneta, have breakfast on the terrace at Bar del Paco or upbeat tapas at Guindilla.

Santa Llúcia Christmas market in front of the cathedral. The rest of the year there is an antiques market on Thursdays.

Dining at Taller de Tapas.

A PASSION FOR FOOD

In Barcelona you will find some of the best food in Spain. An abundance of fresh fish, superb meat, a cornucopia of great vegetables, plus Catalan inventiveness, have produced a distinctive and delicious cuisine.

No one should visit Barcelona without making some attempt to get to know Catalan food. The experience would be incomplete otherwise, and any assessment of its people merely superficial. Eating is an important part of Catalan culture, something to be valued, taken seriously and enjoyed to the full, in true Catalan style.

The acerbic political commentator and eminent writer Manuel Vázquez Montalbán was passionate about food; he bestowed a certain grace on any restaurant where he chose to eat. In his opinion, 'Catalan cooking is one of the most distinguishing signs of the national identity.' It is also a composite of the nation's past, embodying the many influences of the different peoples and cultures that have swept through, settled in or bordered Catalonia, to say nothing of the lands dominated by Catalonia over its millennial history. The original fusion food, perhaps.

The oyster bar at TragaFishh, in the restaurant Tragaluz.

Nature's bounty

Catalan cooking is also a reflection of the geographical and physical characteristics of the country. Many dishes are based on the nuts, garlic, olive oil, tomatoes, herbs and dried fruits that are indigenous to these lands. Catalans are justifiably proud that their region can offer miles of rugged coastline and sheltered beaches, as well as awesome mountain ranges and rich valleys, and all within easy reach of each other.

Similarly, the cooking combines the natural products of the sea, the fertile plains and the mountains in a style known as *mar i muntanya*

(sea and mountain). It makes for strange-sounding, though delicious, marriages on the menu, such as *mandonguilles amb sèpia* (meatballs with cuttlefish), or *gambes amb pollastre* (prawns with chicken).

Simple pleasures

The health-giving properties of a Mediterranean diet are almost a cliché these days, and a selling point in many an advertising campaign, but here such a diet still exists in a pure, unadulterated form. One of the most famous Catalan dishes is perhaps the most simple, yet one of the best: the ubiquitous

> Try to adapt to local timing: have breakfast when Barcelonans do, lunch with them, even have 'tea' with the old ladies and children, and then you'll be able to wait until after 9pm for dinner.

pa amb tomàquet. This fresh 'peasant' bread rubbed with tomato, a trickle of virgin olive oil and a pinch of salt is the Mediterranean answer to northern Europe's sliced bread and butter, and not surprisingly provokes a certain amount of southern pride. It's a delicious accompaniment to meals, and can also be eaten as a snack served with anchovies, cured meats or cheese.

Breakfast time

Breakfast veers wildly from being a dull, cursory affair of milky coffee and biscuits, to a full-blooded *esmorzar de forquilla* (fork breakfast), which is a mid-morning meal of hearty dishes

Local cheeses for sale in the market.

Delectable hams.

like pigs' trotters and bean stews. This is more of a rural market-town tradition, not meant for an efficient morning in the office. It is common, though, to have a large ham sandwich or wedge of traditional Spanish omelette (*truita* in Catalan, *tortilla* in Spanish) with a glass of wine around 10am, and to chase the morning coffee with a *conyac*. For the faint-hearted, bars and cafés serve good *cafè amb llet* (large coffee with milk), *tallat* (a shorter version) or *cafè sol* (small, black and intense) with a range of pastries or croissants.

Lunchtime treats

Visitors can indulge in what is more of a weekend treat for residents: an aperitif around 1pm. This consists of a drink such as red vermouth, often with soda, served with olives and other *tapas* (snacks) like *boquerons* (pickled anchovies) or tinned *escopinyes* (cockles). The temptation to turn this into a light lunch is where visitors often lose the local rhythm.

The advantages of having lunch (*dinar*) are manifold: the food has just arrived from the market and is at its best; it can be slept or walked off; the whole city is tuned in to lunch

El Raval's Rita Rouge, where a Venezuelan chef adds a twist to local produce.

– a sacred quiet descends, especially on Sunday, and many offices and small shops are closed until 4 or 5pm.

Peak lunchtime is 2pm, lingering on to 4pm or even later at weekends – although there is a danger of not being served after 3.30pm. Lunch is also the most economical meal, when nearly every restaurant has a *menú del dia* (set menu). Even the most basic of these offers a choice of starters (soup, salad or vegetables),

OCTOBER HARVEST

October is a great time to be in Barcelona, because it's mushroom season, when fans of wild fungi will be in their element. The market stalls are rich in autumnal colours, and the smell of damp woods is intoxicating. The generic name for the various wild mushrooms is *bolets*. *Rovelló* is one of the best, especially just grilled with garlic and parsley, but also delicious in stewed meat dishes at this time of the year. For the best range of fresh, dried (or, if need be, frozen) mushrooms, and unusual fresh herbs, go to Petras, Fruits del Bosc, at the very back of La Boqueria market, and mingle with restaurateurs picking out choice items.

a main course of meat or fish, a dessert, and wine, beer or a soft drink. Obviously the standard and the price vary from one restaurant to another, but for €10–14 you can expect an excellent, balanced meal.

Sauces may be rich but can be outweighed by a crisp fresh salad and fruit to follow. The option of simple grilled fish or meat, garnished with a *picada* of garlic and parsley, is hard to equal, especially when accompanied by *allioli* (a strong garlic mayonnaise that is also served with rice dishes).

Local specialities

Look out for *menús* that include any of the following: as starters, *arròs negre*, black rice, a more interesting version of paella made with squid and its ink; *escalivada*, grilled peppers and aubergines dressed with oil; *esqueixada*, salad of raw salt cod, onions and peppers; *xató*, a salad from Sitges of frisée lettuce with tuna, salt cod, anchovies and a *romesco* sauce; *espinacs a la Catalana*, spinach sautéed with raisins and pine nuts; *faves a la Catalana*, small broad beans stewed with herbs, pork and sausages (best in spring); *canalons*, a

Oriol Ivern, chef at Hisop restaurant.

Fish being cooked 'a la plancha'.

Catalan tradition brought from Italy, always eaten on 26 December; *fideuà*, an excellent and lesser-known variation on paella, comprising noodles cooked in a fish stock, and *escudella*, the most traditional Catalan soup, a strictly winter dish. *Escudella* is usually followed by *carn d'olla*, that is, the meat and vegetables that have been cooked to make the soup. Now a traditional Christmas dish, this used to be part of the staple diet of every Catalan household.

The main event

Among the main courses, be sure to try the very Catalan *botifarra amb mongetes*, a tasty sausage served with haricot beans; *fricandó*, braised veal with *moixernons*, a small, delicate wild mushroom; *bacallà*, salt cod served in many ways such as *a la llauna* (garlic, parsley and tomato) or *amb xamfaina* (tomato, pepper and aubergine sauce, also served with meat); *suquet*, a seafood stew; *calamars farcits*, stuffed squid; *oca amb naps*, goose with turnip; *conill*, rabbit, either grilled and served with *allioli*, or stewed; *xai*, lamb – the cutlets (*costelletes*) are especially good.

Fish (*peix*) and shellfish (*marisc*) should not be missed in Barcelona: the simplest and perhaps the best way is grilled (a mixed grill, *graellada*, is a good option for two) or baked in the oven, *al forn*. It is worth going to a good restaurant for a paella; cheap imitations are usually disappointing.

If you have any room for dessert, don't miss the famous *crema catalana*, a cinnamon-flavoured custard with a burnt caramel top. Other traditional *postres* include *mel i mató*, a curd cheese with honey, *postre de músic*, a mixture of roast nuts and dried fruits, usually served with a glass of sweet *moscatel*, and *macedonia* (fruit salad).

Berenar and later

The advantage of the light-lunch option is being able to face a *berenar* (afternoon snack). From around 5 to 7.30pm *granjes* (milk bars) overflow as people manage to drink extremely thick chocolate (the authentic version is made with water and needs to be 'drunk' with a spoon – sometimes the spoon will almost stand up in the thick liquid) and very creamy cakes. For a

classic *berenar* try the cafés around the Plaça del Pi, especially in Petritxol, or sit at a marble table in the Granja M. Viader in Xuclà, the oldest *granja* in Barcelona, where *cacaolat* (a children's favourite) was invented.

Shops and offices are open until 8 or 9pm, so family dinner is around 10pm, and is usually quite light: soup and an omelette, for example. Restaurants don't normally start serving until around 9pm.

Creative cooks

Apart from these traditional dishes, the creative spectrum is broadening into many variations on the basic Catalan theme, in both *tapas* and main dishes. There is a new generation of chefs, many inspired or even trained by world-famous Ferran Adrià, and the Roca brothers' El Celler de Can Roca in Girona was named 2013 Best Restaurant in the World by the British magazine *Restaurant*. A rebellious spirit, combined with the essential Catalan love of food and passion for the Mediterranean, is a formula that makes for

Churros and hot chocolate at Granja-Xocolateria La Pallaresa.

You can eat at one of several stalls in La Boqueria market.

exciting results. Get a taste of this in restaurants like Alkimia, Commerç 24 or Hisop, to name but a few.

International influences

As an increasingly cosmopolitan capital, Barcelona has a broad range of restaurants that reflect the tastes and demands of its inhabitants and visitors. There are restaurants from other regions of Spain, particularly Galicia, from top-notch, top-price Botafumeiro with fine oysters and fish, to the average corner bar. And then there are French, Italian, Greek, Lebanese, Moroccan, Mexican, South American, Indian, Pakistani, Chinese and Japanese, plus a growing number of vastly improved vegetarian

EAT YOUR WAY ROUND THE CITY – A GUIDE TO SNACKS

Not traditionally from Catalonia, tapas (*tapes* in Catalan) are available in most bars in Barcelona. The term covers any snack to accompany a drink, ranging from a few olives to a small portion of a main dish, often served here with pa amb tomàquet (see page 72). Regular favourites are ***croquetas*** (croquettes of ham, chicken or mushroom), ***ensaladilla rusa*** (Russian salad – diced vegetables in mayonnaise), ***patates braves*** (fried potatoes doused in a hot spicy sauce), ***pebrots de Padró*** (tiny green peppers, sometimes picante hot) or varied embotits (cured meats and spicy dried sausages). And hanging behind nearly every bar will be legs of pernil salat (cured ham, jamón serrano in Spanish). Treat yourself to jamón ibérico, expensive but melts in the mouth. You may also find on the menu: ***bunyols de bacallà*** (salt cod fritters), formatge (cheese), pescaditos (small fried fish) or pulpo (octopus, a Galician speciality) and, of course, a range of tortillas (Spanish omelette), either potato, spinach, aubergine or francesa (with no filling). Accompany tapas with a canya (glass of draught beer) or wine.

The Basques specialise in *pinchos*, a small tasty montage on a slice of bread, pierced with a toothpick. Basque bars have sprung up across the city. Help yourselves to a pincho then count the toothpicks to assess the bill. Beware how they add up. It's best to drink a txakolí (Basque white wine) to get the full experience.

Scallops at Carballeira.

Customers enjoying a drink and tapas.

restaurants – vegetarians used to have a hard time in Spain, but this, too, is changing. There really is no excuse to resort to one of the fast-food outlets insidiously taking root in some of the most historic streets and squares – the latest, inevitable, sign of cultural colonisation.

So get out there, make new discoveries, and immerse yourself in local culture in one of the most enjoyable ways possible.

PASTRY HEAVEN

In Barcelona the number of pastry shops per square metre must rank among the world's highest. For each feast day and festival there is a corresponding traditional sweetmeat: *bunyols* (a small doughnut) during Lent, *la mona* (an elaborate cake with fancy decorations) for Easter, *panellets* (little marzipan cakes decorated with pine nuts) for All Saints Day and for castanyades (autumnal parties centred on roasting chestnuts). Throughout the summer months the different neighbourhood and village feast days are celebrated with fireworks, cava and cocas (pastries covered in sugar, crystallised fruits and pine nuts).

WINE

The reputation of Spanish wine has changed
enormously in recent years, and Catalonia is one
of the regions that is now attracting attention
from international connoisseurs as well as visitors
with a taste for the good things in life.

There's an extensive range of wines to choose from.

d'Origen Qualificada), the top accolade.
The Rioja is the only other region in Spain
to have this qualification. The D.O. wines
are **Empordà-Costa Brava**, near the French
border; **Alella**, in the Maresme, a tiny area
known for its white wines, on the outskirts
of Barcelona; the well-known **Penedès**, to the
southwest of Barcelona; the most recent, **Pla
de Bages**, near Manresa; **Conca de Barberà**,
with its *modernista* wine cellars, in Tarragona;
Costers del Segre, home of Raimat wines, to
the west in Lleida; and **Tarragona**, **Terra Alta**
and **Montsant** in the south.

In a bid for stronger identity in the international market the large companies, backed

> In restaurants the house wine (vi de la casa)
> is often a young wine or, in rural areas, a
> dark red wine. Don't be surprised if red
> wines are served chilled in summer.

There was a time when Spanish wine meant
plonk, and the only Spanish vintage to
have any international acclaim was Rioja.
Today, these misconceptions are in the past,
and anyone who appreciates a decent glass of
wine will be aware that Spain has many different wine-growing regions, producing a range of
interesting and increasingly high-quality wines.

Catalonia's wine regions

Catalonia has nine wine regions officially clas-
sified as D.O. (*Denominació d'Origen*, similar
to the French *appellation contrôlée*) and one,
the Priorat, which is D.O.Q. (Denominació

by the Generalitat (Catalan autonomous government), introduced a denomination for the
region as a whole, **D.O. Catalunya**, a few years
ago. The smaller denominations continue to
exist within this framework.

The Catalan region with the highest profile
abroad is the Penedès, mostly due to the giant
Torres, a family firm in Vilafranca del Penedès
that exports wine to more than 90 countries, has
vineyards in Chile and California, and is held in
high esteem in the wine world. With the fifth
generation of the family now in the business,
they continue to produce award-winning wines

In the bar La Vinya del Senyor.

such as Gran Coronas Black Label, Fransola, Gran Viña Sol and Viña Esmeralda.

Over the past few years there has been a lot of activity among the smaller bodegas across Catalonia, involving experimentation, new techniques, different grape varieties and maximising of the indigenous grapes such as *xarel. lo* and *macabeo* (white), and *carinyena, garnatxa* and *monastrell* reds. It is reflected in improved quality, and some notable wines are emerging.

Up-and-coming labels

One of the most fascinating areas is the Priorat, traditionally known for cheap, strong wines bought from barrels, but now producing some of the best-quality wine in the country. Large companies from La Rioja and the Penedès have started working there, and some highly prized wines are emerging from its low-yield, high-alcohol-content grapes grown on terraced hillsides rich in slate.

La Ermita, from Riojan wine maker Alvaro Palacios, can sell for over €600 a bottle,

depending on the vintage. Other wines to look out for, not necessarily so highly priced, are **Cervoles**, a red from Costers del Segre, **Can Rafols dels Caus**, **Can Feixes** and the ecological **Albet i Noia** wines from the Penedès, and **Oliver Conti**, from another up-and-coming area, the Empordà. An increasing number of organic wines from small bodegas are available.

THE HOME OF CAVA

Some 95 percent of Spain's cava is produced in Catalonia and the greater part from the Penedès, where it was created by Josep Raventós in 1872. From that celebrated first bottle grew the Codorníu empire, which along with Freixenet leads the cava industry. This sparkling wine, made by the *méthode champenoise*, is obligatory at fiestas and a ubiquitous companion to Sunday lunch (when it is served with dessert). One of the world's great sparkling wines, cava is warmer, earthier and less acidic than champagne (see page 228).

Busy streets in the Barri Gòtic.

Cyclists by El Cap de Barcelona.

ORIENTATION

A detailed guide to Barcelona and its surroundings, with principal sites clearly cross-referenced by number to the maps.

The Places section of this guide is divided geographically, beginning with La Rambla, the Old Town's famous spine, and then exploring the distinctive areas spreading either side, and the waterfront stretching east from the foot of La Rambla.

In the Sagrada Família.

If you can get to one of the city's high points early in your visit – Montjuïc, Tibidabo, the Park Güell, or even Columbus's column – it will put the city into focus. It is not surprising that this is one of the world's densest cities (15,977 inhabitants per sq km): packed in between the Collserola range of hills and the Mediterranean, and bordered by Montjuïc and the River Besòs, all the available space has been consumed. Parks tend to be in rocky knolls where no building could have been erected, or created latterly in disused industrial spaces. The latest developments include planned extensions to the port and the recycling of 19th-century factories into 21st-century business opportunities.

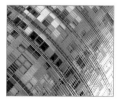

Torre Agbar detail.

The city's layout

Plaça de Catalunya is a good place to get your bearings. From this crossroads between the Old Town (the Ciutat Vella) and the New Town (the 19th-century Eixample), it is easy to get a sense of place and history. The Old Town, containing most of the city's historical landmarks, is divided into the Barri Gòtic, La Ribera and El Raval. The Barri Gòtic (Gothic Quarter) is in the middle, bordered by La Rambla and Via Laietana. La Ribera is the district on the other side of Via Laietana, including some medieval streets, and El Raval lies on the other side of La Rambla, where convents-turned-cultural-centres rub shoulders with the last remnants of the notorious Barri Xino.

Plaça de Catalunya, like an all-encompassing terminal, is also a good departure point for most excursions. Airport buses arrive there, buses to most parts of town and beyond can be caught there, two metro lines run through it and the FGC trains uptown and to the Parc de Collserola leave from there. Even trains to the coast and the mountains depart from beneath this central square.

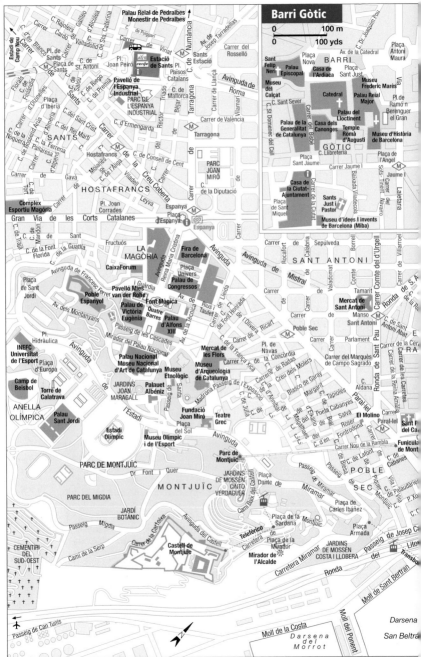

Barri Gòtic

0		100 m
0		100 yds

Palau Reial de Pedralbes
Monestir de Pedralbes

Carrer de Puigpart

C. Rejolers
C. d'Alcolea
C. de Galileo

Pi. Blanco
Pl. de Sants
C. Bordeta
C. de Valladolid
Sta. Caterina

Estadi de Camp Nou

Carrer del Viriat

Av. de Josep Tarradellas

Carrer del Rosselló

Plaça Antoni Maura

BARRI

Plaça Nova

Av. de la Catedral

Sant Felip Neri

Palau Episcopal

Casa de l'Ardiaca

Plaça Sant Just

Museu del Calçat

Museu Frederic Marès

Catedral

Palau Reial Major

Pl. de Ramón Berenguer el Gran

Via Laietana

Palau del Lloctinent

Palau de la Generalitat de Catalunya

Casa dels Canonges

Temple Romà d'Augustí

Museu d'Història de Barcelona

GÒTIC

C. Llibreteria

Plaça Sant Jaume

Plaça de l'Àngel

Carrer Jaume I

Jaume I

Casa de la Ciutat-Ajuntament

Baixada Viladecols

Plaça de Sant Miquel

Sants Just i Pastor

Museu d'idees i invents de Barcelona (Miba)

Carrer de Sepúlveda

SANT ANTONI

Rocafort

Calàbria

Borrell

Viladomat

Comte

de Villarroel

Comte de l'Urgell

Ronda de S.A.

Mistral

Tamarit

Mercat de Sant Antoni

Sant Antoni

C. de Sant Antoni Abat

Manso

M

Parlament

Poble Sec

Carrer del Marquès de Campo Sagrado

Ronda de Sant Pau

Carrer de la Cer...

E RA

Carrer de la Reina Amàlia

El Molino

Paral·lel

Paral·lel

Sant F del Ca

Funicular de Mont

POBLE

SEC

Plaça de Carles Ibáñez

Plaça Armada

JARDINS DE MOSSÈN COSTA I LLOBERA

Passeig de Josep C...

Lito...

Transbo...

Darsena

San Beltrà

Moll de Sant Bertràn

Moll del Ponent

Darsena del Morrot

Moll de la Costa

Estació de Sants

Pavelló de l'Espanya Industrial

PARC DE L'ESPANYA INDUSTRIAL

SANTS

HOSTAFRANCS

Complex Esportiu Magória

Gran Via de les Corts Catalanes

Espanya

Plaça d'Espanya

LA MAGÓRIA

Fira de Barcelona

CaixaForum

Plaça Univers

Palau de Congressos

Pavelló Mies van der Rohe

Poble Espanyol

Palau de Victòria Eugènia

Font Màgica

Quatre Barres

Palau d'Alfons XIII

Plaça de Sant Jordi

INEFC Universitat de l'Esport

Plaça d'Europa

Camp de Beisbol

Torre de Calatrava

ANELLA OLÍMPICA

Palau Sant Jordi

Mirador del Palau Nacional

Palau Nacional Museu Nacional d'Art de Catalunya

Museu Etnològic

JARDINS JOAN MARAGALL

Palauet Albéniz

Mercat de les Flors

Museu d'Arqueologia de Catalunya

Pl. de Navas

Creu dels Molers

Blasco de Garay

Estadi Olímpic

Museu Olímpic i de l'Esport

Fundació Joan Miró

Teatre Grec

Plaça del Sol

PARC DE MONTJUÏC

Parc de Montjuïc

MONTJUÏC

PARC DEL MIGDIA

JARDÍ BOTÀNIC

JARDINS DE MOSSÈN CINTO VERDAGUER

Plaça Dante

Miramar

CEMENTIRI DEL SUD-OEST

Castell de Montjuïc

Teleférico

Mirador de l'Alcalde

Plaça de la Sardana

Plaça de la Mirador

Carretera Miramar

Ronda

Passeig de Can Tunis

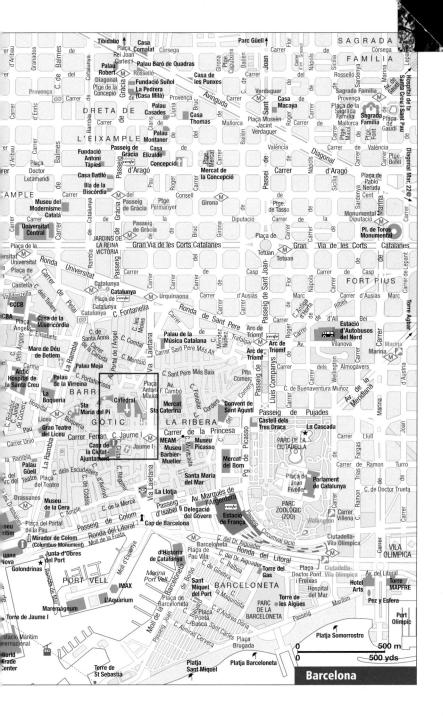

Barcelona

PLAÇA DE CATALUNYA AND LA RAMBLA

The spectacle and colour of the celebrated promenade leading from Plaça de Catalunya to the waterfront is a good starting point for getting to know the Old Town.

At the top end of La Rambla, **Plaça de Catalunya ❶** is not the kind of picturesque square that you might make an effort to visit, but it *is* the kind of place you inevitably pass through on any trip to Barcelona. Whether arriving from the airport by bus, coming into the city from other parts of Catalonia, visiting the Old Town from uptown or vice versa, Plaça de Catalunya is bound to be part of the trajectory. It is more of a pivotal *plaça*, acting as a logistical centre for the city's transport.

CENTRAL SQUARE

Here you'll find the metro underground train service, fgc trains (the Ferrocarrils de la Generalitat de Catalunya, which run to uptown areas and the suburbs), Rodalies de Catalunya (regional trains), city buses and the Aerobús to the airport, the Bus Turístic and taxis. A world of underground corridors leads to the trains, so allow time when travelling.

The main Barcelona city tourist office is also here, marked by a tall 'i' above ground. Run by the tourist board, it offers an efficient and helpful service, dishing out leaflets, maps and all kinds of information, as well as providing a hotel reservation service, money exchange and an internet connection.

For many visitors to the city, Plaça de Catalunya also marks the beginning of another inevitability in Barcelona: a walk down the famous avenue called **La Rambla**.

Before embarking on that flow of humanity down to the sea, pause a moment in the welcome shade of Plaça de Catalunya's trees, or in the bright winter sunshine that fills it with a light and warmth which

Main Attractions
Café Zurich
Font de Canaletes
Palau de la Virreina
Mercat de la Boqueria
Gran Teatre del Liceu
Palau Güell
Arts Santa Mònica
La Mare de Déu de la Mercè
Monument a Colom

Maps and Listings
Map, page 90
Shopping, page 105
Restaurants, page 106
Accommodation, page 250

Choosing cherries at La Boqueria.

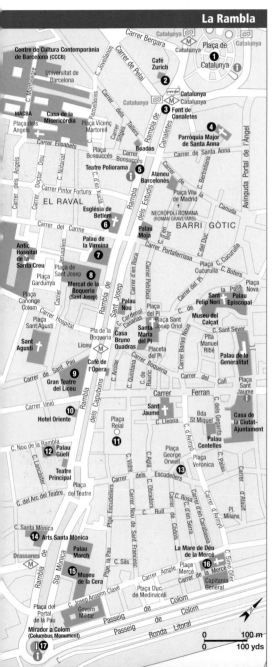

La Rambla

barely reaches the narrowest of the Old Town streets.

Pigeons flock here to be fed by children and old ladies. Tacky stalls sell plastic toys and caramelised nuts. Families wander around aimlessly, lovers meet beneath the gushing fountains and predatory youths lurk, with an eye on swinging handbags and cameras. Men gather to play chess beneath the monument to a much-loved Catalan leader, Macià, designed by contemporary sculptor Subirachs, and tourists in shorts and sun hats queue for the bus tour.

The plaça's past

The square is more of a created centre than one with a real Catalan heart. Consider its history. When the medieval wall of Barcelona was demolished in 1854 to extend the city by making a new district, the *Eixample* (see page 191), the *plaça* was a large field outside the city, traversed by a mountain stream (the stream bed later formed the foundations of La

In Plaça de Catalunya.

Rambla) and connected to the inner city by means of an entrance called the Portal dels Orbs. The entrance was later renamed the **Portal de l'Angel** because, so the story goes, when Sant Ferrer crossed through this doorway with his followers, he was greeted by an angel. The 19th-century Plan Cerdà, a project for the redevelopment of Barcelona, called for the creation of a square a little further inland, at the junction of **Passeig de Gràcia** and the **Gran Via**.

Another rival project presented by Antoni Rovira i Trías proposed an enormous *plaça*, 800 by 400 metres (2,600 by 1,300ft) to be called the 'Forum Isabel II'. Yet another plan for a *plaça*, similar to that which we know today, was designed in 1868 by Miquel Garriga.

While the authorities were trying to reach an agreement, the owners of the corresponding plots of land grew fed up with waiting and began to build. In 1902, Lord Mayor Ledesma ordered the demolition of all these buildings, but it was another quarter of a century before the *plaça* took on its current appearance. Based on a design by Francesc Nebot, the square was officially opened by King Alfonso XIII in 1927.

Winds of change

Ever since this uneasy birth, the winds of change have swept through the square, taking away any vestiges of nostalgia and tradition. Now it is bordered by banks and giant shopping institutions that seem to have been transplanted from Madrid and elsewhere like some kind of late 20th-century colonisation.

On the corner now dominated by the Hard Rock Café and a branch of the El Corte Inglés empire stood the legendary Maison Dorée café. Such was the character of this establishment that, when it closed its doors in 1918, another café of the same

Feeding the pigeons in Plaça de Catalunya.

WHERE

As well as being the hub of Barcelona in terms of transport and city communications, Plaça de Catalunya is the centre of the city in a wider sense. If you look in the middle of the square itself you'll find paving stones arranged in the shape of a star which, they say, marks the centre of the capital of Catalonia.

Fountains in the plaça.

Plaça public art.

name opened at No. 6. 'It was never the same,' wrote Lluís Permanyer, city historian, who relates that it was here that a tradition of 'five o'clock tea' was introduced to Barcelona.

Another meeting point of intellectuals was the old Hotel Colón, which has since been a bank and has just been reborn as a dazzling Apple Store. Older generations of Republicans remember when the facade of the hotel was covered with giant posters of Marx, Lenin and Stalin during the Civil War.

There was no mistaking that this was the headquarters of the Unified Socialist Party of Catalonia (PSUC), then the leading socialist group.

El Triangle

It's difficult to miss the monumental department store **El Corte Inglés**. On the opposite side is El Triangle, a commercial centre which is home to **FNAC**, a mega media store with several slick floors of books, music and technology. On the ground floor is a newsstand with an excellent range of magazines. The broad pavement here forms a tenuous link between La Rambla and the lesser-known Rambla de Catalunya, an elegant boulevard which runs through the Eixample past *modernista* buildings to meet the Diagonal (see page 196).

Café Zurich ❷

At the point of the 'triangle' where **Pelai** meets the top of La Rambla is

Café Zurich, a replica of the original café, which was demolished to build El Triangle. Thanks to its vantage point at a busy crossroads, and with the same old bad-tempered waiters, it has taken on the persona of the former famous landmark, and remains a favourite rendezvous point.

Whether you are seated on Café Zurich's terrace, or emerging blinking from the metro exit, contemplate the panorama ahead.

LA RAMBLA

The city's main pedestrian street is one of the most famous boulevards in Europe, and for many people one of the distinguishing features of Barcelona. This kaleidoscopic avenue throbs day and night, exerting an undeniable magnetism which attracts both visitors and locals, and which never fails to entertain.

The best advice is to plunge in, go with the flow and enjoy the constant weird and wonderful activity. Let yourself be carried past lottery ticket booths, shoe shiners, cheap *pensions*, human statues, northern Europeans in shorts in December,

and locals in sharp suits. Let your senses be assailed by the perfumed air of the flower stalls, the chatter of the gossips and the yells of the porters delivering fruit to the market. Don't miss a thing, especially the gambling con artists and ubiquitous pickpockets who inevitably prey on such a bountiful crowd. After dark La Rambla loses none of its daytime energy, becoming the main artery for anyone going *de juerga* (out for a wild time) in the Old Town.

Dr Masó's Farmacia Nadal has been here for decades.

Tourists flock to the plaça.

of all ages gather there to celebrate yet another victory for their successful team.

Shopping Streets

Just beyond the fountain, at the junction with Bonsuccés, is the pharmacy **Nadal with its** *modernista facade*, and across La Rambla are the diverging streets Santa Anna and Canuda, both pedestrian shopping streets.

Parròquia Major de Santa Anna ❹

Address: Santa Anna, 29
Opening Hrs: Mon–Sat 11am–7pm ; avoid weekends, the time for weddings and Masses
Entrance Fee: free
Transport: Catalunya

Hidden behind the busy shops of Santa Anna on the left is the **Parròquia Major de Santa Anna**, an oasis of peace. The Romanesque church and Gothic cloister are marvellous examples of the architecture of their time.

Return to La Rambla via **Plaça de la Vila de Madrid**, reached from the narrow street Bertrellans almost opposite the church: it is an attractive, landscaped square with some Roman graves dating from the 1st to 3rd centuries and a wonderful jacaranda tree. On the corner, at Canuda No. 6, is the **Ateneu Barcelonès**, a traditional cultural enclave dating from 1796. It's for members only, but you can steal a glimpse of the hushed library and magnificent interiors from the square.

Drinking from the Canaletes fountain.

Teatre Poliorama stages a variety of shows, including flamenco.

RAMBLA DE CANALETES

Between the top of La Rambla and the Columbus monument where it ends there are five different parts to the promenade. The first, **Rambla de Canaletes**, is named after the **Font de Canaletes ❸**, one of the symbols of Barcelona.

A small brass plaque at the foot of this 19th-century cast-iron fountain confirms the legend that all those who drink its waters will be enamoured of Barcelona and always return. It is a favourite meeting place, and posses of retired men regularly gather here for *tertúlies* (chatting in groups and putting the world to rights – often around a table after a large meal). The 'font' is at its most jubilant when Barça football fans

RAMBLA DELS ESTUDIS

Back on La Rambla, the crowd gets denser and the noise level rises as it passes through a corridor of newsstands and kiosks selling Catalan specialities. This is the **Rambla dels Estudis**, so named because the 16th-century university was here.

The Reial Acadèmia de Ciències i Arts on the right also houses the **Teatre Poliorama** ❺, which has regular performances (see page 263). On the exterior of the building, which was designed by Josep Domènech i Estapà, is the clock that has been the official timekeeper of the city since 1891. In *Homage to Catalonia* George Orwell recounts days spent on guard on this roof.

Of all the vast conglomeration of the former university, only the **Església de Betlem** ❻ (just before the smart 1898 hotel) remains, a long and rather depressing bulk. The Baroque facade on **Carme** was built in 1690 but the main structure was not completed until 1729.

Opposite is the **Palau Moja** (also known as the Marquis de Comillas Palace), an important 18th-century neoclassical building housing some offices of the Generalitat (the Catalan government) and occasionally open to show exhibitions. Under the arcades is the Generalitat bookshop, with a few titles of general interest amid weighty tomes of statistics on Catalonia.

The music shop next to the Palau de la Virreina has an attractive façade.

Browsing for music.

BRIEF DETOURS

At the corner, **Portaferrissa** leads into a world of commerce and numerous fashion shops, cafés selling hot chocolate and sticky confectionery, and the central part of the **Barri Gòtic** (see page 109). To the right of La Rambla is Carme, an interesting street going into the heart of **El Raval**, worth a brief detour for **El Indio**, a textiles shop (at No. 24) founded in 1870 and little changed since. Inside there are long wooden counters for proper display of the cloth, and wooden chairs for stout ladies to rest their legs.

RAMBLA DE SANT JOSEP

Back on the **Rambla de Sant Josep** (better known as the **Rambla de les Flors**), the air smells sweet. During the 19th century this was the only place where flowers were sold. The Catalan modernista artist Ramón Casas (1866–1932) picked out one of the flower sellers here to

DRINK

Tucked just inside Tallers, the first street on the right as you head down from Plaça de Catalunya, is Boadas, the oldest cocktail bar in town, with a 1930s interior and walls lined with caricatures of the original owner. The bar is known for its mojitos; the recipe was inherited from Boadas, who learnt his art in Cuba where, like so many Catalans in the 19th century, his parents had emigrated.

From River to Road – the History of La Rambla

Once lined with convents and then a fashionable promenade, today La Rambla offers something for everyone, from opera-goers and children to tourists and thieves.

Originally, La Rambla was the river bed (the Latin name arenno was replaced by the Arab word *ramla*) that marked the exterior limits of the city fortified by King Jaume I. But when Barcelona expanded during the 15th century, La Rambla became part of the inner city. In due course, a number of religious houses were built in the surrounding areas and the river bed came to be known as the 'Convent Thoroughfare'. Only at the beginning of the 18th century did La Rambla become a more clearly defined street, after permission was granted to build on the ancient walls in the Boqueria area. In 1775 a section of the city walls was torn down and a central walkway built, lined with poplar trees and higher than the roadway that ran along either side.

La Rambla has long been a favourite meeting place.

A place to be seen

Within the small and densely populated area of the ancient fortified city, La Rambla was the only street of any significance, and it became the city's focal point. Renovations were constantly under way during the 19th century, and the street settled down to become more exclusive and aristocratic; this change of status was aided by the disappearance of some of the surrounding buildings and convents, creating space for new squares and mansions.

La Rambla assumed its present shape between 1849 and 1856, when all the remaining fortifications were torn down. The first plane trees, brought from Devesa in Girona, were planted in 1851, and the street became 'the fashionable promenade route, where the cream of Barcelona parades on foot, by carriage or on horseback', according to the 19th-century journalist Gaziel.

Madding crowd

Today's promenaders are more mixed and more cosmopolitan, as La Rambla is an essential walk for any visitors, from other parts of Spain or abroad. Listen out for a Babel-like mix of languages as you try to make your way through the inevitable crowds. Since the regeneration of the Old Town in the 1990s, more uptown residents are venturing down to these 'lower' parts to visit art galleries and trendy boutiques, take their children to the chocolate shops in Petritxol or meet friends for dinner in the eclectic selection of new restaurants, though the 'cream' could always be spotted wrapped in furs on their way to the opera at the Liceu. They mingle with tourists, hen parties, pickpockets, petty criminals cheating at dice tricks and prostitutes assailing northern European businessmen. The local youth move in large crowds looking for cheap beer before going clubbing.

And while the fun continues into the night, out come the green municipal cleaners in force, like some kind of eco-angels, sweeping, collecting rubbish and vigorously hosing down the gutters in preparation for a new day, under the watchful eye of the faithful newsstands, which stay open all night.

be his model, and she later became his wife.

Palau de la Virreina ❼

On the right is the **Palau de la Virreina**, a magnificent 18th-century Rococo building set back from the road for greater effect. In 1771 Manuel Amat, Viceroy of Peru, sent a detailed plan from Lima for the construction of the house that he planned to build on La Rambla. The final building was not completed until 1778, and the viceroy died only a few years after taking up residence. It was his young widow who was left to enjoy the palace, which became known as the palace of the 'Virreina' or vicereine.

Today it is an excellent exhibition venue specialising in photography and image-based art as well as being the official cultural information centre, and a booking office. Wander into its handsome courtyard: around fiesta time there is usually some *gegant* (giant) or *drac* (dragon) lurking, before being brought out on parade. Next to it is a music store with a charming *modernista* front.

Mercat de la Boqueria ❽

Address: La Rambla, 91
Opening Hrs: Mon–Sat 7am–8pm
Transport: Liceu

Half a block further down is the entrance to the city's most popular and famous market, the **Mercat de la Boqueria**, or Mercat Sant Josep. The first stone was laid on 19 March 1840, Saint Joseph's day, to appease the saint whose convent on the same spot had been burnt down in the 1835 riots. Again, take plenty of time

Pretty bouquets for sale on one of the many flower stalls in the Sant Josep section of La Rambla.

Shopping in La Boqueria.

THE LICEU

The Liceu, founded by philanthropist Manuel Gibert i Sans, staged its first opera in 1838. Construction of a bigger venue began in 1844. The project was second only to that of La Scala in Milan, with space for 4,000 spectators and every type of performance. Stravinsky, de Falla, Caruso, Callas, Plácido Domingo and Pavarotti have all performed here, as well as Catalonia's own Pablo Casals, Montserrat Caballé and Josep Carreras. In 1994 a fire gutted the interior. Architect Ignasi de Solà Morales doubled its size while conserving its original style and it reopened in 1999 to much public acclaim. In attempts to broaden its appeal, the programme includes cabaret sessions in the foyer, performances for children and opera film cycles.

Details along La Rambla.

to enjoy shopping there, or simply to observe what's going on.

Discerning shoppers – restaurateurs early in the morning, housewives mid-morning and the men in charge of the Sunday paella on Saturdays – queue patiently for the best produce, bark their orders and refuse to be fobbed off with anything below par. The fishwives also shriek, trying to seduce passers-by into the day's best catch. It is a heady experience, despite the frantic crowds, as there is something quintessentially Mediterranean about the noise, human warmth and the serious business of buying and eating wonderfully fresh produce. It is at its best early in the morning before the spectators arrive.

On the opposite side of La Rambla is the **Palau Nou**. The total antithesis to La Boqueria, it is an ultra-modern building that is supposedly completely automated, including 'robot parking' on nine levels underground.

It also provides a short cut through to the **Plaça del Pi**, and effectively frames the beautiful Gothic tower of the *plaça*'s church, Santa Maria del Pi.

Pla de la Boqueria

Continuing on down, La Rambla enters the **Pla de la Boqueria** (marked only by a widening of La Rambla, and a break in the shady avenue of trees). This was the site of executions in the 14th century, when it was paved with flagstones. The name dates from the previous century, when tables selling fresh meat, *mesas de bocatería*, were erected here (*boc* is the Catalan for goat's meat). In the 15th century the tables of gamblers and cardsharps replaced the meat stalls.

Today the flagstones have been replaced by a Joan Miró pavement created in the 1970s – look out for his signature. On one corner stands the **Casa Bruno Quadras**, built by Josep Vilaseca in 1891. The building's colourful, extravagant decoration includes umbrellas, fans and a great Chinese dragon, illustrating the oriental influence on the *modernista* designers.

RAMBLA DELS CAPUTXINS

At this point the **Rambla dels Caputxins** begins, so called because, until 1775, the left side was the site of the Capuchin Convent and its adjacent vegetable garden.

Gran Teatre del Liceu ❾

Address: La Rambla, 51–59; www.liceubarcelona.cat
Tel: 902 533 353 (bookings); 93-485 9900 (information)
Entrance fee: tours (charge), guided 10am; non-guided 11.30am, 12pm, 12.30pm and 1pm
Transport: Liceu

The mood changes slightly now, as this stretch is dominated by the **Gran Teatre del Liceu**, cathedral of the *bel canto* in Spain and launch pad for names such as Carreras and Caballé. The original building, dating from 1861, was badly damaged by fire in 1994, but has since been

extravagantly restored to its former glory. New technology has been installed and a second stage added. The theatre season now covers a wide range of productions, from classical to ambitious avant-garde opera, ballet and recitals.

Alongside the theatre, Sant Pau leads down to the Romanesque church of Sant Pau del Camp in El Raval (see page 147).

Cafè de l'Òpera, an old favourite.

Inside Gran Teatre del Liceu.

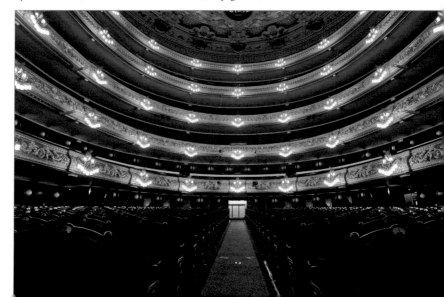

Restaurants and bars line the Plaça Reial. Glaciar is an old favourite, still full of life, and MariscCo is a stylish seafood restaurant. In the nearby streets, too, try traditional Los Caracoles (with sizzling chickens on a blazing grill on the exterior wall), and La Fonda. The latter is related to Quinze Nits in the Plaça and has the same effective formula – reasonably priced Catalan food, served in an attractive interior of palms and pale wood.

Evening dining.

Cafè de l'Òpera

Opposite the opera house is the **Cafè de l'Òpera**, opened in 1929. It remains a good place to read the newspapers in the morning – subdued and peaceful – yet builds up to a giddy pitch late at night.

Carrer Ferran

The Gran Teatre del Liceu ends opposite **Ferran**, one of the most elegant streets in Barcelona in the first half of the 19th century. Remnants of this time can still be seen despite the invasion of fast-food outlets and souvenir shops. Now pedestrianised, the street leads up to the Plaça Sant Jaume at the heart of the Barri Gòtic.

Hotel Oriente ⑩

The legendary Hotel Oriente, a little further down La Rambla, preserves the structures of the Collegi de Sant Bonaventura, founded by Franciscan monks in 1652. The cloister is the ballroom, surrounded by the monks' gallery. A wall plaque reminds guests that this was the first public place in Barcelona to use gas lighting.

Once favoured by the likes of Ernest Hemingway, it has now been absorbed into a large hotel chain.

Plaça Reial ⑪

Back on the other side of La Rambla, an arcaded passageway leads to the **Plaça Reial**, another Barcelona landmark and one of the most handsome yet decadent of its squares. Despite being home to the city's first gastronomic boutique hotel, DO Plaça Reial, it retains its infamous nature, so tourists on terrace bars still jostle with junkies, and backpackers share benches with the homeless. Restaurants, bars and clubs predominate, like the well-established **Jamboree** jazz club, along with its sister club **Tarantos** for flamenco, both open after the shows for dancing. Charismatic new bar Ocaña has quickly become a favourite. **Sidecar**, a fashionable spot, has live music. The buzz never lets up.

On Sunday mornings, stamp and coin collectors gather around the **Font de Les Tres Gràcies** and the two *fanals* (street lamps) designed

by a young Gaudí. Inspired by the French urban designs of the Napoleonic period, this is the only one of the many squares planned in Barcelona during the 19th century that was built entirely according to its original plan. Its uniform, arcaded buildings were constructed by Francesc Daniel Molina on the plot where the Capuchin Convent once stood. Return to La Rambla through Passatge de Bacardí (the Cuban rum was created by a Catalan).

Palau Güell ⑫

Address: Nou de la Rambla 3–5;
www.palauguell.cat
Tel: 93-472 5775
Opening Hrs: Tue–Sun Apr–Sept 10am–8pm, Oct–Mar 10am–5.30pm
Entrance fee: charge
Transport: Liceu or Drassanes

Just off Rambla dels Caputxins on the opposite side to the Plaça Reial is the **Palau Güell**. Built by Antoni Gaudí between 1885 and 1889 as the home of

his patron, Count Güell, it has recently reopened after lavish renovation.

With this early commission, the architect embarked on a period of fertile creativity. The building is structured around an enormous salon, from which a conical roof covered in pieces of tiling emerges to preside over a landscape of capriciously placed battlements, balustrades and strangely shaped chimneys. Designated a World Heritage Site in 1984, this fascinating building displays Gaudí's ingenious solutions concerning light and space, from the wooden cobbles in the basement stables to the rooftop.

Plaça del Teatre

The terraces that line La Rambla along this stretch are pretty well spurned by locals, but as long as you don't expect the ultimate culinary experience it is tempting to pull up a chair, order a cool drink and watch the world go by.

Palau Güell's rooftop.

The Arts Santa Mònica building.

Living statues along La Rambla.

Where the promenade opens up again into the **Plaça del Teatre**, or **Plaça de les Comèdies**, another notorious street, **Escudellers**, leads off to the left. A kind of cross between ingrained seediness and up-to-the-minute trendiness, it is representative of many parts of Barcelona today. Walk along it to feel the pulse of the harsher elements of the city, and to observe its present evolution.

Plaça George Orwell ⓑ

Escudellers opens up at the far end into a square, **Plaça George Orwell**, created in the 1980s as a result of dense housing demolition; trendy bars and restaurants have opened here, and a bike rental company has set up shop. The sculpture on the square is by Leandre Cristòfol.

Now return down Escudellers, passing small grocer's shops, falafel bars, discos and dives. Narrow streets lead off to the right and left, most

hiding late-night bars (see margin tip, page 100).

Teatre Principal

Back on La Rambla you reach the spot where, in the 16th century, the city's first theatre was built. The present **Teatre Principal** replaced the old wooden theatre that was for many years the only stage in Barcelona. A 2,000-seater, it was built on the site of the historical Corral de les Comèdies, a popular early theatre, although it never appealed to the bourgeoisie. Opposite the theatre is a monument to Frederic Soler 'Pitarra', founder of modern Catalan theatre.

RAMBLA DE SANTA MÒNICA

The few prostitutes remaining in this area choose the square surrounding the monument to offer their charms – a reminder of what used to be called the **Barrio Xino** (in Spanish, Barrio Chino). A shadow of its former self, the area has been cleaned up in recent years, but the neon signs of sex shops and the like are still in evidence. The square marks the beginning of the **Rambla de Santa Mònica**, the last stretch of La Rambla before it reaches the harbour.

At this point the pace of the human river slows and the personality of La Rambla seems to fade. The Rambla de Santa Mònica is lined with caricaturists, portrait painters and artisans, and a craft market is held here at the weekend. This is where, in 1895, films were first shown publicly in Spain by the Lumière brothers. Some handsome buildings have been restored and new ones built, notably on the left for the university of Pompeu Fabra.

Arts Santa Mònica 🅮

On the right side as you continue towards the port is the **Arts Santa Mònica** (La Rambla, 7; www.artssanta monica.cat; metro Drassanes), a former convent redesigned as an exhibition space by the highly regarded local architects Piñón and Viaplana, who were instrumental in much of the new Barcelona. It is about to be reinvented as a place that encourages contemporary creativity, but plans remain uncertain. Check the website to see whether it is open to the public. Opposite the centre is the **Palau March** (1780), today the Generalitat's Department of Culture.

Just before the Arts Santa Mònica, a narrow street, Santa Mònica, heads off into the former Barrio Xino, where you'll find a range of seedy and newly fashionable old bars. An evocative French atmosphere is on offer in the timeless **Pastis** at No. 4 Santa Mònica – except on tango nights, when the bar transforms itself into a corner of Buenos Aires.

Museu de la Cera 🅯

Address: Passatge de la Banca, 7; www.museocerabcn.com
Tel: 93-317 2649
Opening Hrs: mid-July–late Sept daily 10am–10pm; rest of year Mon–Fri 10am–1.30pm, 4–7.30pm, Sat–Sun 11am–2pm, 4.30–8.30pm

The façade of the Wax Museum.

La Rambla gets packed – keep an eye on your wallet.

Entrance fee: charge
Transport: Drassanes

Towards the end of La Rambla, on the left, an old-fashioned ticket booth sells tickets for the Museu de la Cera. The roof of Barcelona's wax museum sports Superman, poised to leap from the top of the building, and inside are more than 360 waxworks, giving an insight into some of Catalonia's historic personalities. Recent acquisitions include Prince Charles and Camilla.

Around this part of La Rambla you'll usually find a horse and carriage waiting to whisk tourists off for a trot around town.

Our Lady of Mercy ⑯

A long street on the left, Ample, leads to the 18th-century church of **La Mare de Déu de la Mercè**, usually known simply as **La Mercè**, the patroness of Barcelona, and the name given to many Catalan women. A dramatic statue of the Virgin and Child stands on the top of the church, creating a distinctive element on the waterfront skyline.

Street artists at night on La Rambla.

The square was one of the first urban spaces (1983) to appear as a result of the Socialist city council's long-term project of demolishing old buildings to open up dense areas. It is at its most festive on 24 September, the day of La Mercè, when *gegants* and *castellers* (see page 26) greet the dignitaries coming out of Mass, before the main *festa major* of Barcelona takes off. It is also customary for every member of the Barça football team, whatever his creed, to come and pay his respects to the Virgin after important victories, before going off to parade the trophy in front of the fans in Plaça Sant Jaume.

The last building on the left side of La Rambla before you reach the Waterfront has a curious history. In 1778 the foundry of the Royal Artillery, as well as its workshop, were transferred to this building, known as **El Refino**. The foundry was one of the most renowned cannon factories of its time. From 1844 until 1920 it was occupied by the offices of the Banco de Barcelona and, since the Spanish Civil War (1936–9), it has been converted into the offices of the military governor.

Monument a Colom ⑰

Tel: 93-302 5224
Opening Hrs: daily 8.30am–8pm
Entrance fee: charge
Transport: Drassanes

Looming up at the end of La Rambla is the Columbus Monument, in the **Plaça del Portal de la Pau**, built for the 1888 Universal Exposition. It has an internal lift which takes you to the top for a great view over the city and port.

SHOPPING

The shopping panorama here is large stores surrounding Plaça Catalunya offering global but useful shopping and an excess of souvenirs in La Rambla. In between there are some interesting options for fashionistas and foodies.

Accessories

Alonso
Santa Anna, 27
Tel: 93-317 6085
Family-run since 1905, this modernista shop sells gloves in the winter and a wonderful range of traditional and trendy fans in the summer.

Sombreria Mil
Fontanella, 20
Tel: 93-301 8491
www.sombreriamil.com
Hat shops as they used to be, this traditional establishment from 1917 provides any headgear you could wish for, from cooling Panamas to trilbies, wedding fascinators to Catalan barretinas.

Clothing

Custo Barcelona
La Rambla, 109
Tel: 93-481 3930
http://custobarcelona.com
Home-grown talent from the heart of Lleida, the Dalmau brothers have had a huge hit with their brightly coloured T-shirts, dresses and accessories now sold all over the world.

Desigual
La Rambla, 140
Tel: 93-304 3112
www.desigual.com
Another born-in-Barcelona hit which has gone global, these colourful casual clothes for men, women and now kids brighten your life and make a strong individual statement.

Flora Albacín
Canuda, 3
www.tiendaflamenco.com
A corner of Andalucía just off La Rambla, this tiny shop is bursting at the seams with gorgeous flamenco dresses plus shoes, earrings, beads and fans, which make great gifts. Pure heaven for girls of all ages.

Department stores

El Corte Inglés
Plaça de Catalunya, 14
Tel: 93-306 3800
www.elcorteingles.com
This flagship branch of Spain's leading department store has eleven floors of anything you may need. Open Mon–Sat 10am–10pm, its excellent supermarket covers multicultural tastes and the restaurant on the top floor gives a privileged view of the busy square.

Food

El Celler de la Boqueria
Plaça Sant Josep, 15-B
www.cellerboqueria.com
Tucked into the side alley of the Boqueria market, this friendly shop offers advice on its interesting range of wines from different regions at economical prices.

Escribà
La Rambla, 83
Tel: 93-301 6027
www.escriba.es
The family of the late Antoni Escribà, the famous chocolate 'sculptor', continue his tradition in this beautiful shop, where you can buy small boxes to take home.

Malls

El Triangle
Plaça de Catalunya, 1–4
Tel: 93-318 0108
www.eltriangle.es
Dominated by FNAC's several floors of books, music and the latest tech equipment, this small, user-friendly mall also houses Habitat, Massimo Dutti, fashion for men and women, and Sephora, an emporium of perfume and cosmetics for men and women.

Markets

La Boqueria
La Rambla, 91
Tel: 93-318 2584
www.boqueria.info
The largest and most colourful of the city's many markets. The most exotic and expensive fare is in the entrance; the bargains are to be found in the maze of stalls behind, especially in the adjoining Plaça de Sant Galdric, where there is a farmers' market.

Coin and stamp market
Plaça Reial
Every Sunday 9am–2.30pm collectors gather here to sell and swap their curios, mostly coins and stamps, though all sorts seem to slip in to that category. A timeless gem, worth visiting.

Moll de les Drassanes
The quayside, near Plaça del Portal de la Pau
At the foot of Columbus Monument, this attractive bric-a-brac market by the sea opens every weekend. Bargains can be found if you browse through its old postcards, ancient cameras, pottery and so on.

RESTAURANTS, BARS AND CAFÉS

Restaurants

Consider La Rambla a colourful avenue to walk down and enjoy, rather than a place to eat. With just a few notable exceptions, the restaurants are low on quality and high on price, but there's plenty of choice nearby.

Catalan

ATN
Canuda, 6
Tel: 93-318 5238
www.atnrestaurant.cat
Open: Tue–Sat L & D, Mon L. €€ (set menu €) [❶ p286, B1]
Just off La Rambla in the atmospheric, literary surroundings of the historic Ateneu Barcelonès (cultural organisation), with an attractive terrace overlooking Plaça de la Vila de Madrid. Creative Catalan cooking with an exotic touch.

Can Culleretes
Quintana, 5
Tel: 93-317 3022
www.culleretes.com
Open: Tue–Sat L & D, Sun L. €€ [❷ p286, B2]
This is the second-oldest restaurant in Spain, founded in 1786 and full

Appetising paella.

of character. Adorned with paintings and photos of famous visitors, it mercifully remains authentically Catalan, serving the likes of wild boar stew and spinach *canelones*.

Pinotxo
Mercat Sant Josep (La Boqueria), Parada 466
Tel: 93-317 1731
http://pinotxobar.com
Open: Mon–Sat B & L. €€ [❸ p286, A2]
A high-profile market bar, where the uptown crowd pause from their Saturday shopping for cava and oysters, or whatever the charismatic owner has selected from the season's produce at the neighbouring stalls.

Sagarra
Xuclà, 9
Tel: 93-301 0604
Open: Tue–Sat B, L & D, Mon L. € [❹ p286, A1]
Don't be put off by the somewhat formal, conventional decor – this is a good, honest, local place serving traditional dishes with a touch of flare. Excellent value lunchtime menu and all-day tapas. Eat in the small square for people-watching.

Spanish

Amaya
La Rambla, 20–24
Tel: 93-302 6138
www.restauranteamaya.com
Open: Daily L & D. €€ (set menu Mon–Fri L €) [❺ p286, A3]
This well-established Basque restaurant is a find in the midst of the cheap alternatives surrounding it. It's a good place to try traditional dishes like pebrots de piquillo (fried green peppers) or lluç amb salsa verda (hake in a parsley sauce).

Attic
La Rambla, 120
Tel: 93-302 4866
Open: Daily L & D. €€ [❻ p286, B1]
Part of a chain that produces authentic Spanish cuisine on a large scale, but does so effectively, creating a good ambience. Popular with tourists. The tables overlook-

ing La Rambla provide an irresistible floor show and the roof terrace is perfect.

Bar Cañete
Unió, 17
Tel: 93-270 3458
http://barcanete.com
Open: Mon–Sat L & D. €€ [❼ p286, A2]
A slick spot just off La Rambla serving well-prepared traditional tapas or *platillos* (small dishes) at the long, shiny bar all day, or sitting at a table 'with a cloth' midday and evening.

Los Caracoles
Escudellers, 14
Tel: 93-302 3185
Open: Daily L & D. €€€ [❽ p286, B2]
This old Barcelona favourite still oozes atmosphere, from the moment you walk in through the sizzling, busy kitchen and are settled in its labyrinthine interior, at a table with a crisp white cloth. It specialises in rich meat dishes like lamb and suckling pig.

Irati
Cardenal Casanyes, 17
Tel: 93-302 3084
www.iratitavernabasca.com
Open: Daily L & D. €€ (pintxos all day €) [❾ p286, B2]
The first of a bevy of Basque bars that opened in the 1990s. Grab what you fancy from the great variety of *pintxos* (snacks on a toothpick) that emerge at regular intervals from the kitchen. Serious à la carte Basque dishes are served at the rear.

Kiosco Universal
Mercat Sant Josep (La Boqueria), Parada 691
Tel: 93-317 8286
Open: Mon–Sat B & L. €€ [❿ p286, A2]
Pull up a stool at the bar amid the market's stallholders and eat the freshest of produce, cooked before your eyes. Try their specials, octopus and shellfish.

Luzia
Pintor Fortuny, 1
Tel: 93-342 9628

www.grupotragaluz.com/en/restaurants/luzia/
Open: Daily B, L & D. €€ (set menu L €)
[⓫ p286, A1]
Mediterranean to the gills, this is a
great place to have a healthy
snack at any time of day, from creative sandwiches to pizzas cooked
in a wood-fired oven. Main courses
include vegetarian-friendly dishes

International

Bar Lobo
Pintor Fortuny, 3
Tel: 93-481 5346
www.grupotragaluz.com/restaurantes/bar-lobo/
Open: Daily B, L & D. €€ [⓬ p286, A1]
The hippest member of the Tragaluz empire attracts a cool crowd
with its stylish interior, lounging
terrace in a busy pedestrian street,
and combination of light Mediterranean and Japanese dishes.
Open late for drinks at weekends.

Drassanes
Avinguda Drassanes
Tel: 93-342 9920
Open: Daily B & L. €€ (set menu €)
[⓭ p286, A3]
In part of the medieval building in
which the Maritime Museum is
housed, this is a delightful setting
for lunch or a drink, especially by
the pond in the peaceful garden.

Fresc Co
Carme, 16
Tel: 93-318 7516
www.frescco.com/restaurantes_barcelona.
html
Open: Daily L & D. € [⓮ p286, A1]
Healthy fast food with several
branches around town. Pile up
your plates from a huge choice of
salads, then gorge on the dish of
the day, or pasta and pizza. Kids
love being able to help themselves
to ice cream.

Kasparo
Plaça Vicenç Martorell, 4
Tel: 93-302 2072
www.kasparo.es
Open: Tue–Sat B, L and all-day snacks.
Closed mid-Dec to mid-Jan. € [⓯
p286, A1]
A sought-after terrace bar in this
secluded square just off La Rambla serving delicious and cosmopolitan light snacks and lunch
dishes, the original creations of its

Australian owners. There's a play
area for children in the square.

El Paraguayo
Parc, 1
Tel: 93-302 1441
Open: Tue–Sun L & D. €€ [⓰ p286, A3]
A magnet for passionate carni-
vores, with daily deliveries of
Argentinian and Uruguayan meat,
duly grilled in the inimitable Argen-
tinian style, and irresistible dulce
de leche (rich caramel) to follow.
Always has a lively atmosphere.

Bars and Cafés

Boadas
Tallers, 1
Tel: 93-318 9592
http://boadascocktails.com
[❶ p286, B1]
Cocktail bar par excellence, with
polished wood and brass. Perch on
a sturdy leather stool as you sip
the cocktail of the day. The oldest
cocktail bar in town, its walls are
lined with prints and photographs.

Cafè de l'Òpera
La Rambla, 74
Tel: 93-317 7585
www.cafeoperabcn.com
[❷ p286, A2]
Subdued in the morning for sipping a café con leche and poring
over the newspaper, but buzzing by
night, especially when the opera
crowd drop by. This old favourite
retains its fin-de-siècle charm
despite recent facelifts.

Café Zurich
Plaça Catalunya, 1
Tel: 93-317 9153
[❸ p286, B1]
Strategically positioned at the
head of La Rambla, this legendary
meeting place's spirit has survived
being demolished and rebuilt into
the Triangle shopping centre.
White-jacketed waiters who seem
to date back to its origins attend to
your every need.

Castells
Plaça Bonsuccés, 1
Tel: 93-302 1054
www.barcastells.com
[❹ p286, A1]
A genuine neighbourhood bar
where locals drop in, serving cool

beers and typical tapas, like tortilla
de patatas or cured ham cut from
the leg. You may have to wait to get
an outdoor table in this bustling
square just off La Rambla.

Escribà
La Rambla, 83
Tel: 93-301 6027
[❺ p286, A2]
If you can't resist sticky pastries
with your coffee, this is the place
for you. Enjoy the modernista
decor, best seen from the tables in
the outdoor passageway.

Granja Viader
Xuclà, 4–6
Tel: 93-318 3486
www.granjaviader.cat
[❻ p286, A1]
The oldest and prettiest granja (milk
bar) in town, run by the fourth generation of the family who invented
kids' favourite cacaolat (chocolate
milk). Join families at marble-
topped tables keeping up the tradition of berenar (afternoon snack).

Ocaña
Plaça Reial, 13
Tel: 93-676 4814
www.ocana.cat
[❼ p286, A2]
Named after a colourful former
resident of the square, a much-
loved artist and cross-dresser, this
newcomer quickly established
itself as a super-trendy spot. Enjoy
coffee or cocktails, brunch or tapas
in its distressed, stagey decor or
on its cool terrace.

La Pallaresa
Petritxol, 11
[❽ p286, B1]
One of several traditional spots in
this pretty street serving traditional
xocolata desfeta, a sturdy hot
chocolate not for the faint-hearted.
Prepare to queue at weekends.

La Terrassa del D.O.
Plaça Reial, 1
Tel: 93-481 3666
www.hoteldoreial.com
[❾ p286, A2]
Dip into the luxury of this smart new
hotel by having a drink on its exclusive terrace under the square's
handsome arcade. If you feel really
indulgent, accompany your glass of
cava with an exquisite tapa.

BARRI GÒTIC

There's no finer introduction to Barcelona's Golden Age than a stroll around the warren of narrow streets that constitutes the lovely Barri Gòtic, the oldest part of the city.

The jewel of the Old Town, the Gothic Quarter, or Barri Gòtic, is a dense nucleus of historic buildings that has formed the central part of the Old City since Roman times. Today it represents the centre of municipal administration and is home to the Catalan autonomous government.

The oldest part of the city, it is built around **Mont Tàber**, Taber Hill, a misnomer for what is little more than a mound. This section of the Old Town is surrounded by the remains of Roman walls clearly indicated with descriptive signs. Layer upon layer of different architectural styles illustrate the different periods of Barcelona's history, from remnants of the Roman city to contemporary architectural solutions seen in renovation work and extensions to old buildings. The Gothic period predominates, reflecting the glorious medieval period when Catalonia was at its height.

A TOUR OF THE BARRI GÒTIC

This route is designed to take in the key sites, and constitutes an enjoyable walk through the present-day Gothic Quarter, with its residents, street musicians, cafés and commerce.

Plaça del Rei.

Alternatively, you can simply absorb its atmosphere by wandering aimlessly around its narrow streets, feeling the sense of history and observing the day-to-day comings and goings of the local people.

Approach from Plaça de Catalunya down **Portal de l'Angel**, a wide paved street full of shoe shops, the major fashion chains and a branch of El Corte Inglés, which specialises in music, books, urban fashion, sport and computers, and is housed in a grandiose building. The wide space

Main Attractions
Casa de l'Ardiaca
Catedral
Plaça Sant Felip Neri
Plaça Sant Josep Oriol
Santa Maria del Pi
Plaça Sant Jaume
Plaça Sant Just
Plaça del Rei
Museu d'Història de Barcelona
Museu Frederic Marès

Maps and Listings
Map, page 110
Shopping, page 120
Restaurants, page 122
Accommodation, page 251

Friezes designed by Picasso decorate the exterior of the Col.legi d'Arquitectes (Architects' Association).

lends itself to street performances. Bear left at the fork at the bottom, taking Arcs past a fine *modernista* building now housing a hotel, an Aladdin's cave of a toyshop, and the **Col.legi d'Arquitectes**, the Architects' Association, a 1960s building with friezes designed by Picasso, but executed by Norwegian Carl Nesjar.

Plaça Nova ❶

The street leads into Plaça Nova, and there, in front of you, is one of the main Roman gates to the old city, the **Portal del Bisbe** (Bishop's Gate). The towers date from the 1st century BC but the name came later, from the nearby 18th-century Bishop's Palace. The sculpted letters by Catalan artist Joan Brossa (see page 63) spell out 'Barcino', the Roman name for the city.

Avinguda de la Catedral

Here Plaça Nova merges with **Avinguda de la Catedral**, a wide open space spreading out at the foot of the cathedral steps. The paving hides an underground car park and successfully highlights the drama of the ancient facades, rising theatrically above the Roman walls. Sit on one of the polished stone benches or the terrace of the **Hotel Colón** and take it all in: the constant movement of children, footballs and bicycles, the clicking of cameras, large tour groups from cruise ships, balloon vendors and beggars. An antiques market takes place here on Thursdays, and at the weekend the gatherings of *sardana* dancers form large, impenetrable bouncing circles (6.30pm on Sat, noon on Sun, 7pm on Wed). All this is played out against the surprisingly neo-Gothic front of the cathedral, which was tacked onto its 13th-century origins in the 19th century.

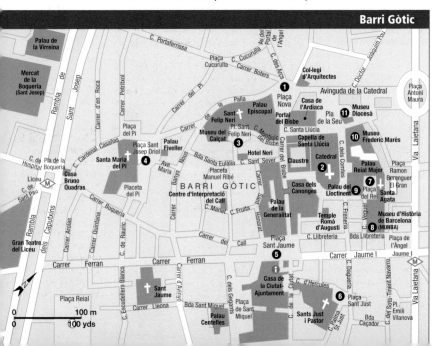

Barri Gòtic

Through the Roman gate

Enter the Gothic Quarter through the Roman gate in Plaça Nova, up the slope into **Bisbe**. On the right is the **Palau Episcopal**, built in 1769 around a 12th-century courtyard, which is the only remaining evidence of the original palace after centuries of modifications. The frescoes on the facade (facing the Carrer Montjuïc del Bisbe) date from the 18th century, while the triple recess windows and large *flamígero* window in the courtyard are from the 14th century. It was the headquarters of Pope Benedict XVI when he visited in 2010 to consecrate the Sagrada Família.

Opposite the palace entrance a short street, **Santa Llúcia**, leads towards the cathedral. On the corner is a chapel dedicated to Santa Llúcia, patron saint of the blind and, curiously, of seamstresses. Built in 1268, it is one of the oldest parts of the cathedral and a fine example of Romanesque architecture, with images of the Annunciation and the Visitation decorating the facade capitals. The holy-water font inside the chapel is from the 14th century. A rear doorway leads into the cloister.

The **Fira de Santa Llúcia**, an atmospheric Christmas arts and crafts fair, fills the cathedral square for most of December. It also sells Christmas trees of all shapes and sizes, plus everything you could possibly need to make your own Nativity scene, from the Three Kings to the *caganer* (see margin, page 111).

The cathedral precincts

Opposite the Capella de Santa Llúcia, on the other corner, is the **Casa de l'Ardiaca** (Archdeacon's Residence), built in the 15th century on Roman ruins. It has one of the most evocative patios in the city. A tall, elegant palm tree rises high above a fountain, which is decorated with flowers at Corpus Christi and

Bridge at Carrer del Bisbe.

is the setting for a curious tradition, *l'ou com balla*, in which a fragile egg 'dances' on the spouting water. The building contains the **Municipal History Archives**, a valuable collection of historical chronicles and documents. Extensions at the rear of the patio have opened up the building, revealing another angle on the Roman tower and part of the first city wall, dating from the 1st century BC. The outer wall, with square towers and the remains of two aqueducts (which can be seen from Avinguda de la Catedral), is from the 4th century AD.

The Cathedral ❷

Address: Pla Catedral de la Seu, 3; www.catedralbcn.org
Tel: 93-342 8260
Opening Hrs: daily 8.30am–12.30pm and 5.15–7pm; free; tourist visit (which includes choir stalls, roof and museum in the Sala Capitular): Mon–Sat 1–4.30pm, Sun

FACT

Wise men, the baby Jesus, donkeys and the *caganer* are all essential figures in the Nativity scene. A curious Catalan tradition, the *caganer*, usually dressed as a local peasant – though sometimes as a star footballer or politician – is supposedly 'fertilising the earth' (defecating) to bring good luck in the New Year.

The Cathedral.

2–4.30pm; Entrance fee: charge (tourist visits only)

Transport: Liceu/Jaume I

Enter the *catedral* by the main door. Its traditional, ornate chapels are a far cry from the simple majesty of Santa Maria del Mar (see page 129). For any kind of spiritual peace it is essential to visit in off-peak hours, such as first thing in the morning, to avoid groups and the accumulation of human traffic; attending Mass is no solution, as the congregation chatters loudly and goes in and out at will.

The construction of the cathedral began in 1298 under the patronage of Jaume II, on the spot where an early Christian church had been destroyed by the pillaging of Al-Mansur, the vizier of Córdoba, in 985. Some signs of it can be seen in the remarkable subterranean world beneath the present cathedral, which can be visited from the Barcelona History Museum (MUHBA, see page 118).

The highlights

The main area consists of three naves and an apse with an ambulatory beneath an octagonal dome. Two 14th- and 15th-century towers rise at each end of the transept. Beneath the main altar is the crypt of Santa Eulàlia, and of particular note are the dome's multicoloured keystones. Some say that this is one of Catalonia's three 'magnetic' points.

The tomb of Santa Eulàlia, behind the altar, is an important 14th-century work of art, executed in alabaster by a disciple of Giovanni Pisano during the same period as the episcopal cathedral. The most outstanding altarpiece is that of the Transfiguration, designed by Bernat Martorell in the chapel dedicated to Sant Salvador, which was built in 1447.

The high-backed choir pews are by Pere Sanglada (1399), and the lower-backed benches were carved by Macià Bonafè towards the end

---

TIP

Next to the entrance of the Casa de l'Ardiaca (see page 111), look out for the letterbox designed by the *modernista* architect Domènech i Montaner. The swallows suggest how fast the post should travel; the tortoise represents the reality.

of the same century. The retrochoir (the extension behind the high altar) was built in the early 16th century by Bartolomé Ordóñez. The Capella del Santo Cristo de Lepanto (Chapel of Christ Lepanto) contains the crucifix borne in the Christian flagship against the Ottomans in the battle of Lepanto. Built between 1405 and 1454, it is considered the finest example of Gothic art in the cathedral.

The oldest part is that of the Porta de Sant Ivo (St Ive's Door), where some of the Romanesque windows and archways can still be seen. Most of the cathedral's more antique furnishings are in the MUHBA, but there is a small collection in the **Sala Capitular** (Chapter House; opening times same as cathedral; charge, or as part of a tourist visit, see page 111).

A small pavilion beside the Porta de la Pietat shelters a 15th-century terracotta statue of St George by Antoni Claperós, and the door to the western end of the transept is made from marble taken from the earlier Romanesque cathedral.

The cathedral cloisters

On one side is the Santa Eulàlia Portal which leads to the **cathedral cloisters**, a quiet haven and perhaps the most atmospheric part of the cathedral, with the sound of running water from the pretty fountain and a romantic garden of elegant palms, medlars and highly perfumed magnolia trees, all enclosed by 15th-century wrought-iron railings. Thirteen geese are the sole residents, symbolising the age of Santa Eulàlia, co-patron saint of Barcelona, when she died.

Plaça Sant Felip Neri ❸

Leave the cloister through the side door, which leads to **Plaça Garriga i Bachs**. To the left, notice the picturesque bridge across the street (another neo-Gothic construction), linking two departments of the Generalitat. Cross the square to **Montjuïc del Bisbe**, a narrow street leading into **Plaça Sant Felip Neri**. This small square is a treasure, enclosed by heavy stone buildings and happily neglected, which increases its historic impact.

TIP

For a gargoyle's view of the city, take a lift to the rooftop of the cathedral (see tourist visiting times, page 111).

The Cathedral's interior.

Geese in the cloisters of the Cathedral.

enormous wooden doors and small dark workshops where furniture is polished and restored. At **Banys Nous** (New Baths), turn right past a shop selling embroidered antique nightdresses. On the wall opposite, a panel of ceramic tiles explains the origin of the street's name.

Plaça Sant Josep Oriol ❹

Where the street joins Palla (which, to the right, runs back to the cathedral past art galleries and antique shops), turn left towards **Plaça Sant Josep Oriol**. This lively square, where artists sell their work at weekends, is dominated by the sought-after terrace of the **Bar del Pi**, and is one of the most popular spots in the Old Town. Along with the adjoining Plaça del Pi and Placeta del Pi, it embraces the church of **Santa Maria del Pi**. Begun in 1322 and completed in the 15th century, this is a fine example of Catalan Gothic architecture, fortress-like on the exterior but ample and welcoming inside. The rose window is magnificent when lit from within.

Adjoining the 18th-century church of Sant Felip Neri is a school, so if you coincide with playtime the peace will be shattered by shrieking children and stray footballs.

In fact, a large number of children were killed here when a bomb dropped nearby during the 1936–9 civil war. The pockmarked church facade tells the tale. The eccentric **Museu del Calçat** (Shoe Museum; Tue–Sun 11am–2pm; charge) was formerly in a street opposite the cathedral, **Corríbia**, cleared to make Avinguda de la Catedral, and was moved to this *plaça*, brick by brick. An enormous shoe made to measure for the Columbus statue in La Rambla and ex-President Jordi Pujol's shoes are among the curiosities.

You could contemplate the square from the shady terrace café of the exclusive boutique Hotel Neri, then take Sant Sever and go down **Baixada Santa Eulàlia** into a world apart, with hidden courtyards behind

Carved details on the Cathedral.

EAT

Recommended restaurants near the cathedral include La Cassola, with tasty Catalan home cooking, in Sant Sever, and El Portalón in Banys Nous. The latter, a timeless bodega, is a good bet in winter, when its warming bean stews go down well (see page 122).

Local producers come in from the country to sell goat's cheese and honey at the market on the Plaça del Pi (first and third weekends of the month, Fri–Sun all day).

Buskers became so numerous here that local residents campaigned to have them banned, except between 6–8pm on Saturday and noon–2pm on Sunday. Guests of the popular Hotel Jardí no doubt appreciate the ruling. Before leaving the square, check out the knife shop (see margin, page 115), dating from 1911, and around the corner from it the very pretty street **Carrer Petritxol**.

Take the narrow street **Ave Maria** that runs down the side of the Palau Fiveller and at the end turn right, back into Banys Nous. Traditional shops are giving way to more commercial enterprises, apart from the faithful Xurreria at No. 8, run by the San Ramon family since the 1960s, and the wonderful **Obach** hat shop, which both remain unchanged. Turn left here and follow **Call**, the main street in Barcelona's Jewish Quarter until 1401 (see page 116), as it winds up to Plaça Sant Jaume.

PLAÇA SANT JAUME ❺

The area that today forms the **Plaça Sant Jaume** was inaugurated in 1823, at the same time as the streets **Ferran** and **Jaume I**. It is the civic heart of the city, home to the **Ajuntament** (City Council), which runs Barcelona, and the **Generalitat** (government of Catalonia), although the Parliament building is in Parc de la Ciutadella (see page 135). The current president of the Generalitat, since the end of 2010, is Artur Mas.

Palau de la Generalitat

The **Palau de la Generalitat** is guarded by the Mossos d'Esquadra, the autonomous police force. Opposite, the town councillors in the **Casa de la Ciutat** are protected by the Guàrdia Urbana. Demonstrations wind up in this square, as do festive parades, Barça fans and players after major football and basketball victories, and, of course, visiting dignitaries. This is where President Tarradellas was given a clamorous reception on his return from exile to attend the birth of the new democracy in 1977.

SHOP

On Plaça del Pi, Ganiveteria Roca is a fascinating shop with a beautiful facade, crammed with thousands of knives and scissors of every kind (*ganivet* is the Catalan word for knife). Fashion victims will delight in Custo, a newcomer to this ancient square.

Plaça Sant Felip Neri.

The Jewish City

In Catalonia the Jewish Quarter of a town or city is known as the *Call*, meaning 'narrow street' or 'lane'. A marked route leads visitors through Barcelona's *Call*.

Situated west of the Roman metropolis in what is now the Gothic Quarter, the *Call* reached its peak of importance during the Middle Ages and had a remarkable cultural reputation. For centuries the only university in Catalonia was the Universidad Judía or Escuela Mayor. This community also had a talent for finance, and monarchs were known to apply for loans. Their knowledge was so advanced that they were made ambassadors at court, but their display of wealth and their superior lifestyle created great jealousy.

Bitter persecution

The fortunes of the Jews began to decline in 1243 when Jaume I ordered the separation of the Jewish Quarter from the rest of the city and made Jews wear long hooded capes with red or yellow circles. Fights erupted, and worsened when a rumour spread that Jews were responsible for bringing the Black Death to Spain. Full-scale rioting in several cities in 1391 was provoked mainly by a group from Seville who encouraged the population to storm houses in the Jewish Quarter and murder the occupants.

The riots began in Valencia and spread to Mallorca, Barcelona, Girona, Lleida and Perpignan. Those in Barcelona were by far the most violent; the *qahqal* (the original Hebrew for *call*) was virtually destroyed and about 1,000 Jews died. The survivors were forced to convert to Christianity or flee, despite the efforts of the national guard to defend the lives and properties of the persecuted.

Joan I ordered the arrest and execution of 15 Castilians responsible for the uprising, but despite this the *Call* was never rebuilt. By 1395 the flow of anti-Semitism had reached such proportions that the synagogue on the street called Sanahuja was converted into a church (Sant Jaume, in Carrer de Ferran). In 1396, the principal synagogue was rented to a pottery maker.

The *Call* disappeared in 1401 when the synagogues were abolished and Jewish cemeteries destroyed. It was not until 1931 that the first new Spanish synagogue was established. It was shut down during the Civil War, reopened in 1948, and later moved to its present site in Carrer d'Avenir.

Jewish Route

Today the only evidence of the prosperous era of the *Call* is certain stretches of the Carrer de Banys Nous and the Carrer del Call. The Barcelona History Museum has signposted a route through the Jewish Quarter and has opened a centre explaining its history, showing artefacts found during excavations and holding temporary exhibitions (Placeta Manuel Ribé; Tue–Fri 11am–2pm, Sat and Sun 11am–7pm, winter until 5pm). The 14th-century building housing the Centre d'Interpretació del Call, known as the Alchemist's House, is well preserved.

The Jewish quarter in Girona is one of the best preserved in Spain and its history is well documented in a museum (see page 235).

Hebrew inscription on a wall in the Call.

Both buildings are of Gothic origin and can be visited on key public holidays, such as Sant Jordi, 23 April, and La Mercè, 24 September. The Palau de la Generalitat can also be visited by booking online (www.gencat.cat) for the second or fourth weekend of the month, while the Ajuntament opens every Sunday (10am–1.30pm). Each has some fine elements: the oldest part of the Casa de la Ciutat (Town Hall) is the **Saló de Cent**, created by Pere Llobet in 1373; the Gothic facade tucked down the side street **Ciutat** is the most delicate. The **Pati dels Tarongers** (a 16th-century courtyard full of orange trees) is the most famous part of the Palau de la Generalitat and the scene of many official photographs. From the square you can glimpse the painted ceilings of a large reception room.

Tourist Information

There is a tourist information office in the Town Hall, on the corner of Ciutat (Mon–Fri 8.30am–8pm, Sat 9am–7pm, Sun 9am–2pm). Take Ciutat out of the square and immediately turn left into Hercules, a quiet street leading to **Plaça Sant Just ❻**. This is an interesting, often overlooked corner of the Barri Gòtic with a strong sense of identity. The *plaça* has all the elements of a village: a church, a *colmado* (grocer's shop), a restaurant, a noble house, and children playing football.

The streets off here are also worth exploring, notably **Palma Sant Just** for the bodega and its breakfasts with wonderful omelettes, and **Lledó** for its medieval houses, one now home to a chic new hotel, Mercer.

The church of **Sant Just and Sant Pastor** was an ancient royal chapel until the 15th century. According to legend, it is built on the site of Barcelona's first Christian temple. The Cafè de l'Acadèmia spills out onto the square (see page 122).

THE ROYAL QUARTER

Behind the cathedral, centring on the Plaça del Rei, is the Conjunt Monumental de la Plaça del Rei, the royal quarter of Barcelona's medieval count-kings. To get there from Plaça Sant Just, follow **Dagueria** past a cheese shop (see margin, page

TIP

From early December until the fiesta of Els Reis (The Kings) on 6 January, the Plaça Sant Jaume is taken over by the largest Nativity scene in town – and the longest queues to visit it. Nativity figures are sold in the Cathedral Square throughout December.

Roman columns in the Museu d'Història de Barcelona.

A ROYAL CITY

The royal palace of the count-kings of Catalonia and Aragón, Palau Reial Major, begun in the 11th century, lies between the cathedral and the northern Roman wall. Its courtyard is now the Plaça del Rei, and beneath it you can see the foundations of the Roman episcopal palace from which it grew. When the crown slipped from Barcelona's grasp and the palace decayed, Madrid's appointed viceroy had his residence built on the left side of the square, the Palau del Lloctinent (see page 119). The 16th-century Gothic mansion that now shelters the Barcelona History Museum was brought here brick by brick to house artefacts amassed for the 1929 Universal Exposition. While re-siting the building, the Roman city beneath was discovered.

Palau de la Generalitat.

In the courtyard of Museu Frederic Marès.

119) and over the street Jaume I, turning right into Baixada Llibreteria and then left into Veguer. This leads to the Museu d'Història de Barcelona (MUHBA) and the Plaça del Rei at the end.

Plaça del Rei ❼

The **Plaça del Rei** is a fine medieval square, testimony to the nobility of the ancient city. It was here that all the flour brought into the city in payment of taxes was collected. The sculpture on the square is by the Basque artist Eduardo Chillida. Entrance to the *plaça*'s former royal buildings, the Palau Reial Major, is from the Museu d'Història, accessed back on Veguer or through its well-stocked bookshop on Baixada Llibreteria.

Museu d'Història de Barcelona ❽

Address: Plaça del Rei, 7–9; www.museuhistoria.bcn.cat

Tel: 93-256 2100
Opening Hrs: Tue–Sat 10am–7pm, Sun 10am–8pm
Entrance fee: charge, free Sun from 3pm
Transport: Jaume I/Liceu

The museum traces the city's history from its origins up to medieval times, following a fascinating chronological route. The highlight is going below ground level to the excavations of the Roman city. Covering 4,000 sq metres (43,000 sq ft) beneath the Plaça del Rei, it offers an intriguing insight not only into Roman building methods, but also into day-to-day commercial and domestic life.

Palau Reial Major

The tour returns to ground level in the **Palau Reial Major**, with its vast vaulted ceilings, 13th-century triple-recess windows and 14th-century rose windows.

The main room of the palace, the great **Salò del Tinell**, was built by Guillem Carbonell, the architect to Pere III in 1359. Its six unreinforced arches span an unprecedented 15 metres (50ft). It was later converted

By a Plaça del Rei café.

to a Baroque church, only to recover its original appearance after restoration work during and after the civil war. In the 15th century the Inquisition held court here. Legend has it that the walls of the tribunal cannot bear a lie to be told, and that if this occurred, the ceiling stones would move, adding further to the victims' terror.

Next door is the **Capella Reial de Santa Agata**, built for Jaume II (1302–12) using the Roman wall as its north side. The decorated ceiling timbers are by Alfonso de Córdoba, the beautiful Epiphany altarpiece painted by Jaume Huguet in 1465, and the Taule de Santa Agata in the Queen's Chapel from around 1500. It also houses the stone on which the saint's breasts were mutilated. Watch out for temporary exhibitions in both the Salò del Tinell and the chapel, which give access to these buildings without doing the museum tour.

The **Torre de Martí I** is sometimes called a *mirador* because of its fine views over both the royal complex and the city. It was built by Antoni Carbonell and is named after Martí I ('the Humanist', 1356–1410), last in the 500-year dynasty of Barcelona count-kings. The silhouette of the box-shaped Renaissance tower built like a dovecote is an outstanding feature of the palace.

On the northern side of Santa Agata chapel, outside the Roman walls, is the Plaça Ramon Berenguer El Gran, distinguished by the statue of the king on his horse. It is well worth a detour to get a feel of the Roman past and see how the medieval city was built on the Roman walls. A metal panel explains which part of the Roman city it was and illustrates an itinerary around what remains of the walls and towers.

Palau del Lloctinent ❾

Address: Comtes, 2
Opening Hrs: daily 10am–7pm

SHOP

The cheese shop at Dagueria, 16 is called Formatgeria La Seu, and is run by a Scottish woman. Open Tue–Sat, it sells only Spanish cheeses, sourced from small independent producers.

SHOPPING

Despite the deluge of brash souvenir shops, many old traditional establishments still stand their ground, selling craftwork or ceramics. The labyrinthine streets around the cathedral hide polished antiques shops and Ferran and Avinyó have independent fashion stores.

Accessories

Almacenes del Pilar
Boqueria, 43
www.almacenesdelpilar.com
Traditional *mantillas* (lace head scarves) as worn by Spanish *señoras*, though usually only seen in Easter processions in Barcelona, as well as beautifully embroidered *mantones de Manila* (shawls), make thoughtful presents or wedding accessories.

Antiques

The streets Palla and Banys Nous have several antique shops.
Heritage
Banys Nous, 14
Tel: 93-317 8515
www.heritagebarcelona.com
A treasure trove overflowing with magnificent pieces of jewellery, hats, textiles, 1920s designer dresses and all kinds of gorgeous accessories, at a price.
Librería Violán
Plaça del Rei, 1
Browse in this attractive shop specialising in old books and prints, with a particularly good collection of Art Deco posters.

Books

La Central
Baixada de Llibreteria, 7
Well-stocked bookshop in the entrance to the Museu d'Història de Barcelona. It also has a good range of mugs, pencils, notebooks and other items related to the city's past, which make stylish souvenirs.

Crafts

La Caixa de Fang
Freneria, 1
This wonderful shop crammed with colourful ceramics, from small tiles to enormous salad bowls, will make you want to check in an extra bag so you can take home a new dinner service. Failing that, you could opt for a spoon in olive wood.
Cereria Subirà
Baixada Llibreteria, 7
One of several candle shops that surround the cathedral, this one has 18th-century elegance. Founded in 1762, it is said to be the oldest shop in the city and is still making candles.
Germanes Garcia
Banys Nous, 15
Traditional basket makers dating back to the mid-19th century, with a wide range of goods, from small shopping baskets to classic wicker chairs and highchairs for kids.
Sabater Hnos
Plaça Sant Felip Neri, 1
Tel: 93-301 9832
The heady aroma of the many flavoured handmade soaps greets you as you walk into this lovely, old shop in one of the most peaceful squares of the Barri Gòtic.

Food

Orolíquido
Palla, 8
An exquisite array of olive oil and olive-based products, ranging from the finest D.O. virgin oils from all over Spain to soap and cosmetics.
Planelles Donat
Portal de l'Àngel, 27
One of the best places to stock up for Christmas speciality *turrón* (a sticky, nougat-like delicacy).
La Seu
Dagueria, 16
Tel: 93-412 6548
www.formatgerialaseu.com
A small shop full of tasty farmhouse cheeses from all over Spain, which the Scottish owner will pack carefully for travel. Check the website for tasting times.

Jewellery

La Basilica Galeria
Sant Sever, 7
Tel: 93-304 2047
www.labasilicagaleria.com
In a narrow street opposite the cathedral cloister, this shop-gallery has the most extraordinary jewellery and objets on display from a selection of artists. If the cockroach necklace doesn't appeal, the earrings made from miniature bags of orange may be more appropriate. Well worth a visit.

Shoes

La Manual Alpargatera
Avinyó, 7
Famous for its huge variety of genuine *alpargatas*, the classic rope-soled canvas shoes, which are handmade on the premises. Unlike the cheap imitations that fall apart after one summer, these are made to last, from the original style to the high-heeled version.

Toys

El Ingenio
Rauric, 6–8
A historic shop full of fun for kids and adults alike, selling everything you would need to join a circus, or go to a fancy-dress party, from practical jokes to carnival masks. Apparently Dalí was a client.
Xalar
Baixada Llibreteria, 4
www.xalar.es
This very tasteful toy shop sells wooden toys, doll's houses, sophisticated dolls and cuddly teddies, as well as reproduction old toys like tin-plated merry-go-rounds or cars. Perfect for kids and collectors.

Museu Frederic Marès has an excellent collection of Spanish sculpture.

Entrance fee: free
Transport: Jaume I

Back in the Plaça del Rei, opposite the chapel is the Palau del Lloctinent, magnificently restored. Part of it is open to the public. When the kingdoms of Catalonia and Aragón were joined with that of Castile, Carlos V created the office of deputy *(lloctinent)* for the court's representative, and this palace, the official residence, was built in 1549 by Antoni Carbonell. The facade is Catalan Gothic, but the inner courtyard is one of the few examples of Renaissance architecture left in the city and has a wonderful carved wooden ceiling. Until recently it was the headquarters of the Arxiu de la Corona d'Aragó (Archive of the Crown of Aragon).

Museu Frederic Marès ➓

Address: Plaça de Sant Iu, 5–6; www.museumares.bcn.cat
Tel: 93-256 3500
Opening Hrs: Tue–Sat 10am–7pm, Sun 11am–8pm
Entrance fee: charge, free Sun from 3pm
Transport: Jaume I

Follow Comtes down the side of the cathedral to a tiny square, Sant Iu, which leads into the charming courtyard of the Museu Frederic Marès. This private collection, donated by the Catalan sculptor Marès in 1946, includes Spanish sculpture, with medieval pieces in the crypt. Upstairs, the Museu Sentimental gives an insight into life in the city in the 18th and 19th centuries.

Comtes leads out into the **Pla de la Seu**, in front of the cathedral. On the right is a beautiful Gothic building, the **Pia Almoina**, where 100 meals were once given to the poor daily. It now houses the **Museu Diocesà** ➓ (Tue–Sat 10am–2pm, 5–8pm, Sun 11am–2pm; charge), with a small collection of religious objects and paintings and which also holds temporary exhibitions.

Palau del Lloctinent.

RESTAURANTS, BARS AND CAFÉS

Restaurants

Modern restaurants designed within medieval buildings, fusion food in old local bars, one of the best Japanese restaurants in town, and economical family-run establishments – this historic quarter has it all.

Catalan

Agut
Gignàs, 16
Tel: 93-315 1709
www.restaurantagut.com
Open: Tue–Sat L & D, Sun L. €€
[**17** p286, B3]
Bustling, traditional restaurant with heaps of atmosphere and walls lined with paintings, which impoverished artists gave in exchange for meals in the lean years of the Franco era. Try succulent Catalan specialities like *trinxat de la Cerdenya* (a tasty bubble and squeak) or *Perdiu amb farcellets de col* (partridge stuffed with cabbage).

L'Antic Bocoi del Gòtic
Baixada de Viladecols, 3
Tel: 93-310 5067
www.bocoi.net
Open: Mon–Sat D. €–€€ [**18** p286, B2]
Inspiring, delicious Catalan specialities like the *coques* (a kind of pizza with interesting toppings), plus imaginative salads. The warm and characterful interior incorporates part of the Roman city wall.

Bosco
Capellans, 9
Tel: 93-412 1370
Open: Tue–Sat L & D, Mon L. €€
[**19** p286, B1]
Hidden from the shopping crowds of Portal de l'Angel is this peaceful res-

taurant with a terrace on the quiet square, where there is a play area for kids. Fresh fish and seasonal vegetables from La Boqueria are on the good-value lunchtime set menu.

Cafè de l'Acadèmia
Lledó, 1
Tel: 93-315 0026
Open: Mon–Fri L & D. €€ [**20** p286, B2]
Delicious new interpretations of classic Catalan dishes have made this low-key place one of the best options in town. Tables in the medieval square. Popular with politicians from nearby Plaça Sant Jaume. Book ahead for dinner. Closed at weekends.

La Cassola
Sant Sever, 3
Tel: 93-318 1580
Open: Mon–Wed L, Thu–Fri L & D. €
[**21** p286, B2]
Get here early for lunch (1.30pm) as this 12-tabled restaurant, two minutes from the cathedral, fills quickly with regular clientele from nearby shops and offices. Enjoy simple but delicious home-made food from sisters Rosa and Carmen.

El Gran Café
Avinyó, 9
Tel: 93-318 7986
www.restaurantelgrancafe.com
Open: Daily L & D. €€ (set menu €)
[**22** p286, B2]
A classic restaurant dating from 1920 with *modernista* decoration. Good, standard Catalan cooking with an economically priced set-lunch menu; the ambience at night is more romantic, accompanied by a pianist.

International

Buenas Migas
Baixada de Santa Clara, 2
www.buenasmigas.com
Open: Daily B, L & D. € [**23** p286, B2]
This picturesque branch of the successful *focacceria* chain, with branches all over town, is tucked behind the cathedral in ancient premises. The savoury pies with

spinach or artichoke are delicious. Good for a light lunch.

Café Babel
Correu Vell, 14
Tel: 93-315 2309
Open: Daily L & D. € [**24** p286, B2]
Pocket handkerchief-sized bar big on atmosphere, with a quiet terrace under one of the remaining Roman towers. It offers all-day snacks and sandwiches and occasional live music.

Can Fly
Baixada de Viladecols, 6
Open: Tue–Sun for snacks. € [**25** p286, B2]
Attractive gay-friendly bar squeezed into a corner overlooking one of the Roman towers. Delicious snacks, unusual salads, *torrades* (toast rubbed with oil and tomato, served with cheese or ham), and the best olives ever.

Koy Shunka
Copons, 7
Tel: 93-412 7939
Open: Tue–Sat L & D, Sun L. €€€€
[**26** p286, B2]
Tucked away in a quiet street near the cathedral, this hidden spot ranks supremely high among the many Japanese restaurants in the city, especially since its chef won a Michelin star in 2013.

Matsuri
Plaça Regomir, 1
Tel: 93-268 1535
www.matsuri-restaurante.com
Open: Daily D. €€ [**27** p286, B2]
Filling a gap in the market, this good-looking restaurant specialises in Southeast Asian food, which is given a personal interpretation by its creative chef.

Les Quinze Nits
Plaça Reial, 6
Tel: 93-317 3075
www.lesquinzenits.com
Open: Daily L & D. € [**28** p286, A2]
The only way to beat the queues for this popular restaurant, which has a winning formula serving cheap Mediterranean food in elegant surroundings, is to follow a

northern European timetable (lunch at 1pm, dinner at 8pm). Sitting on a terrace overlooking the majestic square is a treat.

Spanish

El Club de l'Empanada
Dagueria, 7
Tel: 93-310 7647
Open: Mon–Sat B, L & D. € [29 p286, B2]
A great new bar run by a Galician family who learnt the secret of good empanadas (Galician pie) from la abuela (Granny). Delicious fillings include tuna, salt-cod, octopus and more. They also serve other Galician specialities and an economic lunchtime menu.

La Fonda
Escudellers, 10
Tel: 93-301 7515
www.lafonda-restaurant.com
Open: Daily L & D. € (set menu Mon–Sat D €) [30 p286, A2]
The popularity of this restaurant, part of the expanding Quinze Nits family, comes from its appealing decor and reasonably priced market-fresh food. Keep an eye on your belongings as you stand in the inevitable queue.

MariscCo Reial
Plaça Reial, 8
Tel: 93-412 4536
www.mariscco.com
Open: Daily B, L & D. €€ [31 p286, B2]
Stylish premises that were once a taxidermist's workshop, in prime position in this handsome square. Has appealing outdoor tables and specialises in seafood and rice dishes. Choose your fish from the display and have it cooked in your favourite way.

El Portalón
Banys Nous, 20
Tel: 93-302 1187
http://portalonbarcelona.es
Open: Mon–Sat L & D. € [32 p286, B2]
This old tavern has retained some charm, although you'll no longer find nicotine-stained walls and old men playing dominoes, which used to set the tone. The set menu chalked on a blackboard is still good value and a pitcher of rough wine and some traditional tapas are fun in the evening.

Els Quatre Gats
Montsió, 3
Tel: 93-302 4140
www.4gats.com
Open: Daily B, L & D. €€ (set menu Mon–Sat L €) [33 p286, B1]
The house Puig i Cadalfach built, made famous by Picasso and friends and where an 18-year-old Picasso had his first solo exhibition. Decent food, but it's the decor and atmosphere that counts.

Taller de Tapas
Plaça Sant Josep Oriol, 9
Tel: 93-301 8020
www.tallerdetapas.com
Open: Daily L & D. € [34 p286, B2]
A clever formula whereby you can sit down to tapas instead of fighting for space at the bar has turned this place into a success story, with several branches around town, including one at Argenteria, 51 in the Born and one on the Rambla de Catalunya, 49–51 in Eixample. Perfect for light dinners. The extensive menu includes puddings.

Bars and Cafés

Bar del Pi
Plaça Sant Josep Oriol, 1
Tel: 93-302 2123
www.bardelpi.com
[10 p286, B2]
Run by the same family since 1927, this charismatic bar has an appealing terrace in one of the prettiest squares of the Gothic quarter. It serves traditional tapas and its sticky croissants know no equal.

Cafè d'Estiu
Plaça Sant Iu, 5
Tel: 93-310 3014
www.cafedestiu.com
[11 p286, B2]
This charming café is in the courtyard of the former Royal Palace, now part of the Museu Frederic Marès, and opens only from late March to late September. Serves mint teas and light snacks.

Cala del Vermut
Magdalenes, 6
Tel: 93-317 9623
[12 p286, B1]
As the name suggests, this tiny bar whose barrels spill into the street is the place to stop off for a vermut at aperitif time, just before lunch or dinner. Accompany the house red vermut with olives, anchovies or some escopinyes (tinned cockles doused in a spicy sauce).

Can Conesa
Llibreteria, 1
www.conesaentrepans.com
[13 p286, B2]
Prepare to queue outside this hole-in-the-wall bar in one corner of the Plaça Sant Jaume to try the best toasted bocatas (sturdy sandwiches) in town, like the 'Catalán', made with local sausage.

Ginger
Lledó, 2
Tel: 93-310 5309
www.ginger.cat
[14 p286, B2]
Cool music, including vinyl nights, dim lighting and stylish decor reminiscent of a 1930s cocktail bar, topped by creative tapas make this an essential nightspot. Part cocktail bar and part wine-tasting venue, it has a good range of both.

Magnolia
Ciutat, 5
Tel: 93-304 2376
http://magnoliabarcelona.com
[15 p286, B2]
A laid-back bar a step away from the frenetic political scene of Plaça Sant Jaume, which lends itself equally to coffee and croissants in the morning, mid-day snacks or cocktail hour, complete with Wi-fi.

Mesón del Café
Llibreteria, 16
[16 p286, B2]
Serious coffee enthusiasts should pull up a stool at this quaint bar with heavy wooden decor that looks slightly out of place in this designer city, but remains charming.

Zim
Dagueria, 20
www.barzimbcn.com
[17 p286, B2]
Tiny wine bar which is big on quality and atmosphere, just off Plaça Sant Just, serving carefully selected Spanish wines and cava. The first drink comes with petons (kisses), a small tapa of cheese or spicy cold sausage.

TAPAS

U#1   Minim 2 Persona

eerian Ham
ariety of Cheese
Grilled Shrimps
Squid Andlusian
Entrecote with Roquefort Cheese
Bread with Tomato
21,00€ x person
Drink Include

Minim 2 Persona

t of Sausage

LA RIBERA, BORN AND PARC DE LA CIUTADELLA

The narrow streets and grand mansions of La Ribera resound with reminders of medieval commerce, but the focus is switching to a vibrant bar and restaurant scene.

The *barri* of La Ribera is loosely defined as that part of the Old Town that is separated from the Barri Gòtic by Via Laietana. There is a beaten track to the door of its star museum, the Museu Picasso, but the area has many other attractions, including the modish Born area, so take the long way round to get there and enjoy discovering its many contrasts, from the busy commerce of the Sant Pere district to medieval merchants' houses, from new social and urban developments to the most beautiful church in Barcelona.

Palau de la Música Catalana ❶

Address: Carrer Palau de la Música, 4–6; www.palaumusica.cat
Tel: 93-295 7200
Opening Hrs: guided tours daily 10am–3.30pm (Aug and Easter until 6pm)
Entrance fee: charge
Transport: Urquinaona

Like so many of the city's *barris*, La Ribera is a richly woven texture of contrasts. Nothing is more representative of this than the **Palau de la Música Catalana**, an extravaganza of a concert hall designed by leading

modernista architect Domènech i Montaner in 1908 (see page 55), and declared a World Heritage building by UNESCO. The only concert hall in Europe to be naturally lit, through its huge skylight decorated in magnificent stained glass, it must also be one of the most ornate and splendid. Renovations by leading Catalan architect Oscar Tusquets were completed in 2008, giving it a new space for chamber concerts, the Petit Palau, a rehearsal room and an elegant restaurant.

Main Attractions
Palau de la Música Catalana
Convent de Sant Agustí
Museu Picasso
Santa Maria del Mar
Passeig del Born
El Born Centre Cultural
Parc de la Ciutadella
Arc de Triomf
Castell dels Tres Dragons
Parc Zoològic

Maps and Listings
Map, page 126
Shopping, page 137
Restaurants, page 138
Accommodation, page 252

Ornate horse sculpture, Palau de la Música Catalana.

EAT

For sweet treats, sample the wonderfully rich hot chocolate in the Museu de la Xocolata or visit Brunells *pastisseria* on the corner of Montcada and Princesa. If you are not tempted by the *pastisseria*'s meringue-like *roque de Montserrat*, inspired by the sacred mountain, there are plenty of other cakes and pastries to choose from.

One of the best ways to visit it is to take a guided tour. They are popular, so it is worth booking in advance. Alternatively, pop in for a coffee or tapas in its foyer bar to sample the atmosphere and see plenty of *modernista* detail, or, even better, attend one of the concerts in its busy classical season, or during the International Jazz Festival (see page 261).

Characterful squares

Continue along **Carrer Sant Pere Més Alt** through the heart of today's rag-trade district, the wholesale end of Catalonia's once great textile industry. On weekdays it buzzes with activity, particularly around the 19th-century arcades, like the Passeig Sert, birthplace of painter Josep Maria Sert (1876–1945), where old warehouses have been converted into lofts.

The street emerges into the comparative tranquillity of **Plaça Sant**

The stunning Palau de la Música Catalana.

Pere ➋, site of a much-renovated 10th-century church, **Sant Pere de les Puel.les**, a former Benedictine monastery. In the middle of this triangular square is a *modernista* drinking fountain, designed by Pere Falqués, famed for his benches-cum-lamp-posts on Passeig de Gràcia.

La Ribera, Born and Parc de la Ciutadella

Follow **Basses Sant Pere** down past a vintage shop and local bars, keeping a firm grip on your rucksack and camera, to **Plaça Sant Agustí Vell** ❸. Signs of urban cleansing are evident, but new social housing and created *plaças* have not wiped out local colour altogether. There are several terrace bars in this square, but do not miss **Mundial**, a 1950s time warp, famed for its seafood *tapas* (see page 139).

From here, one option is to take Carrer Carders, where Halal butchers mingle with trendy boutiques, to the delightful Romanesque chapel of **Marcús** ❹, where post horses were blessed on the main route out, being just beyond the city walls and the Portal Major. Turn left into Montcada for the Museu Picasso (see page 128). Alternatively, take one of the narrow alleys to the right, leading to the magnificent Santa Caterina market.

Another option from Plaça Sant Agustí Vell is to meander down Tantarantana, to the former **Convent de Sant Agustí** ❺ at Comerç, 36. Now a civic centre, you can wander through its beautiful 14th-century cloisters. It also houses the **Museu de la Xocolata** (Mon–Sat 10am–7pm, Sun 10am–3pm; charge), which may interest children and chocolate-lovers, and the Arxiu Fotogràfic de Barcelona, which often has fascinating photographic exhibitions on the history of the city (Mon–Sat 10am–7pm; free).

Assaonadors and Princesa

Just before Princesa, turn right into **Assaonadors**, which immediately on the right opens into a long *plaça*, **Allada-Vermell**, a typical Barcelona 'hard' square. Created by the demolition of a row of housing, it brings light and space into the dense *barri*, providing a recreation area, several

The Palau de la Música Catalana's interior.

Figurines on the wall of the concert stage in the Palau de la Música Catalana.

Admiring artworks in the Museu Picasso.

trading was at its height. The merchants' palaces reflect this former prosperity.

Museu Picasso ❻

Address: Montcada, 15–23;
www.museupicasso.bcn.cat
Tel: 93-256 3000
Opening Hrs: Tue–Sun (including public holidays) 10am–7.30pm
Entrance fee: charge; free Sun from 3pm
Transport: Jaume I

The **Museu Picasso** opened in 1963 and now occupies five palaces: Palau Berenguer d'Aguilar, Baró de Castellet, Meca, Casa Mauri and Finestres. The last two, opened in 1999, are for temporary exhibitions; the main entrance is through the 14th-century Meca palace. Take time to enjoy the buildings as you visit the exhibitions. The Palau Berenguer d'Aguilar has a beautiful courtyard, with a surrounding first-floor gallery and pointed archways resting on slender columns, designed by Marc Safont, best known for the inner patio of the **Generalitat** building (see page 115).

bars good for snacks (including a pub) and a weekend craft market.

Continue along Assaonadors, taking the first left which leads into **Princesa**. The Parc de la Ciutadella (see page 132) is at the end of the road, but turn right towards the city centre again. It is a busy, narrow street full of lorries unloading goods and taxis unloading tourists by Montcada. On the corner before turning into Montcada you might be tempted by Brunells *pastisseria* (see margin, page 126).

STREET OF PALACES

The local authorities started renovating the neglected medieval palaces lining Montcada in 1957. Named after members of a noble medieval family who died during the conquest of Mallorca (1229), it was the city's most elegant district from the 12th to the 18th century. It linked the waterfront with the commercial areas, when Catalonia's overseas

SHOP

The Museu Picasso shop has multilingual tomes on this seminal artist, plus every imaginable gift, from mugs to iconic striped T-shirts.

PICASSO IN BARCELONA

Pablo Ruiz Picasso was born in Málaga in southern Spain in 1881. His family moved to Barcelona in 1895, where his father took up the post of painting professor at La Llotja School of Art. The story goes that a brothel in this street inspired the title (and content) of Picasso's landmark painting *Les Demoiselles d'Avignon* (1906–7). Picasso's precocious genius is legendary: aged just 14, he entered his father's school, completing the month-long entrance exams in a single day. He repeated this feat two years later at the Royal Academy in Madrid before abandoning his studies and setting out for Paris. He never again lived in Barcelona, but donated a considerable number of his works to the museum here.

The museum has the most complete collection of Picasso's early works, including sketches in school books and a masterly portrait of his mother, created when he was only 16 years old. The Blue Period (1901–4) is also well represented, as are his ceramics. It is an absorbing collection, although there are only a few of Picasso's later works, including the fascinating studies of *Las Meninas* dating from the 1950s.

Opposite is another noble Gothic palace, the Marquès de Lió, which until recently housed the Textile Museum and then the Disseny Hub Barcelona (DHUB). The DHUB Montcada and DHUB Pedralbes, which had the Textile, Graphic, Ceramic and Decorative Arts collections, have now moved to the much-vaunted Design Museum, in Glòries, due to open in early 2014 (see page 167).

Adjoining it is the Palau Nadal, where the **Museu Barbier-Mueller d'Art Precolombí** is to be replaced by the **Museu de Cultures del Món ❼**, due to open in June 2014. It comprises over 2,000 anthropological pieces from the private Folch collection gathered over many years, mostly from the Far East, Africa, Central America, the Andes and Oceania. Temporary exhibitions will also be held here.

Shops and galleries

Continuing down Montcada you come to the Palau Cervelló, at No. 25, and opposite is the Palau Dalmases, where at a price you can sip a cocktail and hear live opera or flamenco. Bijou shops and fashion boutiques are multiplying here, replacing the traditional local shops.

On the right, just before the Passeig del Born, is **Sombrerers**, named, like many in the area, after the medieval guilds (in this case, 'the hatters'). Follow its shade, with the towering edifice of Santa Maria del Mar on the left, past Casa Gispert, an exquisite grocery specialising in nuts, to reach the **Plaça Santa Maria**, once the church's graveyard. The Gothic fountain is one of the oldest in the city, dating from 1402.

Santa Maria del Mar ❽

Address: Plaça Santa Maria
Tel: 93-310 2390

On Carrer Montcada.

Opening Hrs: Mon–Sat 9am–1.30pm and 4.30–8.30pm, Sun 10am–1.30pm and 5–8.30pm
Entrance fee: free
Transport: Jaume I

On reaching the square, stand back and take in the Gothic facade of the Basílica de Santa Maria del Mar, considered by many – and justly so – to be the city's most beautiful church.

The church was built relatively quickly, between 1329 and 1384, resulting in a purity of style which ranks it as the most perfect example of Gothic church architecture in Catalonia. All the local corporations collaborated in the building, and it became a symbol of the economic and political power of Catalonia during this period.

Main features

The facade exhibits all the characteristics of the Catalan Gothic style: 'prevalence of horizontal lines; flat terraced roofing; wide open spaces; strong buttresses and octagonal towers ending in terraces', according to Alexandre Cirici, the Catalan art historian. It is a much more

down-to-earth style than northern European Gothic, lacking the decorative filigree and pointed spires of the latter.

The rose window is 15th-century, the original having been lost in the earthquake of 1428. The interior is breathtaking in its elegance. The church is built in what is known as the 'salon' design, with three lofty and almost identical naves, which contribute to the sense of space.

Ironically, the drama of more recent history has contributed to this purity: fire during the Civil War destroyed a great deal of the interior, which left it free of over-ornate decoration. The octagonal columns are 13 metres (43ft) apart, a distance no other medieval structure was able to achieve.

Leave through the side door of the church to see the **Plaça Fossar de les Moreres** ❾, a memorial to the fallen in the 1714 siege of Barcelona (see page 39), who are buried here in the former cemetery. Designed in 1986 by Carme Fiol, one of the leading architects in Barcelona's urban space programme, it is a venue for Catalan nationalists to

Inside the beautiful Santa Maria del Mar.

meet on 11 September, La Diada, the day Barcelona fell and the Catalan national holiday.

THE OLD COMMERCIAL DISTRICT

Take d'Espaseria from this side of the church to Consolat del Mar. On one side is **La Llotja ⑩**, the former stock exchange (now in Passeig de Gràcia). Its core is from the 14th century, but the outer shell was completed in 1802. Part of the Acadèmia de Bellas Artes, where Picasso, Gaudí and Miró studied, is still on an upper floor.

The main facade of La Llotja looks over **Pla del Palau ⑪**, where a royal palace once stood. Now devoted mostly to restaurants, it was the political centre of town for a period during the 18th and 19th centuries under the dominant viceroy. There are several good restaurants to choose from and a small playground in the square.

Keeping on the same pavement, walk through to **Plaça de les Olles** (Square of the Cooking Pots), a charming little square with pleasant terrace cafés. One ordinary-looking

bar is in fact one of the city's best places to eat, Cal Pep (see page 138). In the far corner turn into Vidrieria, another street named after a medieval guild ('the glaziers', see box, page 131), to reach the hub of the Born.

The façade of Santa Maria del Mar.

Passeig del Born ⑫

Glass and tin fairs used to be held in the Passeig del Born, as well as jousts and tournaments from the 13th to the 17th century. Take time to wander along this boulevard and its adjoining streets, where the quirky bars, shops and art galleries change hands and style with remarkable frequency, but where a few stalwarts remain. At the end, in Plaça Comercial, there are several good cafés and restaurants.

EL BORN CENTRE CULTURAL ⑬

Address: Plaça Comercial, www.elborn centrecultural.cat
Opening Hrs: Tue–Sun 10am–8pm
Entrance fee: charge for exhibitions

MEDIEVAL GUILDS

Many of the streets in the *barri* of La Ribera are named after trades, a throwback to the medieval boom when guilds were formed to look after the interests of craftsmen. At their height between the 13th and 15th centuries, there were 135 *gremis* (guilds), and 52 streets still carry their names. Watch out for Sombrerers (hatters), Flassaders (blanket weavers), Mirallers (mirror makers), Argenteria (silversmiths), Assaonadors (tanners), Agullers (needlemakers) and Semoleres (pasta makers). The Museu del Calçat in Plaça Sant Felip Neri (see page 114) is housed in the guildhall of the shoemakers, the first guild to be formed and the last to be disbanded in the 20th century, when the Civil War broke out.

SHOP

Just off Plaça Santa Maria is a shop selling the most creative *botifarras* (sausages) imaginable, while in nearby Agullers is an excellent wine shop, Vila Viniteca, which has a wide selection of Catalan and Spanish wines.

The rejuvenated area in and around the Passeig del Born is full of boutiques, speciality food shops, restaurants and bars.

Tapas.

but not for public space. Free Sun after 3pm

Transport: Jaume I/Barceloneta

The magnificent wrought-iron **Mercat del Born,** designed by Fontseré and Cornet in 1873, was Barcelona's central wholesale fruit and vegetable market from 1876 until 1971. After years of indecision about its future, it was relaunched as the Born Centre Cultural on 11 September 2013, symbolically marking the beginning of a year commemorating the 300th anniversary of the siege in 1714 when Barcelona fell to the Spanish troops (see box, page 133). The remains of houses demolished to build the citadel, found while renovating the building, are now on permanent display, along with other exhibitions explaining the history of the area in 1700 as well as the siege, a significant moment in the history of Catalonia. The Born CC embodies emotionally charged political issues for the growing movement for Catalan independence.

PARC DE LA CIUTADELLA ⑭

Address: Passeig de Pujades/Passeig de Picasso
Opening Hrs: summer daily 8am–9pm, winter 8am–8pm
Entrance fee: free
Transport: Jaume I/Arc de Triomf

A walkway through the Born CC leads to Barcelona's oldest and most

visited park, the Parc de la Ciutadella, which is also one of the city's most attractive. It is easy to while away half a day here, simply walking in the fresher air, or enjoying some of

CIUTADELLA'S HISTORY

The name, La Ciutadella (which means citadel, or fortress), has its origins in the use to which Felipe V put this land. After the fall of Barcelona in 1714, following a siege by Franco-Spanish troops, he ordered the building of a fortress capable of housing 8,000 soldiers. To do this, 40 streets and 1,262 buildings were demolished. Remains discovered beneath the Mercat del Born can now be seen in the Born CC. Barceloneta was built to accommodate the evicted residents.

In 1869 General Prim ceded the land to the city for conversion into a public park. Josep Fontseré's plan was approved in 1873 but it was not until 1888, the year of the World Exposition, that the park began to be a reality.

the diverse activities on offer. Located between the Old Town and the new Vila Olímpica, it has two entrances on Passeig de Picasso.

However, one of the most interesting approaches, which also gives the park its historical perspective, is from the northern end of Passeig de Lluís Companys, next to the Arc de Triomf (easily reached by the metro of the same name, or by bus).

Arc de Triomf ⓳

This enormous red-brick arch served as the entrance to the 1888 World Exposition, which was held on the redeveloped land that was previously the site of the citadel of the occupying Spanish forces (see box, page 133). From the top of Passeig de Lluís Companys you can look up **Passeig Sant Joan** – a typical Eixample street with architectural echoes of Passeig de Gràcia, including some fine *modernista* houses – towards the Collserola range.

Outdoor cafés in La Ribera.

Seals in the Parc Zoològic.

The Arc de Triomf is an imposing structure that was built as the entrance to the 1888 World Exposition.

play *petanca* (a southern European form of bowls), while cyclists vie for space with dog-walkers and retired couples who sit on pieces of cardboard playing card games. At the end is the main entrance to the Parc de la Ciutadella.

Park life

Interesting buildings remain from its military past and from its glorious time as the Exposition showground, but the most remarkable aspect of the park is its refreshing tranquillity. It is a real city park, full of skateboards and footballs, prams and toddlers. There are bicycles made for six for hire, as well as rowing boats on the lake. On Sunday large families parade in their best outfits before lunch, and New Age drummers meet for jam sessions. Yet it is still peaceful. Constantly tended by municipal gardeners, it is verdant, scented and shady.

The Arc de Triomf, designed by Josep Vilaseca, includes sculptures by Josep Llimona, among others. It is easy to imagine visitors to the Exposition sweeping down this thoroughfare to the showground, past the magnificent streetlamps, the work of Pere Falqués, who designed the more famous ones in Passeig de Gràcia. Today's palms are some of the most attractive of the many species growing in the city.

In front of the monumental Palau de la Justicia (Law Courts), old men

On the right as you enter is the **Castell dels Tres Dragons** (Castle of the Three Dragons), designed by Domènech i Montaner. It was intended to be the restaurant of the 1888 Exposition, though it never

Boating in the Parc de Ciutadella.

opened as such. However, it was one of the first *modernista* projects in Barcelona. Until 2010 it was the Zoological Museum, now moved to the Museu Blau in the Forum (see page 169).

The Hivernacle 16

Behind the building is the beautiful Hivernacle, an elegant modernista greenhouse now overgrown with tropical plants and sadly still awaiting restoration work. Beyond it is a more classical-looking structure built to be a museum in 1878, the first public one in the city. More recently it has been the Geology Museum, but the collection is now in the Museu Blau.

The Cascada 17

Cross over the inner road and follow signs to the Cascada, the monumental fountain and artificial lake designed by Fontseré in 1875; both the cascade and the lake were intended to camouflage a huge water deposit in the central section of the waterfall, which can be reached by two flanking, symmetrical stairways. Curiously, Gaudí worked on this project as a young architecture student. A landmark and meeting place, its esplanade is often used for concerts or fairs, and Swing dancers bop at weekends in the bandstand.

Catalan Parliament

With your back to the Cascada, follow the boating lake round either way to the Plaça de Joan Fiveller, where there is a serene, oval formal garden designed by French landscape architect J.C.N. Forestier. The statue in the lake is a copy of *El Desconsol* (Desolation), one of Catalan sculptor Josep Llimona's most highly regarded pieces. The original can be seen in the Museu Nacional in Montjuïc.

This square is bordered by the remnants of the citadel era: the Governor's Palace, now a secondary school, the chapel and the arsenal.

This last is now where the **Parlament de Catalunya** ⓲ sits, guarded by the Catalan police, the Mossos d'Esquadra.

Parc Zoològic ⓳

Address: Parc de la Ciutadella;
www.zoobarcelona.cat
Tel: 93-225 6780
Opening Hrs: daily summer 10am–8pm, winter 10am–6pm
Entrance fee: charge
Transport: Barceloneta/Arc de Triomf, Ciutadella Vila Olímpica

Follow the paved road towards the park gates to the Parc Zoològic, or Zoo, founded in 1892. Its most famous inmate was Snowflake (Floquet de Neu), the only albino gorilla in captivity, who died amid much lamenting in 2003, and was succeeded by various non-albino descendants. Highlights include the Aquarama dolphin show (hourly at weekends).

Exiting from the zoo

From within the zoo the **Wellington exit** ⓴ leads to the street of the same name and takes you to the

The Cascada, a monumental fountain designed in 1875.

Vila Olímpica and its beaches (see page 162). A tram runs from here to Plaça de les Glòries, with another route down to Diagonal Mar and the Fòrum site with its beach (see page 169). The metro is also close by, but for further exploration take **Avinguda Icària** into the Olympic Village, or head for the Hotel Arts (the right-hand skyscraper) passing through a small, modern park, **Parc Cascades**, above the Ronda Litoral, with a towering sculpture titled *David i Goliat* by Antoni Llena.

If you'd like to complete your day with a swim on Somorrostro beach and dinner in the Olympic Port but don't want to go through the zoo, there is another exit from the park on Pujades, behind the Cascade. Turn right and follow Wellington past the haunting brick structure, the **Diposit de les Aigües**, which once stored water on its roof. Part of this building has been impressively restored as the library of the nearby University Pompeu Fabra.

The Umbracle ㉑

If you prefer to do full justice to the Ciutadella, from the main entrance

The splendid interior of the Estació de França.

to the zoo head up towards the Arc de Triomf and on your left is the **Umbracle**. This beautiful arched building, with fine iron columns and wooden-slatted roof, was also designed by Fontseré. It offers much-needed shade for the more delicate species in the park. The dim light inside is reminiscent of a jungle.

Passeig de Picasso ㉒

A small gate by the Umbracle leads out of the park to the Passeig de Picasso. The handsome arcaded apartment blocks here were designed by Fontseré as an integral part of his redevelopment plans. Some good bars and a bike-rental shop are located under the arches. Further up the road are the Aire de Barcelona Arab baths, perfect for weary limbs after an excess of sightseeing. A large modern sculpture in a transparent cube on the park boundary by Catalan artist Antoni Tàpies was designed as a homage to Picasso.

Opposite the park entrance is the broad street **Marquès de l'Argentera**. Spain's first railway line was inaugurated here in 1848. The station, the **Estació de França**, was little more than a shack when it opened in 1929, yet was the largest in Europe. Renovated in 1992, it looks more like a grand hotel than a railway station.

SHOPPING

In recent years this neighbourhood has become seriously cool, so the medieval mansions rub shoulders with stylish boutiques. Whichever way you turn off the Passeig del Born you'll find narrow alleyways studded with attractive shops, including some traditional ones.

Food

La Botifarreria de Santa María
Santa María, 4
Tel: 93-319 9123
Catalonia's famed *botifarras* (country sausages) are almost a national dish, but you'll never find such mouth-watering examples as in this shop next to the front door of Santa Maria del Mar. Join the queue to choose between wild mushrooms, apple with curry, squid or 100-percent vegetarian stuffing.

Casa Gispert
Sombrerers, 23
www.casagispert.com
Like a museum piece, this beautiful traditional glass-fronted shop with much of its original shelving and equipment preserved has to be seen. Master roasters since 1851 of nuts and coffee, it also sells dried fruits, preserves, chocolates and more delicacies.

Olisoliva
Mercat Santa Caterina, stall 153–155
Tel: 93-268 1472
Among many enticing stalls in this attractive food market, this shop sells over 200 virgin olive oils as well as vinegars and special salts, beautifully packaged to make good gifts.

Vila Viniteca
Agullers, 7–9
From quite humble origins in the 1930s, this charming shop in medieval surroundings has become one of Spain's leading wine distributors, offering a huge range of national and international wines. Be guided by the helpful personnel and check out the gourmet food section.

Shoes

Nu Sabates
Cotoners, 14
www.nusabates.com
Exclusive handmade shoes for men and women in the softest leather and daring designs, mostly by Californian-based Cydwoq, but also Deux Souliers, from Catalan designer Nunu Solsona based in the Gràcia neighbourhood.

U-Casas
Espaseria, 4
The more casual, sporty side of Casas, who have branches all over town selling a range of good brands and elegant designs.

Women's clothing

Anna Povo
Vidrieria, 11
www.annapovo.com
The only outlet of this local designer who makes simple but very stylish, feminine designs in subtle colours and natural fabrics, which are easy to wear yet striking.

Cortana
Flassaders, 41
www.cortana.es
The outlet store of Mallorcan Rosa Esteva's ultra-feminine, slinky clothes is a great place to find a very smart outfit at a manageable price.

Miriam Ponsa
Princesa, 14
www.miriamponsa.com
This young designer is from a family involved in the famous Catalan textile industry in the 19th century. Her radical designs in earthy, natural colours and heavy cottons have won awards.

RESTAURANTS, BARS AND CAFÉS

Restaurants

At the hub of this area is the trendy Born district, whose recent rise to fame has resulted in a constant turnover of bars, cafés and restaurants, so there's plenty of choice and increasingly multicultural options. There are also many old, established favourites as well as new stars where you need to book, or join the queue, if visiting on a Thursday, Friday or Saturday.

Catalan

Cal Pep
Plaça de les Olles, 8
Tel: 93-310 7961

Senyor Parellada.

www.calpep.com
Open: Tue–Fri L & D, Sat L, Mon D. €€€ [**35** p286, C2]
Jostle and queue to sit at the bar (the dining room at the back is more expensive and less fun), where you can witness the chefs tossing and flipping fat prawns and succulent squid. Mediterranean cooking at its simplest and very best, with atmosphere to match.

Comerç 24
Comerç, 24
Tel: 93-319 2102
www.carlesabellan.es
Open: Tue–Sat L & D. €€€€ [**36** p286, C2]
One of the leading lights in new-wave Catalan cooking, chef Carles Abellán, inspired by several years working in the laboratory-kitchen of El Bullí, has several restaurants in the city. This designer-smart but relaxed space was the first. Choose between two tasting menus, the *Festival de Tapas* or the *Gran Festival* – both are a trip for the taste buds.

Nou Celler
Princesa, 16

Tel: 93-310 4773
Open: Mon–Sat L & D. € [**37** p286, B2]
This attractive, bustling restaurant is very restorative after a long session in the nearby Picasso Museum, serving authentic homely Catalan dishes, like canelons or civet (wild boar stew).

El Passadís del Pep
Pla de Palau, 2
Tel: 93-310 1021
www.passadisdelpep.com
Open: Mon–Sat L & D. €€€€ [**38** p286, C2]
This is a place for people 'in the know', the kind of place you walk past if you are not. The regulars keep returning 30 years on for whatever the chef Joan has on his menu that day. Be prepared to spend a lot, but otherwise relax; you don't even have to choose your food – it is simply brought to you.

Pla de la Garsa
Assaonadors, 13
Tel: 93-315 2413
www.pladelagarsa.com
Open: Daily D. €–€€ [**39** p286, C2]
This tastefully restored medieval stable with attractive decor is a peaceful option for an evening meal. Enjoy Catalan specialities, especially their range of cheeses, pâtés and *embotits* (cured sausages, ham and typical pork products).

Senyor Parellada
Argentería, 37
Tel: 93-310 5094
www.senyorparellada.com
Open: Daily L & D. €€ [**40** p286, B2]
A mixture of unusual and classic Catalan dishes in sophisticated and attractive surroundings, run by the Parelladas, a well-known family of restaurateurs.

Set Portes
Passeig Isabel II, 14
Tel: 93-319 3033
www.7portes.com
Open: Daily L & D. €€–€€€ [**41** p286, B3]
Nearly 180 years old and still going

strong. Sympathetically restored, this good-looking classic restaurant remains popular, especially for family Sunday lunches. It specialises in rice dishes, one for each day of the week. Also has the advantage of remaining open through the afternoon and evening until 1am.

International

Le Cucine Mandarosso
Verdaguer i Callis, 4
Tel: 93-269 0780
Open: Tue–Sat L & D. € [42 p286, B1]
Hidden in a narrow alleyway just opposite the Palau de la Música, this Italian restaurant is a real charm worth hunting down. Specialists in freshly made pasta like Mamma makes, served with unusual sauces and desserts to die for.

Cuines Santa Caterina
Mercat Santa Caterina,
Avinguda Francesc Cambó
Tel: 93-268 9918
www.grupotragaluz.com
Open: Daily L & D. €–€€ [43 p286, B2]
The first market bar for beautiful people in a bustling designer space. Rub shoulders with them at long communal tables as the very visible kitchen whips up deliciously fresh Mediterranean, Asian and vegetarian dishes with a contemporary twist. All day tapas bar in the same space.

Mosquito
Carders 46, Baixos 2a
Tel: 93-268 7569
Open: Tue–Sun L & D. Mon D. €
[44 p286, C2]
The delightful English owners of Mosquito define their food as 'exotic tapas', which is a modest assessment of the delicious, original Asian dishes they create. What's more, it's open from 7pm, which is handy if you are travelling with children and want an early dinner. It's a good idea to eat early as it gets cramped and noisy as the evening goes on. They specialise in Catalan and imported beers.

Spanish

La Candela
Plaça de Sant Pere, 12
Tel: 93-310 6242
Open: Daily L & D. € [45 p286, C1]
Delicious Mediterranean food with an exotic edge and good, plentiful salads in this minute restaurant, which spills out into the surprisingly quiet square. A very attractive place to eat on summer evenings, but get there early for an outdoor table.

Euskal Etxea
Placeta Montcada, 1–3
Tel: 93-310 2185
Open: Daily L, D & tapas. €€€ (tapas €)
[46 p286, C2]
This is a stronghold of Basque cuisine just two minutes from the Picasso Museum, where you can be sure of a good meal. If you prefer tapas, it is advisable to get there early to catch the fresh pintxos at the bar.

Mundial
Plaça Sant Agustí Vell, 1
Tel: 93-319 9056
Open: Daily for tapas. € [47 p286, C2]
May the Mundial never change. A stalwart of traditional Spanish bars, which are fast fading in this up-and-coming district, its solid marble bar is piled with fresh, simple and tasty seafood tapas.

Vegetarian

Bascula
Flassaders, 30 bis
Tel: 93-319 9866
Open: Wed–Sun L & D. € [48 p286, C2]
A new kind of restaurant, run as a co-operative by people from many different countries, in a former chocolate factory in the labyrinth of streets behind the Picasso Museum. Delicious snacks and wholesome meals using organic produce, mostly vegetarian.

Bars and Cafés

Al Sur Café
Sant Pere Més Alt, 4
Tel: 93-310 1286
[18 p286, B1]
A laid-back café opposite the Palau de la Música, where you can snack on home-made pastries and Argentinian empanadas (delicious savoury pasties), while listening to good music and enjoying the free Wi-Fi. Converts into a lounge bar in the evening.

Born CC
Plaça Comercial
www.elborncentrecultural.cat
[19 p286, C2]
Barcelona beer brand Moritz is due to open a gourmet bar in this brand new cultural centre in autumn 2013, which judging by the trendy stamp they've left on other bars in the city will be stylish and serve good tapas.

La Ciutadella
Passeig Pujades, 5
[20 p286, C2]
A typical Spanish cafetería with a sunny terrace, ideal for refreshments or a snack after a long walk in the Ciutadella park.

La Vinya del Señor
Plaça Santa Maria, 5
Tel: 93-310 3379
[21 p286, B2]
A tiny, designer wine bar with an extensive choice of interesting wines from Spain and other countries, which you can taste by the glass accompanied by a snack. Sit on the terrace to admire the majestic Gothic facade of Santa Maria del Mar.

Xampanyet
Montcada, 22
Tel: 93-319 7003
[22 p286, C2]
Amid the explosion of new, fashionable bars in this area it is a relief to see this old favourite still going strong, serving its intoxicating fizzy white wine and house anchovies in pretty, ceramic-tiled surroundings. Not to be missed.

Mosquito's oriental take on tapas.

Relaxing by the CCCB.

EL RAVAL

Contemporary art, music, design and cultural centres plus a new Rambla are rejuvenating the historic but long-neglected quarter of El Raval.

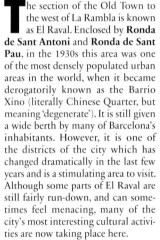

The section of the Old Town to the west of La Rambla is known as El Raval. Enclosed by **Ronda de Sant Antoni** and **Ronda de Sant Pau**, in the 1930s this area was one of the most densely populated urban areas in the world, when it became derogatorily known as the Barrio Xino (literally Chinese Quarter, but meaning 'degenerate'). It is still given a wide berth by many of Barcelona's inhabitants. However, it is one of the districts of the city which has changed dramatically in the last few years and is a stimulating area to visit. Although some parts of El Raval are still fairly run-down, and can sometimes feel menacing, many of the city's most interesting cultural activities are now taking place here.

Religious past

In its medieval past the area was heavily populated by convents and other religious institutions. With the advent of industrialisation in the late 18th century the emphasis switched to factories, and dense urbanisation began. Relics of the religious past still stand out in today's bustling El Raval.

Two pretty squares

Walking down La Rambla from Plaça de Catalunya, take the second road on the right, Bonsuccés, which opens into the **Plaça Bonsuccés ❶**. The large building dominating the square is a former convent dating from 1635, now district council offices. The adjoining modern archway leads into **Plaça Vicenç Martorell**, a square where the convent cloisters would have been. In the far corner of the arches, the popular bar **Kasparo** provides delicious alternative snacks, and a shady terrace on which to relax and watch children playing in the central park.

Main Attractions
Casa de la Misericòrdia
Museu d'Art Contemporani de Barcelona
Centre de Cultura Contemporània de Barcelona
Antic Hospital
La Capella
Rambla del Raval
Església de Sant Pau del Camp

Maps and Listings
Map, page 143
Shopping, page 146
Restaurants, page 148
Accommodation, page 253

A friendly face on the Rambla del Raval.

Gerhard Richter's '48 Portraits' at MACBA.

On one side of the square is the **Casa de la Misericòrdia** (1583), formerly a hospice for abandoned children. It has been cleverly restored, complete with interior palm tree, to make more council offices.

Elisabets

Taking a break.

Return to Plaça Bonsuccés and turn into Elisabets, by the restaurant of

the same name (good for hearty winter dishes and atmosphere), heading towards the **Convent dels Àngels**, a MACBA exhibition space, at the end of the street. There is a good bookshop, Central, in the lofty space of the Misericòrdia chapel and some wonderful tall palms, before you pass ultra-hip hotel Casa Camper (see page 253), discreet in its 19th-century shell. **Doctor Dou** on the left has some interesting bars, good-value restaurants and art galleries. After a couple of designer shops on Elisabets is another well-renovated chapel, part of an orphanage dating back to 1370.

Museu d'Art Contemporani de Barcelona (MACBA) ❷

Address: Plaça dels Àngels;
www.macba.cat
Tel: 93-412 0810
Opening Hrs: Mon, Wed–Fri
11am–7.30pm, Sat 10am–9pm,

Sun 10am–3pm
Entrance fee: charge
Transport: Catalunya/Universitat

At this point you emerge into the **Plaça dels Àngels**, which opens up into the unexpected space dominated by the breathtaking Museu d'Art Contemporani de Barcelona. Opened in 1995 and designed by US architect Richard Meier, the building is dazzling against the Mediterranean sky and gigantic in the context of the humble buildings beyond. The social and urban significance of the architecture in this once declining area has been as much of a talking point as the collection inside, which comprises Catalan, Spanish and some international art, mostly from the second half of the 20th century. The museum also hosts interesting temporary exhibitions.

Its large forecourt has evolved into a world-class space for skateboarding and is also a venue for local fiestas, music festivals and dance events. The Filipino families who live in the narrow streets around **Joaquín Costa** often gather here on warm evenings: the square is a fascinating melting pot of local residents and cosmopolitan visitors.

MACBA was built in the grounds of the enormous Casa de la Caritat (poorhouse), which once provided a home for thousands of children (part of it still stands around the corner in Montalegre). The former 18th-century hospice has now become a centre for contemporary culture.

Centre de Cultura Contemporània de Barcelona ❸

Address: Montalegre, 5;
www.cccb.org
Tel: 93-306 4100
Opening Hrs: Tue–Sun 11am–8pm
Entrance fee: charge
Transport: Catalunya/Universitat

TIP

If you look closely at the Casa de la Misericòrdia you will see a small wooden circle in the wall, where abandoned babies were pushed through and received by nuns on the other side, until as recently as 1931.

Local skateboarders outside MACBA.

El Raval

[Map of El Raval with numbered locations:
C. de Floridablanca
C. del Comte d'Urgell
C. de Tamarit
Ronda de Sant Antoni
Carrer de la Riera Alta
Mercat de Sant Antoni
Sant Antoni
C. de St Antoni Abat
Pl. Joan Coromines
Museu d'Art Contemporani de Barcelona (MACBA) ❷
Centre de Cultura Contemporània de Barcelona (CCCB) ❸
Convent dels Àngels
Joaquín Costa
Plaça dels Àngels
C. del Peu de la Creu
C. Pintor Fortuny
Casa de la Misericòrdia
C. Elisabets
C. Dou
Plaça Bonsuccés ❶
Plaça Vicenç Martorell
Plaça de Catalunya
C. dels Tallers
C. de Pelai
C. d'en Xuclà
EL RAVAL
Plaça Pedró
C. de M.ª Aguiló
Campreny
Carrer del Carme
Carrer de la Cera
Carrer de la Reina Amàlia
Carrer de les Carretes
Carrer de la Riereta
Carrer de
Rambla del Raval
Antic Hospital de la Santa Creu ❹
JARDINS DR FLEMING
Plaça Gardunya
La Capella
Carrer Hospital
St Rafael
C. Robador
Sant Agustí
Plaça Sant Agustí
Filmoteca de Catalunya ❻
Sant Pau
C. Salvador Segui
Pau
Palau de la Virreina
Mercat de la Boqueria (Sant Josep)
Plaça de la Boqueria
Liceu Ⓜ
Gran Teatre del Liceu
Rambla dels Caputxins
C. Marquès de Barberà
C. la Unió
Ronda de Sant Pau
Avinguda
Carrer de Vila i Vila
Carrer del Om
Sant Pau del Camp ❼
Paral·lel Ⓜ
Carrer de les Tàpies
Carrer Nou de la Rambla
Palau Güell
Plaça Reial
Funicular de Montjuïc
PARC TRES XEMENEIES
Paral·lel
❺
0   200 m
0   200 yds]

The Centre de Cultura Contemporània de Barcelona (**CCCB**) is a brilliant centre with a stimulating programme of diverse cultural activities, including dance, music, film, video and seminars, based on urban and contemporary issues. The complex – a renovation of the old hospice by architects Piñón and Vilaplana – rivals MACBA for its architectural interest and has great views from its Sala de Mirador.

Plaça Joan Coromines

Go through the central Patí de les Dones of the CCCB, a courtyard often used for performances or film festivals, into the **Plaça Joan Coromines** which links it with the MACBA art museum. The C3 Bar, with a terrace overlooking the square, is a fashionable place to meet and have a snack, and it converts into a lounge bar at night.

Antic Hospital de la Santa Creu ❹

Address: Carrer del Carme, 47
Opening Hrs: daily 8am–9pm
Entrance fee: free
Transport: Liceu

Weekend market wares.

Return to Plaça dels Àngels. Continue along the tree-lined street of Àngels to Carme, turn left and cross the road into the Antic Hospital de la Santa Creu, a large Gothic complex that was a hospital until the 1920s. On the left is the 18th-century Academy of Medicine and Surgery (open to visitors on Wednesday mornings), and on the right the **Institut d'Estudis Catalans** in the hospital's **Casa de Convalescència**. Wander through the atmospheric cloistered patio, a favourite meeting place for the homeless but full of charm, and with a terrace café serving delicious light meals. The Biblioteca de Catalunya occupies much of the old hospital building, along with the Massana art school.

La Capella

Address: Hospital, 56, http://lacapella.bcn.cat
Opening Hrs: Tue–Sat noon–2pm and 4–8pm, Sun 11am–2pm
Entrance fee: free
Transport: Liceu

As you emerge into the street, Carrer Hospital, check if there is an

A well-placed café outside MACBA.

exhibition in La Capella, once the hospital's chapel, which promotes young experimental artists and has interesting work on display.

MULTICULTURAL RAVAL

With your back to La Rambla, follow Carrer Hospital deeper into El Raval. This is a busy commercial street, even on Sunday, reflecting the increasing number of shops run by Pakistanis, who are the most recent immigrant group in the district. Tandoori restaurants sit side by side with halal butchers, Arabic pastry shops, kebab bars, bazaars crammed with cheap goods and long-established tailors selling uniforms for employees in the catering business. A sign above a narrow doorway, squeezed between two shops indicates the entrance to a *mezquita*, one of the city's mosques.

Trendy vintage clothes shops are another new thread in this multi-coloured fabric. **Riera Baixa**, a short pedestrian street on the right off Hospital, is full of them and has an outdoor market on Saturday.

A heavily illustrated building on Rambla del Raval.

Film screening at the CCCB.

Rambla del Raval ❺

Carrer Hospital then disgorges into the new broad **Rambla del Raval**, not to be confused with the famous Rambla, a model example of the city council's policy of urban regeneration. An entire street of old housing was demolished to create this pleasant promenade bordered with jacaranda and palm trees. Old residents and new immigrants enjoy the space, which is also used as a venue for a colourful weekend market and concerts. The prostitutes, thieves and junkies are still hovering, but on the whole have retreated to the narrower streets behind, where the darker side of urban life is still evident.

The new Rambla is lined with restaurant terraces and kebab bars. The cutting-edge five-star Barceló Raval hotel (see page 253), with its zany night-time lighting, towers over this new scene. Just opposite is the legendary restaurant Casa Leopoldo (see

DRINK

The atmospheric Marsella (on Sant Pau), serving absinthe since 1820, is lamentably threatened with closure by local authorities. But for *modernista* decor try London Bar in Nou de la Rambla, with live music, or Bar Muy Buenas in Carme.

SHOPPING

As this neighbourhood becomes trendier and the cultural centres attract a discerning crowd, the shopping options are changing accordingly. Quirky fashion boutiques, vintage stores and shops with a designer theme await you.

Accessories

Vaho Gallery
Bonsuccés, 13
http://vaho.ws
This creative, socially responsible firm produces a huge range of practical, attractive bags for men and women, all made out of recycled plasticised banners that once hung in the city streets.

Books

La Central del Raval
Elisabets, 6
Take time out in this soothing,

Shoes at Vialis.

huge bookshop, which occupies the 16th-century former chapel of the Casa de la Misericòrdia. Find coffee-table books on art, photography and Barcelona, among the many tomes.

Laie CCCB
Montalegre, 5
www.laie.es/cccb
You could browse for hours in the Contemporary Culture Centre's bookshop, well-stocked with publications on art, architecture, film and other contemporary issues, plus stylish souvenirs like Gaudí tile coasters or vinyl fans.

Clothing

Riera Baixa is a pedestrian street with a concentration of vintage clothing shops, which take their wares, including accessories and records, out onto the street on Saturdays. In other parts of the neighbourhood:

Holala! Plaza
Plaça de Castella, 2
An emporium of second-hand clothes on several levels, mixed with furniture and all sorts of random accessories. Beware that vintage is not synonymous with cheap in Barcelona.

Home

El Indio,
Carme, 24
A wonderful fabric shop that seems to be arrested in time. Behind its untouched modernista facade and entrance is a deep shop, lined with bolts of cloth and long wooden tables for measuring them.

Room Service
Àngels, 16
Somewhere between a studio, shop and gallery, this space shows (and sells) contemporary design, with particular focus on ecological and sustainable issues. It's inspir-

ing to visit, even if a table won't fit into your luggage.

Markets

Mercat Raval
Rambla del Raval
This weekend market runs most of the length of this relatively new *rambla*, bringing a splash of vibrant colour. Independent designers sell clothes, jewellery, accessories and kids' clothes, and you'll also find Moroccan jewellery, babouches and mint tea.

Music

Discos Revolver
Tallers, 11
This is just one of several record shops in this street just off La Rambla, where vinyl collectors are bound to find something they desire.

Etnomusic
Bonsuccés, 6
A small shop with a fantastic collection of world music. If they don't have what you're looking for, they will try to obtain it. Good vibes.

Shoes

Camper
Plaça de los Àngeles, 4
Just beyond the eponymous supertrendy hotel is a small Camper shoe shop. It's not as busy as some branches, which makes it all the better for choosing one of the idiosyncratic designs, which have turned this Mallorcan shoemaker into a world player.

Vialis
Elisabets, 20
www.vialis.es
Another successful Catalan shoemaker, the Menorcan designer behind Vialis creates wonderful shoes in the softest Italian leather, even the sensible lace-ups have a feminine edge.

page 148), which was once hidden down a seedy street.

A left turn on Sant Pau leads back to the Liceu on La Rambla, past the Filmoteca de Catalunya ❻ (Plaça Salvador Seguí, 1–9; www. filmoteca.cat) the film library and theatre housed in a brand new building, another key piece in the urban regeneration scheme. Its busy agenda includes cycles on key film directors.

Església de Sant Pau del Camp ❼

Address: Sant Pau, 101–103
Tel: 93-441 0001
Opening Hrs: Mon–Sat 10am–1pm, 4–7pm
Entrance fee: charge
Transport: Paral.lel/Liceu

Alternatively, from Rambla del Raval turn right on Sant Pau to find the Romanesque church of **Sant Pau del Camp**, generally considered to be the oldest church in Barcelona. Surrounded by greenery, including an olive tree, a cypress and a palm, it is a true survivor in this long-beleaguered area.

Sant Pau del Camp is a fine example of Romanesque architecture, quite rare in the city. The present building dates from the 12th century, but it incorporates elements of an earlier church that was built in 912. Its small cloister, with unusual carvings, is a gem. On the exterior above the main door, look for the simple carving of the Hand of God and a winged creature, a symbolic representation of one of the Evangelists.

Much of the former industrial activity was in this lower part of El Raval – the new park behind the church was created after a fire burnt down a factory – and the park's tall chimney is a fitting memorial to the area's industrial past. A sports centre, Can Ricart (open to the public) has been built in a former textile factory.

Continue along the last block in Sant Pau, past the mirrored shop front of **La Confiteria**, a pastry shop turned stylish bar.

At the end of Sant Pau is the metro Paral.lel, where you can catch the funicular up to the Parc de Montjuïc, not far from the Fundació Joan Miró (see page 184).

Romanesque architecture at Sant Pau del Camp.

Sant Pau del Camp, Barcelona's oldest church.

RESTAURANTS, BARS AND CAFÉS

Restaurants

This once-forgotten neighbourhood is rapidly becoming fashionable. The only difficult aspect of finding a place to eat here is making the choice. There is a wide range of venues for all tastes, tending towards new ideas of fusion, or new concepts in eating, although there's no shortage of genuine local places, plus multicultural options, and several vegetarian choices.

Catalan

Ca l'Isidre
Les Flors, 12
Tel: 93-441 1139
www.calisidre.com
Open: Mon–Sat L & D. €€€€ [49 p284, E2]
This is a family-run business that has grown into one of the city's most respected restaurants. The smart clientele appreciate the meticulous attention to detail in food, decor and service. Classic Catalan dishes exquisitely prepared, using whatever's in season from the nearby Boqueria market.

Can Lluís
Cera, 49
Tel: 93-441 1187
www.restaurantcanlluis.cat
Open: Mon–Sat L & D. €€ [50 p284, E2]
Can Lluís is the kind of genuine Catalan restaurant you would hope to find in a small village, so it's a pleasant surprise to encounter it in the heart of the city. Delicious food, like *favetes minis amb xipironets* (tender broad beans with baby squid) or *suquet* (a rich fish stew) is served amid noise and bustle, and no pretensions. Excellent value lunchtime menu.

Casa Leopoldo
Sant Rafael, 24
Tel: 93-441 3014
Open: Tue–Sat L & D, Sun L (closed Sun June–Sept). €€€ [51 p284, E2]
Just off Rambla del Raval, a family-run Barcelona classic with plenty of history and great atmosphere. Particularly known for its fish and its own version of the Catalan staple, *pa amb tomàquet*.

Suculent
Rambla del Raval, 43
Tel: 93-443 6579
www.suculent.com
Open: Tue–Sat L & D, Sun L. €€ [52 p284, E2]
A great addition to the area with superstar chef Carles Abellan in the wings, though young chef Antonio Romero produces traditional Catalan dishes with a contemporary edge masterfully. Try their take-away fried potatoes if nothing else.

International

Dos Trece
Carme, 40
Tel: 93-301 7306
www.dostrece.net
Open: Daily L & D. €–€€ [53 p286, A1]
Fashionable place with a laid-back attitude and good atmosphere. Unconventional, tasty dishes show the influence of the owner's Mexican/LA background. Serves good brunch at weekends.

En Ville
Doctor Dou, 14
Tel: 93-302 8467
www.envillebarcelona.es
Open: Tue–Sat L & D, Sun–Mon L. €€ (set menu L & D €) [54 p286, A1]
Creative Catalan cooking with a French edge in charming, spacious surroundings. Marble tables, palms and gentle live music (Tue and Wed) complete the picture. Good value.

Iposa
Floristes de la Rambla, 14
Tel: 93-318 6086
Open: Mon–Sat L & D. € [55 p286, A1]
A very popular, lively spot to hang out just behind La Boqueria market with a terrace alongside the Jardins Dr Fleming, where kids can play. Its excellent-value *menú del dia* and snacks reflect the influence of its French owner.

Maharaja
Rambla del Raval, 14
Tel: 93-442 5777
www.maharajarestaurante.com
Open: Daily L & D. € [56 p284, E2]
The ultimate in Spanish-Indian crossover has to be the biryani paella served here on an open-air terrace in the middle of this new *rambla*. The more traditional Indian dishes are good, too, and there are plenty of vegetarian options.

Rita Blue
Plaça Sant Agustí, 3
Tel: 93-342 4086
www.ritablue.com
Open: Mon–Sat L & D, Sun L. €–€€ [57 p286, A2]
Serves 'Tex-Med' fusion food featuring light snacks as well as more substantial mains. Try a cocktail in the basement lounge bar or on the popular terrace on the square alongside the church, which houses St Rita, saint of the impossible.

Silenus
Àngels, 8
Tel: 93-302 2680
www.restaurantsilenus.com
Open: Mon–Sat L & D. €€ (set menu Mon–Fri L €) [58 p284, E2]
Comfortable and arty café/restaurant with an appetising selection of Mediterranean and international dishes, including plenty of seafood. In warm weather, tables are set up in the street.

La Verònica
Rambla del Raval, 2–4
Tel: 93-329 3303

Open: Daily L & D. € [**59** p284, E2]
This ultra-trendy spot selling *pizzas del mercat* topped with whatever is in season has moved here from the Gothic Quarter, a sure sign of just how up-and-coming the new Raval really is. Eat alfresco on their terrace on the Rambla. A great option for before or after the Filmoteca just down the *rambla*.

Spanish

Elisabets
Elisabets, 2
Tel: 93-317 5826
Open: Mon–Thu & Sat L, Fri L & D. €
[**60** p286, A1]
A bustling local bar, serving hearty winter stews and a good-value set menu, conveniently en route to the MACBA and CCCB. Only serves tapas in the evenings, except on Fridays.

Fonda Espanya
Sant Pau, 9–11
Tel: 93-550 0010
www.hotelespanya.com/es/fonda-espana/
Open: Mon–Sat L & D, Sun L. €€€ [**61** p284, A2]
Radical refurbishment in this legendary hotel has included installing Basque star chef Martín Berasategui in the kitchen. Top-notch cooking in a dining room decorated by *modernista* architect Domènech i Montaner.

Romesco
Sant Pau, 28
Tel: 93-318 9381
Open: Mon–Sat L & D. € [**62** p286, A2]
The fluorescent lighting and Formica-topped tables deter no one. Old favourite Romesco is famous for its *frijoles* (black beans, rice, minced meat, fried egg and fried banana, all on one plate) to fill the hungriest poor student, as well as simple grilled fish.

Vegetarian

Biocenter
Pintor Fortuny, 25
Tel: 93-301 4583
http://restaurantebiocenter.es
Open: Mon–Sat L & D, Sun L. € [**63** p286, A1]
This was one of the first vegetarian restaurants in the city. You can

choose between an enormous, nutritious *menú del día* (four courses) or a substantial *plato combinado* (one dish with accompaniment). Either way you will enjoy a hearty meal in soothing surroundings. Good-value set menu in the evening.

Juicy Jones
Hospital, 74
Tel: 93-443 9082
Open: Daily L & D. € [**64** p284, E2]
Latest branch of this vegan restaurant selling organic juices all day, as well as tasty Hindu and European dishes. Excellent value for money.

Organic
Junta de Comerç, 11
Tel: 93-301 0902
Open: Daily L & D. € [**65** p286, A2]
Wholesome organic food in an impressive former industrial space. The set menu offers a self-service salad bar, soup and bread for starters, then a choice from three or four main dishes (if you can manage more). Massages are also available.

Bars and Cafés

Almirall
Joaquín Costa, 33
[**23** p286, A1]
This old timer, dating from 1860, stands out in the middle of this buzzy street where kebab houses and Asian grocers alternate with trendy cocktail bars. Enjoy beer or wine at small tables surrounded by exquisite *modernista* decor.

Barceló Raval
Rambla del Raval, 17
Tel: 93-320 1490
www.barcelo.com
[**24** p286, A2]
The rooftop terrace of this cutting-edge hotel that towers over some of the darker streets of the area is a great place for Sunday brunch or sunset cocktails with a panoramic view.

Betty Ford's
Joaquín Costa, 56
[**25** p286, A1]
One of the trendy bars that's attracted the night crowd to this

Raval street with its eclectic mix of furniture and good atmosphere. Also serves burgers.

El Colectivo
Pintor Fortuny, 22
Tel: 93-318 6380
[**26** p286, A1]
With its pale wood and clean lines, this peaceful coffee bar has a serene atmosphere, perfect at breakfast time when there is a range of cereals, croissants and pastries to accompany the excellent coffee.

El Jardi
Hospital, 56
Tel: 93-329 1550
www.eljardibarcelona.es
[**27** p286, A2]
Charming terrace café away from the din in the medieval courtyard and gardens of the Antic Hospital de Santa Creu. A peaceful spot for coffee, a light lunch (delicious salads) or early evening cocktail.

La Paciencia
Rambla del Raval, 53
Tel: 93-441 5387
[**28** p286, A2]
A real local bar with a trendy edge, attracting both locals and film buffs from the nearby Filmoteca. You may have to queue to catch a table on its terrace on this crossroads, where there's plenty of world to watch going by.

A few drinks at Betty Ford's.

THE WATERFRONT

Rejuvenated for the Barcelona Olympics in 1992, the waterfront area has added an exciting new dimension to the city. Bold development is continuing, with the creation of Diagonal Mar and the Fòrum to the north and new projects at the southern end.

t is ironic that Barcelona, a city on the shores of the Mediterranean with a large industrial port and strong maritime tradition, gained a 'waterfront' only in the last decade of the 20th century. As the popular saying went, Barcelona lived with its back to the sea.

Being bordered on one side by the Mediterranean, the city's residential and commercial areas expanded inland, first with the construction of the 19th-century Eixample and then by moving further up the hill towards Collserola during the 20th century. Investment tended to be linked with this movement, and as a result the Old Town and Barceloneta were neglected.

Regeneration

The rediscovery of the waterfront began in the 1980s as part of the Socialist city council's vision, but the 1992 Olympics were the vital catalyst. The development, perhaps the most radical transformation of any city in Europe, represented an investment of 400 billion pesetas (2.3 billion euros). Some 5km (3 miles) of beaches were renovated or newly created, landscaped and equipped with facilities. The Vila Olímpica was built, creating what is now a new residential

district and its port. The old city wharves, once hidden under tumbledown sheds, emerged, blinking, into the sun. Barceloneta was transformed. Since 1992 the momentum has been sustained with projects like Maremàgnum and, more recently, Diagonal Mar and the Fòrum area (see page 163), and, for better or worse, there are more to come. The port area beyond the W hotel is due for major development.

For energetic walkers or cyclists, this route could be one long itinerary

Port Vell.

right along the front. However, to be able to enjoy the walk and fully appreciate the extensive renovations, to take in the many colourful details and have time to pause in the right places (such as the fish restaurants in Barceloneta), the route should be split into two (or more) days. What's on offer on Barcelona's waterfront is something quite extraordinary for a large cosmopolitan European city.

Museu Marítim ❶

Address: Av de les Drassanes, s/n; www.mmb.cat
Tel: 93-342 9920
Opening Hrs: daily 10am–8pm
Entrance fee: charge
Transport: Drassanes

A model of Magellan's Santa María de la Victoria, the first ship to circumnavigate the world (1519–1522), is on display at the Maritime Museum.

A good place to begin is the Maritime Museum, which brings to life Catalonia's seafaring past. Housed in the massive **Drassanes Reials** (Royal Shipyards), at the foot of La Rambla just before it meets the port, the building alone makes

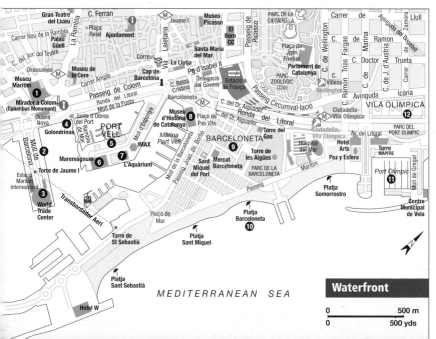

Waterfront

a visit worthwhile – the magnificent Gothic-style shipyards, parts of which date from the 13th century, are a fine and rare example of civic architecture from that period. The art critic Robert Hughes described this stunning building as 'perhaps the most stirring ancient industrial space of any kind that has survived from the Middle Ages: a masterpiece of civil engineering'.

After major renovation work to the building, during which interesting archaeological ruins were found, a new-format exhibition is being prepared. Until it opens in 2014, temporary exhibitions and the schooner on the quayside, *Santa Eulàlia* (see page 155), can be visited.

A wooden submarine designed by Catalan Narcís Monturiol.

Exhibits

The new exhibition space will include the former collection of real fishing boats from the Catalan coast, representing the importance of both fishing and boatbuilding in the country's history, and prized models of vessels from all ages. Also on display will be a modern Olympic winner, a model-making workshop, maps, instruments and other sea-related artefacts. The highlight will still be the full-scale replica of the 16th-century galley in which Don Juan of Austria led the Christian fleet to defeat the Turks in the battle of Lepanto in 1571. Like so many vessels over the centuries, it was built here in one of the slipways then on the water's edge.

THE PORT OF BARCELONA

Today you have to cross a wide road, full of traffic, leading to the Ronda

View over Monument a Colom and Junta d'Obres del Port.

Passeig Marítim is hugely popular with afternoon strollers, cyclists and rollerbladers.

For a bird's-eye view of Port Vell and the length of the waterfront, take the cable car, which runs between Montjuïc and the Torre de Sant Sebastià, or just go as far as the Torre de Jaume I.

Litoral, before reaching the water. Leaving the **Mirador a Colom** (see page 105) to your left, go down the side of the rather overbearing former **Duana Nova** (New Customs House), built between 1895 and 1902 from a project drawn up by Enric Sagnier and Pere García. Crowned by a massive winged sphinx and other mythical flying beasts (Barcelona's port buildings seem to specialise in fine rooftop silhouettes), the Duana Nova is designed in the form of the letter 'H', the most practical design for processing cargoes.

To the left of the Columbus statue as you look out to sea is the **Junta d'Obres del Port** (Port Authority Building), designed by the engineer Julio Valdés and built in 1907. Its original use was as the reception for passengers arriving in the city from the sea. The interior is somewhat eclectic in style, while the exterior of the building is impressively ornate.

To the right, the **Moll de Barcelona ❷** and, beyond it, the **Moll de Sant Bertran** are the centre for ferry services to the Balearic Islands. This quay also has the 119-metre (390ft)-high **Torre de Jaume I** link for the cross-harbour cable car, which comes from Montjuïc and goes to the tower on the other side of the harbour, the **Torre de Sant Sebastià** (an alternative route to the beach). The cable car has hardly changed since its introduction in 1931 – unlike the spectacular views it affords of the city and port, which are constantly changing.

World Trade Center ❸

At the end of the quay stands the **World Trade Center**, designed by the architect I.M. Pei (who also designed the Louvre glass pyramid in Paris); it makes a loud statement in the middle of the port, looking remarkably like the luxury cruisers moored alongside it. Unlike most waterfront developments, this building is not used for social or leisure activities: it is a commercial centre with offices, a smart restaurant and a very grand hotel.

Las Golondrinas ❹

Address: Moll de Drassanes; www.las golondrinas.com
Tel: 93-442 3106
Opening Hrs: summer daily 11.30am–8.30pm, winter hours vary
Entrance fee: charge
Transport: Drassanes/Barceloneta

A popular way of seeing the harbour is to take a ride on one of the Golondrinas, or ferries, which are moored on the Moll de Drassanes.

'The Lobster' sculpture by Mariscal.

Apart from a pause during the civil war, they have been plying these waters since the 1888 Exhibition. Half-hour trips in the older pleasure boats take you out to the new entrance to the port and back past the fishing boats.

More modern catamarans head out of the harbour and along the coast to the Olympic port and the Fòrum, where you can disembark to explore, then catch a later return boat.

PORT VELL ❺

Just beyond the Golondrinas is Port Vell, the old port, now a yacht harbour. A sleek, sinuous walkway and footbridge, the **Rambla de Mar**, leads across the water to Maremàgnum, on the **Moll d'Espanya**, Port Vell's main quay.

Moored alongside the palm-lined **Moll de la Fusta** ('Wood Quay', where wood was stored in the past) is the *Santa Eulàlia* (Tue–Fri, Sun 10am–5.30pm, Sat 2pm–5.30pm,

CAPITAL OF THE MED

The port of Barcelona plays an important commercial role, covering a huge area winding south towards the airport. Recent expansion involved diverting the River Llobregat and current construction work will double its size. The authorities' much vaunted aim is to establish it as 'Europe's southern port', tying in with the city's aspiration to be regarded as the 'capital of the Mediterranean'. While massive container ships line the docks beneath the Castell de Montjuïc, enormous white cruise ships moored against the Moll Adossat are now part of the landscape. As the largest cruiser terminal in Europe, it regularly disgorges hundreds of passengers into La Rambla for sightseeing.

KIDS

There's plenty to keep children distracted around the port. The wavy design of the Rambla de Mar footbridge appeals, especially when it opens up to let yachts through. Once across the bridge, there's the Aquarium, an IMAX cinema and a replica of the world's first combustion-powered submarine.

Diners are reflected in the Maremàgnum mall.

later in summer; charge, or free with ticket to Museu Marítim). Restored to its original glory, this schooner dates from the beginning of the 20th century, when it took cargo to the Americas. Its moment of glory is on 5th January, when it brings in the three Wise Kings to parade around the city (see page 260).

Maremàgnum ❻

Address: Moll d'Espanya;
www.maremagnum.es
Tel: 93-225 8100
Opening Hrs: daily, shops 10am–10pm, restaurants until 1am
Transport: Drassanes/Barceloneta

Crowds head over the Rambla de Mar footbridge to Maremàgnum, the Aquàrium and the IMAX cinema. The complex has a wide range of shops and places to eat and a cinema with eight screens. The bars and restaurants are dominated by fast-food outlets but there are some exceptions, like **L'Elx al Moll**, with an irresistible terrace overlooking the fishing boats (see page 165). Despite the commercial context, enjoying some tapas while watching

Santa Eulalia is moored in Port Vell.

the yachts or looking across the harbour to Barcelona's Gothic towers and 19th-century chimneys takes some beating.

Aquàrium ❼

Address: Moll d'Espanya;
www.aquariumbcn.com
Tel: 93-221 7474
Opening Hrs: daily 9.30am–9pm, until 11pm in July and Aug
Entrance fee: charge
Transport: Drassanes/Barceloneta

Since opening in 1995, the Aquàrium, the most important for Mediterranean species in the world, has become one of the most successful crowd-pullers in Barcelona, second only to the Sagrada Família. With 11,000 animals and 450 different species, the colourful marine communities of the Mediterranean and the tropical seas are shown off in all their glory. A glass tunnel leads visitors through the sharks and rays, while experienced divers can book to swim among them.

Around Passeig d'Isabel II

Pass the historic submarine, a reproduction of the *Ictineo II*, invented by Catalan Narcís Monturiol, and follow the path that leads up to the **Mirador del Port Vell** (a slightly raised lookout point). On Moll de la Fusta is American pop artist Roy Lichtenstein's **El Cap de Barcelona** (Barcelona Head), a striking sculpture made in 1992 to commemorate the Olympics; the mosaic-work pays homage to Gaudí's *trencadís* technique. On the corner of Via Laietana is the headquarters of **Correus** (the post office), a very grand building completed in 1927. The enormous vestibule was decorated by the prestigious *noucentiste* artists (from the 1900s) Canyellas, Obiols, Galí and Labarta. It is easier to buy stamps in an *estanc* (the tobacconists' shops found in every district) but not nearly as interesting. It is not hard

Crowds on Rambla de Mar.

to see why the facade has been used by film-makers as a stand-in for American law courts.

With your back to Correus, walk towards the sea. On the left is **Reina Cristina**, a street full of cheap-and-cheerful electro-domestic shops. At No. 7 is Can Paixano, a popular cava bar selling sparkling wine and hefty sandwiches at rock-bottom prices, frequented by locals and tourists alike. Nearby is the first Galician seafood restaurant to open in Barcelona, **Carballeira** (see page 165). If you are passing when the *arròs a la banda* (a delicious rice dish) is coming out of the kitchen, cancel all other plans: stand at the bar and request a portion with *allioli* (garlic mayonnaise) and a glass of Galician *vino turbio*.

Back on the quayside, the promenade sweeps on round to the **Moll de la Barceloneta**. These once busy working quays now shelter the **Marina Port Vell**, where some of the most exclusive motor and sailing

yachts in the Mediterranean winter or pass through on their way to the Balearics or the Caribbean. The marina is currently being upgraded to accommodate super yachts.

Museu d'Història de Catalunya ⑧

Address: Plaça de Pau Vila 3; www.mhcat.cat

Up close and personal with a shark at the Aquàrium.

Strolling in Barceloneta.

Tel: 93-225 4700
Opening hrs: Tue–Sat 10am–7pm, Wed until 8pm, Sun 10am–2.30pm
Entrance fee: charge
Transport: Barceloneta

This fascinating museum is housed in the Palau de Mar, a former warehouse complex (the Magatzem General de Comerç, 1881, the last one in the area), beautifully renovated in 1992. True to its name, the museum elucidates Catalan history, but also looks at it from a wider historical perspective, with various bits of technical wizardry and plenty of interactive spaces – try walking in a suit of armour, or building a Roman arch – which kids of all ages love.

BARCELONETA ⑨

Beyond the museum is Barceloneta. Once home to the city's fishing community, it retains a strong sense of neighbourhood, especially in its interior. The main focus along the quayside is leisure and eating out.

EAT

The Museu d' Història de Catalunya is a good place for lunch or dinner. The restaurant on the top floor, Restaurant 1881, offers Mediterranean dishes and fine views over the harbour (tel: 902-520 522).

Sunday lunch at one of the restaurants in front of the Palau de Mar has become a regular pastime for those who can afford it. This is an

WOODY'S BARCELONA

When Woody Allen came to town in 2007, supposedly in love with its Mediterranean charms, the feeling was mutual. Red carpets were rolled out and local politicians rushed to shake his hand and, controversially, open their coffers. It became commonplace to run into the inimitable director, in his trademark cap, putting his stars through their paces on the Waterfront and other emblematic locations around the city, like La Rambla or Park Güell. Starring Javier Bardem, Penélope Cruz, Scarlett Johansson and Rebecca Hall, *Vicky Cristina Barcelona* garnered one Oscar, for best supporting actress (Penélope Cruz), and the postcard scenes of Barcelona spread the city's fame further than ever around the globe.

attractive place to sit and watch the world go by, and is sheltered even in winter. The charms of outdoor eating often outweigh the gastronomic shortcomings, so as long as you don't expect haute cuisine you will be spoilt for choice along the whole length of **Passeig Joan de Borbó**. Even for Barcelona residents it is a thrill to eat on a pavement in the December sun.

Fishermen's Wharf

At the end of the promenade is an expensive but excellent fish restaurant called Barceloneta (see page 164); it features in Woody Allen's film *Vicky Cristina Barcelona* (see box, page 158). Just beyond are glimpses of the hard-working fishing boats moored up against the **Moll dels Pescadors** (Fishermen's Wharf). The distinctive clock tower, **Torre del Rellotge** (closed to the public), started life as a lighthouse. Close by is the fish market (*mercat de peix*, first opened in 1924), where the boats come in twice a day (from 6.30am and 4.30pm) to supply the fishmongers.

Towering above the scene is the **Torre de Sant Sebastià**, whose 78-metre (257ft) height marks the end, or the beginning, of the route of the cable car, which completes its 1,300-metre (4,200ft) journey on Montjuïc.

At the foot of the tower, **Club Natació Atlètic Barceloneta** (also known as Banys Sant Sebastià) has an excellent heated outdoor pool (tel: 93-221 0010; Mon–Sat 6.30am–10.30pm, Sun 8am–7.30pm, winter Sun 8am–4.30pm). It also has a large

Drinking in the sunshine.

Hotel W on Barceloneta beach.

indoor pool and small spa area and overlooks the beach of Sant Sebastià.

The landscape has changed here recently as the promenade has been developed to reach the domineering new landmark of the Hotel W Barcelona, designed by local architect Ricardo Bofill. If your budget does not run to the €10,000 Extreme Wow suite, you may at least be able to have a *copa* in the Eclipse bar on its 26th floor, or a drink at its beach bar. The sea wall beyond the hotel is free, giving a great new perspective on both port and city. Some feel, though, that the intelligent town planning of the 1980s is now being compromised.

Origins of Barceloneta

Town planning in the 18th century was also of questionable merit. The streets behind the quayside are in a grid formation, the pattern of which was born of a military decision. It was to Barceloneta that the inhabitants of La Ribera were relocated when their homes were demolished to make way for the building of the fortress La Ciutadella, after the siege and conquest of Barcelona by

Felipe V. The streets were built in a series of narrow, rectangular blocks all facing in the same direction (towards La Ciutadella), facilitating easy military control (volleys from the citadel could be directed down the streets).

This residential area is now an appealing mix of traditional and modern; washing hangs along the narrow balconies, while the bars and restaurants have become popular nightspots, and apartments are being restored and let to tourists.

Mercat Barceloneta

In the square in the middle of Barceloneta is the **Mercat Barceloneta** (Plaça Font; tel: 93-221 6471), built in *modernista* style in 1884 but recently renovated and given the designer treatment. Inside, along with the fish, meat, fruit and vegetable stalls, are various bars with terraces on the square.

Platja Barceloneta ❿

By cutting through the streets of Barceloneta to the **Passeig Marítim**, or wandering along from Platja

'Homenatage a la Natació' by Alfredo Lanz, on Sant Sebastiá beach.

Sant Sebastià (*platja* means beach), you arrive at a series of beaches with wooden walkways, palms and designer showers that run along the post-Olympic seafront. They are all easily accessible by public transport, and both the sand and the water's surface are cleaned daily, with weekly sanitary checks on top of that.

It's clear that the people of Barcelona, as well as tourists, derive enormous pleasure from these wide-open beaches. Every morning, locals come down in their towelling dressing gowns to swim in all weathers, play cards, gossip and get fit. In summer the beaches get very crowded and noisy by midday, but then comes the lunchtime exodus. If you can't make it in the early morning, wait until the early evening sun brings a new tranquillity – an eight o'clock swim here in mid-summer is sheer bliss.

The beaches are now an essential part of Barcelona's famed nightlife. New *xiringuitos* or beach restaurants serve drinks and snacks by day, but at sunset the DJs start spinning, young people come out to play and a cool scene emerges.

Part of Barceloneta beach has been renamed Somorrostro in homage to the shanty town and its inhabitants who were there until the mid-1960s. The famous and much-loved gypsy flamenco dancer Carmen Amaya was born there.

Parc de la Barceloneta and onwards

On the eastern edge of Barceloneta is the Parc de la Barceloneta, a fine setting for the *modernista* water tower, **Torre de les Aigües**, by Josep Domènech i Estapà (1905), virtually the only original industrial building left in this area.

It stands in dramatic contrast to the avant-garde Gas building, **Torre del Gas**, on one side of the park and the gleaming Hospital del Mar on the other. The formerly gloomy hospital underwent a metamorphosis for the Olympics and is now more reminiscent of an international airport than a major public hospital.

Along the promenade at beach level are several hip bars and one of the best restaurants on the beach, Agua (see page 164).

Buskers on Barceloneta beach.

A busy day at the beach.

Volleyball on Platja Nova Icària.

PORT OLÍMPIC ⑪

You can't miss the Port Olímpic: two skyscrapers tower above a huge woven copper fish sculpture (*Pez y Esfera*, meaning 'fish and sphere') by Frank Gehry, who is best known as the architect of the Guggenheim Museum in Bilbao.

The first skyscraper is the luxurious **Hotel Arts** (see page 254), designed by Bruce Graham (architect of Chicago's Sears Tower and the Hancock Centre). You can wander beneath Frank Gehry's awesome fish sculpture and imagine the heady view from the exclusive suites high up in the Arts, favoured by rock stars, actors and jet-setters. At ground level is the **Barcelona Casino**. The other building is the MAPFRE tower, housing offices.

Here, bars and restaurants proliferate, with entrances on the promenade overlooking the strikingly modern marina. If you don't mind paying extra for the location, this is a colourful place to stop and eat, watching the yachts and dinghies coming and going. If you want a quiet drink, though, think again. At night the clubs and cocktail bars seem to attract the whole of Barcelona.

At the end of the **Moll de Gregal**, jutting out to sea, is the Centre Municipal de Vela (municipal sailing school), offering courses for the public and short trips along the seafront with a skipper (book on www. barcelonaturisme.com).

Vila Olímpica ⑫

It is worth taking time to go inland a block or two, to see the feats of architecture that comprise the Olympic Village. On the way you'll come to the **Parc del Port Olímpic**, behind the towers. In the **Plaça dels Campions** (Champions' Square) are listed the names of the 257 gold medallists of the 1992 Olympics, as well as the handprints of Pele and cyclist Eddie Merx, along with numerous other sporting heroes. The Vila Olímpica was built according to a master plan developed by architects Mackay, Martorell, Bohigas and Puigdomènech, on land formerly occupied by 19th-century ramshackle warehouses and tumble-down factories.

The flats accommodated athletes in 1992 and since then have been gradually sold. The development was a major undertaking, and a vital part of Barcelona's wider plan of achieving long-overdue improvements to the city's infrastructure. It involved major changes, like moving the railway lines into Estació de França underground.

The 200 buildings cover 74 hectares (183 acres), and are in 200 different designs. The area did not become a new neighbourhood of Barcelona overnight, but it is now looking more established, has become a desirable place to live, and is beginning to merge with the remaining buildings of Poble Nou that surround its outer limits. In the midst of a clinical shopping mall is one of the few magnetic points that attract people in the evenings: the 15-screen cinema complex, Icària Yelmo, which specialises in *v.o.* (original-language) films.

THE BEACHES

Return to the front to walk along the series of beaches after the Port Olímpic. Tons of sand were imported to create **Platja Nova Icària** (named after the original industrial neighbourhood), **Bogatell**, **Mar Bella, Nova Mar Bella** and, most recently, **Llevant**, reclaiming a seafront that

had been cut off by railway lines, yards and warehouses. The strategic Ronda Litoral (ring road) runs all along here but at a lower level, and is cleverly hidden beneath parks, playgrounds and bridges that connect with the residential areas behind. The promenade is popular with joggers, skaters, cyclists and walkers.

The waterfront ends with the **Fòrum** area (see page 168). A huge solar panel marks the spot. It also has a swimming area without sand, an enclosed area landscaped into the sea.

This part of the city, along with the former industrial area of Poble Nou (inland from Bogatell and Mar Bella beaches), has been the scene of frenetic construction in recent years. Although these developments were initially subject to criticism, the new residential area Diagonal Mar is slowly becoming established, alongside a new hi-tech business district (see page 166).

From here one could wander inland to get a taste of the latest developments, walk back along the everexhilarating seaside or catch a tram, metro or bus back into the centre.

This is 'Marc', by Robert Llimós (1997), who welcomes you to the Parc del Port Olímpic.

A climbing frame on Platja Nova Icària.

RESTAURANTS, BARS AND CAFÉS

Restaurants

The 4km (2.5 miles) of waterfront
makes an endlessly tempting
place to walk, eat and drink, especially in the winter when there is
nothing like the luxury of eating a
paella outdoors. Sea views are a
treat that sometimes requires a
sacrifice, either financially or in
food quality, but is often worth it.
However, don't miss some of the
best options hidden in the backstreets of Barceloneta.

Catalan

Agua
Passeig Marítim, 30
Tel: 93-225 1272
www.grupotragaluz.com
Open: Daily L & D. €€€ [⑥⑤ p286, D4]
This stylish, relaxed restaurant,
serving modern Mediterranean
food, is virtually in the sand near
the Vila Olímpica. The combination
is bliss, especially at lunchtime, so
book days in advance for the terrace, especially at weekends.

Arola
Marina, 19-21
Tel: 93-483 8090
Open: Wed–Sun L & D. €€€€ [⑥⑦ p286,
D3]
In the luxurious surroundings of
the Hotel Arts, overlooking Gehry's
sculpted fish and the Olympic Port,
is one of top Catalan chef Sergi
Arola's restaurants. His delicacies
are served as tapas. In the warmer
months you can eat out on the terrace.

Can Majó
Almirall Aixada, 23
Tel: 93-221 5455

www.canmajo.es
Open: Tue–Sat L & D, Sun L. €€€
[⑥⑧ p286, C4]
This is one of the best and longest
established of the Barceloneta seafood restaurants, where it's worth
paying a bit extra to be sure of a
good paella. Pretty decor indoors,
but it also has a terrace on the
pavement within sight of the sea.

Puda Can Manel
Passeig Joan de Borbó, 60–61
Tel: 93-221 5013
www.pudacanmanel.com
Open: L & D Tues- Sun. €€ [⑥⑨ p286, B4]
A good middle-range fish restaurant on this parade bursting with
places that try to tempt you in.
Here they don't have to bother. Get
there early to find a place on the
pretty terrace overlooking Port Vell.

El Suquet de l'Almirall
Passeig Joan de Borbó, 65
Tel: 93-221 6233
www.suquetdelalmirall.com
Open: Tue–Sun L & D. €€€ [⑦⓪ p286, B4]
This comfortable, tastefully decorated restaurant with a small terrace overlooking Port Vell is in a
different league to its numerous
neighbours. Chef Joan Marqués
has given new interpretations to
traditional Mediterranean favourites such as rice dishes and *suquet*
(fish stew).

Xiringuito Escribà
Avinguda del Litoral, 42
Tel: 93-221 0729
Open: Summer daily L & D, winter Tue–Sun
L. €€ [⑦① p286, E3]
One of the more elegant *xiringuitos*
(beach bars) just above Nova Icària
beach, known for its paellas. Fab
desserts, as you'd expect from this
famous pastry maker.

International

Bestial
Ramón Trias i Fargas, 2–4
Tel: 93-224 0407
www.grupotragaluz.com
Open: Daily L & D. €€ [⑦② p286, D4]
Sea views, minimalist interior, mul-

tilevel outdoor terrace, beautiful
clientele – this is more of a place
to be seen in than to eat in, though
their unusual risottos and Italian-
inspired pasta dishes are good.
Reasonably priced set menu
Mon–Fri.

Sal Café
Passeig Marítim
Tel: 93-224 0707
http://salcafe.com
Open: Summer daily L & D, winter Sat–Sun
L & D, depending on weather. €
[⑦③ p286, C4]
Down on the Barceloneta beach
near the climbing frame is this
slick restaurant-cum-bar, the
trendiest *xiringuito* around, serving
exotic flavours. Handy for kids,
with special menus and plenty of
sand to play in.

Spanish

Barceloneta
L'Escar, 22
Tel: 93-221 2111
www.restaurantbarceloneta.com
Open: Daily L & D. €€€ [⑦④ p286, B4]
Barceloneta's outdoor terrace in a
privileged position, jutting out
above the fishing boats and super
yachts of the Port Vell marina,
makes this one of the most
delightful places to enjoy high-
quality seafood dishes.

La Bombeta
Maquinista, 3
Tel: 93-319 9445
Open: Thu–Tue L & D. € [⑦⑤ p286, C3]
Down a side street in Barceloneta
is one of the most genuine tapas
bars you could hope to find, devoid
of designer details, busy, crowded
and fun, serving well-prepared traditional tapas, like their namesake
bomba, (deep-fried stuffed potato,
basically).

Can Solé
Sant Carles, 4
Tel: 93-221 5012
www.restaurantcansole.com
Open: Tue–Sat L & D, Sun L. €€€ [⑦⑥
p286, C4]

In the heart of Barceloneta, literally and metaphorically, and a favourite with locals and Barcelona celebrities, Can Solé has been cooking great seafood and fish since 1903.

Carballeira
Reina Cristina, 3
Tel: 93-310 1006
http://carballeira.com
Open: Tue–Sat L & D, Sun L. €€€€
[77] p286, B3]
Excellent Galician fish and seafood dishes in an old-style restaurant. At lunchtime try a simple *tapa* of *arròs a la banda* (delicious rice cooked in fish stock) at the bar. Accompany it with a glass of Ribeira (Galician white wine), in particular, the cloudy variety, *turbio*.

L'Elx al Moll
Moll d'Espanya, 5, Maremàgnum
Tel: 93-225 8117
http://elxrestaurant.es
Open: Daily L & D. €€ [78] p286, B4]
As a close relative to the Elx in the Paral.lel, known for its rice dishes since 1959, you can be sure of a good rice dish here. Try the *pica-pica* (assorted starters), followed by the rice of your choice. A cut above most of the other eating options in this commercial centre, with a quayside terrace and great views of the port.

Torre d'Alta Mar
Passeig Joan de Borbó, 88
Tel: 93-221 0007
www.torredealtamar.com
Open: Tue–Sat L & D, Sun–Mon D. €€€€
[79] p286, B4]
Perched 75 metres (250ft) above the port in Torre Sant Sebastià, this smart restaurant is in competition with L'Orangerie for the title of 'best dining room with a view'. The gourmet experience does not quite measure up to such heights, but the panorama is spectacular.

Bars and Cafés

Can Paixano
Reina Cristina, 7
Tel: 93-310 0839
www.canpaixano.com
[29] p286, B3]
Cheap cava and ultra-tasty sandwiches are the winning formula that has made this cavernous bar an essential stop, particularly for *guiri* (foreign) students and low-budget travellers.

Fastnet Bar
Passeig Joan de Borbó, 22
Tel: 93-295 3005
http://thefastnet.com
[30] p286, C4]
This Irish bar by the sea serves good pub food (Irish stew, cottage pie) and fills with yachtsmen and sports enthusiasts when any big event is shown on its large screen.

Filferro
Sant Carles, 29
Tel: 93-221 9836
[31] p286, C4]
This attractive bar with a terrace is proof that it's worth exploring the backstreets of Barceloneta rather than being commandeered by waiters into seafront or harbour-front joints. A low-key spot to relax over a quiet beer or coffee away from the beach bustle

Vaso de Oro
Balbao, 6
Tel: 93-319 3098
[32] p286, C3]
This long narrow *cervecería* is a classic, with white-jacketed waiters who are old pros. The golden beer is served in long, narrow glasses, which somehow makes it all the more thirst-quenching. Be pushy like the locals to get to the bar lined with traditional tapas.

Xiringuitos
Xiringuitos (*chiringuitos* in Spanish, beach bars in English) are a phenomenon that has taken hold in recent years and are dotted all along the waterfront. Every beach has at least one serving breakfast and coffee in the morning, lunchtime snacks, winding up with mojitos by night when the DJs start spinning and the day cools down enough to dance in the sand.

A shady spot to cool off on Platja Nova Icària.

21ST CENTURY BARCELONA

Never content to sit on its laurels, Barcelona launched itself into the new millennium with an ambitious goal of creating a new knowledge-based business district in an industrial wasteland. Its evolution makes fascinating viewing.

The area which stretches from Plaça de les Glòries, the arterial roundabout at the extreme right of the Eixample, down to the Fòrum and Diagonal Mar and between Avinguda Diagonal and the waterfront is a curious landscape of 19th-century industrial land morphing into a high-tech business district with pockets of residential zones and green spaces. This is the **22@ Innovation district**, which has merged with the original community of **Poble Nou** and the new residential district **Diagonal Mar** to give a new dimension to the city and is an area worth exploring for locals and visitors alike. This is an ever-changing panorama as wasteland transforms into star architect-designed skyscrapers, and red-brick former factories find new life as cultural centres or university faculties.

The story goes that after the highly successful Olympic Games and consequent urban regeneration programme the city authorities invented another challenge, a new goal to generate work, investment and vital infrastructure. The idea of creating a new knowledge-based industrial district was agreed in 2001. Since then, despite recession and financial crises, huge strides have been made, although there are still forests of cranes, placards promising new energy-efficient buildings and a supposed completion date of 2020. Many key companies in ICT, medical technology, energy and media have bought into it and are established in state-of-the-art skyscrapers, graduates stream into their brand new faculties and locals have been re-housed in sustainable buildings.

DHUB to Ca l'Aranyó

A good starting point is **Glòries** ❶ metro. As you emerge from the

Torre Agbar.

station, three attention-grabbing constructions herald what's to come. The new location for **Els Encants** flea market is marked by a high undulating roof that seems to float in mid-air and reflects the commercial activity below. Then comes the imposing **DHUB** 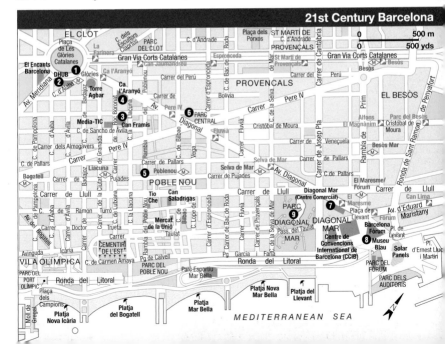 (Design Hub building; Plaça de les Glòries, 37–38; tel: 93-256 6713; www.museudeldisseny.bcn.cat), which houses the **Museu del Disseny de Barcelona** (Design Museum), comprising the collections from the former museums of textiles, ceramics, decorative arts, industrial design and graphics, as well as various design bodies and organisations. Due to open in 2014, it straddles a monumental concrete landscape with an interactive light installation (9pm–1am) and a lake, which contributes to the building's sustainability. Jean Nouvel's **Torre Agbar**, landmark on the city skyline, rises high above the scene. Visit at night to see the kaleidoscopic colours of the

two buildings. Stretching down to the sea is the redeveloped Avinguda Diagonal, with different lanes for different means of transport, including some of the new 30km (18.5 miles) of bicycle lanes.

Turn right off Diagonal down Roc de Boronat, where local architect Enric Ruiz Geli's **Media-TIC** building, clad in energy-saving material, houses part of the distance-learning UOC (Open University). Opposite is **Can Framis** ❸ (Roc Boronat, 116–126; tel: 93-320 8736; Tue–Sat 11am–6pm, Sun 11am–2pm, closed Aug; charge), an award-winning conversion from ruined wool factory to contemporary art museum, housing the Fundació Vilacasas' private collection. The juxtaposition of the old factory chimney against the surrounding steel, concrete and glass is the leitmotif in this area, repeated in the magnificent **Ca l'Aranyó** ❹ in Llacuna, a former textile

EAT

The striking contrasts in this area are also echoed in its restaurants, from lofty gourmet cuisine with a view at the Torres twins' Dos Cielos restaurant, high in the ME hotel, or the more down-to-earth endearing bars of the Rambla del Poblenou.

Skateboarders in Parc Diagonal Mar.

The old community

Follow any of the streets on the left into the **Rambla del Poblenou ❺**, and turn right towards the sea. Still the heart of the old community which grew up in the area's industrial heyday, this is like a thread of real life in the midst of the high-tech environment. Here in the shade of the plane trees normal *barrio* life goes on: babies in prams, kids playing football, old ladies gossiping over their shopping trolleys as they return from the market and retired gents sipping their pre-lunch *vermuts*. There are numerous bars and restaurants running its length, with terraces on the *rambla*, but an essential stop is **Tio Che** at No. 44, for a cool *orxata* or ice cream, a favourite with local families on Sundays. Meander through the side streets that cross the *rambla* and you'll be rewarded with small squares and narrow streets with one-storey *modernista* houses and shops that seem timeless.

You can either continue down to the beach at the end of the *rambla*, or head back up towards Avinguda Diagonal along a parallel street like Bilbao, where the local library is located in another former textile factory, the imposing **Can Saladrigas**. Cross over Diagonal to Jean Nouvel's **Parc Central ❻**, a designer green space surrounded by modern blocks and some still-empty cement skeletons.

The Fòrum

Catch a tram down Diagonal, running between original housing for migrant workers from other parts of Spain in the 1950s and '60s on one side and towering new builds like the 29-storey, luxurious ME hotel on the other. Travel as far as **Diagonal Mar ❼**, where there is a large shopping centre, several hotels and a conference centre, the CCIB. Jutting into the sea is the **Fòrum**

factory now housing the faculty of Communication of the University of Pompeu Fabra. Buildings like this explain why the 19th-century **Poble Nou** (New Town) was nicknamed the Catalan Manchester, not just because of the textile industry that dominated but because of the style of industrial architecture, a fusion of Manchester-style iron structures with Catalan vaulting.

SHOPPING

Traditional neighbourhood shops in the Poble Nou area may change with the area's evolution, but apart from the commercial centre, shopping is low key here.

Malls

Diagonal Mar
Avinguda Diagonal, 3
www.diagonalmarcentre.es
Enormous, well-equipped shopping mall a few metres from the sea with chain stores ranging from Alcampo hypermarket to Zara. Open

until 10pm, but closed on Sundays.

Markets

Els Encants
Avinguda Meridiana 69/Plaça de les Glòries
www.encantsbcn.com
The main flea market moved to this 21st-century designer location in 2013 from its dishevelled premises on the other side of Plaça de les Glòries. Sift through the eclectic mix of goods to find a bargain. Mon, Wed, Fri, Sat 9am–8pm.

Parc Diagonal Mar is divided into seven areas linked by one theme: water.

proposed new Diagonal-Besòs (CIDB) university campus building, centred on Zaha Hadid's Spiralling Tower, starts to take shape.

This is all work in progress and fascinating to watch, albeit a regular source of controversy and slowed down by the current economic climate. Meanwhile another project regarded as a white elephant a few years ago, the residential area and its **Parc Diagonal Mar ❾** designed by the late Enric Miralles, is beginning to take root and look more established. This inspired park, with creative games for kids and landscaped lakes, is a pleasant oasis amid the high rises. Return to the centre on the 41 bus to complete the tour as it follows the newest part of the waterfront and then passes through the **Vila Olímpica**, which was itself an earlier brainchild of the enterprising municipal authorities.

Exhibits at the natural science museum.

area, legacy of a world symposium in 2004 and now used for large-scale events like music festivals and the April Fair, the annual celebration of Catalonia's Andalucian community. The original Fòrum building, designed by Herzog and de Meuron, has been adapted to house the **Museu Blau ❽** (Plaça Leonardo da Vinci, 4–5; tel: 93-256 6002; www.museuciencies.bcn.cat; Tue–Sat 10am–7pm; Sun 10am–8pm; charge, free from 3pm Sun), the natural science museum formerly in the Ciutadella Park. It has a permanent exhibition of planet earth and its history, as well as a section entitled *Laboratorios de la vida*, exploring life from microbes to reproduction.

Beyond the museum is the **Parc del Fòrum**, which has a sense of no-man's land under the shadow of an enormous solar panel. However, its marina, landscaped bathing pool and other facilities may develop in the next few years, as more locals start to come to the area and the

RESTAURANTS AND BARS

PRICE CATEGORIES

Prices for a three-course dinner per person with a bottle of house wine:

€ = under €25
€€ = €25–40
€€€ = €40–60
€€€€ = over €60

Restaurants & Bars

Catalan

Els Pescadors
Plaça Prim, 1
Tel: 93-225 2018
www.elspescadors.com
Open: Daily L & D. €€€€ [off map]
This charming restaurant specialising in seafood and game is a complete surprise. Find it tucked away in a pretty square amid the former textile factories and new developments of Poble Nou. Worth tracking down.

Spanish

Bar Llacuna
Llacuna, 88
Tel: 93-300 8957
Open: Mon–Thu L, Fri L & D. € [off map]
A great find amid the high-tech 22@ blocks, this is a local corner bar with a difference. Subtly spruced up by its young Catalan owners, it still welcomes the old clientele while serving traditional dishes with a modern twist. Offering excellent value and a good atmosphere, it's best to get there early for lunch to beat the office crowd.

Barlovento
Rambla del Poble Nou, 21
Tel: 93-225 2109
Open: Tue–Sun B, L & D. € [off map]
A great corner bar, located just inland from the waterfront on the bustling Rambla del Poble Nou. The tapas are genuinely home-cooked and are good enough to meet with local residents' approval.

BESIDE THE SEASIDE

Few cultural capitals visited for their history, architecture, art or gourmet restaurants can also boast a seashore with boardwalks, palm trees and nightlife.

It was the 1992 Olympics that transformed Barcelona's heavily industrial coastline into today's glamorous waterfront. Until then people had little contact with the Mediterranean on their doorstep, as the shores were taken over by industries or the sprawl of shanty housing. Essential work in preparation for the Games rewarded Barcelona's inhabitants with a string of golden beaches and a long, landscaped promenade.

Today these beaches are a well-established playground for Barcelonans and visitors, easily reached from all parts of the city by public transport. It is often warm enough to eat at one of the many xiringuitos (beach bars) or restaurants between Barceloneta and the Fòrum area. In the summer the nearly 5km (3 miles) of beaches are thronged with kids, grandparents and the bronzed and beautiful who flop from sun lounger to beach bar as the sun sets. By nightfall the DJs start spinning, making the beach a cool place to be on a summer night. Overnight, an army of cleaners prepare the nine beaches for the next day.

In nearby Sitges you can combine time on the beach with exploring this pretty whitewashed town with its shops, restaurants and museums.

The Essentials

Address: www.bcn.cat/platges
Tel: 010 (general info line)
Transport:L4 Barceloneta; Ciutadella; Bogatell; Llacuna; Poble Nou; Selva de Mar; El Maresme; 6, 14, 17, 36, 41, 45, 59, 64, 71, 92, 99,

The promenade is perfect for joggers of all ages.

Fun in the sun on Nova Icària beach.

Frank Gehry's giant sculpture 'Pez y Esfera' overlooks Platja Somorrostro and pinpoints the Olympic Port and Village.

It's worth observing the flags: green is fine, yellow suggests swimming with caution and the red flag means don't go in the water. The sea may be flat but it could be polluted or infested with jellyfish.

CITY BEACHES

Sant Sebastià
Southernmost beach, sheltered beneath the skyscraper W Hotel (aka 'The Sail'), quieter than Barceloneta beach. Trendy bars. Disabled swimming service (daily July–early Sept; weekends in June).

Looking out over the W Hotel.

Nova Icària
Attractive beach with the municipal sailing school and facilities for various other water sports. Disabled swimming service.

Mar Bella
Newly created in 1992, this beach is full of fun for kids, with a skateboarding area in the park just behind. Also has a nudist section.

A SHORT TRAIN RIDE AWAY

Sitges
Only 40 minutes by train but a world apart, often with better weather than Barcelona. Several beaches to choose from and the pretty town to explore.

Montgat Nord
The furthest point you can get to on the Maresme coast using the basic T10 transport ticket (Zone One). Long, open sandy beach popular with surfers. A mere 15 minutes from Plaça de Catalunya.

Caldes d'Estrac
Also known as Caldetes, this charming spa town has a long peaceful beach overlooked by *modernista* villas. A pleasant 45-minute train ride along the coast.

Surfer at Sitges.

Escalators were installed on Montjuïc for the 1992 Olympic Games.

MONTJUÏC

The lofty setting for the 1992 Olympic Games has superb views of the city, two world-class museums, an inspiring cultural centre, gardens and the entertaining Poble Espanyol (Spanish Village).

The small hill of Montjuïc is only 213 metres (699ft) high, but it has an undeniable physical presence that is noticeable from most parts of the city. From along the waterfront it marks the end of the leisure port, and from the Ronda Litoral it acts like a barrier between the inner residential area of the city and the industrial sprawl of the Zona Franca, the gateway to the south.

From high points around Barcelona you can see how densely packed a city this is – the result of its growth having been contained within the natural limits of the River Besòs, the Collserola range, the Mediterranean and Montjuïc.

Montjuïc past and present

The rocky promontory of Montjuïc has also featured in some of the key events in Barcelona's history. A pre-Roman civilisation made a settlement here, preferring its rough heights to the humid plain that the Romans later opted for. The Romans did, however, build a temple to Jupiter here, which is thought to explain the origin of the name: Mons Iovis eventually evolved into Montjuïc.

In 1929 the hill was landscaped and used as the grounds of the

Universal Exposition. More recently, it was seen by millions of people worldwide as it hosted the opening and closing ceremonies and core events of the 1992 Olympic Games. It was regarded as the 'nerve centre' of the Games.

Today it is a large city park offering a wide range of cultural, leisure and sporting activities – a playground used by both residents and tourists. It is a wonderful space for walking dogs and allowing children to run wild, or just for clearing the head and getting

Main Attractions

Font Màgica
Pavelló Mies van der Rohe
CaixaForum
Poble Espanyol
Museu Nacional d'Art de Catalunya
Estadi Olímpic
Jardí Botànic
Fundació Joan Miró
Castell de Montjuïc

Maps and Listings

Open-air concert in Poble Espanyol.

*Plenty of help to find
your way around.*

a bird's-eye view of Barcelona, especially its maritime area. Apart from the cable car that crosses the harbour, this is the only place where you can piece together the waterfront at a glance, and watch the comings and goings of the busy industrial port.

PLAÇA D'ESPANYA ❶

One of the best approaches to Montjuïc is from **Plaça d'Espanya**, which has good metro and bus connections. (If you are heading for a specific destination, such as the Fundació Joan Miró or the castle, the funicular from Paral.lel metro station is a better option.) Plaça d'Espanya is a large, noisy junction at the southern end of town. Glaring and hot, surrounded by an incoherent mixture of buildings and with little or no shade, it is not a place to linger.

Spare a brief moment, however, to look at the monument to Spain in the middle of the square's roundabout, commissioned for the 1929 Universal Exposition. The most intriguing thing about it is that Josep Jujol was the sculptor; it is difficult to reconcile this monumental piece with the same artist's brilliant ceramic serpentine bench in Park Güell (see page

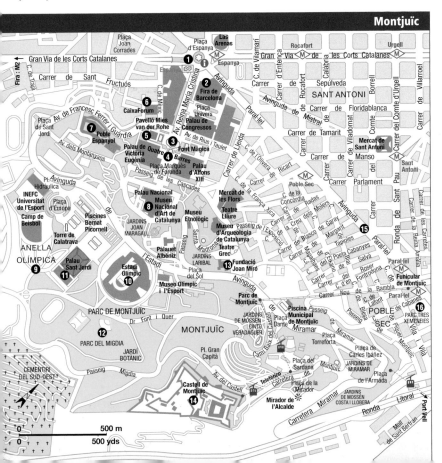

220), built at least 15 years earlier. The explanation for the two opposing styles was that the Primo de Rivera dictatorship in Madrid controlled the design of Jujol's monument to Spain.

Las Arenas

The former bullring, **Las Arenas**, on the other side of the square opened in 1900 with a capacity for 15,000 spectators. It has been converted into a popular commercial centre with shops and restaurants, after standing empty for years. In 2004, city councillors became the first in Spain to declare their opposition to bullfighting, and in 2010 the Parliament of Catalonia passed the law prohibiting it in Catalonia. The last *corridas* were in the Monumental bullring, near Plaça de les Glòries, in 2011.

HEADING UP THE HILL

Turning your back on the roundabout, head past the twin Venetian-style towers, designed by Ramón Reventós, that formed the main entrance to the Universal Exposition of 1929. Most of the buildings here were designed for this event, with

a sweeping vista up to the **Palau Nacional**, the enormous, rather overbearing building at the top of the steps. The Exposition, opened by King Alfonso XIII, had industry, art and sport as its themes, and was a political *tour de force* for the Primo de Rivera dictatorship. The hillside was landscaped in accordance with a plan drawn up by Forestier and Nicolau Maria Rubió i Tudurí. Some 15 palaces were built, as well as national and commercial pavilions, a stadium,

The view from MNAC over Barcelona.

The Palau Nacional, designed for the Universal Exposition of 1929, houses a wonderful art museum.

Puppet show during the Festa de la Tolerancia, Poble Espanyol.

Passeig de la Cascades, on the approach to MNAC.

a swimming pool, ornamental fountains, the Poble Espanyol (Spanish Village), the Greek amphitheatre, several towers and the access avenue.

Fira de Barcelona ❷

It still looks very much like a showground, and today acts as the main headquarters of the Barcelona Trade Fair organisation, the **Fira de Barcelona**. The showground has additional new premises on Gran Via, the total amounting to 295,000 sq metres (3,175,000 sq ft), including two congress centres. If a trade fair is being held, you may be diverted, but there will be a way to reach all the different activities.

The upper esplanades are reached by escalator; the system of escalators was created for the 1992 Olympics, the next major event after the Exposition to bring enormous change to this district.

Font Màgica ❸

Tel: 010
Opening Hrs: Son et lumière shows May–Sept Thu–Sun every half hour from 9–11.30pm, Oct–Apr Fri–Sat

7–9pm, closed for maintenance at some stage in winter
Transport: Espanya

The imposing Font Màgica, designed by Carlos Buïgas for the Exposition in 1929, has been restored and still delights thousands of visitors during the *son et lumière* shows, which change every half hour.

Quatre barres ❹

Just behind the fountain four very symbolic columns (les quatre barres) have been erected. Representing the stripes on the Catalan flag, they were originally installed by Puig i Cadafalch in 1919, but demolished by the Primo de Rivera regime in 1928. Their reinstatement has been a moral victory for the Catalan independent movement.

Pavelló Mies van der Rohe ❺

Address: Av. de Francesc Ferrer i Guàrdia, 7; www.miesbcn.com
Tel: 93-423 4016
Opening Hrs: daily 10am–8pm
Entrance fee: charge
Transport: Espanya

Don't miss the Pavelló Mies van der Rohe, lying low among greenery across the esplanade. Built by Ludwig Mies van der Rohe as the German Pavilion for the 1929 Exposition, it was later dismantled, but, at the instigation of some leading architects, rebuilt in 1986 to celebrate the centenary of the architect's birth. Its clean lines are quite breathtaking, and clarify the significance and beauty of minimalism. The contrast with some of the other, pompously ornate, buildings of the same time is extraordinary. Van der Rohe's professor wrote at the time: 'This building will one day be remembered as the most beautiful of those built in the 20th century.'

CaixaForum 6

Address: Av. de Francesc Ferrer i Guàrdia, 6–8; www.fundacio.lacaixa.es
Tel: 93-476 8600
Opening Hrs: daily 10am–8pm
Entrance fee: charge
Transport: Espanya

Across the road is a fascinating former textile factory, Casaramona, built by Puig i Cadafalch in 1911. A gem of *modernista* industrial architecture, it has been converted by the cultural organisation Fundació 'la Caixa' into its centre, the CaixaForum, a wonderful space with an entrance designed by Arata Isozaki. Apart from its own contemporary collection, it holds temporary exhibitions, concerts, debates and music festivals. It's always worth checking what's on in this inspiring space, and the building itself is worth a visit.

Summer concert at Poble Espanyol.

Watching a puppet show at Poble Espanyol.

Poble Espanyol ⑦

Address: Av. de Francesc Ferrer i Guàrdia, 13; www.poble-espanyol.com
Tel: 93-508 6300
Opening Hrs: Mon 9am–8pm, Tue–Thu, Sun 9am–midnight, Fri 9am–3am, Sat 9am–4am
Entrance fee: charge
Transport: Espanya

The ceiling at MNAC's dome room.

Further up the hill is the Poble Espanyol, also built for the 1929 Exposition. The shady green of **Avinguda de Francesc Ferrer i Guàrdia** is a welcome relief after the exposed areas of the Fira. The Poble Espanyol has reinvented itself recently and now provides many diversions both day and night, from well-organised activities for kids including treasure hunts in English and arts and crafts workshops, to a *tablao*, where you can watch flamenco dancing. It is not just 'family' entertainment: young people flock here for the buzzy night scene, especially in summer. The village is one of the most popular venues in Barcelona.

Modern Art at Palau Nacional.

It was built as a showpiece for regional architecture, handicrafts, and cultural and gastronomic styles from all over Spain. It has a Plaza Mayor, typical of many squares you might find in any part of the country, where popular fiestas take place. The square is at its best when it stages jazz and rock concerts during the summer months.

Innovations in the village

The entrance is through San Vicente de Avila Portal. Javier Mariscal, one of Barcelona's most popular designers (he was responsible for the Olympic mascot), put the Poble Espanyol into the limelight in the early 1990s by creating a trendy bar within the gateway, the **Torres de Avila**. One of the city's most popular open-air clubs, La Terrazza, opens here in the summer. The village has also opened some new spaces for contemporary art like the Fundació Fran Daurel, with more than 300 pieces, including works by Picasso, Barceló, Miró and Tàpies, and a sculpture garden.

Approaching the Palau Nacional

From here, you can either walk up the hill, following signs to the **Palau Nacional**, or take a longer walk up Avinguda de l'Estadi straight to the

Olympic Stadium. The easiest route, however, is to go back down to the Font Màgica and take the escalator.

In some lights, or at a distance, the Palau Nacional can look imposing and quite dramatic, but on the whole it looks somewhat out of place in Barcelona. However, the museum in this massive building should not be missed.

Museu Nacional d'Art de Catalunya ❽

Address: Parc de Montjuïc; www.mnac.cat
Tel: 93-622 0376
Opening Hrs: Tue–Sat 10am–8pm, Oct–Apr 10am–6pm; Sun 10am–3pm
Entrance fee: charge; free first Sun of every month and Sat from 3pm
Transport: Espanya

Since 1934 the Palau Nacional has housed the Museu Nacional d'Art de Catalunya , which has the most important Romanesque art collection in the world, including murals that were peeled from the walls of tiny churches in the Pyrenees in the province of Lleida and brought down

by donkey. There is also an excellent Gothic collection and a selection of Renaissance and Baroque art (see photo feature, page 188).

However, after major renovation work under the direction of the Italian architect Gae Aulenti, it also now houses a complete collection of Catalan art, ranging over a millennium. The original collection has been complemented by the 19th- and 20th-century works from the former Museu d'Art Modern, which includes work by Casas, Rusiñol, Nonell and Fortuny, and the decorative arts, including pieces by Gaudí and Jujol.

The sign of the cat at the Font de Gat in Jardins Laribal.

Roman mosaic at Museu de Arqueologia de Catalunya.

Teatre Grec's gardens.

The museum also holds part of the Thyssen collection of paintings, a coin collection, drawings, engravings and photography. The former Throne Room houses an attractive restaurant, Òleum, while the Terrace bar is perfect for a snack or drink looking over the city. From the steps of the Palau, turn right if you fancy a detour to the museums of archaeology and ethnology on Passeig Santa Madrona.

Museu Etnològic

Address: Passeig Santa Madrona, 16–22; www.museuetnologic.bcn.cat
Tel: 93-424 6807
Opening Hrs: summer Tue–Sat 10am–6pm; winter Tue, Thu 10am–7pm, Wed, Fri, Sat 10am–2pm, Sun 10am–2pm and 3–8pm (but currently closed for restoration)
Entrance fee: charge, free Sun from 3pm
Transport: Espanya/Poble Sec

The Museu Etnològic has collections from all over the world, notably Latin America and the Philippines. A section on Japan, the *Espai Japó*, is an indication of the new cultural (and commercial) exchange between Catalonia and Japan. The museum remains closed for renovation work. Check the website before visiting.

On the same street and in the midst of lovely gardens (the **Jardins Laribal**) is a small, pretty café and restaurant, La Font del Gat. Further down the hill is the **Teatre Grec** (Greek amphitheatre; see margin note, page 180).

Museu d'Arqueologia de Catalunya

Address: Passeig Santa Madrona, 39–41; www.mac.cat
Tel: 93-423 2149
Opening Hrs: Tue–Sat 9.30am–7pm, Sun 10am–2.30pm
Entrance fee: charge
Transport: Espanya/Poble Sec

Just beyond the Teatre Grec is the recently renovated Museu

d'Arqueologia de Catalunya, with finds relating to the first inhabitants of Catalonia, including those in the Greek and Roman periods.

From here, the route will take you down the hill as far as the complex of theatres including the **Teatre Lliure** and the **Mercat de les Flors**, which specialises in contemporary dance and movement, featuring many top-level international companies, and the **Institut del Teatre**, a drama school. The productions here are generally interesting and of a good standard. However, if your main goal is to check out the Olympic legacy on Montjuïc, this detour should be left for another day as it takes you a long way downhill.

ANELLA OLÍMPICA ❾

The Anella Olímpica (Olympic Ring) is spread across the hillside behind the Palau Nacional and easily accessible from there by escalator. The buildings here appear to be sculpted out of the ridge, with open views to the south dropping down behind them. Despite the passage of time, they are dazzling in the abundant light of Montjuïc.

There are eight Olympic-standard sports centres and three athletics tracks in the area, but if you stick to the road you will see only a fraction of what was created. Fortunately, a walkway on the inland (downhill) side of the main stadium gives access to the central square.

Estadi Olímpic ❿

Address: Av. de l'Estadi, s/n
Opening hrs: summer daily 10am–8pm, winter 10am–6pm
Entrance fee: free
Transport: Espanya/Paral.lel funicular

The Estadi Olímpic was actually built for the 1929 Universal Exposition, following a design by Pere Domènech. Its opening football match was a victory for the Catalan side against Bolton Wanderers – a little-known fact. It remained open until the Mediterranean Games in 1955, then fell into disrepair. Extensive works for the 1992 Olympics involved lowering the arena by 11 metres (36ft) to create the extra seating needed for 55,000 spectators. Most of the track events and the opening and closing ceremonies were held here.

EAT

During the Grec Festival in June and July an attractive open-air restaurant operates near the Greek amphitheatre (see page 180).

The Piscina Municipal de Montjuïc was used for diving events in the 1992 Olympics.

TIP

International sporting events are often held in the Olympic complex, like the FINA World Aquatic Championships in 2013.

Just outside the stadium a new museum has opened, the **Museu Olímpic i de l'Esport** (summer Tue–Sat 10am–8pm, winter Tue–Sat 10am–6pm, Sun 10am–2.30pm; charge). It's the first in Europe giving a global view of sports with interactive exhibits, multimedia installations and, of course, coverage of the 1992 Games.

Olympic installations

Below and west of the stadium stretches the immense **Olympic Terrace**, lined with pillars. In the middle of the main terrace is a lawn with an artificial stream flowing through it; on the left is a small forest of identical sculptures. The terrace drops down to a second level in the middle distance, and then to a third – the **Plaça d'Europa** – a circular colonnaded area built on top of a massive water tank containing 60 million litres (13,200,000 gallons) of drinking water

for the city. The whole has the atmosphere of a recreated Roman forum.

On each side of the terrace are key installations: to the left the **Palau Sant Jordi**, to the right the **Piscines Bernat Picornell**. In the far distance is the **INEFC Universitat de l'Esport**.

Torre de Calatrava

There is one highly visible landmark here that caused great controversy at the time, not least with the architects who created the whole Olympic Ring: the great white **Torre de Calatrava** communications tower (188 metres/616ft), designed by Spanish architect Santiago Calatrava, known for his elegantly engineered bridges. Olympic architects Frederic Correa, Alfonso Milá, Joan Margarit and Carles Buxadé hated the tower project, and rallied dozens of intellectuals to their cause. Nevertheless, the

A walk in the Parc del Migdia.

Telefònica tower went ahead, and the result is stunning.

Palau Sant Jordi

Other than the stadium itself, the installation most in the public eye is the **Palau Sant Jordi** ⑪, an indoor stadium designed by Japanese architect Arata Isozaki. The ultramodern design in steel and glass can seat 15,000, with not a pillar in sight.

Since the Olympics, the Palau has proved popular for concerts and exhibitions, as well as sporting events.

Parc del Migdia ⑫

Just beyond the stadium is an expanse of hillside known as the **Parc del Migdia**, a great spot for picnics. The beautifully landscaped botanical garden, **Jardí Botànic** (June–Aug daily 10am–8pm, Sept–May 10am–6pm; charge, free Sun from 3pm), is a sustainable garden in keeping with Barcelona's aspirations for the new century. It contains species from the different Mediterranean climates around the world and has a prized Bonsai collection.

Palauet Albéniz

Returning to Avinguda de l'Estadi, opposite the stadium are the smaller, more peaceful and elegant gardens of Joan Maragall surrounding the **Palauet Albéniz**. This 'little palace' is now the official residence of visiting dignitaries to Barcelona. It was built as a royal pavilion for the 1929

The Olympic Stadium lit up for the closing ceremony of the 1992 Games.

The Palau Sant Jordi, Torre de Calatrava and Olympic Terrace.

In Fundació Juan Miró.

One of the largest collections in the world of Miró's work, it includes paintings, drawings, sculptures and tapestries, as well as his complete graphic work. It also contains the mercury fountain designed by Alexander Calder for the Spanish Republic's Pavilion in the 1937 Paris Exhibition. It seems fitting that this should be here now: the Spanish Pavilion was intended as a political statement, coinciding as it did with the civil war, was designed by Sert and included Miró's work and Picasso's *Guernica* (see box on page 50). Contemporary exhibitions and concerts are also held here regularly.

Montjuïc gardens

Just before the municipal swimming pool on the left, scene of Olympic diving in 1992, is the funicular station, Parc de Montjuïc, with the **Jardins de Mossèn Cinto Verdaguer** close by.

Continue along the road for magnificent views of the port from the **Jardins de Miramar**, where there are several bars serving food and

Exposition, and during the years of self-government in Catalonia – from 1931 until the end of the civil war – it was a music museum.

Exhibits at the Fundació Miró.

Fundació Joan Miró ⑬

Address: Parc de Montjuïc, s/n; www.fundaciomiro-bcn.org
Tel: 93-443 9470
Opening Hrs: Tue–Wed, Fri–Sat 10am–7pm, summer until 8pm, Thu 10am–9.30pm, Sun 10am–2.30pm
Entrance fee: charge
Transport: Paral.lel + funicular

Cable cars can take you back down the hill.

With the stadium on your right, follow the main road until it becomes **Avinguda de Miramar**. On the left is the **Fundació Joan Miró**, an understated yet powerfully impressive gem on this sporting hill. Designed by Josep Lluís Sert, eminent architect and friend of Miró, the gallery has been open since 1974.

A Mediterranean luminosity floods the striking building and shows Miró's work in its best light.

refreshments, and the impressive **Jardins de Mossèn Costa i Llobera**. Once a strategic defence point, the Buenavista battery, this is now a cactus garden, described by the *New York Times* as one of the best gardens in the world. It has cacti from Mexico, Bolivia, Africa and California. A five-star hotel has also opened here, with extraordinary views of the port (see page 255).

Alternatively, you could catch the funicular back down to Paral. lel metro station, or complete the Montjuïc experience and take the cable car up to the Castell de Montjuïc for an even better view.

Castell de Montjuïc ⓮

Address: Carretera de Montjuïc, 66
www.bcn.cat/castelldemontjuic
Tel: 93-256 4445
Opening Hrs: winter daily 9am–7pm, summer until 9pm
Entrance fee: free
Transport: Paral.lel + funicular, cable car

The Castell de Montjuïc was built in the 17th century during the battle between Catalonia and Spain's Felipe IV, known as the War of the Reapers. At the beginning of the 18th century Bourbon troops ransacked the castle; it was rebuilt between 1751 and 1779. The new fortress was in the form of a starred pentagon, with enormous moats, bastions and buttresses. It was a place where torture and executions took place over many years. To Catalans, it has represented oppression by the central government in Madrid.

It was here that Lluís Companys, Catalan Nationalist leader and president of the Generalitat, was shot in 1940. A statue of Franco was removed from the courtyard soon after his death in 1975. The castle has finally been ceded to the city by central government in Madrid and there are various proposals for its future. The military museum was closed and the rooms around the central courtyard now hold exhibitions related to the historic memory of Catalonia, or themes of repression universally.

The citizens of Barcelona are enjoying reclaiming their castle and it is being used more for leisure activities. An open-air cinema in its

FACT

Joan Miró was born in Barcelona in 1893 and studied here, but in 1920 he went to Paris, where he was influenced by the Surrealists. He spent the latter years of his long life – he was 90 when he died – in Palma de Mallorca, home of his wife, Pilar. For more on Miró's life and work, see page 60.

Castell de Montjuïc.

grounds is a popular event during the summer.

THE ROUTE DOWNHILL

Descending the hill on foot, you pass through the **Plaça del Sardana**, with its circle of stone dancers, sculpted by Josep Cañas in 1966. Nearby is the **Mirador de l'Alcalde** (the Mayor's Lookout Point), with panoramic views over the waterfront. A new walkway, the Camí del Mar, runs from here to the Mirador de L'Anella Olímpica, giving a new perspective southwards over the delta of the River Llobregat.

Return to Plaça d'Espanya by the escalators, or from the castle take the scenic route down by catching the cable car from the Plaça de l'Armada, in the area known as Miramar, and cross to the port.

There is a pleasant walking route down the hill beginning opposite the Plaça Dante near the Fundació Miró, and leading down steps into Poble Sec, the unspoilt neighbourhood that slopes down the hill. Follow the steep street Margarit and make a detour into Plaça Sortidor, which has

Taking in the view from Castell de Montjuic.

Performers in the 'Made in El Molino' show, El Molino theatre.

an attractive old bar that offers a set lunch menu. Meander downwards through this bustling district, a genuine neighbourhood, where pedestrianised street Blai is full of unusual and attractive bars and restaurants, making it a good nightlife spot.

Alternatively wander down through the Mirador del Poble Sec, a newly landscaped park, or opt for the funicular, which you can board near Plaça Dante. The rail descends a distance of 760 metres (2,500ft) and disembarks at Avinguda Paral.lel, not far from the church of Sant Pau (see page 147).

Avinguda Paral.lel ⓯

Avinguda Paral.lel was originally called Calle Marqués del Duero, until in 1794, a Frenchman, Pierre François André Méchain, discovered that the avenue's pathway coincided with the navigational parallel 44º44'N.

This neighbourhood has always been known as the centre of variety theatre and vaudeville. Its most famous theatre was El Molino, a colourful music hall which, after being closed for years, reopened in 2010 after major refurbishment. It now offers lunch and dinner shows with content ranging from vaudeville to tango, burlesque to flamenco. Its reopening is bringing life back to what used to be known as the 'Broadway of Barcelona'. Even the world's most famous chef, Ferran Adrià, has made a serious investment in the area by opening Tickets, arguably the most expensive tapas bar in town.

Parc Tres Xemeneies ⓰

Parc Tres Xemeneies, just down the avenue towards the sea, is dominated by three enormous 72-metre (235ft)-high chimneys. This is a fine example of a 'hard' urban park, with interesting design ideas. The chimneys are the remains of the 'Grupo Mata', an electricity-producing plant dating from the turn of the 20th century.

RESTAURANTS, BARS AND CAFÉS

PRICE CATEGORIES

Prices for a three-course dinner per person with a bottle of house wine:

€ = under €25
€€ = €25–40
€€€ = €40–60
€€€€ = over €60

Restaurants

The hill is more an open space for picnics than somewhere for dinner, but the cultural centres have attractive cafés and there are *xiringuitos* (kiosks) in the parks. In the Paral.lel and Poble Sec districts, options range from corner bars to state-of-the-art tapas.

Catalan

Òleum
Museu Nacional d'Art de Catalunya
Parc de Montjuïc
Tel: 93-289 0679
www.laierestaurants.es/mnac_oleum
Open: Tue–Sat L & D. €€–€€€
[80] p284, B2]
Enjoy contemporary Catalan dishes within the gracious surroundings of the Throne Room in the Palau Nacional (today's National Museum), where Alfonso XIII officially opened the 1929 Exposition. Stunning views by day and night.

International

Fundació Joan Miró
Avinguda de Miramar, 1
Tel: 93-329 0768
Open: Tue–Sat L. €–€€ [81] p284, C3]
Choose from the select menu of pasta, wok and Indian dishes in the setting of the Miró museum or have a snack in the courtyard.

Spanish

Barramón
Blai, 28–30
Tel: 93-442 3080
www.barramon.es
Open: Mon–Fri D, Sat–Sun L & D. €
[82] p284, D2]

This bar-cum-restaurant, on a lively pedestrian street in Poble Sec, has a great young atmosphere and serves various risottos.

La Caseta del Migdia
Parc del Migdia
Tel: 693-992760 (mobile)
www.lacaseta.org
Open: summer Wed–Sun L & D, winter Sat–Sun L. € [83] p284, B4]
Alfresco rustic eating with an amazing view. One of the few spots you can watch the sun set in the city. Try grilled sardines accompanied by rumba on summer nights.

Elche
Vila i Vilà, 71
Tel: 93-441 3089
http://elcherestaurant.es
Open: Daily L & D. €€€ [84] p284, D3]
Famous for its paella and other rice dishes since 1959, when the parents of the present owners brought the recipes from Valencia.

Quimet i Quimet
Poeta Cabanyes, 25
Tel: 93-442 3142
Open: Mon–Fri L & D (tapas), Sat L. €
[85] p284, D2]
You'll find wall-to-wall wine bottles (with an unusually wide choice by the glass) and excellent tapas in this tiny, authentic bar run by the third generation of 'Quims'.

Tablao de Carmen
Poble Espanyol, Av. de Francesc Ferrer i Guàrdia, 13–27
Tel: 93-325 6895
www.tablaodecarmen.com
Open: Tue–Sun D. €€€€ (includes show) or tapas menu €€€ [86] p284, B1]
One of several restaurants in the Spanish Village. Touristy but fun. This one has a good flamenco show twice a night, with set dinner, or you can have lunch on the patio.

Tickets
Av. Paral.lel 164
www.ticketsbar.es
Open: Tue–Fri D, Sat L & D, Sun L. €€€–€€€€ [87] p284, D1]
Word has spread so fast about Ferran Adrià's hot cheese and ham

airbags that you need to book months in advance via the website to get a look in at this high-end tapas bar with staff in circus garb.

La Tieta
Blai, 1
Tel: 93-186 3595
Open: Tue–Sun L & D. € [88] p284, D3]
A small but very *simpático* bar recently opened by two sisters, with a range of gourmet tapas like salmon tartare as well as traditional favourites like *tortilla de patatas*. Drinks include some interesting wines sold by the glass, beers and the house special *vermut*.

La Tomaquera
Margarit, 58
Open: Tue–Sat L & D, Sun L. €€
[89] p284, D2]
No phone, no reservations, no credit cards, but always packed. A rough-and-ready spot where large portions of grilled meat are served with a dollop of *allioli* and house wine. Snails are the speciality.

Bars and Cafés

La Confiteria
Sant Pau, 128
[93] p284, E2]
This beautiful, *modernista* former pastry shop is a great place to stop off for a coffee or a cocktail.

Gran Bodega Saltó
Blesa, 36
http://bodegasalto.net
[94] p284, D3]
This wonderful old *bodega* has become an essential stop in Poble Sec's increasingly trendy scene. Like an unofficial cultural centre, its quirky decoration, Sunday lunchtime *vermut* and live music attract a colourful crowd.

Sirvent
Parlament, 56
http://turronessirvent.com
[95] p284, D2]
One of the best places in town to try *orxata* – a cooling, traditional drink made from *xufas* (tiger nuts).

THE HOME OF CATALAN ART

The Palau Nacional is home to the Museu Nacional d'Art de Catalunya, which brings together collections spanning 1,000 years of Catalan art.

At the end of 2004, after a decade of refurbishments, the Palau Nacional opened its doors for the first time to the fully integrated collections of Catalan art in the city. The original collection of the umbrella museum, the Museu Nacional, runs from Romanesque through to Baroque and has the finest assemblage of medieval art in Europe. To this has been added various collections, including that of the Museu d'Art Modern that previously had its own home next to the Parlament de Catalunya in the Parc de la Ciutadella. The Palau Nacional was originally redesigned as a museum after relinquishing its function as host centre for the Universal Exposition of 1929, for which it was built. There are plans to take over the two palaces just beneath it to extend the scope of the museum's activities in cooperation with the other key cultural centres on this hillside.

Unmissable above the exhibition halls and shooting fountains of Montjuïc, the imposing neo-Baroque 'palace' is lit up at night. Take time to have a drink on its terrace with expansive views over the city.

Romanesque art is well represented here.

The formidable Sala Oval has been splendidly restored and is often used for events.

The Essentials

Address: Palau Nacional, Parc de Montjuïc, www.mnac.cat
Tel: 93-622 0376
Opening Hrs: Tue–Sat 10am–8pm, Oct–Apr until 6pm, Sun and public hols 10am–3pm
Entrance Fee: charge
Transport: L1 and L3 Espanya

THE HIGHLIGHTS

'Poble Escalonat' (Terraced Village), by Joaquim Mir.

Romanesque The greatest collection of Romanesque art in Europe includes many wall paintings from churches in the Pyrenees, rescued from decay at the beginning of the 20th century. Dating from the 11th to the 13th centuries, these paintings, along with altar screens, chests, madonnas and crucifixes, are brightly coloured and executed with a powerful simplicity that has inspired many modern Catalan painters.

Gothic Catalonia's exceptional period of architecture was also rich in fine art. From the 13th to the late 15th centuries, religious paintings by Jaume Huguet, Bernat Martorell and many others are complemented by sculpture, metal and enamel work.

Renaissance and Baroque Between the 14th and 19th centuries, Catalonia had no artists of international standing. This European collection, has works from Italy, the Netherlands and Spain, such as El Greco, Goya, Velázquez and Zurbarán.

Modern Art This collection runs from the early 19th century until the Civil War (1936), and is important for understanding *modernisme* and *Noucentisme*, the driving art forces of the modern city. *Modernista* furniture, decorative arts and interiors can also be seen.

Other Collections These include coins, prints and drawings from the 17th to the 20th centuries, and photography. Its temporary exhibitions are top-quality.

MNAC also hosts many temporary exhibits, in addition to its rich collection.

Depiction of the 13th-century 'Assault on the City of Mallorca'.

A golden casket, one of many magnificent chests, caskets, screens and crucifixes.

Gaudí's magnificent Casa Batlló.

EIXAMPLE

Cerdà's 19th-century grid system of streets allowed the city's wealthy elite to commission some of the most innovative buildings of the age, including Gaudí's fabulous Sagrada Família.

The Eixample is one of the most characteristic districts of Barcelona, and has some of its most distinctive elements, such as the Sagrada Família and much of the city's famed *modernista* architecture. It stands as a symbol of the 19th-century boom that initiated Barcelona's modern era, and today is the most populated district in the city.

Layout of Eixample

After the narrow, irregular streets of the Old Town, where history has left layer upon layer of building styles, the Eixample can feel like a new town. Its regular structure forms a repeated pattern. Traffic roars down one street and up another in a well-structured one-way system, all the way from its southern boundary by Plaça d'Espanya to its northern limit leading up from Plaça de les Glòries.

Plaça de les Glòries is the axis for three main roads crossing the city: La Meridiana, Gran Via and Avinguda Diagonal. From here the tram goes through Diagonal Mar and the Fòrum, and heads out to Sant Adrià, a suburb on the other side of the River Besòs.

Plaça de les Glòries is pinpointed by the **Torre Agbar**, headquarters of a water company. Designed by the

French architect Jean Nouvel, it has an outer casing of glass vents reflecting 40 colours and is spectacular by night.

An expanding city

The Eixample is broken into two halves, *la dreta* (right) and *l'esquerra* (left) on either side of **Balmes** as you look inland towards the summit of Tibidabo. Within the two halves are well-defined neighbourhoods, such as those of the **Sagrada Família** and **Fort Pienc** (on the right) and **Sant Antoni** (on the left).

Main Attractions
Passeig de Gràcia
Illa de la Discòrdia
Casa Batlló
Rambla de Catalunya
Palau Robert
La Pedrera
Sagrada Família
Hospital Sant Pau
Parc Joan Miró

Maps and Listings
Map, page 192
Shopping, page 200
Restaurants, page 202
Accommodation, page 255

On the rooftop of La Pedrera.

Mansion houses, Passeig de Gracia.

The best way to appreciate the Eixample is to wander aimlessly. Peep into doorways to see *modernista* lamps and ceramic tiles, look up at balconies and stained-glass *tribunes* (enclosed balconies), notice the decorative facades, as well as the plants, washing and other elements of real life that go on inside these museum pieces. Take time to visit the art galleries that abound, to notice old shop signs, to shop in ancient *colmados* (grocer's stores).

Whenever possible, catch a glimpse of the inner patios of these *illas*, the name of each four-sided block of buildings: sadly not used for the greater good, as Cerdà, the brilliant town planner behind this scheme, would have wished (see box, page 193), but mostly for car parks, commercial or private use. They still make fascinating viewing though, particularly the backs of the elegant houses and some well-established private gardens.

Most of Barcelona's *modernista* landmarks can be found in *la dreta*, while *l'esquerra* is more modern and residential. Since the 1960s *la dreta* has undergone a profound transformation. With the earlier inhabitants moving to uptown districts, the larger houses have been converted into offices and flats.

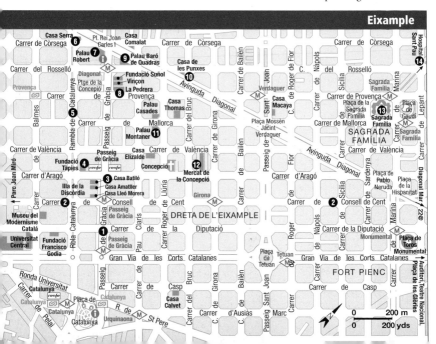

PASSEIG DE GRÀCIA ❶

The tour outlined here will focus on the central area and some key areas leading off it. Using Plaça de Catalunya as a pivotal point, cross over to Passeig de Gràcia. This wide, tree-lined avenue originally linked the Old City and the former village of Gràcia even before the ancient walls of the city were torn down. Cerdà increased its width to 60 metres (200ft), which makes it distinctive from the uniform streets of the rest of the Eixample; more recently, the pavements have been widened. The beautiful wrought-iron streetlamps, which are incorporated with mosaic benches, were designed by Pere Falqués in 1906.

Notice the hexagonal pavement tiles designed by Gaudí and unique to the Passeig de Gràcia. Everywhere you look there are fascinating details.

Junction with Gran Via

This is a broad, busy thoroughfare that brings traffic in from the airport and the south. The fountains in the middle and the impressive buildings around it prevent it from being merely a major through-road, however. As you cross over, don't miss a fine example of 1930s architecture by Sert, prestigious architect of the Fundació Miró, now taken over by Tous jewellers.

Consell de Cent ❷

Continue up Passeig de Gràcia to Consell de Cent, which demands a detour. Cross Passeig de Gràcia and wander a block or two, to see some of the city's best art galleries, which are concentrated in Consell de Cent, such as the Sala Dalmau or Galeria Carles Taché.

Illa de la Discòrdia

The most famous, and no doubt most visited, block on Passeig de Gràcia is between Consell de Cent and Aragó. The block, known as the **Illa de la Discòrdia** (the 'Block of Discord') gained its name because of the juxtaposition of three outstanding buildings, each of which is in a conflicting style, although they are all categorised as *modernista.*

CERDÀ

Barcelona recently celebrated the 150th anniversary of the enlightened town plan designed by liberal-minded civil engineer Ildefons Cerdà i Sunyer. When the Old Town could no longer be contained by the city walls, Cerdà's radical proposal for its extension *(eixample)* was adopted in 1859. He planned a garden city in which each block *(illa)* of housing would have a huge central open space, and there would be shady squares, as well as public facilities. In contrast to the dark lanes of the dense Old Town, his wide streets and geometric layout would let light and air into the city. Cerdà's plan was not adopted in its entirety. His 'utopian socialism' did not appeal to the more conservative elements in the city, and speculation inevitably reared its ugly head. However, its spirit has informed the strong sense of urbanism visible in Barcelona today.

There is plenty of upmarket dining in L'Eixample.

A pavement detail.

Casa Lleó Morera, designed by Lluís Domènech i Montaner and decorated with the sculptures of Eusebi Arnau, is on the corner, with an exclusive leather shop occupying the ground floor. Slightly further up is the **Casa Amatller** by Josep Puig i Cadafalch, and next door to it is Casa Batlló. Unfortunately, the Casa Lleó Morera cannot be visited, but take a peek at the extraordinary ceramic work inside its entrance. The Casa Amatller is being renovated but should open to the public in early 2014.

Casa Batlló ❸

Address: Passeig de Gràcia, 43; www.casabatllo.cat
Tel: 93-488 0666
Opening Hrs: daily 9am–9pm
Entrance fee: charge
Transport: Passeig de Gràcia

Shoppers on Passeig de Gracia.

Casa Batlló, remodelled by Gaudí in 1906 and considered the ultimate Gaudí masterpiece, has recently opened to the public for the first time in its history, despite the upper floors being occupied. The visit includes the *planta noble* (the main

This is a great part of town for shopping.

floor where the Batlló family lived), the terrace, the attic and the rooftop with its extraordinary chimneys, as well as the beautiful light well.

Declared a World Heritage site in 2005, the Casa Batlló is perhaps the most dazzling of the architect's buildings. At any time of day or night there is a small crowd on the pavement staring up at its colourful facade. The pale stone, extracted from quarries on Montjuïc hill, is delicately sculpted and, together with the balconies, almost bone-like.

The extraordinary decoration continues inside, from Sr. Batlló's office, through grand public rooms, including furniture designed by Gaudí for the Batlló family, to the roof. Ahead of his time, Gaudí came up with ingenious building solutions for ventilation or lighting which always had an attractive decorative finish. Batlló recommended his architect to Milà, and so began La Pedrera three blocks up (see page 197).

Just around the corner on busy Aragó is another Domènech i Montaner work, built in 1886 for the publishers Montaner i Simón and now the Fundació Tàpies.

Fundació Tàpies ❹

Address: Aragó, 255; www.fundacio tapies.org
Tel: 93-487 0315
Opening Hrs: Tue–Sun 10am–7pm
Entrance fee: charge
Transport: Passeig de Gràcia/ Catalunya

Observe this extraordinary building from across the street to get the full perspective, and pick out the chair in the Tàpies sculpture which crowns it, *Núvol i Cadira* (Cloud and Chair.)

Reputedly the first *modernista* building, it reflects the more rationalist ideas of Domènech i Montaner compared with Gaudí's expressionism in the ornate facade of Casa Batlló. The interior spaces make a good setting for the large collection of work by Antoni Tàpies (1923–2012), who is considered Spain's greatest artist of recent times. Excellent temporary exhibitions of modern art are also held here.

RAMBLA DE CATALUNYA ❺

After the Tàpies museum, continue to the next corner and turn right into Rambla de Catalunya, which runs parallel with Passeig de Gràcia, one block away. It is like an elongation of the Old Town's La Rambla through

The façade of Illa de la Discòrdia.

TIP

The Centre del Modernisme has information on a do-it-yourself tour of *modernista* buildings in the city, including bars and restaurants, plus discounts on entrance charges (basement of the Tourist Office, Plaça de Catalunya 17; www. rutadelmodernisme.com).

On Rambla de Catalunya.

the central part of the Eixample. The atmosphere, though, is quite different: the central boulevard is quiet and sedate, the pavement cafés are patronised by smart, middle-aged Catalans, and the shopping is sophisticated. Pop into the new shop of **Antonio Miró** (**No 125**). One of the first designers to put Catalan fashion in the limelight in the 1970s, he also designed the uniforms for the *Mossos*, the Catalan police force. Even the Liceu opera house (see page 99) has a Miró label on its velvet designer stage curtain.

REACHING THE DIAGONAL

At the end of Rambla de Catalunya, the Eixample meets the Diagonal, where there is more high-end shopping. On the right is **Casa Serra** ❻, built by Puig i Cadafalch in 1908. It was controversially adapted to accommodate the **Diputació de Barcelona**, the central government body that occupied the Palau de la Generalitat in Plaça Sant Jaume during the Franco regime, and had to be relocated with the return of democracy. In the complex designed by Milà and Correa, the new steel building seems like a large shadow of the older one.

Palau Robert ❼

Address: Passeig de Gràcia, 107; www.gencat.cat/palaurobert
Tel: 93-238 8091
Opening Hrs: Mon–Sat 10am–8pm, Sun 10am–2.30pm
Entrance fee: free
Transport: Diagonal; FGC Provença

Walk along the short stretch of Còrsega, and turn right into the gardens of the Palau Robert, a cool haven in midsummer. The house was built by a French architect and is home to the Generalitat tourist offices, with information on the rest of Catalonia (useful for daytrips or longer excursions), and regular exhibitions on general issues in Catalonia. Concerts are held in the gardens in midsummer.

Fundació Tàpies.

Cut through the side entrance to return to Passeig de Gràcia, at the busy junction of **Plaça Rei Joan Carles I**, where a constantly traffic-filled Diagonal runs across the top of the Eixample, up to Plaça Francesc Macià and the upper reaches of the city, and down towards Diagonal Mar, where it meets the sea; above it the district of Gràcia begins.

OFF THE MAIN DRAG

Back on Passeig de Gràcia, head down towards Plaça de Catalunya, cross **Rosselló** and halfway along the next block you will come to another characteristic feature of the Eixample – a passageway running through the inner part of the block. **Passatge de la Concepció** has decorative iron gates across it, but is open to the public (see margin, page 197).

Have a wander through it then return to Passeig de Gràcia via Provença. Pause on this corner to give yourself time to take in the extraordinary spectacle of Gaudí's **Casa Milà**, more often known as **La Pedrera** (the Quarry) because of its rippling grey stone facade.

La Pedrera ❽

Address: Provença, 261–265; www.lapedrera.com
Tel: 902-202 138
Opening hrs: daily Mar–Oct 9am–8pm, Nov–Feb 9am–6.30pm
Entrance fee: charge to visit building; temporary exhibitions free
Transport: Diagonal, FGC Provença

Over recent years this splendid apartment building has been cleaned and refurbished by its owners, the foundation of the savings bank CatalunyaCaixa.

At the time of its construction in 1910 it was the subject of passionate debate between enthusiasts and denigrators. For many years it was left to fall apart, but then Unesco declared it a Monument of World Interest and CatalunyaCaixa stepped in.

Take time to visit this exceptional building, which has the *Espai Gaudí*, an enlightening exhibition of the architect's work, in the attic; a spectacular roof, whose chimneys have been dubbed the 'witch-scarers'; and *El Pis*, one of the flats now open to the public and decorated as it would have been when the building was

EAT

The Passatge de la Concepció contains three chic restaurants: **Tragaluz**, meaning skylight, a fabulous example of which can be seen upstairs (see page 203), **El Japonés**, serving trendy *kushiyaki*, and newcomer **Petit Comitè**, with its traditional Catalan dishes by a star chef.

La Pedrera is one of L'Eixample's most famous buildings.

Exploring La Pedrera's rooftop.

first occupied. Major temporary exhibitions are held on the first floor (*principal*) and are open to the public free of charge.

Temple of interior design

Just up from La Pedrera, at Passeig de Gràcia, 96, is contemporary design shop **Vinçon**, based in the former home of 19th-century painter Ramón Casas, and an essential stop for design enthusiasts. Its growing empire is quietly taking over the block, so you can actually cut through the shop to **Pau Claris** or **Provença**. Before leaving, have a look at the inner patio of the block from the first floor, including a privileged rear view of La Pedrera.

Fundació Suñol

Address: Passeig de Gràcia 98; www.fundaciosunol.org
Tel: 93-496 1032
Opening Hrs: Mon–Fri 11am–2pm, 4–8pm, Sat 4–8pm
Entrance fee: charge
Transport: Diagonal, FGC Provença

Next to Vinçon is the Fundació Suñol, an important newcomer to the contemporary art scene. This huge private collection contains 20th-century works by Spanish, Catalan and some international artists. It is housed in a magnificently redesigned building now open to the public. It also has a space called 'Nivell Zero' which shows the work of emerging young artists.

More *modernista* creations

After this, turn right into Rosselló and pass the back of Puig i Cadafalch's **Palau Baró de Quadras** ❾, turning into Diagonal to reach its splendid entrance (Av. Diagonal 373). Built in 1904, it has recently been the headquarters of **Casa Asia** but is to become part of the Ramon Llull University. If public access is possible when it becomes part of the university, wander into its vestibule

Fundació Suñol.

to see the elaborate *modernista* decoration.

Walk down the Diagonal a short way to see another building by Puig i Cadafalch, the **Casa Terrades** (1903–5), also known as the **Casa de les Punxes ⑩**, at Nos 416–420. Sadly, it is not possible to go inside, but the exterior is impressive enough. Like Casa Quadras and Casa Serra, it displays Nordic neo-Gothic influences typical of Puig i Cadalfach.

At this point delve deeper into everyday Eixample and see how these architectural gems form part of a normal neighbourhood. Follow Bruc and turn right into Mallorca to **Casa Thomas** (No. 293), designed by Domènech i Montaner. At the end of the block on the opposite corner is the **Palau Montaner ⑪** (No. 278), a grand work by the same architect. Now housing government offices, it can no longer be visited.

Go down Roger de Llúria and on the next corner left again into València. On the opposite *xamfrà* (the typical chamfered corner designed by Cerdà) is **J. Múrria**, an exceptional delicatessen frozen in time, which is worth visiting for the sheer aesthetics of the place, to say nothing of its mouth-watering display of hams, cheeses and fine wines. Walk along València, past **Navarro's**, the best flower shop in town (open 24/7), until you reach the **Mercat de la Concepció ⑫** (www.laconcepcio.com). This is a fine example of a 19th-century market, remodelled in late 20th-century style with striking results.

From here zigzag block by block until you reach Mallorca and see the towering spires (and cranes) of the Sagrada Família. If you get footsore, hail a yellow and black cab to complete the journey. They are never too pricey for short rides.

The Sagrada Família is under constant construction.

SAGRADA FAMÍLIA ⑬

Address: Mallorca, 401; www.sagrada familia.cat
Tel: 93-513 2060
Opening Hrs: daily Apr–Sept 9am–8pm, Oct–Mar 9am–6pm
Entrance fee: charge
Transport: Sagrada Família

Here, in this ordinary neighbourhood, the symbol of Barcelona for many, and the reason the name Antoni Gaudí spread around the world, is a staggering sight.

Fresh produce at the Mercat de la Concepció between Carrer d'Aragó and València.

SHOPPING

The central part of the Eixample is high-end shopping, its main avenue, Passeig de Gràcia, now studded with the major international fashion houses and some Spanish and Catalan designers. The streets that crisscross have interesting smaller names and some traditional establishments remain, from bespoke tailors to high-class grocers.

Accessories

Guantes Victoriano
Mallorca, 195
A real find: in this family-run business you can still have gloves made to measure in the finest leather, choosing your own colour and style.

Loewe
Passeig de Gràcia, 35
www.loewe.com
Classic Spanish leather-makers since 1846 but constantly up-to-the-minute with fashion trends. Their iconic handbags are collectors' items, shown at their best here in the privileged setting of the Casa Lleó Morera.

Books

BCN Books
Roger de Llúria, 118
An English bookshop with a good range of travel guides, children's books and some novels, including English translations of Spanish literature.

Clothing

Adolfo Dominguez
Passeig de Gràcia, 32
The man who made it cool to wear crushed linen is still producing elegant clothes for men and women and recently has introduced a kids' line.

Antonio Miró
Rambla de Catalunya 125

www.antoniomiro.com
King of the new wave of Catalan fashion which emerged in the post-Franco era, Antonio Miró's classics for men and women are now complemented with his household designs in this new kind of shopping space, where you're invited to enjoy a coffee.

La Coqueteria
Girona, 60
A real boutique, this attractive small shop in the middle of a residential zone specialises in independent designers, always with a romantic flavour.

Purificación Garcia
Provença, 292
www.purificaciongarcia.com
Where some Spanish designers have dropped by the wayside, Galician Purificación Garcia has managed to resist and now has shops all over the world. Practical, well-designed fashion for men and women, and accessories.

Food

Colmado Quilez
Rambla Catalunya, 63
A wide selection of traditional food, wines and spirits, served by charming and attentive staff in blue smocks.

J.Múrria
Roger de Llúria, 85
www.murria.cat
This traditional grocer's shop purveys exquisite fine fare in immaculately preserved *modernista* surroundings where the service also seems to come from another era. Go to see this shop even if you don't intend to buy.

Home

Pilma
Avinguda Diagonal, 403
www.pilma.com

A surprisingly huge space for the centre of town, crammed with desirable objects for the home, from stylish sofas to designer kitchenware, including tasteful gift solutions.

Vinçon
Passeig de Gràcia, 96
Tel: 93-215 6050
www.vincon.com
See how trendy Barcelonans decorate their homes by wandering around this temple of interior design in the former *modernista* home of painter Ramón Casas. Be sure to visit the furniture display on the magnificent first floor and go out to see a fine example of an Eixample inner patio (plus a privileged view of La Pedrera).

Malls

Bulevard Rosa
Passeig de Gràcia, 55
www.bulevardrosa.com
A small-scale mall which never seems noisy or overcrowded, housing independent boutiques rather than chains, like the luscious leather bags and belts of Beatriz Furest or the hilarious T-shirts and accessories from Basque company kukuxumusu.

Shoes

Carmina
Passeig de Gràcia, 108
www.carminashoemaker.com
You'll find immaculate brogues for men and women in soft leather and suede among this range of classical shoes hand-crafted in Mallorca. Don't expect to pay less than €300.

Tascón
Rambla de Catalunya 42
There are several branches of this store around town, all selling the best Spanish brands like Dorotea and Lottusse and some international brands.

The temple was actually begun in 1882 as a neo-Gothic structure under the direction of the architect Francesc P. Villar. Gaudí took over the project a year later, using Villar's plans as a starting point, but greatly expanding their scale and originality. It became Gaudí's main project for the rest of his life. He realised long before he died that he would not live to see its completion, but he compared it with the building of great Gothic cathedrals in the past: 'It is not possible for one generation to erect the entire temple.'

At the time of his death in 1926 only the crypt, apse, part of the Nativity facade and one tower had been completed. Today, nearly 90 years after Gaudí's death, work progresses well under successive architects, aided by the latest technology but always interpreting Gaudí's plans. By 2010 the naves were finally roofed over and Pope Benedict XVI came to consecrate them, granting the church the status of basilica.

This extraordinary building is best tackled in the morning rather than at the end of a long day's sightseeing, as there is much to see, though you may find shorter queues and fewer tour groups in the afternoon. Purchase tickets online to avoid the queues that wind around the block (http://visit.sagradafamilia.cat). For more information on the Sagrada Família's main features, see page 204.

Along Avinguda de Gaudí is the less well-known *modernista* complex, the **Hospital Sant Pau** ⑭ (1902–12), a fascinating World Heritage site. Made up of over 20 buildings, it is the work of the prolific Domènech i Montaner. A public hospital until 2009, it is now being renovated to accommodate various institutions. In theory it can be visited on a guided tour but this may be subject to changes. Check with tourist offices (English tours daily 10am, 11am, noon, 1pm with discounts).

Parc Joan Miró

Venturing beyond the central part of the Eixample is a good way to complete the picture of Barcelona from the mid-19th century to the present day. On the extreme left of the Eixample is one of the first urban parks created in the 1980s. Covering four Eixample blocks above Plaça d'Espanya, where Diputació and Aragó meet Tarragona (metro Espanya or Tarragona), is the **Parc Joan Miró**. It is a great area for kids to run wild in. The 22-metre (70ft)-high Miró statue *Dona i Ocell* (Woman and Bird) is striking in its simple setting on a small island in the middle of a pool. One of Miró's last works, it was unveiled in 1983, just a few months before he died.

You could link a visit to the park with a trip to Montjuïc (see page 173). Alternatively, combine it with a walk along Gran Via or a parallel street to get a sense of the day-to-day life of the city. The apartment blocks along this route follow the Cerdà plan, even though, on the whole, they grew up later and are more modest than earlier buildings in the central Eixample.

Parc Joan Miró is also known as the Parc de l'Escorxador, because it was the location of the municipal slaughterhouse until 1979.

Hospital Sant Pau, by Domènech i Montaner.

RESTAURANTS, BARS AND CAFÉS

Restaurants

Catalan

Alkimia
Industria, 79
Tel: 93-207 6115
www.alkimia.cat
Open: Mon–Fri L & D. €€€€ [⑨⓪ p288, D2]
A shining example of the new talent in Catalan cuisine, young chef Jordi Vilà is the alchemist in question, working wonders on ordinary Catalan dishes and converting them into something quite delicious. With its Michelin star, it is one of Barcelona's leading restaurants.

El Caballito Blanco
Mallorca, 196

Tragaluz.

Tel: 93-453 1033
Open: Tue–Sat L & D, Sun L. €€€ [⑨① p288, A3]
This is an old-fashioned, popular place that always has traditional Catalan dishes from which to choose. The fresh ingredients are selected according to what is in season. It's a relief to find places like this have escaped being redesigned and relaunched in 21st-century Barcelona.

Casa Amalia
Passatge Mercat, 4
Tel: 93-458 9458
www.casamaliabcn.com
Open: Tue–Sat L & D, Sun L. €€ (set menu L Tue–Fri €) [⑨② p288, C3]
This bustling, local spot serves the freshest food sourced from the Concepció market nearby, in a family atmosphere dating back to 1950. Excellent-value *menú del día*.

Cata 1.81
València, 181
Tel: 93-323 6818

www.cata181.net
Open: Mon–Sat D (from 6pm). €€ [⑨③ p288, A3]
The main point of this sophisticated little bar is to taste an excellent range of different wines (*cata* is a tasting), served in quarter-litre decanters. However, the tiny accompanying dishes have taken on equal importance and come in a wild mixture of flavours in true new-Catalan style.

Fastvínic
Diputació, 251
Tel: 93-487 3241
www.fastvinic.com
Open: Mon–Sat L & D. € [⑨④ p288, B4]
The first restaurant in Catalonia to receive the LEED Gold certificate, this new-concept, good-looking, sustainable place serves unique sandwiches using locally sourced seasonal products based on Catalan dishes. Try a pig's trotter or river trout and fennel sandwich accompanied by one of 24 Catalan wines.

Ferrum
Còrsega, 400
Tel: 93-457 7610
www.ferrum.es
Open: Mon–Sat L & D. €€€ [⑨⑤ p288, C2]
Attentive discreet service and soothing atmosphere combined with top-quality creative Catalan cooking at a reasonable price add up to a winning combination. Half-portions available. The cocktail bar next door makes a good starting point.

Ponsa
Enric Granados, 89
Tel: 93-453 1037
Open: Daily L & D. €–€€ [⑨⑥ p288, A2]
A highly polished classic from the 1940s. Old-fashioned good taste and great traditional Catalan food, in one of the most attractive streets of the Eixample.

Roca Moo
Hotel Omm, Rosselló, 265
Tel: 93-445 4000
www.hotelomm.es/roca-barcelona

Open: Tue–Sat L & D. €€€€ (midday menu €€€) [**97** p288, B2]
Designer food for the very fashionable Hotel Omm. Sleek surroundings and delectable modern Catalan cuisine supervised by the award-winning Roca brothers. For a less formal snack, try the Roca Bar in the hotel lobby, where 'street food' is served all day.

International

Au Port de la Lune
Pau Claris, 103
Tel: 93-412 2224
Open: Daily L & D. €€ [**98** p288, B4]
A poster of Serge Gainsbourg and a sign saying 'No coca cola, nor will there ever be' are the only clues to this neutral-looking café's provenance. However, the menu features steak tartare, *cassoulet* and herrings. Even the salad dressing tastes French. This is genuine 'cuisine'.

Tragaluz
Passatge de la Concepció, 5
Tel: 93-487 0621
Open: Daily L & D. €€–€€€ [**99** p288, B2]
The flagship of this unfailingly successful group, this place shot to fame in the early '90s as one of the first designer restaurants. It has recently been brought up to 21st-century speed, but retains its original charms and excellent Mediterranean cuisine. The eponymous skylight (*tragaluz*) is bigger than ever so you feel as if you are on a sunlit terrace. On the ground floor is El Japonés, with a Japanese charcoal grill for making *kushiyaki*.

Spanish

Bodega Sepúlveda
Sepúlveda, 173
Tel: 93-323 5944
www.bodegasepulveda.net
Open: Mon–Fri L & D, Sat D. €€–€€€ [**100** p284, E1]
Atmospheric old bodega run by the same family since 1952, with tiled walls and crisp white tablecloths. Delicious traditional tapas like *tortilla de bacalao* (salt-cod omelette) or scrambled eggs with wild mushrooms and squid.

La Bodegueta
Rambla de Catalunya, 100
Tel: 93-215 4894
http://rambla.labodegueta.cat
Open: Mon–Sat L & D (tapas), Sun D. € [**101** p288, B3]
Spain was once full of bodegas like this one, with massive old fridges, barrels and marble tables where you can accompany the rough red wine with olives, *tacos de manchego* and a plate of *jamón serrano*. Happily, here you can still do so. It now has tables on Rambla de Catalunya, but the atmosphere inside is better.

Bars and Cafés

Bracafé
Casp, 2
Tel: 93-302 3082
www.bracafe.com
[**36** p288, B4]
For a business-like shot of coffee at any time of day at the bar or a leisurely *cafè amb llet* on the terrace, this is the place. Just off Passeig de Gràcia, it has attracted office workers and elegant shoppers since 1929.

Café Adonis
Bailén, 188
Tel: 93-459 1292
www.bracafe.com
[**37** p288, C2]
The original 1940 café has been revived and rejuvenated, making for an appealing combination with Parisian overtones. It's a great place to stop for coffee or *una copa* (a drink) on your way to or from the Sagrada Família.

Cornelia & Co
Valencia, 225
Tel: 93-272 3956
www.corneliaandco.com
[**38** p288, B3]
Aka 'The Daily Picnic Store', this good-looking space sells delicious, top-level produce to take away, or to eat with a coffee or drink at one of their long tables getting to know the local executives. Very helpful staff.

Dry Martini
Aribau, 162
Tel: 93-217 5072
[**39** p288, A2]
Whether you like your martini shaken or stirred, go no further for the perfect cocktail. Sink into a leather armchair and enjoy the moment in this legendary bar, one of the top 25 bars in the world according to *Drinks International* magazine.

Laie Librería Café
Pau Claris, 85
Tel: 93-318 1739
www.laie.es/pauclaris
[**40** p288, B4]
An excellent bookshop that now has branches in many of the leading cultural centres around the city, but in this one you can enjoy a coffee or have lunch in the attractive surroundings of a typical Eixample building, with a terrace at the back.

Mauri
Rambla de Catalunya, 102
Tel: 93-215 1020
www.pasteleriasmauri.com
[**41** p288, B2]
A time-honoured pastry shop selling delicate cakes and sandwiches as well as ready-made savoury dishes to its elegant clientele, who chat in the tea room. Its new terrace on Rambla de Catalunya makes an ideal spot for watching the well-dressed Catalans strolling.

Primavera Café
Bruc, 121
Tel: 626-651 544 (mobile)
[**42** p288, C3]
Small neighbourhood café with friendly atmosphere offering a broader range than the usual croissant-and-coffee breakfast, including muffins, bagels and different teas. By the evening, cocktails join the mix.

Xixbar
Rocafort, 19
Tel: 93-423 4314
www.xixbar.com
[**43** p284, D1]
A former dairy where two cows provided the daily milk, lined with the original blue and white checked tiles, makes a pretty backdrop for this bar, whose mission is to provide the most perfect gin and tonics in town.

THE SAGRADA FAMILIA

The Sagrada Família, unofficial symbol of the city and the most visited of its sights, was dreamed up by a religious patriot with astonishing vision.

Antoni Gaudí i Cornet was born in Reus in 1852 and studied in Barcelona's School of Architecture. His principal patron, industrialist Eusebi Güell, certainly believed in him, commissioning him to design Palau Güell (see page 101), Park Güell (see page 207) and the crypt at Colònia Güell (see page 225). La Pedrera, his best-known town dwelling, is a Unesco monument (see page 197).

Undoubtedly Gaudí's greatest work, however, was the Temple Expiatori de la Sagrada Família (Expiatory Temple of the Holy Family), which he embarked on at the age of 31. Deeply religious and a passionate Catalan, Gaudí spent his last years devoted to this enormous project, which he knew future generations would have to finish. When he was fatally injured by a tram in 1926, the only parts of the church completed were the Nativity facade, one tower, the apse and the crypt, where he is buried. By 2010 the nave was covered and consecrated by Pope Benedict XVI in a grand ceremony. Today the work continues, with an optimistic completion date of 2026, the centenary of the great architect's death.

The Pasión (Passion) facade, with sculptures of gaunt, tormented characters by Josep Maria Subirachs.

The Essentials

Address: Mallorca, 401, www.sagradafamilia.cat
Tel: 93-513 2060
Opening Hrs: daily Apr–Sept 9am–8pm, Oct–Mar 9am–6pm; guided vists in English available 4 times a day
Entrance Fee: charge
Transport: Sagrada Família

Stained glass windows are just one of the cathedral's features.

The cathedral has been under construction since 1882 and is yet to be completed.

Interior details include stained glass and carvings.

THE HIGHLIGHTS

The intricacy of the exterior up close.

Passion Facade Visitors enter through the west face, where angular figures of Christ's Passion have been sculpted by contemporary Catalan artist Josep Maria Subirachs, an avowed atheist.

The Nave Running north–south, the nave has a forest of tree-like pillars. Gaudí eschewed straight lines.

The Towers For a view over church and city, you have to take a lift to the top of one of the spindly towers that rise above the east and west facades, sparkling with Venetian mosaics and tinkling with bells. When it is complete, there will be 18 towers, the tallest rising to 172.5 metres (566ft).

Nativity Facade On the east side of the building is the only facade completed by Gaudí, in 1904. Elaborately carved and dripping with symbolism, its doorways represent Faith, Hope and Charity.

Ambulatory This external cloister will provide a sheltered walkway all the way round the outside of the building.

The Crypt and Museum The neo-gothic crypt, by the original architect, Francesc de Paula Villar i Lozano, who was employed for just one year before Gaudí took over. The museum is a must, with models of the church, photographs and an informative audiovisual. most of Gaudí's plans and models were destroyed during the Civil War but they have been painstakingly reconstructed.

A close-up of one of the cathedral's towers.

ABOVE THE DIAGONAL

Avinguda Diagonal effectively cuts the city in two. In the little-explored area above this divide are some of the city's most distinctive districts and worthwhile excursions.

The Diagonal is the name of the arterial road that slices through the city at an angle, from its western boundary in the Les Corts district right down to where it meets the sea. Two well-worn clichés about the city are that it has traditionally turned its back to the sea, and that people who live above the Diagonal never venture below it. Neither are now true. The development of the waterfront in the 1990s succeeded in dispelling the former and, along with the whole urban-renewal programme, has drawn uptown people downtown.

Many visitors to Barcelona never make it above the Diagonal, but the Park Güell is among the few isolated pockets here that are well trodden.

PARK GÜELL ❶

Address: Olot, 1–13
Tel: 010
Opening Hrs: fpark daily, May–Sept 10am–9pm, Apr and Oct 10am–8pm, Mar and Nov 10am–7pm, Dec–Feb 10am–6pm
Entrance fee: charge for park, Casa-Museu Gaudí and Casa del Guarda
Transport: Lesseps, then 20-minute walk or Vallcarca, then escalators; buses 24, 92

Designed by Antoni Gaudí, Park Güell is the second-most visited park in Barcelona after the Ciutadella. Gaudí's faithful patron, industrialist Eusebi Güell, commissioned him to build it along the lines of an English garden suburb.

The estate was to encompass 60 building plots, but only five buildings were completed: the two pavilions flanking the entrance, both designed by Gaudí, and three others inside the park, one of which is today the Casa-Museu Gaudí. One of the

The view back from Tibidabo hill.

TIP

Getting to the main sites above the Diagonal is easy. For Park Güell take metro line 3 to Lesseps and walk, or Vallcarca and take the escalators up to a side entrance. The Palau Reial de Pedralbes is also on metro line 3.

pavilions, the Casa del Guarda, has a permanent exhibition on the park, Gaudí and Barcelona in the time of *modernisme*.

(For more information on Park Güell, see page 220)

GRÀCIA

The Park Güell is in the upper part of the district of **Gràcia** ❷, also 'above the Diagonal' but without the connotations described on page 207. On the contrary, it is a neighbourhood with its own history and distinctive personality, preserved in the narrow streets and squares,

which have managed to keep out large-scale projects and expensive residential developments.

Traditionally Gràcia was a *barri* of artisans. Generations of families remain loyal to the district, and since the 19th century a strong gypsy community has been well integrated here. There are few newcomers, apart from a small number of young people, students and a sprinkling of foreigners charmed by the district's down-to-earth character.

The *vila* (a cut above 'village') of Gràcia was once reached from Barcelona by a track through open

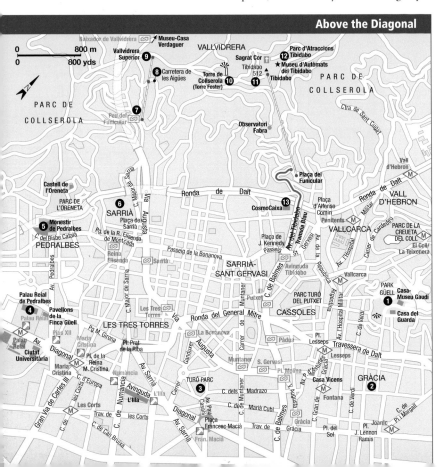

Above the Diagonal

A drink in Plaça del Sol.

doors open to reveal an array of bars and restaurants, ranging from typical Catalan to Lebanese. You need to visit Gràcia both during the day and in the evening to appreciate its charms fully.

Plaça del Sol

The whole area is dotted with attractive *plaças*; look out for the lively Plaça del Sol, which functions as an unofficial centre for the district. Nearby is the **Verdi** multiscreen cinema in a long street of the same name; it always shows *v.o.* (original version) films.

There is an early Gaudí house, **Casa Vicens** (closed to the public), in **Carolines**, a street on the other side of Gran de Gràcia, just above metro Fontana. It is worth a quick detour to see the facade of this striking house, which Gaudí built for a tile manufacturer.

TURÓ PARC ❸

By contrast with Gràcia, a classic example of residential life 'above the Diagonal' is the area around Turó Parc, pinpointed by the roundabout

fields (today's Passeig de Gràcia, see page 193). Its established buildings imposed the upper limit on the Eixample, Cerdà's 19th-century expansion plan for Barcelona; the streets of **Còrsega** and **Bailèn** were built right up to its sides. The upper boundary is loosely **Travessera de Dalt**, and on the western side **Príncep d'Astúries**, although the official municipal district extends a little further.

Gran de Gràcia

The main route into Gràcia is along Gran de Gràcia, the continuation of Passeig de Gràcia, but it is also well served by the metro (Fontana and Lesseps L3; Joanic L4; Gràcia FGC line). Gran de Gràcia is a busy but elegant street full of shops and *modernista* apartment blocks. It also has one of the best and most expensive fish restaurants in the city, the Galician **Botafumeiro** (see page 219).

Walking up the hill, take any of the turnings to the right and zigzag up through streets bustling with small businesses, workshops, wonderfully dated grocer's shops and trendy fashion shops. At night, shuttered

Posing in Park Güell.

Plaça Francesc Macià (on many bus routes), where one begins to leave the 19th-century Eixample and enter the upper reaches of the Diagonal. Modern office blocks, hotels, smart shops and expensive properties are the trademark. In the park, just at the end of **Pau Casals** (a monument to the famous Catalan cellist is at the entrance), it is not uncommon to see children playing under the watchful eye of a fully uniformed nanny.

Also known as **Jardins Poeta Eduard Marquina**, the park was a project of landscape architect Rubió i Tudurí, and has two distinct areas. One is made up of lawn, hedges and flowerbeds laid out in a classic geometric pattern, the other contains children's playgrounds, a small lake and an open-air theatre. Sculptures by Clarà and Viladomat, among others, dot the interior of the park.

From Plaça Francesc Macià the Diagonal is wider and the traffic faster, revving up for one of the main routes out of town. Walk, or catch a bus or tram, to the gardens of the Palau Reial de Pedralbes, passing the shopping centre L'Illa on the left.

Statue of Isabel II presenting her son Alfonso XII, outside the Palau de Pedralbes.

Palau Reial de Pedralbes ❹

Address: Diagonal, 686
Opening Hrs: grounds daily 10am–nightfall
Entrance fee: free
Transport: Palau Reial

The Royal Palace is the result of a 1919 conversion of the antique Can Feliu into a residence for King Alfonso XIII during his visits to Barcelona. It is elegant, and the

Palau Reial de Pedralbes.

classical garden peaceful, but it has little sense of history.

The palace is currently closed to the public as its former collections have been moved to the brand new Design Museum (see page 167) and it is only used for official occasions. However, the gardens make a pleasant place to stroll and unwind and provide an ideal setting for a new summer music festival featuring an eclectic mix of stars like Julio Iglesias and Antony and the Johnsons (www.festivalpedralbes.com).

The grounds

The garden, built to a 'geometric decorative outline' in the 1920s, also by Rubió i Tudurí, integrated the existing palace garden with land ceded by Count Güell. What remains of his neighbouring estate are the lodge and gates, the **Pavellons de la Finca Güell** (Avinguda Pedralbes, 7; access by guided tour only, Sat–Sun am; charge), designed by Gaudí. Guarded

by an awesome iron dragon gate, also created by Gaudí, one building was the caretaker's lodge and the other was the stable block. The lodge interior is simple but with the distinct stamp of Gaudí, particularly the use of brightly coloured ceramic tiles. Built between 1884 and 1887, this was one of his earlier commissions.

Monestir de Pedralbes ⑤

Address: Baixada del Monestir, 9; www.museuhistoria.bcn.es
Tel: 93-256 3434
Opening Hrs: summer Tue–Fri 10am–5pm, winter until 2pm, Sat 10am-7pm, Sun 10am–8pm, winter until 5pm
Entrance fee: charge (combined ticket with MHCB available, see page 118), free Sun from 3pm
Transport: Palau Reial; FGC Reina Elisenda

At the top of Avinguda Pedralbes, by the Creu (cross) de Pedralbes, are the welcomingly old stones of the

The Monestir de Pedralbes.

Soaking up the views from Tibidabo.

Monestir de Pedralbes. This is one of the most peaceful corners of the city.

The monastery was founded in 1326 by Queen Elisenda de Montcada, widow (and fourth wife) of King Jaume II. She herself took the vows of the Order of St Clare, and today some 20 nuns are still in residence in an adjacent building. The fine Gothic architecture, most notably the unusual three-tiered cloister, evokes the spiritual side of monastic life, while the rooms that are open to the public provide an insight into the day-to-day life of the monastery's inhabitants. There are some remarkable 14th-century murals by the Catalan artist Ferrer Bassa.

SARRIÀ

While up here, take the opportunity to visit **Sarrià** ❻ by taking Passeig Reina Elisenda de Montcada, which leads straight into **Plaça Sarrià** (also reached in under 10 minutes from Plaça de Catalunya and other central stations on the FGC line). Recognisable as a former village, despite being a sought-after city residence today, it is more charming than Pedralbes, and the wealth more discreet.

This is a real neighbourhood with a market, old ladies in cardigans queuing for lottery tickets, local bars, and the attractive church of **Sant Vicenç** at the centre of things. The main street leading down from the church, **Major de Sarrià**, encourages strolling. The pastry shop **Foix de Sarrià**, founded in 1886, makes an elegant corner. **Casa Joana**, another old established business and little changed, still serves good home cooking at a reasonable price.

Parc de Collserola

From Sarrià you can get a taste of the **Parc de Collserola** by taking a walk on the city side of the hill, overlooking the whole of Barcelona (see box, page 214). The trip is equally

The Torre de Collserola from below.

manageable from the centre with the efficient and frequent FGC train service from Plaça de Catalunya.

The Parc de Collserola is a green belt measuring 17 by 6km (11 by 4 miles), which is on the city's doorstep. Its 8,000 hectares (20,000 acres) of vegetation border the Ronda de Dalt ring road, and spread over the Collserola range of hills to Sant Cugat and beyond.

This easily accessible area is a bonus to city living. It is best known for its highest peak, Tibidabo (512 metres/1,680ft) and its distinctive skyline, with the Sagrat Cor church, a 20th-century confection, and the Torre de Collserola communications tower forming a dramatic backdrop to Barcelona.

The funicular

Reach the Parc by taking the FGC train to **Peu del Funicular** 7 ('foot of the funicular'), which leads up to Vallvidrera, a suburban village on the crest of the hill where the desirable homes come with a spectacular view. There are frequent services from this station, which, by particular request (at the press of a button), will stop halfway to Vallvidrera at **Carretera de les Aigües** 8 (see box, page 214), where you may want to continue on foot.

Alternatively, take the funicular as far as **Vallvidrera Superior** ❾, an attractive *modernista* station in this pleasant village, evocative of the days when city dwellers would spend the summer up here for the cooler air. The air still feels a few degrees cooler, even in the height of summer, and definitely cleaner.

Torre de Collserola ❿

Address: Carretera Vallvidrera–Tibidabo, 8–12; www.torredecollserola.com
Tel: 93-211 7942
Opening Hrs: July–Aug Wed–Sun noon–2pm, 3.15–8pm, Mar–June and Sept–Dec Sat–Sun noon–2pm, 3.15–7pm; check website for earlier closing times off season
Entrance fee: charge
Transport: No. 111

View from the Torre de Collserola.

Inside the Torre de Collserola.

High flying at the Parc d'Atraccions.

The No. 111 bus will take you to the striking communications tower, the **Torre de Collserola**, designed by Norman Foster for the Olympics and sometimes known as the **Torre Foster**. Up close it is even more impressive than from afar, with giant stays anchoring it to the hill. A lift will take you up to the observation deck on the 10th floor for a panoramic view 560 metres (1,837ft) above sea level. On clear days you can see as far as Montserrat or the Pyrenees.

The other side of the hill

The Collserola Park on the other side of the hill is another world, yet it is only a short train ride through the tunnel after the Peu del Funicular stop to **Baixador de Vallvidrera** station (just 13 minutes direct from Plaça de Catalunya). The contrast of the pine-scented cooler air that hits you as the train doors open is quite extraordinary. Walk up a path to the information centre, the **Centre d'Informació del Parc de Collserola** (www.parcnaturalcollserola.cat; daily 9.30am–3pm), a helpful base with an exhibition about the park's wildlife, maps and a bar/restaurant.

Close to it is **Villa Joana**, also known as the Museu-Casa Verdaguer

RECOMMENDED WALK

If you take the funicular, or 'funi', up to Vallvidrera, consider getting off at the Carretera de les Aigües, a track cut into the side of the hill that winds around to beyond Tibidabo. Popular with joggers, cyclists, ramblers and dog-walkers, it is perfect for stretching city legs, particularly on bright blue, pollution-free days, when the views are breathtaking. For an enjoyable round trip, walk as far as the point where the track crosses the Tibidabo funicular, where a badly indicated footpath leads down to the Plaça del Funicular. Once here, catch the tram, or walk to Avinguda Tibidabo FGC station, which will return you to the city centre.

(Carretera de l'Església, 104; Sat–Sun 10am–2pm; free; FGC: Baixador de Vallvidrera), an atmospheric 18th-century house. This is where the much-loved Catalan poet Jacint Verdaguer lived until his death in 1902. It is now a museum dedicated to the poet, with some rooms preserved from the year he died. Various footpaths lead off into the woods of pine and cork oak to *fonts* (natural springs) and picnic spots. After several days in the steamy city, this area is the perfect antidote.

TIBIDABO ⑪

The best-known summit of the Collserola range is Tibidabo, with its legendary funfair. Its popularity means moving in large crowds and queuing, but it still has its charms. You can reach the summit from Sarrià, by walking along Bonanova, which leads to Avinguda del Tibidabo, becoming Passeig Sant Gervasi at the end. It is a tiring street to walk along as it is always congested. The bus journey is more pleasant and offers an interesting slice of life.

However, a trip to Tibidabo is more likely to be a day's or half-day's excursion directly from the centre of town. The FGC train goes to Avinguda Tibidabo station. Coming out in **Plaça de John Kennedy**, pause a moment to take in the colours of La Rotonda, a *modernista* house opposite, which is due for renovation.

The Tramvia Blau

At the base of Avinguda Tibidabo, the ancient Tramvia Blau (blue tram) rattles up the hill, passing beautiful *modernista* houses. The avenue's former elegance is now diminished, many of the large houses having been converted into institutions, advertising agencies or flats.

The tram stops at the **Plaça del Funicular**, where there are attractive

Find a planetarium and giant Pirarucu fish at CosmoCaixa.

bars and **La Venta**, a good restaurant with a pretty terrace (see page 219).

The Top of Tibidabo

From Plaça del Funicular you can catch the funicular to the funfair at the summit. This lofty playground has been a popular tradition since the turn of the 20th century. It tends to look more interesting from a distance, but the views are spectacular – and children love it. The church,

Sagrat Cor church.

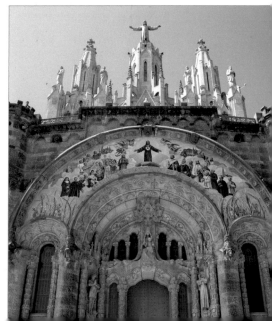

In the aquarium.

the **Sagrat Cor**, topped by the figure of Christ, has little charm, but this doesn't prevent the crowds flocking to it. Floodlit at night, it forms a dramatic part of the Barcelona skyline.

Parc d'Atraccions ⑫

Address: Plaça del Tibidabo; www.tibidabo.cat
Tel: 93-211 7942
Opening Hrs: Mar–Apr Sat–Sun

SHOPPING

You'll find a wide range of shopping opportunities in this large area, from the small boutiques of Gràcia to classy fashion names on and around the Avinguda Diagonal.

Clothing

Camiseria Pons
Gran de Gràcia, 49
www.camiseriapons.com
A shirt shop from 1900 relaunched in the 1980s to sell contemporary designer clothes for men and women, behind a wonderfully preserved shop front and respecting plenty of original interior detail.
Jean Pierre Bua
Avinguda Diagonal, 467–469

http://jeanpierrebua.com
A reference point in the fashion world, this was one of the first shops to bring in major Paris labels and now has one of the best selections you'll find in Barcelona of top international designers.
Lydia Delgado
Minerva, 21
www.lydiadelgado.es
This Barcelona-based ballerina-turned-fashion-designer creates feminine clothes in gorgeous fabrics and now works in conjunction with her daughter-designer Miranda Makaroff.
El Piano Tina Garcia
Verdi, 20

This small shop and its brother, Piano Man, at number 15 sell well-designed kit at reasonable prices, in this buzzy street in the heart of Gràcia, where you'll also find plenty of other options.

Malls

L'illa Diagonal
Avinguda Diagonal 557
www.lilla.com
A cut above most shopping centres, as befits its uptown location, with a good range of designers and up-market brands as well as the favourite chains like Zara and Mango. Also offers a good range of restaurants and snack bars.

noon–8pm, May–June & Sept Sat–Sun noon–9pm, July Wed–Fri noon–9pm, Sat noon–11pm, Sun noon–10pm, Aug Mon–Thu noon–10pm, Fri–Sun noon–11pm, Oct Sat noon–9pm, Sun noon–8pm, Nov–mid-Dec and mid-Jan–Feb Sat–Sun noon–6pm

Entrance fee: tickets allow unlimited access to the rides; cheaper tickets for just six rides are also available

Transport: Tramvia Blau/funicular from Plaça del Funicular or Tibibus from Plaça de Catalunya

This funfair has a wonderful retro air. Some of its attractions date back to 1901, when the funicular first reached the top, and some are from renovations that took place in 1986. There is also a museum of automatons, the **Museu d'Autòmats**, displaying pieces made between 1901 and 1954. The tram, funicular and bus run in conjunction with the opening times.

CosmoCaixa ⑬

Address: Isaac Newton, 26; www.obrasocial.lacaixa.es
Tel: 93-212 6050

Opening Hrs: Tue–Sun 10am–8pm, also Mon during late June–Sept
Entrance fee: charge
Transport: FGC Avinguda Tibidabo; 196

A few minutes' walk from Plaça John Kennedy (walk up Avinguda Tibidabo from the FGC station and turn left onto Teodor Roviralta) is one of the most exciting science museums in Europe, the CosmoCaixa, with plenty of hands-on exhibits and interesting temporary exhibitions for all ages. Even three- to six-year-olds are catered for in the 'Clik dels Nens', a space to play and learn in created by the high-profile designer Javier Mariscal.

There are many other innovative ways to enlighten the public on the subjects of science and technology. Among the highlights are the Flooded Forest, a recreation of part of the Amazon rainforest, the Geological Wall and the large outdoor Plaça de la Ciència, with interactive modules. The museum is funded by the affluent cultural foundation of La Caixa savings bank.

The view from Tibidabo's hill, over the theme park and city.

RESTAURANTS, BARS AND CAFÉS

PRICE CATEGORIES

Prices for a three-course dinner per person with a bottle of house wine:
€ = under €25
€€ = €25–40
€€€ = €40–60
€€€€ = over €60

Restaurants

This area covers a lot of ground, so it has an equally broad range of restaurants, cafés and bars, from inexpensive student haunts and 'ethnic' restaurants in the Gràcia neighbourhood to top-notch Michelin-starred restaurants in the smarter zones and rustic outdoor restaurants in Collserola Park.

Catalan

A Contraluz
Milanesat, 19
Tel: 93-203 0658
www.acontraluz.com
Open: Daily L & D. **€€€** (set menu **€**)
[off map]
In a quiet street in the smart residential Tres Torres area (en route to the Monestir de Pedralbes), this

Retro chic at Flash-Flash.

house and garden make a relaxing place to dine, and frequented by a fashionable clientele. The reasonably priced lunchtime menu is a good option.

Abac
Av. Tibidabo, 1
Tel: 93-319 6600
www.abacbarcelona.com
Open: Tue–Sat L & D. **€€€€** [off map]
With three Michelin stars to his name, young chef Jordi Cruz continues to reach creative heights in this exclusive restaurant in its own garden, which comes with 15 hotel rooms and a spa. An indulgent night for travelling gourmets is guaranteed.

Casa Joana
Major de Sarrià, 59
Tel: 93-203 1036
Open: Mon–Sat L & D. **€** [off map]
Very good value for this generally expensive part of town, especially the midday menu. A genuine, family-run restaurant where it's good to choose traditional dishes like *canelons*.

Casa Trampa
Plaça de Vallvidrera, 3
Tel: 93-406 8051
www.restaurantecasatrampa.com
Open: Tue–Thu & Sun L, Fri–Sat L & D. **€**
[off map]
Traditional, homely Catalan restaurant with food to match, right in the centre of this charming 'village' that is part of the city. Their *croquetas* are a must. It is just a funicular ride away and well worth the trip. Combine a meal here with a walk in the Collserola Park. Closed in August.

Hisop
Passatge Marimon, 9
Tel: 93-241 3233
Open: Mon–Fri L & D, Sat D. **€€€** [102 p288, A1]
Catalan chef Oriol Ivern practises the latest culinary art of deconstructivism with amazing results in this minimalist restaurant, much acclaimed by foodies and proud

winner of a Michelin star.

Roig Robí
Sèneca, 20
Tel: 93-218 9222
www.roigrobi.com
Open: Mon–Fri L & D, Sat D. **€€€€** [103 p288, B2]
Mercè Navarro's famed restaurant is a beautifully subtle, elegant space with an inner garden, and food and service to match the high standard of the surroundings. A favourite with locals in the know.

International

Amir de Nit
Plaça del Sol, 2
Tel: 93-218 5121
Open: Daily L & D. **€** [104 p288, B1]
There are quite a few Lebanese places in Barcelona now, but this has always been a firm favourite. It has a large choice of well-prepared, delicious dishes, and its location in one corner of this popular square in Gràcia is perfect, especially for eating alfresco on a summer evening.

Flash-Flash
Granada del Penedès, 25
Tel: 93-237 0990
www.flashflashbarcelona.com
Open: Daily L & D. **€–€€** [105 p288, A1]
Almost a period piece now, this bar was super-trendy in the 1970s. Its wonderful white leatherette seating and black-and-white Warhol-type prints on the walls still have a lot of style and it's a great place for tortillas (there are over 50 varieties to choose from) and hamburgers; the cheesecake is legendary.

Fragments Café
Plaça de la Concòrdia, 12
Tel: 93-419 9613
Open: Tue–Sat L & D. **€–€€** [106 p282, C1]
In a quiet square away from the tourist throngs, this pretty bar-restaurant serves *vermuts* and tapas on its terrace and delicious meals, including creative pasta dishes, at the bar or in its prized garden.

Spanish

Bilbao
Perill, 33
Tel: 93-458 9624
Open: Mon–Sat L & D. €€ [107 p288, C2]
Find an animated atmosphere in this traditional eatery in Gràcia, frequented mainly by journalists, artists and writers. Especially busy at lunchtime. Try to get a table in the main part downstairs to enjoy the scene.

Botafumeiro
Gran de Gràcia, 81
Tel: 93-218 4230
www.botafumeiro.es
Open: Daily L & D. €€€€ [106 p288, B1]
This smart Galician restaurant, haunt of the rich and famous, has a long-running reputation as *the* place to eat seafood in Barcelona. Oysters are served at the bar.

Envalira
Plaça del Sol, 13
Tel: 93-218 5813
Open: Tue–Sat L & D, Sun L. €€–€€€ [109 p288, B1]
A classic in the heart of Gràcia whose decoration does not seem to have changed in all the years the family has run it, but where you can be sure of an excellent *arroz* (rice dishes, including paella). The house speciality is *arroz a la milanesa*. This is Spanish cooking at its most genuine.

El Jardí de l'Abadessa
Abadessa d'Olzet, 26
Tel: 93-280 3754
www.jardiabadessa.com
Open: Mon–Sat L & D. Sun L. €€ [off map]
A very attractive uptown spot in a large garden, ideal for a peaceful lunch after a visit to the Monestir de Pedralbes, or to possibly rub shoulders with a Barça star on a summer evening. Serves light Mediterranean dishes. A great place to sip a glass of cava.

Roure
Riera Sant Miquel, 51
Tel: 93-218 7387
Open: Mon–Sat L & D. € [110 p288, B1]
A real Barcelona corner bar that is always bustling, especially when there is a Barça match being broadcast. Popular with a strong band of regulars, it serves tapas all day long and meals at lunchtime (it's worth coming for the paella on Thursday). Good value in every sense.

La Singular
Francisco Giner, 50
Tel: 93-237 5098
Open: Mon–Fri L & D, Sat D. € [111 p288, B1]
This is a wonderful little Gràcia restaurant with a warm, friendly atmosphere and great cooking, using seasonal local produce but giving it a creative edge.

La Venta
Plaça Doctor Andreu, 1
Tel: 93-212 6455
www.restaurantelaventa.com
Open: Tue–Sat L & D. Sun L. €€€ [off map]
One of the prettiest restaurants in the city, at the foot of the funicular to Tibidabo. High-class Mediterranean food – the perfect setting for springtime lunches or summer nights on the leafy terrace. **El Mirador de la Venta** is a more exclusive space upstairs, with magnificent views over the city.

Bars and Cafés

L'Astrolabi
Martínez de la Rosa, 14
[44 p306,B2]
This small bar with a big personality, thanks to its welcoming owner Jordi and his loyal clientele, embodies the essence of Gràcia. Live music on some nights, usually of the singer-songwriter variety.

Bar Tomás
Major de Sarrià, 49
Tel: 93-203 1036
off map]
People come to this happily untouched local bar from all over town to enjoy Tomás's renowned *patatas bravas* (fried potatoes served with a spicy sauce and mayonnaise), made according to his own secret recipe.

Café del Sol
Plaça del Sol, 16
Tel: 93-237 1448
[45 p306,B1]
Gràcia is characterised by narrow streets which open up into squares like this one, and each has a range of terrace bars. Café del Sol has a long history and is a landmark in the area, buzzing by day and well into the night.

Café Vienés
Passeig de Gràcia, 132
Tel: 93-255 3006
[46 p306,B2]
Teas and cocktails are served in what was once a meeting place for the literati of the city, a legendary café which is now part of the exclusive Hotel Casa Fuster. Enjoy the chance to sit back and absorb the *modernista* decoration, with live jazz on Thursday evenings.

La Cervesera Artesana
Agustí, 14
Tel: 93-237 9594
www.lacervesera.net
[47 p306,B2]
As craft beer festivals begin to gain momentum in Catalonia, interest is rising. In this bar in Gràcia you can try a tasty brew made on the premises.

Sol Soler
Plaça del Sol, 21
Tel: 93-217 4440
[48 p306,B1]
A charming bar on this lively square with a peaceful, tiled interior, antique mirrors and small marble tables under the old beams. The cool staff serve delicious alternative tapas, with plenty of vegetarian options.

Tortilla, or Spanish omelette.

PARK GÜELL

A high point in the city is the park designed by Antoni Gaudí to be an avant-garde suburb, a project which floundered, giving the city a colourful open space.

The 'park' of Park Güell is officially spelt the English way because its developer, the industrialist Eusebi Güell, intended it to be a suburban 'garden city' along the English lines. Sixty houses were planned in a 15-hectare (38-acre) environment designed by Antoni Gaudí, and although only five were completed, the park remains one of the architect's most appealing works.

Always aware of the struggle between man and nature, Gaudí used shapes which harmonised with the landscape, building a complex of staircases, zoomorphic sculptures, sinuous ramps and viaducts. The most important single element of the park is a two-tiered plaza; the lower part is the Sala Hipóstila, a hypostyle of Doric columns leaning inwards and with hollow central cores to collect water from the terrace above. This was designed to be the estate's marketplace. The overhead terrace is an open area with wonderful views, surrounded by an undulating bench 100 metres (328ft) long, covered in the inimitable *trencadís* (mosaics) by Josep Jujol, one of Gaudí's close collaborators.

Built between 1900 and 1914, the park was taken over by the city council in 1918 and is today a Unesco World Heritage site.

The method of decoration using broken glazed ceramics (incorporating old crockery and bottle bottoms at times) is a hallmark of Gaudí buildings, known as trencadís.

It's also easy to spend time gazing at the endlessly fascinating details of the ceramic decorative work.

The Essentials

Address: Olot, 1–13
Tel: 010
Opening Hrs: daily May–Sept 10am–9pm, Apr and Oct until 8pm, Mar and Nov until 7pm, Dec–Feb until 6pm
Entrance Fee: charge for park, Casa-Museu Gaudí, Casa del Guarda
Transport: bus 24, 92

Jujol's bright ceramic serpentine bench outlines the terrace – a popular place to sit and relax or take stock of the city which stretches out below.

Gaudí designed two Hansel and Gretel-like pavilions with fantastical roofs to flank the park entrance. The Casa Guarda, open to the public, has a small but interesting exhibition.

CASA-MUSEU GAUDÍ

In the Casa-Museu Gaudí.

Park Güell's original showhouse was the work of a collaborating architect, Francesc Berenguer. Gaudí himself moved into this house, which he called Torre Rosa, in 1906 after no buyers were found, and it remained his home until his death in 1926. Today the three-storey **Casa-Museu Gaudí** contains his bed, prie-dieu and crucifix, as well as drawings and a collection of furniture designed by him and taken from different parts of the city. Although Gaudí was the mastermind of the proposed 'garden city', it was never intended that he should be the architect of the 60 houses. Plots were to be sold with the provisos that buildings took up no more than one-sixth of the ground area, and garden walls should be no more than 40cm (16 inches) high. A second house, Casa Trias, was built by Juli Batllevell in 1903 for a lawyer, Martín Trias Domènech, and it remains in the Trias family hands.

Count Güell died in Casa Larrard, the original house on the estate, in 1918, knowing that nobody else wanted to share his dream.

The columns at Sala Hipóstila.

Begur on the Costa Brava.

Barefoot on Sitges' promenade.

AROUND BARCELONA

The Catalonian hinterland as far as the Pyrenees and long stretches of coastline on either side of Barcelona provide exceptional opportunities for excursions from the city, most of which are possible on public transport.

Barcelona

Barcelona is a great city to be in, but there are also beaches, mountains, wine country, religious retreats and historic provincial cities all within relatively easy reach. Travelling to and from the city by hire car is best avoided in weekday rush hours, Friday and Sunday evenings and at the start and end of Christmas, Easter and August holidays. Visitors who travel outside these times will enjoy straightforward, stress-free journeys. Travelling by train and bus is also manageable from the city.

EXCURSIONS

Some of these excursions are day trips but it would be worth taking two or three days for the longer ones.

There are two options for journeys to the south of Barcelona (Sitges and Tarragona), two to the west (the Penedès region and Montserrat), three inland to the north (Montseny, Vic and the Pyrenees), two up into the province of Girona (Figueres and Girona), one to the Maresme coast just north of Barcelona (Caldetes), and one to the Costa Brava.

Sitges, Caldetes and the Costa Brava all have fine beaches; Montserrat, the Montseny and the Pyrenees are

mountain-top retreats; Vic, Tarragona, Figueres and Girona are historic provincial centres.

Colònia Güell ❶

Address: Santa Coloma de Cervelló; www.gaudicoloniaguell.org
Opening Hrs: summer Mon–Fri 10am–7pm, winter until 5pm, Sat–Sun 10am–3pm
Entrance fee: charge for church
Transport: FGC trains from Plaça d'Espanya to Colònia Güell station

Main Attractions
Colònia Güell
Sitges
Tarragona
Penedès
Montserrat
Vic
Aigüestortes
Girona
Caldes d'Estrac
Begur

Maps and Listings
Map, page 226
Restaurants, page 238
Accommodation, page 257

The Costa Brava is popular for family holidays.

TIP

Using a T10 metro card (zone 1) you can travel up the coast on a train as far as Montgat Nord (a favourite for surfers) or down to Platja de Castelldefels (and even the airport).

One easy trip that can be done in half a day is to the Colònia Güell **in Santa Coloma de Cervellò. This** 19th-century textile-industry estate, with a church crypt designed by Antoni Gaudí, is a fascinating place. The crypt, named a World Heritage site in 2005, is a must for Gaudí enthusiasts, illustrating his ingenious building techniques and fantastical decorative ideas. It is worth getting the audioguide to capture the wealth of details and to be guided round the interesting buildings in the village, though they are not open to the public.

SITGES ❷

A smooth 40-minute train ride or a quick drive through the Garraf tunnels on the C32 motorway will whisk you south to **Sitges**, the closest clean and uncrowded bit of the Mediterranean coast. Sand and sun can be enjoyed at Castelldefels, 20 minutes from Barcelona, but the whitewashed houses and flower-festooned balconies of Sitges are worth the extra journey time, making you feel a world away. A day on the beach, with a paella for lunch, is a great idea. What's more, the weather is reputed always to be better in Sitges, so you

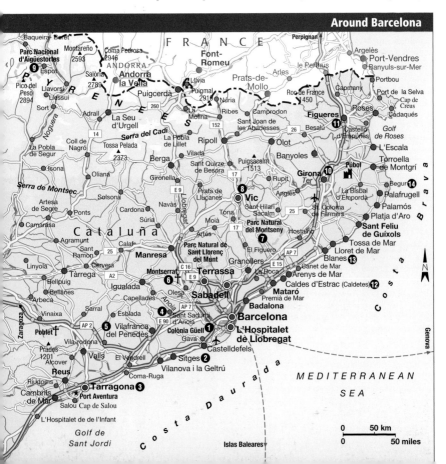

Around Barcelona

could leave Barcelona in cloud and arrive to find glorious sunshine.

An international party atmosphere pervades Sitges in summer, and the town has a full calendar of festivals year round, including a notoriously wild Carnival, thanks to its gay community, and an International Film Festival in October.

The beaches are fringed by palms and an elegant promenade. They start on the other side of the 17th-century Església Sant Bartomeu i Santa Tecla, on the headland, and extend south past the Hotel Terramar.

Museu Romàntic Can Llopis

Address: Sant Gaudenci, s/n; www.museusdesitges.com
Opening Hrs: summer Tue–Sat 10am–2pm, 4–8pm, Sun 10am–3pm, winter Tue–Sat 10am–2pm, 3.30–7pm, Sun 11am–3pm

The Museu Romàntic Can Llopis gives a good insight into the life of a 19th-century bourgeois family in this handsome building and also houses the **Lola Anglada** antique-doll collection. Also in Sitges, in Fonollar

street, the atmospheric **Museu Cau Ferrat**, studio-home of Santiago Rusiñol, leading light in the *modernista* movement, is due to reopen after extensive refurbishment. Containing a huge collection of art, glass and ceramics, it is very evocative of the period. Check the above website for opening times.

TARRAGONA ❸

Around 90 minutes from Barcelona by train or car, **Tarragona** still has the feel of a provincial capital of the Roman Empire. Captured by Rome

The beach at Sitges.

Tarragona's Roman amphitheatre.

On Tarragona's Rambla.

The Pont del Diable is a Roman aqueduct in Tarragona.

in 218BC and later the capital of the Spanish province of Tarraconensis under Emperor Augustus, the town was the major commercial centre until Barcelona and Valencia overshadowed it following the Christian Reconquest in the early 12th century.

Rich in Roman ruins still being unearthed and stunningly beautiful ancient buildings, it was declared a World Heritage site in 2000.

The cathedral

Tarragona's **cathedral**, the centrepiece of the top part of the city, has been described by Catalonia's own travel writer Josep Pla as 'easily and serenely mighty, solid as granite, maternal – a cathedral redolent of Roman virtues projected onto carved stone – a lion in repose, drowsy, unabashedly powerful.'

Passeig Arqueològic

Explore the walled upper part of the city surrounding the cathedral,

then tour the wall itself, the Passeig Arqueològic (Archaeological Promenade; (www.tarragonaturisme.cat). It offers views south over the city, west out to the mountains, north to the hills and trees surrounding the city, and finally east to the coastline and sea.

Below the walls is the middle section of Tarragona, with the wide and stately **Rambla** ending in the **Balcó del Mediterrani** (Mediterranean Balcony) looking over the beach, port and impressive Roman amphitheatre. The city's luminosity at this point has been much commented on and is indeed remarkable: a crisp elegance and clean air shimmer over the golden sandstone of 2,000-year-old Roman structures.

The port

The **Serrallo** section of the port is the main attraction in the lower part of the city, the multicoloured fishing fleet unloading their catch every afternoon, the fish auctioned off within minutes. A lunch at a dockside restaurant – featuring fine Tarragona wines and seafood just out of the nets – makes a delicious end to a visit.

Salou and Port Aventura

Just 8km (5 miles) south of Tarragona is the seaside resort of **Salou** and its neighbouring theme park **Port Aventura**, the largest in Europe after Disneyland Resort Paris (www.portaventura.es; end Mar–end Oct daily, Nov–Dec Fri–Sun only; see website to confirm opening times; charge). People travel for miles to experience the thrills and spills it offers. There are several hotels on the site and a new golf course.

SANT SADURNÍ D'ANOIA ④

If you wish to experience the more indigenous pleasures of Catalonia, the Penedès wine-growing region can be easily reached from the city. Begin in **Sant Sadurní d'Anoia**, a small town responsible for 80 percent of

Café outside Tarragona's splendid cathedral.

cava production, the sparkling wine made in Catalonia.

A 45-minute train ride from Sants or Plaça de Catalunya stations in Barcelona will drop you in Sant Sadurní, right next to Freixenet, the world's leading producer of cava, with vineyards in California and operations in China.

Cava has been produced in Sant Sadurní since 1872 by Josep Raventós, founder of the Codorníu empire, who studied the *méthode champenoise* of Dom Pérignon and made Catalonia's first bottle of cava. It is an important part of life in Catalonia: baptisms, weddings, even routine Sunday lunches are occasions for popping corks. On 20 November 1975, the day Franco died, cava was given away free in Barcelona.

VILAFRANCA DEL PENEDÈS ❺

About 14km (8 miles) from Sant Sadurní is **Vilafranca del Penedès**. The Penedès region has more than 300 wine and cava-producing companies, most of which can be visited, including the winery and extensive vineyards of the world-famous Torres, which dominates the region. Information is centralised through the tourist office in Vilafranca (tel: 93-818 1254; http://turisme.vilafranca. cat). Around Sant Sadurní even children have opinions on *bruts, secs* and *brut natures*.

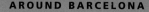

EAT

Sant Sadurní offers excellent gastronomic opportunities at local restaurants well known for fine cava and seafood. Between late January and mid-March, the *calçotada* is a traditional feast starring long-stemmed *calçots* (something between a spring onion and a leek), dipped in a romesco sauce of oil, peppers, garlic and ground nuts. Cava flows freely at these rustic banquets, accompanied by lamb or rabbit grilled, as are the *calçots*, over coals.

Sant Sadurní d'Anoia produces 80 percent of Spain's cava.

Stained glass at the Vinseum.

The Vinseum, Vilafranca del Penedès.

Vinseum: Museu de les Cultures del Vi de Catalunya

Address: Plaça Jaume I, Vilafranca del Penedès; www.vinseum.cat
Tel: 93-8900 582
Opening Hrs: Tue–Sat 10am–2pm and 4–7pm, Sun 10am–2pm
Entrance fee: charge

One of Europe's best wine museums, explaining the history of wine in Catalonia, has reopened in a renovated 13th-century palace, displaying its interesting collection of over 17,000 objects related to wine.

MONTSERRAT ❻

Address: www.montserratvisita.com
Tel: 93-877 7701
Opening Hrs: Basilica daily 7.30am–8pm, museum daily 10am–5.30pm, closes slightly later in mid-summer
Entrance fee: free; charge for museum
Transport: FGC Plaça Espanya to Aeri de Montserrat (for cable car) or Monistrol de Montserrat for Cremallera (zip-train)

Situated 48km (30 miles) west of Barcelona, and looming 1,236 metres (4,055ft) over the valley floor, Montserrat, the highest point of the lowlands, is Catalonia's most important religious site (see page 240). Here athletes pledge to make barefoot pilgrimages if their prayers are answered and vital competitions won. Groups of young people from all over Catalonia make overnight hikes at least once in their lives to watch the sunrise from the heights.

'La Moreneta' (the Black Virgin), said to have been made by St Luke and brought to Barcelona by St Peter, resides in the sanctuary of the Mare de Deu de Montserrat. There is a separate door at the front of the basilica for people wanting to see and touch this statue of Madonna and Child, but be prepared to queue.

Montserrat can be reached easily and spectacularly by train, but the advantage of going by car is the opportunity of seeing it from different angles. In the words of Catalan poet Maragall, from varying perspectives Montserrat resembles 'a bluish cloud with fantastic carvings, a giant's castle with 100 towers thrown towards the sky... above all an altar, a temple'.

The basilica is packed with works by prominent painters and sculptors, including paintings by El Greco in the sanctuary's museum. Catalan poets have dedicated some of their most inspired verse to Montserrat, while maestros such as Nicolau and Millet have composed some of their finest pieces in its honour. Goethe is said to have dreamed of Montserrat, and Parsifal sought the Holy Grail here in Wagner's opera.

Excursions

There are several excursions to be made from the monastery. Via Crucis, the Way of the Cross (behind Plaça de L'Abat Oliba) leads to the hermitage of **Sant Miquel**. From Plaça de la Cru a cable car runs down to **Santa Cova**, a chapel in a grotto where the Virgin is said to have been hidden during the Moorish occupation.

On a clear day it is worth taking the funicular (plus a 20-minute walk) up to **Sant Joan**, one of the 13 *ermitas* inhabited by hermits until Napoleon's troops hunted them down and killed them. Montserrat's highest point is **Sant Jeroni**, from where Catalonia spreads out before you – the view sometimes extends as far as Mallorca.

Montseny hills ❼

Montserrat and the Montseny range of mountains in the **Parc Natural de Montseny** (www.turisme-montseny.com) occupy polar extremes in Catalonian spiritual life. Montserrat is vertical, acute and passionate, Montseny is smooth, horizontal, massive and placid. *Seny* in Catalan means sense, patience, restraint, serenity, and is a byword for a description of the national characteristics.

Best explored by car, this monumental mountain forest is presided over by four peaks: Turó de l'Home,

Agudes, Matagalls (all around 1,500 metres/5,000ft) and Calma i Puigdrau, a lower peak at 1,215 metres (4,050ft). Lesser terrain features and watercourses connect and define these pieces of high ground, tracing out an autonomous geographical entity which always appears mistenshrouded on the horizon, often confused with cloud formations.

The village of **Montseny** can be reached via Santa Maria de Palautordera and Sant Esteve de

Looking down on the monastery at Montserrat.

The Parc Natural de Montseny.

Palautordera on the BV-5301. This road continues on to Brull, through the pass at Collformic and over to Tona, near Vic (see page 232), traversing the entire Montseny massif. The road up from Sant Celoni, just off the *autovia* towards France, via Campins and Fogars de Montclus, arrives at the **Santa Fe** hermitage, a vantage point which seems only a stone's throw from Montseny's highest points. The oaks and poplars are colourful in autumn, which is an unusual sight in Catalonia, where forests of deciduous trees are uncommon.

VIC ❽

An easy hour's journey north by train or car, **Vic** (www.victurisme. cat) is an elegant market town with interesting medieval buildings, sophisticated shops and good food. It is the meeting place of industry, commerce and agriculture and a mixture of rural and urban life. With a strong ecclesiastical and cultural tradition, the town is an entity quite distinct from Barcelona, and the Vic accent is unmistakable.

Aigüestortes National Park.

Inside the basilica at Montserrat.

The magnificent **Plaça Major**, surrounded by low arcades, has a lively Saturday market and is a pleasant place to have a drink.

Cathedral

Vic's **cathedral**, a neoclassical structure completed in 1803 and with a graceful 11th-century Romanesque

bell tower, is best known for Josep Maria Sert's epic murals covering the interior walls. Sert left his personal vision in the voluptuous, neo-Baroque figures performing colossal deeds. His triptych on the back of the western door depicts the injustices in the life of Christ and, by association, in the history of Catalonia. With the cathedral in ruins as his background, Jesus expels the moneylenders from the temple and is, in turn, condemned to be crucified while Pilate washes his hands and Barabbas, the thief, is cheered by the crowd. Certain faces (Pilate, Barabbas) are said to be those of Franco's lieutenants, but El Generalísimo himself, visiting while Sert's work was in progress, did not see the resemblance.

The philosopher Jaume Balmes (1810–48), a native of Vic, is buried in the cloister, as is Sert.

Museu Episcopal

Address: Plaça Bisbe Oliba, 3
Opening Hrs: Tue–Sat 10am–7pm, closed lunchtime Mon–Fri in winter, Sun 10am–2pm
Entrance fee: charge

The museum has a large, impressive collection of Romanesque and Gothic pieces, including altarpieces and sculpted figures collected from local chapels and churches.

Its treasures have now been rehoused in a new building designed by leading Barcelona architects Correa and Milà. Note especially the Romanesque textiles and *El Davallament de la Creu* (The Descent from the Cross), an especially fine 12th-century sculptural work in polychrome wood.

AIGÜESTORTES ⑨

Although many parts of the Pyrenees can be visited in a day from Barcelona – keen skiers dash up to La Molina for as many downhill runs as they can pack in before returning for dinner on the coast – the **Parc Nacional d'Aigüestortes i Estany de Sant Maurici** (www.gencat.cat/parcs/aiguestortes), in the province of Lleida, deserves at least two or three days. A three- to four-hour car journey from the city, Catalonia's only national park is stunningly beautiful and a stimulating antidote to the city. It

TIP

A mere 70km (43.5 miles) away from Barcelona, the Montseny range is the perfect rural antidote to the city. A favourite retreat for feeling remote is the much-loved Hotel Sant Bernat, with breathtaking views, traditional mountain fare and – of course – a collection of St Bernard dogs to keep you company.

The Old City rises on the banks of the River Onyar.

Girona is home to many historical and cultural sights.

has some 200 lakes, dramatic peaks, walks for all ages and a rich cultural heritage. Many of the Romanesque pieces of art in the Museu Nacional in Barcelona (see page 179) and the Museu Episcopal in Vic came from 11th-century churches that can still be visited in this area.

Espot

The village of **Espot** makes a good base. It is just outside the Parc, and easily reached on the C13 following the roaring Noguera Pallaresa river, a favourite for whitewater rafting. It has several hotels and some good restaurants serving hearty mountain fare like *estofat de porc senglar* (wild boar stew). There are easy trails straight from Espot, or from the car park beyond the village. Alternatively, catch a four-wheel drive taxi to take you deeper into the park before you start walking. Seriously keen hikers can stay in one of several *refugis* (shelters), so

as to cover as much of this extensive 14,000-hectare (34,594-acre) national park as possible.

During the skiing season there is a small resort nearby, **Espot Esqui**, or you could opt for **Port Ainé**, slightly closer to Barcelona, which has a hotel at the foot of the slopes.

Another approach to Aigüestortes is through the **Boí Valley**, reached through El Pont de Suert on the N230. This valley has been made a World Heritage site for the wealth of its Romanesque architecture. Don't miss the churches of Sant Climent and Santa Maria in **Taüll**, Sant Joan in **Boí** itself and Santa Eulàlia in **Erill la Vall**. Avoid rush hour and try to find a solitary moment in any one of these simple but majestic mountain churches. Catalans and people from other parts of Spain tend to flood into the main tourist centres in the Pyrenees in August, but there are still plenty of river banks and woods far from the madding crowd.

GIRONA ⑩

Girona and Figueres can be combined for a memorable excursion from Barcelona. **Girona**, the provincial capital, is a most attractive city (www.girona.cat/turisme), full of history, tasteful shops and high-class restaurants (including El Celler de Can Roca, named best restaurant in the world in 2013 by *Restaurant* magazine, and only an hour's drive or train ride from Barcelona. It is known for its **Ciutat Antiga** (Old City), especially the 13th-century **Jewish Quarter**, the **Call**, considered one of the two most important and best-preserved in Spain (the other is Toledo's). The River Onyar separates the Old City from the modern section, which lies west of the river.

The footbridges over the Onyar provide some of Girona's most unforgettable views, including reflections of the colourful buildings on the banks of the river. The 12th-century **Església de Sant Pere de Galligants** is one of the city's oldest monuments, with a delightful Romanesque cloister built before 1154. From here you can walk around the city walls as far as Plaça de Catalunya.

Girona's Old City, built on a hill, is known for its lovely stairways, such as those up to the **Església de Sant Martí**, or the Baroque *escalinata* of 96 steps leading up to the cathedral.

Santa Maria Cathedral

Opening Hrs: Visit includes the museum; Mon–Sat summer 10am–7.30pm, winter 10am–6.30pm, Sun all year Treasury and Cloisters only, 10am–2pm
Entrance fee: charge (free on Sun)

Described by Josep Pla as 'literally sensational', Girona's cathedral was built by Guillem Bofill, who covered the structure with Europe's largest Gothic vault. It includes several treasures, the most notable being the *Tapis de la Creació*, a stunning 12th-century tapestry depicting God surrounded by all the flora and fauna, fish and fowl of Creation. Equally impressive is Beatus's *Llibre de l'Apocalipsi* (Book of the Apocalypse), dated 975.

The **Església de Sant Feliu**, the **Arab Baths** and the Call, with its **Museum of Jewish History** (summer Mon–Sat 10am–8pm, Sun 10am–2pm, winter Tue–Sat 10am–6pm, Sun–Mon 10am–2pm; charge), are other important landmarks of this ancient city.

FIGUERES ⑪

Figueres, another half-hour north on the AP7 motorway, is the major city of the **Alt Empordà**. The **Rambla** is the scene of the traditional *passeig*, the midday or evening stroll.

Teatre-Museu Dalí

Address: Plaça Gala-Salvador Dalí, 5; www.salvador-dali.org
Opening Hrs: July–Sept daily 9am–8pm, Oct–June Tue–Sun, times vary so check website
Entrance fee: charge

Figueres is best known as the birthplace of the Surrealist artist Salvador Dalí, whose museum is aptly located

EAT

Figueres has many good restaurants. Hotel Empordà, on the outskirts of town, has one of Catalonia's most famous restaurants (see page 238).

Steps up to the cathedral nave, Girona.

The Costa Brava is lined with sandy coves.

In the Teatre-Museu Dalí.

in the former municipal theatre. This is one of the most visited museums in Spain and has a wide range of Dalí's work, including the *Poetry of America*, painted in 1943, a portrait of his wife Gala as *Atomic Leda*, and the huge ceiling fresco dominating the Wind Palace Room on the first floor. Whether you regard him as a genius or not, there is no denying that this museum, with its tricks and illusions, provides an entertaining show.

A new space, **Dalí.Joies** (entrance charge, or entry with ticket to main museum), in an annexe, exhibits 37 pieces of jewellery by Dalí and sketched designs.

Figueres is a good base for Dalí tourism in the region: both Dalí's house in **Port Lligat**, near Cadaqués, and the castle he bought for his wife, in **Púbol**, are open to the public (see box, page 237).

COSTA DEL MARESME

The beaches just north of Barcelona have a much lower profile than Sitges, and are much maligned for the railway line that runs alongside them. As a result, they are often less

crowded. In recent years most have been overhauled, with some beaches being widened, promenades landscaped and marinas built. It is worth travelling beyond Badalona, though its promenade is a pleasant place for lunch. However, if you only have half a day, both Masnou and Vilassar de Mar are very acceptable, with *xiringuitos* (snack bars) on the beach.

Caldes d'Estrac ⑫

One of the most attractive resorts is **Caldes d'Estrac**, also known as **Caldetes**. The slightly longer journey – about 40 minutes from Barcelona by car on the speedy C32 and about 45 minutes on the train from Plaça de Catalunya – is well rewarded. Caldetes is a spa town – several hotels have thermal baths – and it has many pretty *modernista* houses. The long, sandy beaches never get too crowded, and the sea is usually clear.

Early evening is a particularly pleasant time, when families dress up in smart-casual clothes to promenade and have a drink on the esplanade, or an ice cream on the seafront. You can enjoy all this, have dinner and get

The castle at Tossa de Mar.

back to Barcelona for the night without too much effort.

Seaside villages

The beaches of Caldetes merge with those of **Arenys de Mar**, known for its attractive fishing port and famous restaurant, the **Hispania**, favoured by King Juan Carlos (see page 239).

The next town north, **Canet de Mar**, has a refurbished waterfront and interesting 19th-century architecture. The home of Lluís Domènech i Montaner (see page 54), one of the leading *modernista* architects in Barcelona, can be visited (Tue–Sun 10am–2pm; Fri–Sat also 5–8pm; closed last weekend of month; charge).

Just beyond Canet de Mar is **Sant Pol**, a pretty, whitewashed village.

THE COSTA BRAVA

To get away entirely from city beaches it is worth going as far as the Costa Brava. The southernmost parts of this rocky coastline (*brava*) can be reached in a day, like **Blanes** ⑱, where it officially begins. However, with more time you can get further north to the really magical

parts, from **Tossa de Mar** up to the French border. Most of these places can be reached by bus from Estació del Nord bus station, though it is well worth renting a car to allow maximum freedom to explore.

The beaches and medieval inland villages of the area known as El Baix Empordà were until recently a well-kept secret. Some of the villages have been prettified, their honey-coloured houses tastefully renovated by middle-class weekenders from Barcelona, but they remain endlessly charming. A good base could be **Begur** ⑭, a pretty hilltop village with a cosmopolitan edge, just inland from some of the prettiest *calas* (sandy inlets) that punctuate the rocky coastline. You will be spoilt for choice between the sheltered cove of **Tamariu**, lined with seafood restaurants, the clear azure of the different bays of **Aigua Blava** or the atmosphere of generations of family summers in **Sa Riera**.

SALVADOR DALÍ

Through the endeavours of the Gala-Salvador Dalí Foundation, the surreal world of Dalí now includes his home in Port Lligat, his wife Gala's castle in Púbol and the museum in Figueres. To get a broad view of the art and a vivid idea of the man, the best introduction is the **Teatre-Museu Dalí**. Some 30km (20 miles) away on the coast, near Cadaqués, is the **Casa-Museu Salvador Dalí**, giving a fascinating glimpse of Dalí's life. These old fishermen's cottages have limited space, so small groups are admitted every 10 minutes. It is essential to book in advance and obey strict rules (check website for the conditions; tel: 972-251 015; www.salvador-dali.org; summer daily 9.30am–9pm, winter Tue–Sun 10.30am–6pm, closed Jan–early Feb). Bought by Dalí for his wife in 1970, the **Castell Gala Dalí** is atmospheric, set in a landscaped garden in Púbol in the Baix Empordà district (summer daily 10am–8pm, winter Tue–Sat 10am–5pm, closed Jan–mid-Mar).

RESTAURANTS

Restaurants

In rural areas all over Catalonia you'll find well-kept roadside restaurants, popular for weddings, baptisms and other family occasions, where you can be sure of a good, traditional meal, with *pa amb tomàquet* and pork dishes as staples, as well as the regional or seasonal speciality. Catalonia is also hitting the headlines for its wave of avant-garde restaurants, where chefs create wonders and garner Michelin stars (advance booking essential). Explore villages where the local bar may have a wholesome dish of the day,

Tapas at a Girona bar.

unpretentious and delicious, cooked for local workers. Eating hours tend to be earlier than in the city.

Baro

El Carro
La Vinya s/n
Tel: 973-662 148
www.restaurantelcarro.com
Open: Early July–early Sept daily L & D, rest of year Sat–Sun L & D. €€
Succulent local meat cooked in a woodburning oven, or *a la brasa* (charcoal grilled), and served in the shade of the garden close to the gushing Noguera Pallaresa river is an experience not to be missed. In a small village en route to the Aigüestortes National Park, though better to do the hiking before lunch.

Begur

La Pizzeta
Ventura i Sabater, 2
Tel: 972-623 884

http://lapizzeta.com
Open: June–Aug daily D, mid-March–May, Sept–Oct Thu–Mon D. Closed Nov–mid-March. €€
This creative restaurant in the garden of a beautiful old village house serves not only imaginative pizzas and pasta, but also great salads, grilled local meat, a few Asian dishes and plenty for vegetarians. Charming and trendy, so book early.

Castelldefels

Mar Blanc
Ribera de Sant Pere, 17
Tel: 93-636 0075
www.marblanc.com
Open: Tue–Sat L & D, Sun L. €€€
The plus here is that you can eat seafood on a terrace looking straight over the long beach and Mediterranean sea, which on a sunny day in mid-winter takes some beating. Rice dishes and *calderetas* (fish stews) are the speciality.

Figueres

El Motel
Av. Salvador Dalí, 170
Tel: 972-500562
http://ca.hotelemporda.com
Open: Daily L & D. €€€
Its founder, the late Josep Mercader, has become a legend as one of the first chefs to reinvent Catalan dishes back in the 1950s. His charisma and inspiration live on in this well-established restaurant offering creative cooking using local ingredients. The hotel makes a good base for visiting the Dalí museums.

Girona

El Celler de Can Roca
Can Sunyer, 48
Tel: 972-222 157
www.cellercanroca.com
Open: Tue–Sat L & D. €€€€
One of the most established of the new wave of avant-garde restau-

rants in Catalonia, with three Michelin stars, this place was named top restaurant in the world in 2013. It's run by the Roca brothers: Joan is the chef who conjures up dishes like a carpaccio of pigs' trotters with vinaigrette, Josep advises expertly on wines and Jordi concentrates on the exotic desserts.

Maresme

Fonda Manau
Sant Josep, 11, Caldes d'Estrac
Tel: 93-791 0459
www.manau.cat
Open: July–Sept Wed–Mon L & D, Oct–June Fri, Sat L & D, Wed, Thu, Sun, Mon L.
€€
This small *fonda* (inn) serves good, simple food in its pretty courtyard, although the creative flair of Xavi Manau, son of the former owner, is now coming to the fore, resulting in delicious dishes like squid tossed with wild mushrooms.

Hispania
Reial, 54, Carretera N11, Arenys de Mar
Tel: 93-791 0306
www.restauranthispania.com
Open: Mon, Wed–Sat L & D, Sun L. Closed Oct. €€€€
A classic of Catalan cuisine, which has been in the same family for 60 years. Known for their seasonal dishes using fresh local produce, such as peas from Llavaneres or fresh clams from the port of Arenys. Their *crema catalana*, the national dessert, is legendary.

Petit Moll
Platja l'Espigó de Garbí, Vilassar de Mar
Tel: 600-520 000
Open: Mid-May–early Sept daily L & D.
€–€€
Very charming *xiringuito* (beachside restaurant) on a small beach, great for fresh sardines and salad after a swim. Only a 20-minute train ride from Barcelona but it feels more like Ibiza among the fishing boats.

Pizzeria Estrac
Camí Ral, 5, Caldes d'Estrac
Tel: 93-791 3188
www.pizzeriaestrac.com
Open: Sat–Sun L & D, (also Mon–Fri D July–mid-Sept). €

Pasta, salads and particularly good home-made pizzas in an attractive restaurant in the heart of this pretty village. Pizzas can also be taken away.

Penedès

El Mirador de les Caves
Carretera Sant Sadurní–Ordal, Subirats
Tel: 93-899 3178
Open: Tue–Sun L. €€
When visiting cava country, this is a good spot to sample the end product – and indulge in a good meal – while gazing across the vineyards that have produced it. Penedès wine and cava can be bought here, too.

Saldet

La Sal
Carretera de l'Armentera
Tel: 972-521 874
www.lasalrestaurant.com
Open: Mid-June to mid-Sept Mon–Fri D, Sat–Sun L & D, mid-Sep to mid-June Fri D, Sat L & D, Sun L. €€ (€ tapas)
This newcomer, in a handsome old mill with vaulted ceilings and a peaceful garden just inland from the Costa Brava beaches in the Alt Empordà, is quite a discovery. Delicate and delicious creative dishes like deep-fried squid with black garlic mayonnaise or pumpkin and smoked cheese cannelloni make the journey worth it.

Sant Celoni

Can Fabes
Sant Joan, 6
Tel: 93-867 2851
www.canfabes.com
Open: Wed–Sat L & D, Sun L. €€€€
People come from far and wide to enjoy the legacy of renowned avant-garde chef Santi Santamaria, who died in 2011. His disciples and family keep the creative standard high in this attractive restaurant in the Montseny with an indulgent boutique hotel attached.

Sitges

The temptation to eat a paella overlooking the sea is irresistible, and there are several places along

the seafront to choose from. You'll be able to find more unusual options in the narrow streets leading up to the centre.

Al Fresco
Pau Barrabeig, 4
Tel: 93-894 0600
www.alfrescorestaurante.es
Open: July–early Sept daily D. Rest of year, check website. €€€
Excellent fusion between Mediterranean and the Far East results in delicious flavours in this very attractive whitewashed restaurant and pretty courtyard.

La Santa Maria
Passeig de la Ribera, 52
Tel: 93-894 0999
www.lasantamaria.com/restaurant
Open: Daily L & D. Closed mid-Dec–Feb.
€€
La Santa Maria is a traditional hotel restaurant where large families meet for Sunday lunch. Be sure to wait for a table on the terrace overlooking the main promenade – it's a good spot for paella.

Vilanova i la Geltrú

La Fitorra
Hotel César, Isaac Peral, 4–8
Tel: 93-815 1125
www.lafitorra.com
Open: Tue–Sat L & D, Sun L. Daily in mid-summer. €€
Delicious Mediterranean food at a reasonable price, with immaculate and friendly service in this delightful hotel with a personal touch. The lunchtime buffet can be eaten in the shady garden, bursting with hibiscus flowers. Many options for vegetarians.

Vic

Ca L'U
Riera, 25
Tel: 93-889 0345
www.restaurantcalu.com
Open: Thu–Sat L & D, Sun, Tue, Wed L.
€€€
In the extremely elegant surroundings of an 18th-century town house just off the magnificent Plaça Major of this market town you can eat fine local fare, mostly produce from the rich plains of Vic.

MONTSERRAT

Catalonia's iconic sacred monastery is an inspiring excursion from the city, full of interest for families, hikers, mountaineers, picnickers and pilgrims alike.

La Moreneta, the Black Virgin of Montserrat, is the patron saint of Catalonia, and her statue is the object of pilgrimage for every Catalan Catholic. Reached by cable car (travel to Aeri de Montserrat from FGC Plaça Espanya) or the Cremallera rack-and-pinion railway (from Monistrol de Montserrat), the mountain-top monastery caters well for some 2.3 million visitors a year. They also come to hear the Escolania boys' choir (Mon–Thu 1pm and 6.45pm, Fri 1pm, Sun noon and 6.45pm, except late Jun–late Aug and late Dec–mid-Jan). Visitors also want to see the rich art collection and enjoy the mountain air and walks in the stunning, flower-strewn hills. Try to avoid weekends if you can. To find some peace, take the funicular to a greater height (1,000m/3,280ft) and wander across this extraordinary 'serrated' mountain. An excellent audiovisual show explains the daily lives of the Benedictine monks, who offer accommodation (see page 258). The museum's art collection, with icons, masterpieces from Caravaggio to modern art, including works by Picasso, Dalí, Casas and Rusiñol, as well as archaeological artefacts from the Bible Lands, should not be missed.

A late 16th-century depiction of the Virgin of Montserrat.

The Essentials

Address: 01899 Montserrat; www.montserrat visita.com
Tel: 93-877 7701
Opening Hrs: basilica daily 7.30am–8pm; museum daily 10am–5.30pm, later in mid-summer
Entrance fee: free; charge for museum

The basilica has some incredible stained glass.

Plaça Santa Maria, the main square, with the entrance to the basilica through the five arches to the right. The art museum lies beneath the square.

MONASTERY MILESTONES

The monastery before its destruction by the French in 1812.

880 Image of the Virgin Mary found in cave.
1025 Oliba, Abbott of Ripoll, founds monastery.
12th–13th centuries Romanesque church built, current carving of Virgin Mary made.
1223 Mention of boys' choir, Europe's first.
1409 Pope grants the monastery independence.
1476 Gothic cloisters built.
1490 Printing press installed. Library becomes famous. Books are still published here today.
1493 Bernat Boïl, a local hermit, sails with Columbus on his second trip; his statue can be seen on the monument to Columbus in Barcelona; an Antilles island is named Montserrat.
1592 Present-day church consecrated.
1811–12 Napoleonic forces destroy monastery.
1844 Monks return and monastery is rebuilt.
1939–74 Monastery becomes symbol of Catalan resistance to Franco regime.
1982 Museum of Catalan painting opened.
1987 Mountain designated a national park.
1996 Art collections housed in one new building.
2012 Radical nun Teresa Forcades, one of the Benedictine community living here, publicly supports the Catalan independence movement in a meeting in Montserrat.

The children's choir singing in the Benedictine Abbey.

Pilgrims queue to see their beloved La Moreneta (the Black Virgin) and touch her golden orb, although she remains behind protective glass.

Strolling on Rambla del Poble Nou.

INSIGHT GUIDES **TRAVEL TIPS**

BARCELONA

TRANSPORT

GETTING THERE AND GETTING AROUND

GETTING THERE

By Air

Iberia (www.iberia.com), the national carrier, and other major airlines connect with most parts of the world, sometimes via Madrid. There are numerous low-cost airlines flying to Barcelona from European cities. Among the most popular from the UK are **easyJet** (www.easyjet. com), **Monarch** (www.monarch. co.uk) and **Jet2** (www.jet2.com). Spanish low-cost airline **Vueling** (www.vueling.com) has some UK flights and is good for onward destinations in Spain and Europe.

Ryanair (www.ryanair.com) flies to Girona (90km/56 miles from Barcelona) and Reus (80km/50 miles from Barcelona) from several UK cities and has a few flights to El Prat, the main Barcelona airport. There are shuttle-bus connections to Barcelona from Girona (tel: 902-130 014; www.sagales.com) and Reus (tel: 902-447 726; www.hispanoi gualadina.net). Tickets (around €14 single, €24 return) are available at the airports; the journey takes 60–90 minutes, depending on traffic.

Direct flights from the US are operated by **Delta** (from Atlanta and New York; www.delta.com), **American Airlines** (from Miami and New York; www.aa.com), **United** (from Newark; www.united. com), **Iberia** (from several US cities; www.iberia.com) and **Air Europa** via Madrid (www.aireuropa. com). **Air Canada** (www.aircanada. com) flies from Toronto and Montreal, while **Singapore Airlines** flies directly from Singapore to Barcelona and on to Sao Paulo.

Advance passenger information: Since 2007, Spain has demanded that all air carriers supply passport information about passengers flying into the country, prior to travel. Check with your airline before travelling; more details on www.dft.gov.uk.

Barcelona Airport

Barcelona Airport (El Prat; tel: 902-404 704; www.aena-aeropuertos.es) is 12km (7 miles) south of the city. There are two terminals T1, the new one, and T2, which mostly handles budget flights. (For information on transport to and from the airport, see *Getting Around*.)

Airlines flying out of Barcelona to other parts of Spain include:
Iberia: tel: 902-400 500
Air Europa: tel: 902-401 501
Air Nostrum: tel: 902-400 500
Vueling: tel: 807-200 100

DISTANCES

Distances to other cities in Spain by road from Barcelona:
Tarragona: 98km (60 miles)
Girona: 100km (62 miles)
La Jonquera (French border): 149km (93 miles)
Valencia: 349km (217 miles)
San Sebastián: 529km (329 miles)
Bilbao: 620km (385 miles)
Madrid: 621km (386 miles)
Salamanca: 778km (483 miles)
Málaga: 997km (620 miles)
Sevilla: 1,046km (650 miles)

By Train

A more eco-friendly and relaxing option from other parts of Europe is to take the **Trenhotel**, aka the Tren Joan Miró, which runs daily overnight from Paris Austerlitz to Estació de França in Barcelona (www.renfe.com or www.elipsos. com). During the day there are several TGVs, the French high-speed train from Paris Gare de Lyon to Figueres Vilafant, where you can change onto the AVE, the Spanish high-speed train to Barcelona Sants. This recently inaugurated route cuts the journey from Paris to Barcelona to only 6.5 hours. Soon it should be possible to do this without changing at Figueres. All other international connections involve a change at the French border, in Port Bou on entering Spain and Cerbère when leaving. These trains have few facilities. There is also a line from Barcelona to La Tour de Carol on the French border, further west in the Pyrenees, from Sants and Plaça Catalunya.

For international train information and reservations, tel: 902-243 402. A helpful website is www.seat61.com.

Most national long-distance trains terminate in Estació de Sants, some in Estació de França. For national train information: tel: 902-240 202; www.renfe.es. The AVE high-speed train to Madrid is one option.

The T1 terminal at Barcelona's airport.

By Bus

Eurolines (tel: 902-405 040; www.eurolines.com) offers a service from London which involves a change in Paris. Most services arrive at the bus station Barce-lona Nord (tel: 902-260 606), but some go to Estació d'Autobusos Sants (tel: 93-490 4000). More information and timetables on www.barcelonanord.com. In the UK, contact National Express (tel: 08717 818 178; www.national express.com).

TAKING TAXIS

All Barcelona taxis are black and yellow, and show a green light when available for hire. There are taxi ranks at the airport, Sants station, Plaça de Catalunya and other strategic points, but taxis can be hailed on any street corner.

Rates are standard and calculated by meter, starting at a set rate and clocking up at a rate governed by the time of day: night-times, weekends and fiestas are more expensive. Travelling by taxi is still affordable here compared to many European cities. If you travel outside the metropolitan area, the rate increases slightly.

Drivers do not expect a tip, but a small one is always appreciated.

Taxis equipped for wheelchairs are available (tel: 93-420 8088).

By Car

Barcelona is 149km (93 miles) or 1.5 hours' drive from La Jonquera on the French border and can be reached easily along the AP7 (or E15) motorway (*autopista*; toll payable, around €14 from the border to the city) and then, nearer Barcelona, the C33. Alternatively, the national route N11 is toll-free but tedious.

Be careful when you stop in service stations or lay-bys: professional thieves work this territory. If you stop for a drink or a meal don't leave the car unattended.

The worst times to travel, particularly between June and September, are Friday 6–10pm, Sunday 7pm–midnight or the end of a bank holiday, when tailbacks of 16km (10 miles) are common. Normal weekday rush hours are 7–9am and 6–9pm.

The ring roads (*cinturones*) surrounding the city can be very confusing when you first arrive; it is worth studying a road map beforehand. The Ronda de Dalt curves around the top part of the city, and the Ronda Litoral follows the sea.

GETTING AROUND

From the Airport

Barcelona is only 12km (7 miles) from El Prat airport and is easily reached by train, bus or taxi.

Trains to Sants and Passeig de Gràcia depart every 30 minutes from 6am–11.38pm and take about 25 minutes. The approximate cost is €3, but the best value is a T10 card for Zone 1, which can be shared between travellers and can be used on the metro and buses in the city. It costs about €10. A shuttle bus connects Terminal 1 with the train station, which is near Terminal 2. The **Aerobús**, an efficient bus service, runs to Plaça de Catalunya from each terminal every 5 minutes, stopping at strategic points en route. It operates from 6am–1am; a single fare is about €6, a return €10. You can buy tickets from a machine at the stop or from the driver, but have change ready. Note that the return ticket is only valid for up to nine days after purchase (www. aerobusbcn.com).

From Plaça de Catalunya the buses run from 5.28am–12.30am. Be sure to get on the one for your terminal when returning to the airport. A nightbus, the N17, runs from Plaça de Catalunya/Ronda Universitat from 11pm–5am.

To reach most central parts of Barcelona by taxi will cost about €25–30 plus an airport supplement. To avoid misunderstandings, ask how much it will cost before getting into the taxi: '*Cuánto vale el recorrido desde el aeropuerto hasta ...* (e.g.) *Plaça de Catalunya?'* Get the taxi driver to write down the answer if necessary.

Julia Tours
Tel: 93-317 6454; www.barcelona citytour.com

Public Transport

Barcelona is a manageable city to get around, whether on foot or by public transport. The latter is efficient and good value and a far better option than having a car. Parking is expensive and on the street you run the risk of being towed away or vandalised.

Metro

The metro has eight colour-coded lines but the main ones are 1, 2, 3, 4 and 5. Some stations are equipped with lifts for wheelchairs and prams. Trains are frequent and cheap, with a set price per journey, no matter how far you travel. It is more economical to buy a card that allows 10 journeys (Targeta T10), available at stations, banks and *estancs* (tobacconists). It can be shared and is valid for FGC trains, RENFE trains within Zone 1 (see page 247) and buses. If you change from one form of transport to another within 1 hour and 15 mins, the ticket will still be valid, so you won't be charged again. Trains run 5am–midnight Mon–Thu and Sun, 5am–2am Fri and all night Sat. Tel: 010 for metro and bus information.

Along the Passeig de Colom near the waterfront.

FGC

The local train service, Ferrocarrils de la Generalitat de Catalunya (FGC), interconnects with the metro, looks like the metro and functions in the same way, but extends beyond the inner city to towns on the other side of Tibidabo, such as San Cugat (from Plaça de Catalunya) and to Manresa and Montserrat (from Plaça d'Espanya). It is a useful service for reaching the upper parts of Barcelona and for parts of Tibidabo and the Parc de Collserola.

The metro ticket is valid on this line within Zone 1, but travel beyond is more expensive. The FGC lines can be recognised on the metro map by their distinctive logo. Within the city the timetable is the same as the metro, but beyond it varies according to the line. Check in a station or tel: 012 for FGC information (www.fgc.cat).

Bus

The bus service is good for reaching the areas the metro doesn't, and for seeing more of Barcelona. Single tickets are the same price as metro tickets and can be bought from the driver, or a multiple card (Targeta T10) of 10 journeys can be punched

TOURIST BUSES

A convenient way of getting an overall idea of the city is to catch the official city Tourist Bus (**Barcelona Bus Turístic**), which takes in the most interesting parts of the city. You can combine three different routes, and get on and off at the 44 stops freely. It also offers discounts on entrance charges.

The buses operate year-round with frequent services, the first leaving Plaça de Catalunya at 9am. The fleet includes buses equipped for wheelchairs and open-air double-deckers.

For information and tickets, ask at a tourist information office such as the one on Plaça de Catalunya, or book online at www.barcelonaturisme.com. The two-day ticket is better value.

An alternative tourist bus, Barcelona City Tour, run by Julia Tours, covers roughly the same route, starting from Plaça de Catalunya. Its main advantage is that there are fewer queues.

inside the bus, but not bought on the bus (see Metro, page 246). Most buses run from 4.25am–11pm. There are night services (the **Nit bus**) that run from Plaça de Catalunya, but lines vary, so check on the map or at bus stops.

The **Tibibus** runs from Plaça de Catalunya to Plaça del Tibidabo (on the top of the hill).

Cycling

Barcelona is now a cyclist-friendly city, with over 180km (112 miles) of bike lanes, parking facilities and many great traffic-free places to cycle, such as the port, marinas, and along the beachfront from Barceloneta to Diagonal Mar. Bicycles can be taken on trains free of charge, and a useful map of the cycle lanes can be found at www.bcn.

cat/bicicleta. It may soon become obligatory to wear helmets, after a current debate in the government. Check the latest situation when you arrive.

'Bicing'

The red-and-white bicycles parked at strategic points all over town are unfortunately not for rent. These 'Bicing' bikes are exclusively for resident/long-term use: membership is paid annually, and any use over 30 minutes is charged to a credit card. The idea is to complement the public transport system, to get you to the metro or station and not for touring, so maximum use is two hours. Luckily, though, there are plenty of enterprising companies that rent bicycles and organise cycling tours by day and night (see page 265).

Barcelona on Foot

Walking is one of the best ways of getting around Barcelona – despite the traffic fumes. It is ideal for seeing the many details that cannot be charted by maps or guidebooks – *modernista* doorways, ancient corner shops, roof gardens and balconies.

'Bicing' dock.

The tourist office Turisme de Barcelona (Plaça de Catalunya; tel: 93-285 3832) offers guided walking tours, which include:
Barcelona Walking Tours Gothic Quarter: daily in English at 10am.
Picasso Route: a glimpse of the artist's life in Barcelona, ending with a tour of the museum. There are also **Modernista**, **Gourmet**, **Literary** and **Marina** routes, to name a few.
The Route of Modernisme: A do-it-yourself route using a book available from the Centre del Modernisme (www.rutadelmodernisme.com) in the tourist office in Plaça de Catalunya, or bookshops.
Guided Tours of Palau de la Música Catalana: best to purchase in advance at the concert hall (10am–3.30pm; tel: 902-475 485; www.palaumusica.org).

Travelling outside Barcelona

By Train

The following stations currently function as described, but before planning any journey it is advisable to call **RENFE** (the national train network) for the latest information and ticket deals, tel: 902-240 202. It is wise to buy long-distance tickets in advance (on this number), especially at holidays. If you pay by credit card, tickets can be collected from machines at Sants and Passeig de Gràcia stations.

Estació de Sants, in Plaça Països Catalans, is for long-distance national and international trains, including the AVE high-speed train to Madrid. Some of these will also stop in **Passeig de Gràcia** station, which is convenient for central parts of town. Confirm beforehand that your train really does stop there.

Regional trains leave Sants for the coast south and north of Barcelona, including a direct train to Port Aventura theme park and the high-speed Euromed to Valencia and Alicante, which makes a few stops in between. In Sants station, queues can be long and

ticket clerks impatient.
Estació de França, Avinguda Marquès de l'Argentera: international and long-distance national trains.
Plaça de Catalunya: apart from the metro and Generalitat railways (FGC), RENFE/Rodalies de Catalunya has a station in Plaça de Catalunya, where trains can be caught to Manresa, Lleida, Vic, Puigcerdà, La Tour de Carol, Mataró (Maresme Coast) and Blanes. These routes also stop in Arc de Triomf station, which is convenient, depending on where you are staying.
Plaça d'Espanya: FGC trains to Montserrat, Igualada and Manresa.

By Long-Distance Bus

There are regular long-distance bus lines running all over Spain, which leave from the Estació d'Autobusos Barcelona Nord, Alibei 80, or Sants bus station. For information: tel: 902-260 606; www.barcelonanord.com.
Bus services to other parts of Catalonia are operated by:
Costa Brava: Sarfa
Tel: 902-302 025
Costa Maresme: Casas
Tel: 93-798 1100
Montserrat: Autocares Julià. A daily bus leaves Sants bus station (c/Viriato) at 9.15am and returns late afternoon. Buy tickets on the bus.
Pyrenees: Alsina Graells
Tel: 902-422 242

Tours

Several companies offer day trips to different parts of Catalonia, such as Figueres and Girona (to the north), including the Dalí Museum, or Sitges (to the south), Montserrat and a visit to a wine producer in the Penedès, from April to October. Companies include **Catalunya Bus Turístic** (information available from tourist offices, or tel: 93-285 3832; www.catalunyabusturistic.com). **Julià Travel** is another well-established company with a range of tours (www.juliatravel.com).

BREAKDOWNS

In case of a breakdown on the road, call the number given to you by your car hire company. If this is not possible, the general emergency number, **112**, has a foreign-language service and can connect you to the relevant service. On motorways and main roads, there are SOS phone boxes.

By Sea

There is a regular passenger and car service between Barcelona and Mallorca, Menorca and Ibiza, as well as Morocco, with the **Acciona Trasmediterránea** company, based at the Estació Marítima, Moll de Sant Bertran (tel: 902-454 645; www.trasmediterranea.es). It also has a service to Italy in conjunction with **Grimaldi Ferries** (www.grimaldi-lines. com). **Baleària** has a regular service to the Balearics and in the summer a fast service – four hours as opposed to the usual eight. For information and bookings, tel: 902-160 180; www. balearia.com.

Driving in Catalonia

Driving is the most flexible way to see the rest of Catalonia, but cars are better left in a parking place while you are in the city. Avoid parking illegally, particularly outside entrances and private garage doors: the police tow offenders away with remarkable alacrity, and the charge for retrieval is heavy. If this happens, you will find a document with a triangular symbol stuck on the ground where your car was. This paper will give details of where you can retrieve your vehicle. Street parking, indicated by blue lines on the road and a nearby machine to buy a ticket, is limited. Avoid green zones, which are exclusively for residents. Convenient (but expensive) car parks are in Plaça de Catalunya, Passeig de Gràcia and Plaça de la Catedral.

Drivers are supposed to stop for pedestrians at zebra crossings and when the green man is illuminated on traffic lights, but often they don't. Be sure to lock all doors when driving in town – thieving is common at traffic lights. Beware of anyone asking directions or saying you have a puncture. It is probably a trap.

The drink-driving rules have become tougher in recent years in Spain, and the police often do spot checks, so don't risk it.

Car Hire/Rental

Hiring a car is a good way to explore the area around Barcelona. It may be cheaper to make arrangements before you leave home as there are some good deals on the internet and often tied in with your flight booking. The main companies are based in the airport and in central locations in the city, notably at Sants station.

Avis: tel: 902-180 854; www.avis.es
Europcar: tel: 902-503 010; www.europcar.es
Hertz: tel: 902-402 405; www.hertz.es
National-Atesa: tel: 902-100 101; www.atesa.es
Over: Josep Tarradellas, 42; tel: 902-410 410; www.over-rentacar. com. Good-value local company.
Sixt: useful central locations; www.sixt.es
Vanguard: Londres, 31; tel: 93-439 3880; www.vanguardrent. com.

Scooters also for hire.

www.pepecar.com can be a good option if you book well in advance on the internet, but beware of added extras. It now has an office at the airport and several in the city centre.

Scooter Rental

Scooters are a popular way of visiting the city. Several companies rent out scooters or give tours. Explore different options via the tourist office (www.barcelonaturisme.com). Be warned, traffic in the city is dense and there is a

SPEED LIMITS

These have been fluctuating recently in an attempt to reduce petrol consumption, and are currently being reviewed. The police are staunchly vigilant and there are many radar points, so beware. The following may be changed, so check the latest situation when you arrive.
Urban areas: 50kmh (30mph)
Roads outside urban areas: 80–110kmh (50–68mph)
Dual carriageways outside urban areas: 110kmh (68mph)
Motorways: 120kmh (74mph)

tendency for some drivers to ignore traffic lights, so be cautious, especially at junctions.

Licences and Insurance

Citizens of the EU can use their national driving licence. Those from outside the EU need an international driving licence. Most UK insurance firms will issue a Green Card (an internationally recognised certificate of motor insurance) on request for drivers who are taking their own car to Spain – check with your insurer what this does and does not include. If you are hiring a car, you can select the kind of insurance coverage you want as part of the rental charge. Whether taking your own car or hiring a vehicle, always make sure you have adequate insurance cover.

GOCARS

A new transport option in Barcelona is sightseeing by GoCar. Guided by a GPS system and a recorded voice, these hazardous-looking vehicles are no doubt fun. There is also an electric vehicle, GoCar Twizy.
GoCar
Freixures 23 (outside Santa Caterina market); tel: 93-269 1792; www.gocartours.es

ACCOMMODATION

SOME THINGS TO CONSIDER BEFORE YOU BOOK THE ROOM

Accommodation

As Barcelona has become an increasingly desirable destination, the last few years have seen a boom in hotel construction and renovations of old buildings to provide quality accommodation. There are now nearly 400 hotels, rated from one-star to five-star GL (Gran Luxe), as well as innumerable guesthouses *(pensions)*, ranging from basic rooms accommodating three or four beds to boutique bed and breakfasts.

At the top end of the scale establishments are suitably indulgent, in avant-garde or historic buildings, with privileged views, rooftop pools and impeccable service at a very high price. Boutique hotels, with exquisite interior design and a more intimate feel, are on the increase.

In the moderate range there is a wide choice, with an equally diverse price range according to the services offered or the location. Further from the centre there are better deals – these can be a good option considering the city's efficient public transport system, which can whisk you to the centre in a matter of minutes.

The inexpensive range has improved, with more economic deals in attractive surroundings and giving good service. *Pensions* range from basic to decent, with just a few notable exceptions where an effort has been made to modernise or give some extra value. There are plenty in the centre, mostly in the Old Town, particularly in the streets leading off La Rambla. Some do not accept bookings in advance, but at least that gives you the advantage of checking out the rooms first, though many are accessible through internet booking agencies.

Rates vary dramatically, mostly on a supply-and-demand basis. Now that there are more rooms available, the client has more chance of getting a rate way below the standard price quoted, especially at weekends or off-peak times of the year. However, if there is a trade fair or large congress taking place, prices may double. Ironically – and fortunately for the many northern European and American travellers who take their holidays in midsummer – July and August are not considered peak times, whereas September and October are high season. Good deals can also be found through internet booking, directly with the hotel or through the many booking services on the web. Special offers are advertised, often with bargains for families. A small tourist tax is also charged. There are several new hotels along the recently developed waterfront near Diagonal Mar where high-standard accommodation can be found at a reasonable price. As they are a taxi or metro ride from the centre they are less popular, but the advantages of sea views and more peaceful nights, not to mention speedy access to the beach, are well worth considering.

Self-catering has become a popular choice in the city as it offers the opportunity to select the area you wish to stay in and to buy fresh food from the local market, as well as giving favourable rates.

Bed and breakfast accommodation is also widely available now, and has the advantage of friendly local advice and a closer insight into Barcelona life.

Hotel Chains

Aside from the recommended hotels listed below, you could also contact the central offices of the following hotel chains, which offer good quality and a range of prices.

Derby Hotels
Tel: 93-366 8800
www.derbyhotels.com
Group H 10
Tel: 902-100 906
www.h10hotels.com
Hoteles Catalonia
Tel: 900-301 078
www.hoteles-catalonia.com
NH Hotels
Tel: 902-115 116
www.nh-hotels.com

TRANSPORT
ACCOMMODATION
ACTIVITIES
A – Z
LANGUAGE

LA RAMBLA

1898
La Rambla, 109
Tel: 93-552 9552
www.hotel1898.com
€€€€ [1] p286, A1]
A major renovation of the Philippines Tobacco Company headquarters produced this smart, comfortable hotel with a suitably colonial air in its decor and indulgences, which include a personal shopping service, two year-round pools and top-floor suites with private garden and jacuzzi.

Bagués
La Rambla, 105
Tel: 93-343 5000
www.derbyhotels.com
€€€ [2] p286, A1]
The jewel in the Derby Hotels crown is, fittingly, a former jewellery shop in prime position on La Rambla, right next to La Boqueria market. It's all about attention to detail and elegant finishes using gold leaf and ebony. Even the swimming pool on the roof is slimline.

Barcelona House
Escudellers, 19
Tel: 93-343 7167
www.hotel-barcelonahouse.com
€€ [3] p286, A2]
Recently renovated in a funky, colourful style and located close to the nightlife in the Plaça Reial in a slightly edgy street, this good-value hotel is ideal for a youngish crowd. Rooms have basic comforts plus en-suite bathrooms.

Catalonia Plaza Cataluña
Bergara, 11
Tel: 93-301 5151
www.hoteles-catalonia.com
€€€ [4] p286, B1]
The magnificent modernista entrance hall inevitably gives way to modernised bedrooms, but the place still has charm and is well located just off Plaça de Catalunya. Surprisingly, it has a small pool and terrace.

Catalunya Plaza
Plaça de Catalunya, 7
Tel: 93-317 7171
www.h10hotels.com

€€€ [5] p286, B1]
Recently refurbished into a plush boutique hotel with elaborate decoration that brings out the best of the original 19th-century features. The chill-out garden is an oasis in this vibrant, strategic square. It's hard to get more central than this.

Citadines Barcelona-Ramblas
La Rambla, 122
Tel: 93-270 1111
www.citadines.com
€€ [6] p286, B1]
Good value for money in this aparthotel in a prime location. Food shopping can be done at the nearby Boqueria market or local supermarket. Enjoy the breakfast buffet bar, with privileged views of life on the city's most famous boulevard.

Continental
La Rambla, 138
Tel: 93-301 2570
www.hotelcontinental.com
€€ [7] p286, B1]
This historic hotel's individual character is a welcome change. Swirling carpets and floral decor can be forgiven when you can sit on a balcony watching the world go by on the famous Rambla – and at a reasonable price. Ask for a room at the front if you don't mind the noise.

D.O. Plaça Reial
Plaça Reial, 1
Tel: 93-481 3666
www.hoteldoreial.es
€€€€ [8] p286, A2]

A pool with a view at 1898.

The city's first gastronomic boutique hotel is in a handsome building, with smart interior decor, overlooking this legendary square. Enjoy the contemporary Catalan cuisine of Pere Moreno in La Cuina restaurant or on the exclusive rooftop, where there is also a small plunge pool.

Internacional
La Rambla, 78–80
Tel: 93-302 2566
www.hotelinternacionalcool.com
€€€ [9] p286, A2]
With rooms giving views of the opera house and Miró's mosaic, laptops with Wi-fi in each room, a rooftop terrace and reasonable rates, this refurbished hotel really lives up to its full name Internacional Cool Local hotel.

Kabul
Plaça Reial, 17
Tel: 93-318 5190
http://kabul.es
€ [10] p286, A2]
This long-established youth hostel, in a privileged position on this magnificent square just off La Rambla, now has a sun terrace on the roof. Rooms extend to dorms for up to 20. Renowned for a party atmosphere.

Le Meridien Barcelona
La Rambla, 111
Tel: 93-318 6200
www.lemeridienbarcelona.com
€€€€ [11] p286, A1]
A large, comfortable hotel, well positioned on La Rambla, born

again after major renovations gave it a more contemporary feel. The 360-degree Barcelona Suite, with a panoramic view of the Old Town, will set you back around €1,500, but it is some view.

Onix Liceo
Nou de la Rambla, 36
Tel: 93-481 6441
www.onixliceohotel.com
€€€ [12 p286, A2]
This elegant eco-friendly hotel, just off the lower part of La Rambla near the Palau Güell, has a minimalist style showing off the handsome decorative details of the grand building it occupies. The inner patio, with a sleek pool, is a haven away from the throngs in the street.

Oriente
La Rambla, 45
Tel: 93-302 2558
www.hotelhusaoriente.com
€€€ [13 p286, A2]
Once a charismatic old favourite, the 19th-century Oriente, in the heart of La Rambla, has been thoroughly refurbished to become a standard, efficient hotel, perhaps at the expense of its personality. It remains a great location.

Pulitzer
Bergara, 8
Tel: 93-481 6767
www.hotelpulitzer.es
€€€ [14 p286, **B1**]
The latest in this street of classy hotels just off Plaça de Catalunya

is sleek, smooth and wonderfully luminous for such a central location. A cocktail on the roof terrace is a must.

Regina
Bergara, 4
Tel: 93-301 3232
www.reginahotel.com
€€€ [15 p286, B1]
After recent renovation, this well-established hotel offers high-quality rooms and service in a central location just off Plaça de Catalunya, within easy reach of shopping and history.

Rivoli Ramblas
La Rambla, 128
Tel: 93-481 7676
www.hotelrivoliramblas.com
€€€ [16 p286, B1]
Behind the elegantly cool 1930s facade is a modern hotel with tasteful rooms. The barman of the cocktail bar downstairs plays great music.

Roma Reial
Plaça Reial, 11
Tel: 93-302 0366
www.hotel-romareial.com
€€ [17 p286, B2]
The no-frills, clean rooms overlook the stunning square, which is a treat. For a good night's sleep, though, request an interior room. You run the risk of hen-night groups at weekends.

Royal Ramblas
La Rambla, 117
Tel: 93-304 1212
www.royalramblashotel.com

€€€ [18 p286, B1]
The rather mediocre 1970s exterior gives way to a recently refurbished smart interior. Considering its position near the top of La Rambla, it is good value.

Silken Ramblas
Pintor Fortuny, 13
Tel: 93-342 6180
www.hoteles-silken.com/hotel-ramblas-barcelona
€€€ [19 p286, A1]
Comfortable rooms and a small rooftop pool make this hotel a pleasant retreat from the bustle but within very easy access of all the history of the Old Town and the cutting-edge cultural centres of El Raval.

The lobby of the Grand Hotel Central.

BARRI GÒTIC

La Casa de les Lletres
Plaça Antonio López, 6
Tel: 93-319 3723
www.cru2001.com
€€€ [20 p286, B3]
This tall, slim, listed building houses several self-catering apartments, including a penthouse with a terrace. The extremely stylish apartments have a literary theme, so you can choose between a one-bedroomed Orwell or a duplex Josep Pla.

Catalonia Portal de l'Àngel
Portal de l'Àngel, 17
Tel: 93-318 4141
www.hoteles-catalonia.com
€€€ [21 p286, B1]
Many vestiges of its former life as a palace remain, including the splendid staircase and tiled floors. Combined with modern details and tasteful décor, this is a really good option, well-situated between the Gothic Quarter and the Eixample, with an attractive pool in the inner courtyard.

Colón
Avinguda Catedral, 7
Tel: 93-301 1404
www.colonhotelbarcelona.com

PRICE CATEGORIES

Prices for a standard double room without breakfast or IVA (VAT):
€ = under €50
€€ = €50–100
€€€ = €100–200
€€€€ = over €200

€€€ [22 p286, B2]
A legendary hotel overlooking the cathedral. The classically decorated bedrooms seem more English than Spanish. To feel really privileged, request a top-floor room with a private terrace so you're eye-to-eye with the spires.

Denit
Estruc, 24–26
Tel: 93-545 4000
www.denit.com
€€€ [23 p286, B1]
A new concept in B&B, this functional but very stylish hotel has the advantage of being associated with the Hotel Majestic, so clients can use some of its facilities, like the luxurious spa. Very central, near the airport bus stop.

Gran Hotel Barcino
Jaume I, 6
Tel: 93-302 2012
www.hotelbarcino.com
€€€ [24 p286, B2]
A bit expensive for what it is, but there's no denying the luxury of being a stone's throw from Plaça Sant Jaume, the seat of government and nucleus of all fiestas.

Grand Hotel Central
Via Laietana, 30
Tel: 93-295 7900
www.grandhotelcentral.com
€€€ [25 p286, B2]
As grand as they come, this luxurious hotel has a 1930s Manhattan feel, a restaurant run by Michelin-starred chef Ramón Freixa and one of the city's slickest rooftop swimming pools.

Jardí
Plaça Sant Josep Oriol, 1, Plaça del Pi
Tel: 93-301 5900
www.eljardi-barcelona.com
€€ [26 p286, B2]
An extremely sought-after hotel with fairly basic accommodation, but overlooking two of the most attractive squares in the Barri Gòtic. Book well in advance.

Hostal Lausanne
Portal de l'Àngel, 24,1º,1ª
Tel: 93-302 1139
www.hostallausanne.es
€€ [27 p286, B1]
In a dream location for shoppers in this pedestrian street between Plaça de Catalunya and the cathedral, this homely place has retained some of the 19th-century elegance of the building where it is located.

Mercer
Lledó, 7
Tel: 93-310 7480
www.mercerbarcelona.com
€€€€ [28 p286, B2]
Feel the multi-layered history of the city in this stunning new boutique hotel in a former Gothic palace located on part of the Roman wall. Feast on gourmet delicacies, relaxed tapas and uplifting cocktails or chill in the rooftop pool between two Roman watchtowers.

Neri
Sant Sever, 5
Tel: 93-304 0655
www.hotelneri.com
€€€€ [29 p286, B2]
This was the first of Barcelona's several boutique hotels and is arguably the most unique. It's in a 17th-century palace giving on to Plaça Sant Felip Neri, one of the most atmospheric squares in the
Gothic Quarter. Only 22 rooms, so early booking is needed.

NH Barcelona Centro
Duc, 15
Tel: 93-270 3410
www.nh-hotels.com
€€€ [30 p286, B1]
Reasonably priced for what it offers, this modern hotel in a quiet location between La Rambla and the cathedral is surprisingly friendly.

Nouvel
Santa Anna, 20
Tel: 93-301 8274
www.hotelnouvel.es
€€€ [31 p286, B1]
Located strategically in a pedestrian street between La Rambla and Portal de l'Àngel, this attractive old building has a modern interior and comfortable, spacious rooms.

Racó del Pi
Pi, 7
Tel: 93-342 6190
www.hotelh10racodelpi.com
€€€ [32 p286, B2]
Small hotel built within an 18th-century palace in a pretty pedestrian street in the heart of the neighbourhood. Only 37 rooms, so book early.

Suizo
Plaça de l'Àngel, 12
Tel: 93-310 6108
www.hotelsuizo.com
€€ [33 p286, B2]
Lost some of its personality when renovated but in a great location on the border of the Gothic Quarter and fashionable El Born. Request a room on Baixada Llibreteria for more peace.

LA RIBERA

Banys Orientals
Argenteria, 37
Tel: 93-268 8460
www.hotelbanysorientals.com
€€€ [34 p286, B2]
Still one of the best options in town, with impeccable, slick interiors and stylish details, and it's in the hottest spot for shopping, wining and dining. Unbeatable value, so book well in advance.

chic&basic Born
Princesa, 50
Tel: 93-295 4652
www.chicandbasic.com
€€€ [35 p286, C2]
In an elegant 19th-century building close to the Parc de la Ciutadella and the buzz of the
Born, this utterly chic hotel is so fashion-conscious that even the rooms come in XL, L or M.

K&K Hotel Picasso
Passeig de Picasso, 26–30
Tel: 93-547 8600
www.kkhotels.com/en/hotels/barcelona
€€€ [36 p286, C2]
A new business-like hotel made appealing because of its position

overlooking the Parc de la Ciutadella, especially from a lounger by the rooftop pool.

Park Hotel
Avinguda Marquès de l'Argentera, 11
Tel: 93-319 6000
www.parkhotelbarcelona.com
€€€ [🖲 p286, C3]
A gem of well-preserved 1950s architecture, quite rare in Barcelona, on the edge of the Born district and within walking distance of the beach. Well-designed

rooms and a tapas bar on the ground floor run by Jordi Cruz, chef of the uptown restaurant Abac.

Pensió 2000
Sant Pere Més Alt, 6, 1°
Tel: 93-310 7466
www.pensio2000.com
€€ [🖲 p286, B1]
A noble marble staircase leads to this friendly family-run guesthouse, which is a cut above the average *pensión* and right oppo-

site the Palau de la Música. Great value.

Pension Ciudadela
Comerç, 33, 1°,1a
Tel: 93-319 6203
www.pension-ciudadela.com
€€ [🖲 p286, C2]
Opposite the Estació de França, this humble guesthouse has decent rooms at a very reasonable price, and is within staggering distance of the Born nightlife and the beach.

EL RAVAL

Barceló Raval
Rambla del Raval, 17–21
Tel: 93-320 1490
www.barceloraval.com
€€€ [🖲 p286, A2]
This cutting-edge, 11-storey hotel in the middle of what's still a fairly shady area is typical of the city's bold urban regeneration policies. Striking design, with panoramic views from every room, rooftop pool and terrace bar.

Casa Camper
Elisabets, 11
Tel: 93-342 6280
www.casacamper.com
€€€ [🖲 p286, A1]
The famed Majorcan shoemakers' first venture into hotel management, incorporating the aesthetics of design mecca Vinçon, has created an eco-friendly boutique hotel as revolutionary as a Camper shoe. Stylish, functional rooms all have their own mini lounge across the corridor.

chic&basic Ramblas
Passatge Gutenberg, 7
Tel: 93-302 7111
www.chicandbasic.com
€€€ [🖲 p286, A3]
The creativity of this ingenious small Catalan chain is irrepressible. Their latest venture has a 1960s theme, in keeping with its funky building. The comfortable rooms and communal areas are fun and colourful as well as being excellent value.

España
Sant Pau, 9–11
Tel: 93-550 0000
www.hotelespanya.com
€€€ [🖲 p286, A2]
Extensive renovation work stripped some of the old faded charm but added welcome comforts and highlighted the original Domènech i Montaner *modernista* details. The legendary dining room is now in the hands of Michelin-starred chef Martín Berasategui.

Gaudí
Nou de la Rambla, 12
Tel: 93-317 9032
www.hotelgaudi.es
€€€ [🖲 p286, A2]
A modern hotel without much personality, but the treat is the view: get a room at the front, so you can feast your eyes on Gaudí's Palau Güell opposite. The top-floor rooms have small terraces, which are worth fighting for.

Hosteria Grau
Ramelleres, 27
Tel: 93-301 8135
www.hostalgrau.com
€€€ [🖲 p286, A1]
Book early for this popular family-run *pensión*, which has had a recent facelift. It's in a good position for shopping and visiting the Eixample and Old Town. Excellent breakfasts are served in the adjoining bar.

Inglaterra
Pelai, 14

Tel: 93-505 1100
www.hotel-inglaterra.com
€€€ [🖲 p286, A1]
A good-looking hotel behind an old facade, equally well located for the bohemian Raval or the elegant Eixample. Now has a small pool on its roof.

Mesón de Castilla
Valldonzella, 5
Tel: 93-318 2182
www.mesoncastilla.com
€€€ [🖲 p286, A1]
The furniture is old-fashioned and rustic in style and the place is a bit quirky, but at least it has individual character. Very good location near the CCCB, university and shops. The owners are friendly and helpful.

Sant Agustí
Plaça Sant Agustí, 3
Tel: 93-318 1658
www.hotelsa.com
€€€ [🖲 p286, A2]
The oldest hotel in the city overlooks a quiet square. Recently spruced up, it is worth paying more for one of the luxury rooms on the fourth floor.

PRICE CATEGORIES

Prices for a standard double room without breakfast or IVA (VAT):
€ = under €50
€€ = €50–100
€€€ = €100–200
€€€€ = over €200

THE WATERFRONT

Arts
Passeig de la Marina, 19
Tel: 93-221 1000
www.hotelartsbarcelona.com
€€€€ [49 p286, D3]
Its ranking as the hotel with the highest profile on the seafront has been challenged by the new W hotel, but it is still a favourite with celebs. Rooms with panoramic views and every indulgence are only bettered by the recently renovated suites.

Duquesa de Cardona
Passeig Colom, 12
Tel: 93-268 9090
www.hduqesadecardona.com
€€€ [50 p286, B3]
A classically elegant hotel, in one of the handsome buildings giving onto the original waterfront and the old harbour. The pool and terrace on the roof are a hidden

treasure. Luxurious details at a moderate price.

Equity Point Sea Hostel
Plaça del Mar, 4
Tel: 93-224 7075
www.equity-point.com
€ [51 p286, B4]
An unbeatable spot for a youth hostel right on Barceloneta beach. Also has branches in La Ribera (Equity Point Gothic) and Passeig de Gràcia (Equity Point Centric).

Grand Marina
World Trade Centre, Moll de Barcelona, 1
Tel: 93-603 90 00
www.grandmarinahotel.com
€€€€ [52 p286, A4]
You feel as if you are aboard a luxurious cruise ship. Some of the bedrooms, with hydro-massage baths, jut out into the port, while those at the rear have a pano-

ramic view of the city.

Hotel 54
Passeig Joan de Borbó, 54
Tel: 93-225 0054
www.hotel54barceloneta.es
€€€ [53 p286, B4]
A modern hotel in an extraordinary location in Barceloneta overlooking the port and city, so you can enjoy the sea, but still easily walk to the centre. The building was once the fishermen's headquarters.

Marina Folch
Mar, 16, pral (1st floor)
Tel: 93-310 3709
Email:marinafolchbcn@hotmail.com
€€ [54 p286, C3]
This is a family-run gem with only 11 rooms, so book in advance. Request a room overlooking the busy waterfront for fun, or at the rear for a more peaceful night.

21ST CENTURY BARCELONA

Barcelona Princess
Avinguda Diagonal, 1
Tel: 93-356 1000
www.hotelbarcelonaprincess.com
€€€€ [off map]
On the cutting edge in all senses: designed by leading Catalan architect Oscar Tusquets, situated in Diagonal Mar, and offering all possible facilities. Prices can be subject to radical cuts, too, so it is worth trying to bargain to sleep at this giddy height with views of sea and city.

Diagonal
Avinguda Diagonal, 205
Tel: 93-489 5300

www.hoteldiagonalbarcelona.com
€€€ [off map]
Designed by award-winning Barcelona architect Juli Capella, this eye-catching hotel rubs shoulders with the Torre Agbar and the new Design Museum in Plaça de les Glòries and the 22@ business district.

Front Marítim
Passeig García Faria, 69–71
Tel: 93-303 4440
www.hotelfrontmaritim.com
€€ [off map]
One of the hotels on the waterfront between Vila Olímpica and Diagonal Mar. Being just a taxi

ride away from the inner-city buzz can be advantageous, especially if you wake up to sea views.

Poble Nou Bed & Breakfast
Taulat, 30
Tel: 93-221 2601
www.hostalpoblenou.com
€€ [off map]
In this very pretty bed and breakfast a stone's throw from the beach and the lively bustle of Poble Nou's Rambla you can have breakfast in the terrace-garden. With stylish decor and warm, attentive service, this place is a find.

MONTJUÏC

Mambo Tango Hostal
Poeta Cabanyes, 23
Tel: 93-442 5164
www.hostelmambotango.com
€ [55 p284, D2]
Private rooms are available but

the fun begins in the dorms. Lively, good-value hostel with very friendly staff in a great position amid the nightlife of Poble Sec.

Milleni
Ronda Sant Pau, 14

Tel: 93-441 4177
www.hotel-millennibarcelona.com
€€€ [56 p284, E2]
This medium-sized modernised hotel lies on the edge of the Old Town so is within easy reach of

the historical treasures, Montjuïc and the trade fair site. Good deals for family rooms.

Hotel Miramar
Plaça Carlos Ibáñez
Tel: 93-281 1600
www.hotelmiramarbarcelona.es
€€€€ [57 p284, D3]
In prime position on the hilltop, these former TV studios have been transformed by local star architect Tusqets into a luxury hotel offering full-on indulgence. For the best views, ask for a room overlooking the port.

EIXAMPLE

Actual
Rosselló, 238
Tel: 93-552 0550
http://hotelactual.com
€€€ [58 p288, B2]
A great little hotel in an unbeatable location with some rooms overlooking Gaudí's La Pedrera. It has attractive minimalist decor yet maintains a warm, personal atmosphere. Book early.

Alma
Mallorca, 271
Tel: 93-216 4490
www.almabarcelona.com
€€€€ [59 p288, B3]
An exquisite new boutique hotel in a 19th-century grand building typical of the Eixample. Despite being so central it exudes calm, especially in its lush interior garden, where you can have dinner.

Avenida Palace
Gran Via, 605–607
Tel: 93-301 9600
www.avenidapalace.com
€€€ [60 p288, B4]
Classic old-world gilt and chandeliers and new-world comfort. You can even stay where The Beatles slept on their one visit to the city in 1965.

Axel
Aribau, 33
Tel: 93-323 9393
www.axelhotels.com/barcelona
€€€ [p284, A3]
This hetero-friendly gay hotel located in the 'Gayxample' is one of the most beautiful in the city. Behind the modernista facade of stained-glass balconies there are stylish rooms and an urban spa. Every indulgence.

Hostal Cèntric
Casanova, 13
Tel: 93-426 7573
www.hostalcentric.com
€€ [62 p288, A4]

New-generation guesthouse, fresh, clean, modern and recently renovated. Excellent value and within walking distance of the Old Town and the Eixample.

Hostal Ciudad Condal
Mallorca, 255
Tel: 93-215 1040
www.hostalciudadcondal.com
€€ [63 p288, B3]
Very clean, respectable 14-roomed *pensión* in the heart of the best part of the Eixample. All rooms come with en-suite bathroom.

Claris
Pau Claris, 150
Tel: 93-487 6262
www.derbyhotels.com
€€€€ [64 p288, B3]
The Claris's strikingly designed interior was built behind the original facade of the Palace of Vedruna and is crammed with valuable artwork. Its roof terrace, open for lunch, dinner or cocktails, is probably one of the most glamorous in town.

Condes de Barcelona
Passeig de Gràcia, 75
Tel: 93-445 0000
www.condesdebarcelona.com
€€€ [65 p288, B3]
Contemporary elegance in two *modernista* buildings facing each other in the Quadrat d'Or. Rooms available with private balcony; roof terrace with mini pool.

Constanza
Bruc, 33
Tel: 93-270 1910
www.hotelconstanza.com
€€ [66 p288, C4]
This small hotel with a slick, modern interior, in a quiet residential neighbourhood, is very good value. Attractive terrace overlooking rooftops.

Cram
Aribau, 54

Tel: 93-216 7700
www.hotelcram.com
€€€ [67 p288, A3]
High design, impeccable style and all the latest mod cons in the warm interiors of this renovated, handsome 19th-century building. It now has a pool on the roof with fabulous views over the city.

Gallery
Rosselló, 249
Tel: 93-415 9911
www.galleryhotel.com
€€€ [68 p288, B2]
Well situated between Passeig de Gràcia and Rambla de Catalunya, with a brand new pool on the roof. Very pleasant bar on the first floor overlooking the street, and a restaurant that has tables outside in the garden.

Gran Hotel Havana
Gran Via, 647
Tel: 93-341 7000
www.granhotelhavana.com
€€€€ [69 p288, C4]
A comfortable, pleasant hotel with stylish rooms and an attractive, luminous interior. Good location.

Granados 83
Enric Granados, 83
Tel: 93-492 9670
www.derbyhotels.com
€€€€ [70 p288, A2]
One of the latest to come from this chain of smart hotels, this one, with its slick interiors, is in possibly the prettiest street of the

PRICE CATEGORIES

Prices for a standard double room without breakfast or IVA (VAT):
€ = under €50
€€ = €50–100
€€€ = €100–200
€€€€ = over €200

Lobby of the Omm, the height of cool.

Eixample, semi-pedestrianised, with many terrace bars and restaurants.

Indigo
Gran Vía de les Corts Catalanes, 629
Tel: 93-165 1381
www.indigobarcelona.com
€€€ [71 p288, B4]
The boutique branch of InterContinental has just opened this bright, cheerful hotel in an enviable location, just off Passeig de Gràcia. Handsome building, with a contemporary interior and a huge terrace with a pool.

Majestic
Passeig de Gràcia, 68
Tel: 93-488 1717
www.hotelmajestic.es
€€€€ [72 p288, B3]
This warm, sophisticated classic in prime position on the city's most elegant street has every comfort, including a luxury spa on its top floor. Gaze at the Sagrada Família and other key buildings from its magnificent roof terrace.

Market
Comte Borrell, 68
Tel: 93-325 1205
www.andilanahotels.com/es/hoteles/hotel-market
€€ [73 p284, D1]
Probably the best value in town, with an attractive neo-colonial theme running through the restaurant, bedrooms and indulgent bathrooms. A stylish find tucked

behind bustling Sant Antoni market.

Murmuri
Rambla de Catalunya, 104
Tel: 93-492 2244
www.murmuri.com
€€€ [74 p288, B2]
The award-winning modern elegance of this boutique hotel fits in perfectly with the sophisticated surroundings of the upper part of Rambla de Catalunya and carries on through its apartments, housed in an adjacent building. This is high-end living.

Omm
Rosselló, 265
Tel: 93-445 4000
www.hotelomm.es
€€€€ [75 p288, B2]
The ultimate designer hotel is seriously cool and *the* place to be seen. Whether you're in the Roca Moo restaurant, the rooftop pool, the sublime spa or chilling in the Omm Session club, you'll feel like you're in a fashion shoot

Palace
Gran Via, 668
Tel: 93-510 1130
www.hotelpalacebarcelona.com
€€€€ [76 p288, C4]
No longer part of the Ritz group but still eminently high-class, the Palace has reopened after major refurbishment, making it even more sumptuous. Dalí had a permanent suite here.

Paseo de Gràcia
Passeig de Gràcia, 102
Tel: 93-215 0603
www.hotelpaseodegracia.es
€€ [77 p288, B2]
Recently renovated in a simple manner but very effectively. Ask for a room with a balcony for the best views. This place is quite a find for this prime location, and is good value.

Praktik Rambla
Rambla Catalunya, 27
Tel: 93-343 6690
www.hotelpraktikrambla.com
€€€ [78 p288, B4]
An amazingly stylish hotel, making the most of the building's *modernista* features but mixed with fresh, clean design and creative ideas. Has an attractive terrace in a typical Eixample interior patio. Great location between Old Town and Eixample.

Regente
Rambla de Catalunya, 76
Tel: 93-487 5989
www.hcchotels.es
€€€ [79 p288, B3]
Pleasant hotel in an excellent position with some attractive original *modernista* features. Rooftop pool open in summer.

SixtyTwo
Passeig de Gràcia, 62
Tel: 93-272 4180
www.sixtytwohotel.com
€€€€ [80 p288, B3]
You'll find low-key elegance in this stylish newcomer. Its claim to individuality is the 'Ask Me' service: a team of switched-on young people who can answer your cultural, gastronomic or shopping queries. There's a small, oriental-style garden.

Violeta Hostel
Girona, 39
Tel: 93-500 5999
www.violetahostel.com
€€ [81 p288, C4]
Only 9 rooms in this friendly, personal hostel, well located in a quiet part of the Eixample midway between Sagrada Família and the Old Town. Great terrace in a typical Eixample inner patio, where drinks are served.

ABOVE THE DIAGONAL

A suite at the Gran Hotel la Florida.

Bonanova Suite
Bisbe Sevilla, 7
Tel: 93-253 1563
www.bonanovasuite.com
€€€ [off map]
In a quiet uptown residential area a short train or bus ride from the centre, these functional apartments are ideal if you want to get away from the noisy centre. Reserve one with a terrace if you can.

Casa Dover
Còrsega 429, pral. 1a
Tel: (mobile) 672 250 387
www.casadover.com
€€ [p288, C2]
High-class B&B with a stylish café on the ground floor. Well-designed and decorated rooms, in a perfect location on the edge of Gràcia, within short walking distance of the Sagrada Família. A great addition to the accommodation scene.

Generator
Còrsega, 377
Tel: 93-220 0377
http://generatorhostels.com

€€ [p288, C2]
This state-of-the-art hostel just landed in Barcelona is in a huge 1960s building bordering Gràcia and the Eixample, offering modernista monuments by day and the buzzy Gràcia scene by night. Targeted at a young crowd, though private twin rooms with bath and terrace are available.

Gran Hotel La Florida
Carretera Vallvidrera–Tibidabo, 83–93
Tel: 93-259 3064
www.hotellaflorida.com
€€€€ [off map]
This Grand Luxe hotel is the ultimate in luxury, perched high on Tibidabo hill. Brought back to life from its former 1940s glory, when the likes of Ernest Hemingway and James Stewart were clients, it has impeccable service and unbeatable views.

Hotel Husa Tres Torres
Calatrava, 32–34
Tel: 93-417 7300
www.husatrestorres.com

€€ [off map]
The Tres Torres is a small hotel, very reasonably priced for this smart residential area. It's nothing spectacular, but it sits in a quiet leafy street and the centre of town is only minutes away on the FGC trains. A good-value, peaceful option.

Hostal Lesseps
Gran de Gràcia, 239
Tel: 93-218 4434
www.hostallesseps.es
€€ [off map]
Recently refurbished so every room has an en-suite bathroom, and close to Lesseps metro in Gràcia, this is a good-value base in a great area.

Melia Barcelona
Avinguda Sarrià, 48–50
Tel: 93-410 6060
www.melia-barcelona.com
€€€ [p282, D2]
You could easily forget you're in Barcelona in this smart hotel, which could be anywhere in the world but guarantees good service, and is especially suitable for business travellers.

Rey Juan Carlos I
Avinguda Diagonal, 661–671
Tel: 93-364 4040
www.hrjuancarlos.com
€€€ [off map]
A vast glass and steel construction at the upper end of Diagonal and therefore a taxi ride away from everything. It offers maximum comfort and security, which may be why it is favoured by royalty and politicians. Stunning gardens and pool.

FURTHER AFIELD

Efficient and frequent suburban train lines *(Rodalies)* make staying out of town a good option. A cool, comfortable 45-minute train ride will take you from a quiet beach-side hotel to the centre of Barcelona. Rooms are usually easier to book and rates better value.

There are several top-quality hotels, including *paradores*, and an increasing number of self-catering options and rural guesthouses, which range from simple rooms in a traditional farmhouse to more exclusive country houses. An internet search will throw up contacts, but a good start is the

PRICE CATEGORIES

Prices for a standard double room without breakfast or IVA (VAT):
€ = under €50
€€ = €50–100
€€€ = €100–200
€€€€ = over €200

Catalan tourist office: www.cata lunya.com.

Badalona

Hotel Miramar
Santa Madrona, 60
Tel: 93-384 0311
www.hotelmiramar.es
€€

A traditional beach-side hotel, fairly recently renovated with all mod cons included. A quirky but fun choice, it's only 10 minutes from Plaça de Catalunya by train, and a pleasant walk along Badalona's elegant promenade.

Caldes d'Estrac

Kalima
Passeig de les Moreres, 7
Tel: 93-791 4890
www.kalima-caldes.com
€€€

Charming B&B in a small *modernista* villa on the promenade overlooking one of the less-frequented beaches, open from June to mid-September. The devoted owners take care of every small detail. A gem, at a reasonable price.

Capellades

Hostal Can Carol
Font de la Reina, 5
Tel: 93-801 0330
www.hostalcancarol.com
€€

Only half an hour inland from Barcelona near the Penedès wine region and Montserrat, this small hotel in a 14th-century farmhouse gives a warm welcome with its attractive, individually decorated bedrooms and rural surroundings. Wine tastings and other activities can be organised.

L'Escala

Hostal Empúries
Platja de Portitxol
Tel: 972-770207
www.hostalempuries.com
€€€

Rubbing shoulders with the Greek and Roman ruins of Empúries, overlooking a golden beach, this new-generation designer hostal offers pure bliss. It was the first hotel in Europe to win a Gold LEED certificate, and its leitmotiv is eco-responsibility, right down to its eco-Mediterranean cuisine.

Espot

Hotel Saurat
Plaça San Martí, 1
Tel: 973-624 162
www.hotelsaurat.com
€€

A comfortable family-run mountain hotel, right in the heart of the village, it is a perfect base for all the different activities in the Aigüestortes National Park and surrounding area. Now run by the fifth generation, its restaurant serves traditional, home cooking.

Girona

Aiguablava
Platja de Fornells, Begur
Tel: 972-622 058
www.aiguablava.com
€€€

This stylish, historic, traditional family hotel dates back to the 1930s. It overlooks one of the prettiest beaches on this spectacular coastline and makes for memorable holidays.

Bellmirall
Bellmirall, 3
Tel: 972-204 009
http://bellmirall.eu/
€€

Friendly and charming, this family-run bed and breakfast between the cathedral and city walls is a perfect base for discovering this historic city.

Montserrat

Cel.les Abat Marcet
Montserrat
Tel: 93-877 7701
www.montserratvisita.com
€€

The perfect way to capture the peace of Catalonia's sacred mountain – spend the night in a former monk's cell and avoid the busloads which descend in daytime. Good-value self-catering, ranging from one-person studios to four-person apartments.

Palamós

Trias
Passeig del Mar, s/n
Tel: 972-601 800
www.andilanahotels.com/es/hoteles/hotel-trias
€€€

This once typical beach-side hotel has reinvented itself into an extremely stylish place to stay with a good restaurant and pool, at a very moderate rate.

Ripoll

Mas El Reixac
Sant Joan de les Abadesses
Tel: 972-720 373
www.elreixac.com
€€

Self-catering accommodation in tastefully restored farm buildings just outside a historic village. Walks on the doorstep and skiing 30 minutes away. Log fires and duvets make it cosy in winter.

Vic

Parador de Vic-Sau
Paraje el Bac de Sau
Tel: 93-812 2323
www.parador.es
€€€

Traditional *parador* outside Vic, on the edge of a huge reservoir.

Vilanova i la Geltrú

Hotel César
Isaac Peral, 8
Tel: 93-815 1125
www.hotelcesar.net
€€

A delightful hotel run by two sisters, one creative in interior design, the other in the kitchen. It has a tiny pool in a shady garden a stone's throw from the beach, a good restaurant and is full of personal charm. Only 45 minutes by train from Barcelona.

PRICE CATEGORIES

Prices for a standard double room without breakfast or IVA (VAT):
€ = under €50
€€ = €50–100
€€€ = €100–200
€€€€ = over €200

ACTIVITIES

THE ARTS, FESTIVALS, NIGHTLIFE, SPORTS AND CHILDREN'S ACTIVITIES

THE ARTS

Festivals and Cultural Events

The combination of Catalonia's rich cultural heritage and the dynamism of contemporary movements has made Barcelona one of Europe's cultural capitals. Apart from its architecture and more than 50 museums, there is a busy calendar of music, festivals, opera, visiting exhibitions and constant activity in design, theatre, dance and the arts in general.

Posters, banners, the daily and weekly press and multiple websites all herald what's on in Barcelona. The city council has a cultural information centre in the Palau de la Virreina (the Institut de Cultura, Rambla, 99), which is crammed with leaflets from the different venues and acts as a ticket office for many events. Its website is very informative (http://barcelonacultura.bcn.cat/en). Also check the city council's website www.bcn.cat or http://guia.bcn.cat. The tourist information office in Plaça de Catalunya sells two-for-the-price-of-one tickets on the day of a performance. Two of the savings banks

also have an efficient system for ticket sales:

CXTelentrada of the CatalunyaCaixa, tel: 902-101 212; www.telentrada.com.
ServiCaixa of La Caixa, in most branches of the bank, tel: 902-332 211; www.servicaixa.com.

The Grec Festival

Venues: Teatre Grec; theatres and squares all over town
Held in July, Barcelona's biggest summer cultural event brings together a high standard of national and international talent in theatre, music, circus and dance, including activities for kids. Performances take place all over the city, but one of the most impressive and appealing venues on a summer night is the Greek amphitheatre on Montjuïc.

For information and booking: Palau de la Virreina, Rambla, 99; tel: 93-316 1000; www.bcn.cat/grec.

Film festivals

Barcelona holds several film festivals throughout the year, including: **DocsBarcelona** International documentary festival usually held in June, but dates may vary. www.docsbarcelona.com/en
L'Alternativa Festival of independent cinema held in November, based in the CCCB. http://alternativa.cccb.org

International Women's Film Festival Usually held in May/June, including outdoor venues. www.mostrafilmsdones.cat
Sitges Festival Internacional de Cinema Fantàstic de Catalunya A well-established event held every October specialising in fantasy, which attracts major players in the industry. www.sitgesfilmfestival.com

Music festivals

Sónar International Festival of Advanced Music and New Media Art Held in mid-June, this is an essential in the electronic music calendar, drawing an international crowd. Takes place in the Fira Montjuïc and Fira Gran Via. www.sonar.es
International Jazz Festival Oct–Dec. Running for over 45 years, this brings together legends of jazz and new talent in contrasting venues, from small jazz clubs to the Palau de la Música. www.theproject.es
Festival de Música Antiga This festival of ancient music, based in L'Auditori concert hall, usually features the extraordinary music-making of Jordi Savall, one of Catalonia's most renowned musicians internationally. www.auditori.cat
Festival de Peralada A glamorous music festival held in July and August in a castle near Girona,

often featuring opera singers, ballet dancers and popular crooners.
www.festivalperalada.com

Cultural Centres

The following centres regularly hold temporary exhibitions of the visual arts, festivals and other events. Consult local press or websites for details:
CaixaForum, the cultural centre of La Caixa Foundation
Av. Francesc Ferrer i Guàrdia, 6–8
Tel: 93-476 8600
www.fundacio.lacaixa.es
Exciting space in modernista industrial building holding exhibitions of contemporary art, historical heritage, concerts and talks.

TRADITIONAL FESTIVALS

Every district *(barri)* of the city has its own annual fiesta, known as the Festa Major, centred on its own patron saint. Giants *(gegants)* and comic characters parade the streets and *castellers* perform during fiestas. These troupes, made up of local people, erect human towers capped with the youngest and smallest. The *sardana*, the national dance of Catalonia, can also be seen every Sunday in Plaça Sant Jaume at 7pm (6.30pm in winter), and in the Plaça de la Catedral on Sundays at noon.
Christmas. In early December the Santa Llúcia Fair of arts and crafts plus Christmas trees is held around the cathedral.
Sant Esteve (St Stephen's Day), 26 Dec. Families meet for an even larger meal than on the 25th.
Reis Mags (Epiphany), 6 Jan. Children receive presents from the Three Kings, though modern commerce now indulges them with presents at Christmas as well. In Barcelona the Kings arrive from the Orient by boat the evening before and parade around the city.
Carnival (Carnestoltes), Feb or Mar. Wild pre-Lent celebrations

close with the 'Burial of the Sardine' on Ash Wednesday, a riotous mock funeral. The most extravagant Carnival parades are at Sitges, on the coast.
Sant Jordi, 23 April. A Catalan festival, St George's Day is also World Book Day, on which men give a rose to their lady, and receive a book in return.
Fira de Sant Ponç, 11 May. Aromatic and medicinal herbs, crystallised fruit and honey are sold in Carrer de l'Hospital.
Sant Joan, 23–4 June. Midsummer's Night, the eve of the Feast of St John, is a big event in Catalonia. It is celebrated with fireworks, cava and *coca*, a Catalan cake.
Diada de Catalunya, 11 Sept. Catalonia's national day is less a traditional fiesta than an occasion for political demonstrations and national anthems, gaining strength as the 300th anniversary of the fall of Barcelona is in 2014.
The Feast of La Mercè, 24 Sept. Barcelona's main fiesta is held in honour of the city's patroness. A week of merriment is crowned by the *correfoc*, a nocturnal procession of devils and fire-breathing dragons.

Centre de Cultura Contemporània de Barcelona (CCCB)
Montalegre, 5
Tel: 93-306 4100
www.cccb.org
Hosts seminars and a range of activities, as well as installations, exhibitions of contemporary art, and film and music festivals.
CX La Pedrera
Provença, 261
Tel: 902-202 138
www.lapedrera.com
Apart from the Gaudí architecture itself, and the Espai Gaudí permanent exhibition on the man and his work, there are free temporary shows on totally different themes in the exhibition space on the first floor.

Fabra i Coats
Sant Adrià, 20
Tel: 93-256 6150
www.bcn.cat/fabriquesdecreacio
Off the beaten track (metro: Sant Andreu), this fabulous space in a former fabric and thread factory is now devoted to 'manufacturing creativity' in the visual arts, performing arts and multimedia. It groups together various studios in this industrial area and holds exhibitions.
Fundació Antoni Tàpies
Aragó, 255
Tel: 93-487 0315
www.fundaciotapies.org
Permanent collection of work by the artist himself plus very good shows by other internationally acclaimed artists. Beautiful art library upstairs which can be consulted.
Palau de la Virreina
Rambla, 99
Tel: 93-316 1000
http://lavirreina.bcn.cat
Cultural information centre run by the city council. Exhibition spaces devoted to photography and the moving image.

Art Galleries

Art galleries are usually open Tue–Sat 10.30am–1.30pm and 4.30–8.30pm. They tend to be concentrated in two areas of the city.
In the Eixample: Passeig de Gràcia, Rambla de Catalunya and on interconnecting streets, but especially notably Consell de Cent:
Carles Taché, Consell de Cent, 290.
Galería Estrany·De la Mota, Passatge Mercader, 18.
Galería Senda, Consell de Cent, 337.
Joan Prats, Rambla de Catalunya, 54.
Sala Dalmau, Consell de Cent, 349.
In the Old Town around Plaça Sant Josep Oriol, in the Born and in El Raval district, near the MACBA:
Àngels Barcelona, Pintor Fortuny

MUSIC HALL AND CABARET

Barcelona has a long and colourful tradition of show business, centred on the Paral·lel area, with the more decadent shows in the dark alleys of what was the Barri Xino, much of which has disappeared with the new urban planning. After a period of decline there is a revival of this kind of entertainment, stimulated by the reopening of **El Molino** (Vila i Vila, 99; www.elmolinobcn.com), the most famous and colourful of this type of theatre. Here you'll find vaudeville, burlesque,

tango and a weekly flamenco night, with the option of dinner. Alternative cabaret can be found at:

Café Concert Llantiol, Riereta 7; tel: 93-329 9009
Circol Maldà, Pi, 5, Pral. 2b
Intimate space in an old palace for theatre, music and cabaret.
Gran Bodega Saltó, Blesa, 36
Tiny and colourful, with a bohemian crowd.
Tinta Roja, Creu dels Molers, 17; tel: 93-443 3243
Cabaret plus tango and Argentinian flavours.

27.
Artur Ramon Art, Palla, 10.
Ras, Doctor Dou, 10.
Sala Pares, Petrixtol, 5.
Trama, Petritxol 5, first floor.

Music and Dance

Classical Music

A busy season of concerts by the Orquestra Simfònica de Barcelona i Nacional de Catalunya (OBC) and visiting orchestras and soloists runs from September to early July.
The main places to hear classi-

cal music are:
L'Auditori
Plaça de les Arts
Tel: 93-247 9300
www.auditori.cat
A huge music auditorium which includes a Music Museum and now hosts the major concerts.
CaixaForum (see page 177)
Palau de la Música Catalana
Palau de la Música, 4–6
Tel: 93-295 7200/902-442 882
www.palaumusica.cat
If you have an opportunity to go to a concert in this extravagant *modernista* concert hall by Domènech i Montaner, then you

should. Its programme

Contemporary Music
CCCB
Montalegre, 5
Tel: 93-306 4100
www.cccb.org
(See page 143)
Fundació Miró
Montjuïc
Tel: 93-443 9470
This museum hosts a season of 20th-century music, with particular emphasis on Catalan composers. L'Auditori (see page 261) also has a programme of contemporary music.

Jazz
The Terrassa Jazz Festival in the spring and the International Jazz Festival in the autumn gather together some leading names. In addition there is a jazz festival in the Old Town (Ciutat Vella), from mid-October to mid-December, and regular jazz and blues sessions in an ever-increasing number of venues. To name a few:
Harlem Jazz Club, Comtessa de Sobradiel, 8; www.harlemjazz club.es
Jamboree Jazz and Dance Club, Plaça Reial, 17; www.masimas. com/jamboree
Jazz Sí Club, Requesens, 2; http://

At Harlem Jazz Club.

tallerdemusics.com/jazzsi-club

Rock/Pop

Barcelona is on the itinerary of most major international tours. Booking for these is usually online or through music shops, notably in Carrer de Tallers, just off La Rambla. FNAC in the Triangle shopping centre at Plaça de Catalunya sells tickets for most of the well-known groups performing. On a smaller scale, some interesting offbeat musicians and eternal old timers often pass through. Check the listings. Some key venues:

Bikini, Diagonal 547; www.bikini bcn.com. A well-loved club that was born again in this new venue in the 1990s. It has a well-selected, varied programme of live music, as well as a nightly disco of rock, funk and reggae.

Luz de Gas, Muntaner, 246; www. luzdegas.com. Formerly a music hall, this is a pretty place for concerts of many descriptions: jazz, ethnic, rock, soul. It turns into a dance place later on, but by then you can consider going elsewhere – it's not their forte.

Palau Sant Jordi and Sant Jordi Club, Montjuïc. The former Olympic venue is a favourite for huge concerts, while the Club hosts smaller bands. http://www.bsmsa.cat

Razzmatazz, Almogàvers, 122; www.salarazzmatazz.com. This remains one of the best nightspots, for hot-tipped international bands or old legends. Different spaces for different moods, with a range of DJs and VJs.

Sala Apolo/Club Nitsa, Nou de la Rambla, 113; www.sala-apolo. com. Once a music hall, now a trendy club with nightly music from visiting DJs as well as live events. Different spaces have different styles, from the latest techno to jazz-swing. It's always worth checking what's on.

Celtic

The city's Irish pubs nearly all have live music sessions. Check the local listings.

Opera and Ballet

Gran Teatre del Liceu
Rambla, 51–59
Tel: 93-485 9900/902-533 353 (tickets)
www.liceubarcelona.cat

Barcelona's opera house reopened in 1999 having been rebuilt after a devastating fire. Despite better technology and more productions, it is still difficult to get tickets. The repertoire has been broadened to have popular appeal, and avant-garde productions are on the rise. Good ballet season.

Contemporary Dance

Local companies and visiting groups perform in the city throughout the year.
Mercat de les Flors
Lleida, 59
Tel: 902-101 212
www.mercatflors.org
This venue is the former flower market converted into a theatre complex which specialises in dance and movement. Its busy programme of national and international cutting-edge performers is currently suffering because of budget cuts, so the season may be limited.

In addition there are dance seasons at the Liceu, the Teatre Nacional and at outdoor locations during festivals.

In the Gran Teatre del Liceu.

Flamenco

A *tablao* is a bar/restaurant that has a flamenco show. *Tablaos* are not strictly Catalan, but this import from Andalucía has quite a following. Check the times of the shows and whether or not dinner is obligatory.

El Patio Andaluz, Aribau, 242; tel: 93-209 3378

El Tablao Cordobés, La Rambla, 35; tel: 93-317 5711

El Tablao de Carmen, Arcs, 9, Poble Espanyol; tel: 93-325 6895. A good authentic show and reasonable dinner.

Los Tarantos, Plaça Reial, 17; tel: 93-304 1210. One of the most genuine shows.

Salsa

Some key venues:

Antilla BCN Latin Club, Aragó, 141–143

Sabor Cubano, Francisco Giner, 32

Samba Brasil, Lepant, 297

Theatre

Most theatre productions are in Catalan or Spanish, but for true enthusiasts the theatrical experience should compensate for language problems.

Among the main theatres are:

CASINOS

The Spanish are avid gamblers, and playing the various lotteries is a favourite pastime. If you want to do more serious gambling, you have the following waiting for you:

Casino Castell de Perelada
Perelada
Tel: 972-53 8125
In the province of Girona, 20km (13 miles) from the French border.

Gran Casino Costa Brava
Lloret de Mar
Tel: 972-361 166

Gran Casino de Barcelona
Marina, 19–21
Tel: 93-225 7878
www.casino-barcelona.com

Lliure
Plaça Margarida Xirgu
Tel: 93-228 9747
www.teatrelliure.com
Good contemporary productions.

Poliorama
Rambla, 115
Tel: 93-317 7599
www.teatrepoliorama.com
Accessible theatre performances, including flamenco spectacles.

La Puntual
Allada Vermell, 15
www.lapuntual.info
Alternative space in El Born, which occasionally has shows for kids.

Romea
Hospital, 51
Tel: 93-301 5504
www.teatreromea.com
A small, historic theatre in the Old Town now known for its avant-garde productions, mostly in Catalan.

Teatre Nacional de Catalunya
Plaça de les Arts
Tel: 93-306 5700
www.tnc.cat
Ricardo Bofill's neoclassical building is next to the L'Auditori concert hall near Plaça de les Glòries. It has the space to stage large-scale productions and smaller workshops.

Tívoli
Casp, 8
Tel: 93-412 2063
Old theatre with pretty facade; sometimes has ballet performances.

Victoria
Avinguda Paral·lel, 67
Tel: 93-443 2929
www.teatrevictoria.com
Often stages musicals and ballet performances, as well as flamenco shows.

Cinema

Barcelona has a great cinema-going tradition. The following usually show *versió original* films (*v.o.* in listings) – foreign films that have been subtitled rather than dubbed.

Most showings begin around 4pm. The last and most popular screening will be around 10.30pm, although sometimes at weekends there will be a very late-night show, called the *sesión de madrugada*.

Filmoteca de la Generalitat de Catalunya, Plaça Salvador Seguí. A film theatre showing less commercial films and retrospectives.

Icària Yelmo, Salvador Espriu, 61. Fifteen screens in the Vila Olímpica.

Renoir Floridablanca, Floridablanca, 135. Always something good to see on one of the five screens, and good bars nearby for after-film chat.

Verdi (Verdi, 32), and, around the corner, **Verdi Park** (Torrijos, 49). Together they have nine screens. Interesting and reliable selection.

NIGHTLIFE

Barcelona is internationally known as being the city that never sleeps. Wander down La Rambla and through the squares of Gràcia after midnight and it becomes obvious why. The streets are buzzing, and this is just the beginning: lounge bars are slowly filling and clubs have hardly opened their doors. Most people are still finishing dinner (restaurants tend to open from 9pm) having had a cocktail before, or they are having an after-dinner drink before finding a place to dance. When the clubs close between 3 and 5am there are still the 'Afters' – bars where the die-hards can continue until 8 or 9am.

This is the usual programme from Thursday to Saturday, though there is still plenty happening on other days of the week. It's easy to understand, especially in summer when 2am is the most cool and comfortable time of day, and the party spirit is infectious. Amazingly, the hard-working Catalans still make it to their offices bright and early the next day. An app for nightlife venues is available at www.bcnight.es.

TRANSPORT · ACCOMMODATION · ACTIVITIES · A – Z · LANGUAGE

Partaking in a Fat Tire bike tour.

Bars

The range is infinite, from neon-lit local bars to the designer bars of the 1980s and more recently cool, sophisticated bars in hotels, often on their roof, from milk bars (*granja*) and New Age cafés serving juices and infusions to *cocteleries* (cocktail bars) and *xampanyeries* (champagne bars). In addition, there are bars with live music, dance halls, chill-out lounges, restaurants which transform into bars when the DJs move in after dinner, and *xiringuitos* along the waterfront. The great majority are found in the Old Town, especially El Born and El Raval, but also in the central part of Eixample and a few uptown haunts. See the relevant neighbourhood chapters.

Clubs

Club venues are ever-changing. Check in the local listings for what's current, or better still, ask around. The bars lining the Plaça Reial make a good starting point. There is quite a scene around the Port Olímpic, at the foot of the Hotel Arts.

Club Ommsession, Rosselló, 265. If you can't stay in the trendiest hotel in town, at least enjoy its club. A seriously cool place to see and be seen in, from Thursday to Saturday.

Dot, Nou de Sant Francesc, 7. Small and very popular. In-house and visiting DJs play the best of current styles every night of the week. You can drink, dance and watch films all at the same time.

Eclipse, Hotel W, Plaça de la Rosa dels Vents, 1. Way up on the 26th floor you'll find the latest cool venue, where the view (and probably the cost of a cocktail) will take your breath away.

KGB, Alegre de Dalt, 55. An old favourite going through a revival, with live music sessions on Friday. A young crowd.

Moog, Arc del Teatre, 3. Found down an alleyway off La Rambla. A small place but very good for techno/electronic. You can dance until 5.30am if you so desire, and even later at weekends.

Otto Zutz Club, Lincoln, 15. One of the first designer discos. Best after 2am. Occasional live music.

La Terraza, Avinguda Francesc Ferrer i Guàrdia, 13. This is up on Montjuïc, part of Poble Espanyol and a great summer venue. Dance to electronic music in the open air until the early hours of the morning, with a fashionable crowd. Open from May to Oct.

When the summer crowds get too much, a dip in a pool can be the perfect antidote to city fatigue.

Club Natació Atlètic Barceloneta
Plaça del Mar
Tel: 93-221 0010
Large indoor pool and two outdoor pools, one acclimatised and one for kids. Has loungers overlooking the sea.

Parc de la Creueta del Coll
Mare de Deu del Coll, 87
Tel: 93-211 3599
Large outdoor pool/lake in one of Barcelona's urban parks up behind Park Güell but it can be reached by metro. Boats can be hired in the winter. Swimming from June to end of August Mon–Fri 10am–4pm, Sun and holidays 10am–7pm. Ideal for small children.

Piscines Bernat Picornell
Avinguda de l'Estadi, 30–40
Tel: 93-423 4041
Olympic pool in a beautiful location on Montjuïc.

Piscina Municipal Montjuïc
Avinguda Miramar, 31
Tel: 93-443 0046
Two pools with a superb, panoramic view. The Olympic diving events took place here, against the dramatic backdrop of the city.

Universal, Marià Cubí, 184. Striking decor on three floors. Dance to house music downstairs, funk, pop and 1980s sounds upstairs, or just enjoy a drink in plush surroundings.

Dance Halls

Nueva Epoca, Gran Via, 770. Old-time dancing to the sound of a live orchestra (Thu–Sun 6–9.30pm).

Sala Apolo, Nou de la Rambla, 113. A multifaceted old dance hall that's mostly disco and clubbing, but one Sunday a month it has a jazz-swing night with an excellent big band (see also Rock/Pop on page 262).

The Gay Scene

If you start off with these places, you'll soon get to know where all the rest are. For more details, see page 271.

Arena, Diputació, 233. A lively, easy-going club in the heart of the Gayxample – the name given to this part of the Eixample, full of cool gay bars and clubs.

El Misterioso Secreto de Amparo, Platja de Mar Bella. Every summer this lesbian *xiringuito* opens on Mar Bella, the beach near Poble Nou. Sunday evening is party night with DJs. This hetero-friendly beach bar is just along from the gay bar **El Dulce Deseo de Lorenzo**, epicentre of the gay scene from June to September.

Metro, Sepúlveda 185. A well-known gay club. Best after 1.30am.

SPORT

Participant Sports

The city council has been very active in providing sports facili-

FOOTBALL

Football is close to a religion in Barcelona. When the favourite local team, Barça, is playing, you will know all about it: firstly from the traffic jams to get to the the match or to the television, secondly because the town goes silent during the match, and thirdly thanks to the explosion of fireworks, car horns and bugles following a victory.

The stadium, Nou Camp, is one of the largest stadiums in the world, and has a museum that can be visited. **Fútbol Club Barcelona**, Arístides Maillol; tel: 93-496 3600; www.fcbarcelona.com.

ties for the community. Some are the legacy of the Olympic Games.

Bowling

Pedralbes Bowling
Avinguda Doctor Marañón, 11
Tel: 93-333 0352
Sun–Thu 10am–2am, until 4am Fri–Sat

Cycling

Cycling has become very popular in Barcelona. The city council issues a guide/map, available in tourist offices, which shows suggested routes and cycle lanes, and gives advice on taking bicycles on public transport.

Barcelona by Bicycle
Esparteria, 3
Tel: 93-268 2105
www.biketoursbarcelona.com
Accompanied cycling tours of the Old Town, with a meal included in the price. Also has bicycles and skates for hire.

Classic Bikes
Tallers, 45
Tel: 93-317 1970
www.barcelonarentbikes.com
Classic and folding bikes for hire, in a central location. Also offers guided tours, which can include tapas.

Fat Tire Bike Tours
Plaça George Orwell
Tel: 93-301 3612
City tours on US bicycles.

Rollerblading by Port Forum.

Filicletos
Passeig de Picasso, 40
Bicycles, tandems and child seats for hire. Open weekends and holidays 10am–dusk. Easy access to Parc de la Ciutadella, the port and the beach.

Golf

There are many courses all over Catalonia (visit www.catgolf.com to see a full list). To play, it is essential you can prove membership of a recognised club. Be aware that weekend fees are usually double the weekday fee. Three courses close to Barcelona are:

Port Aventura Golf
Tel: 902-202 220
Attraction at Salou's theme park. Two of the three courses are designed by Greg Norman.

El Prat
El Prat de Llobregat
Tel: 93-728 1000
www.rcgep.com
A premier course, often host to international competitions. Hires out clubs and trolleys.

Sant Cugat
Sant Cugat del Vallès
Tel: 93-674 3908
Includes a bar, restaurant and swimming pool. Clubs and trolleys available to hire. Closed Monday.

Terramar
Sitges
Tel: 93-894 0580
www.golfterramar.com

At L'Aquàrium de Barcelona.

Dating from the 1920s, this pleasant course amid pine trees runs down to the Mediterranean.

Horse Riding

Hípica Sant Cugat
Finca La Palleria, Avinguda Corts Catalanes, Sant Cugat
Tel: 93-674 8385
A bus from Sant Cugat to Cerdan-yola will drop you off. Pony treks range from one hour to the whole day in the Collserola hills.

Rollerblading

Cooltra
Passeig Joan de Borbó, 80–84
Tel: 93-221 4070
Skates to buy or hire.

Skiing

During the ski season cheap weekend excursions are available from Barcelona to the Pyrenean resorts, some of which can be reached by train (check out www.lamolina.com or www.catneu.net).

Tennis

Club Vall Parc
Carretera de l'Arrabassada, 97
Tel: 93-212 6789
www.vallparc.com
The courts, all clay, are open from 8am to midnight.

Water Sports

Agencia de Viajes Tuareg
Consell de Cent, 378
Offers organised boat trips near and far.
Base Nautica de la Mar Bella
Espigó del Ferrocarril, Platja de Bogatell, Avinguda Litoral
Tel: 93-221 0432
All types of boats available for hire by qualified sailors. Offers sailing courses for the inexperienced, as well as windsurf hire.
Orsom
Alongside Las Golondrinas at the quayside in Moll de les Drassanes
Tel: 93-441 0537
www.barcelona-orsom.com
Hourly and daily sails or charters in this enormous catamaran. Evening trips have live jazz.

Spectator Sports

Check the weekly entertainment guides or the sports magazines like *El Mundo Deportivo* for a calendar of events. The daily papers also have good sports coverage.
    Most local fiestas have various sporting activities as part of their programme, notably the Barcelona fiesta of La Mercè around 24 September.

Basketball

Basketball is gaining almost as ardent a following as football. The Barça basketball team is part of the football club and matches are played in the Palau Blaugrana, next to Nou Camp, tel: 93-496 3600.

Motor Racing

The Catalunya Circuit, home to the Spanish Formula 1 Grand Prix every May, is about 20km (12 miles) from Barcelona, in Montmeló. Cars and motorbikes can be rented for 30-minute practice sessions. For information: tel: 93-571 9700; www.circuitcat.com.

Tennis

The Conde de Godó trophy is an annual event at the Real Club de Tenis Barcelona, Bosch i Gimpera, 5; tel: 93-203 7562; www.rctb 1899.es.

CHILDREN'S ACTIVITIES

Barcelona, like everywhere else in Spain, is very child-friendly, and there will be few places where kids will be excluded.

Spanish children are allowed to stay up much later than elsewhere, particularly in the summer. Eating out is quite easy with children; the variety of local food means that there will always be something to appeal to a child's palate, and restaurants are welcoming.

However, take care when out in Barcelona. Busy roads and inconsiderate drivers call for extra care. You can escape from the traffic in the Old Town, where there are many pedestrianised streets. The city's beaches are obviously wonderful options and nearly all parks now have children's play areas. When you really need to let them run wild, take the 10-minute train ride to the Parc de Collserola (see page 212).

An invaluable website in English is www.kidsinbarcelona.com, which covers what's on for kids and suitable flat rentals.

Attractions for Children

L'Aquàrium de Barcelona
Moll d'Espanya, Port Vell
Tel: 93-221 7474
A very popular venue. For full details, see page 156.

Parc de la Ciutadella
Open green spaces for riding bicycles and having picnics, a play park to keep toddlers amused, and boats for hire on the pond (see page 132).

Poble Espanyol
Montjuïc
This pastiche of a Spanish village built in 1929 (see page 178) organises activities for kids.

Skating
Roger de Flor, 168
Tel: 93-245 2800
A popular ice-skating rink.

Tibidabo Funfair
Parc d'Atraccions de Tibidabo, Plaça del Tibidabo
Tel: 93-211 7942
A good old-fashioned funfair. Take the FGC train, then the little blue tram and the funicular to the top of the hill (see page 216).

Zoo
Tel: 93-221 2506
Enter via the Parc de la Ciutadella or Carrer Wellington if you're coming from the seafront (see page 136).

The following museums should also appeal:

CosmoCaixa
Isaac Newton, 26
Tel: 93-212 6050
The renovated science museum

is magnificent, with plenty of interactive games to keep the kids happy for hours (see page 217).

Museu de la Cera
Passatge de la Banca, 7
Tel: 93-317 2649
The waxworks museum is usually a hit with older children (see page 103).

Museu Marítim
Av. de les Drassanes
Tel: 93-342 9920
Contains lots of vessels from different eras, plus a chance to board a schooner (see page 152).

Places further afield:

Illa de Fantasia
Finca Mas Brassó, Vilassar de Dalt
Tel: 93-751 4553
www.illafantasia.com
An aquatic park 24km (15 miles) from Barcelona in Premià de Mar, easily reached by train.

Port Aventura
Near Tarragona, 108km (67 miles) from Barcelona
Tel: 977-779 090
www.portaventura.es
A theme park based on five world locations: the Mediterranean, Mexico, the Wild West, China and Polynesia.

Ride at PortAventura.

TRANSPORT

ACCOMMODATION

ACTIVITIES

A – Z

LANGUAGE

A – Z

AN ALPHABETICAL SUMMARY OF PRACTICAL INFORMATION

A

Addresses

Addresses are indicated by street name, number, storey, door. So Muntaner, 375, 6° 2a means Muntaner Street No. 375, 6th floor, 2nd door. The first floor of a building is *Principal*, often abbreviated to *Pral*. Some buildings have an *entresol* or mezzanine. An *àtic* is a top floor or penthouse, usually with a terrace. Street names are sometimes prefaced with C/ or Av. or Pg, meaning carrer (street), avinguda (avenue) and passeig (passageway).

Admission Charges

Museums have an entry charge ranging from €4 to €10 for the main ones and as little as €2 for the smaller ones, although entry to the Gaudí buildings is more. They have the usual reductions for students and pensioners, and many are free or reduced in price one day, often the first Sunday, of each month. People eligible for discounts should carry evidence of their identity. All municipal museums are free from 3pm to closing time on Sundays.

An Articket (around €30) allows entry to six key museums: Museu Nacional d'Art de Catalunya, the Picasso Museum, Fundació Miró, Fundació Tàpies, CCCB and MACBA. The ticket, which lasts three months but is valid for only one visit per museum, is available from tourist offices, from one of the relevant museums or through Tel-Entrada CatalunyaCaixa; tel: 902-101 212 (from abroad tel: +34 933-262 946); www.telentrada.com.

B

Budgeting for Your Trip

Gone are the days of cheap holidays in Spain. What you save on budget flights can easily be spent on meals, accommodation, shopping and clubbing. Accommodation is the main culprit, although for budget travellers there are hostels where beds are available in dormitories from €18. Self-catering is now widely available and is a good solution for families; shopping in the market is an enjoyable experience and an obvious saving.

Good restaurants are expensive but usually better value and quality than in northern Europe.

Bargain-hunters should opt for a lunch-time set menu, excellent value at anything from €8–15. Even some smart restaurants offer a lunch-time menu for around €25.

On the whole, fashion items and some household goods are slightly cheaper than in northern Europe, but probably not less than in the USA.

Cinema tickets cost from €5–8, with discounts on certain days of the week – Dia del espectador, usually Monday or Wednesday. Check listings in the daily press.

Public transport is good value with a T10 card for 10 journeys about €10 for use on the metro, bus, FGC and even RENFE trains within Zone 1 (see page 246). Taxis are not prohibitively expensive: a short journey within the centre could be as little as €3, but the fare quickly rises on longer journeys, late at night and when stuck in the frequent traffic jams.

One option for serious travellers who intend to cover a lot of ground in a short stay is the Barcelona Card, a ticket valid for anything from two to five days which gives free public transport and entry to museums, plus discounts on some leisure centres, restaurants, bars and shops. An adult card for two days is €37 and for five €62. This, the Articket and

Information gathering.

other offers can be purchased online at http://bcnshop.barcelonaturisme.cat.

Low-budget travellers can take comfort from the fact that, Barcelona being a Mediterranean city, life on the streets is free and endlessly entertaining, and no one charges for basking in the sun or swimming at the city's many beaches.

C

Climate and Clothing

Average temperature: 10°C (54°F) in winter, 25°C (75°F) in summer. December and January have the lowest temperatures, though the cold is often accompanied by bright sunshine.

Rain tends to fall in November and February to April. Spring and autumn are pleasant, with mild, sunny days. July and August are hot and humid. There are 2,500 hours of sunlight a year.

What to Wear

Catalan men and women dress elegantly, though casually. Ties are worn in formal situations and some offices, but not when going out to dinner. In July and August cotton and loose-fitting garments are necessary. Respect local traditions: bathing costumes and bikinis are strictly for the beach and you now risk paying fines if you are not fully clothed in the street. A light jacket is useful any time of the year. In winter, bring a warm jacket which can accommodate various layers, especially in January and February, when the wind blows. Be sure to bring comfortable shoes – Barcelona is a very walkable city.

Consulates

Canada
Pl. Catalunya 9, 1° 2a
Tel: 93-270 3614

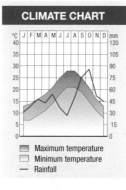

CLIMATE CHART

°C / mm chart with months J F M A M J J A S O N D

Legend:
- ▦ Maximum temperature
- ▢ Minimum temperature
- — Rainfall

Ireland
Gran Via Carles III, 94
Tel: 93-491 5021
UK
Avinguda Diagonal, 477, 13°
Tel: 902-109 356
US
Passeig Reina Elisenda, 23
Tel: 93-280 2227

Crime and Safety

Take care, as in any large city. Loosely swinging handbags, ostentatious cameras, mobile phones and even rucksacks are regularly snatched in broad daylight, especially from bars and terrace cafés. Barcelona is not a den of iniquity, and with due care and attention, you can avoid dangerous situations. Be streetwise and don't get distracted by someone asking you a question so you look the other way while their partner snatches your bag.

The Old Town has a bad reputation for petty crime, so be alert when wandering through it or watching street artists. Wear your handbag across your chest, keep your camera hidden and do not flash your wallet around. Carry enough money for the day, leaving the rest in the safe-deposit box at your hotel.

At airports and railway and bus stations, keep your luggage

TRANSPORT

ACCOMMODATION

ACTIVITIES

A – Z

LANGUAGE

together and don't leave it unattended. Never leave anything valuable in a car, even in a crowded street. Take special care when arriving in town from airports, as the professional thieves watch these spots.

Don't get caught by a few small gangs who perpetrate various tricks to waylay you, like commenting on the dirt on your back and, while 'helping' you to remove it, slip the purse from your pocket. Another is a game known as *trila*, a variation of the three-card trick, played by crooks (regulars on La Rambla), in the guise of innocent bystanders. You will *never* win. When travelling by car, be careful at traffic lights: a familiar scam is where one person causes a diversion while the other pinches your bag from the back seat, or slashes your tyres. The latest scam is performed by individuals claiming to be plain-clothed police officers and even showing their 'identity'. Do not show them yours.

In the case of a theft, assault or loss, call the general emergency number, 112. You will probably be advised to go to a police station to make a statement *(denuncia)*. This is vital if you want to claim on an insurance policy or seek further help from the city police or your consulate. It may soon be possible to make a *denuncia* in hotels to ease the process.

Police

The main police station is at Nou de la Rambla, 76. There are two main types of police in the city:
Policia Municipal. Tel: 092. The city police, known as the *Guàrdia Urbana*, are responsible for traffic, civilian care and security. They are recognisable by the blue-and-white checked band around their caps and on their vehicles.
Mossos d'Esquadra. Tel: 088. The autonomous police of Catalonia have taken over all responsibilities from the state police, the Policia Nacional, in Catalonia. The Policia Nacional in Barcelona just handle bureaucratic paperwork

like issuing IDs, passports, etc. Occasionally you see the Guardia Civil, who are responsible for customs and border controls at ports and airports.

Assistance for Tourists

The city police have a special scheme for tourists at their headquarters (La Rambla, 43; tel: 93-256 2430; 24-hour service), offering legal advice, medical assistance, provision of temporary documents in the event of loss or robbery and an international telephone line for the speedy cancellation of credit cards, etc.

The general emergency number, 112, can attend to calls in English and French and has a translation service for other languages.

Customs

Visitors from outside the EU can bring limited amounts of cigarettes, alcohol, perfume, coffee and tea. If your camera, computer, etc is new and you do not have the purchase receipt, it is wise to ask a customs official to certify that you brought it into the country with you. There is no restriction on the movement of goods between EU countries, although there are guidance levels for alcohol and tobacco for personal use: 3,200 cigarettes, 90 litres of wine, 110 litres of beer and 10 litres of spirits.

Disabled Travellers

Huge advances have been made recently for people with disabilities thanks to new local authority policies. Over 190 hotels are equipped with facilities for people with disabilities. Details can be found at www.bcn.es/turisme or through the tourist office, tel: 93-285 3834. Some 28 city

museums are wheelchair-accessible, as are many public and historic buildings; a complete listing can be found on www.bcn.es/cultura by clicking on the Directories category.

All the beaches have suitable access, and there are 14 adapted public toilets.

On public transport, nearly all bus and metro lines have disabled facilities; for details click on Transport for Everyone at www.tmb.net.

Regarding car rental, with warning Hertz can provide automatic cars.

For an accessible taxi service, tel: 93-420 8088 for information.

A very helpful organisation is Accessible Barcelona (tel: 93-428 5227; www.accessiblebarcelona.com), run by British wheelchair-user Craig Grimes, who has road-tested all his recommendations.

For general information, see www.tourspain.co.uk/disabled, or for queries specific to Barcelona, contact: Institut Municipal de Persones amb Disminució, Diagonal 233, 08013 Barcelona; tel: 93-413 2775; sap@mail.bcn.es.

Electricity

British or US plugs do not fit Spanish sockets, because wall sockets for shavers, hairdryers, etc, take plugs with two round pins. It is advisable to bring an adaptor, which can be bought at supermarkets, chemists and airports, or in Barcelona at El Corte Inglés. The voltage is 220v, so US visitors with 110v appliances will need a transformer.

Emergencies

In an emergency call 112 or go to the 'Urgències' department (A & E) at one of the main hospitals, or visit an *ambulatorio* (medical centre). They can be found in every

A student in the Barri Gòtic.

district – ask in any pharmacy for the nearest one. With the drastic cutbacks to Spain's public health system in 2013, some EU visitors have been presented with a bill even if they have a European Health Insurance Card (EHIC), which should make them eligible for emergency treatment. Check the latest situation with the relevant authorities. It is wise to take out travel and medical insurance before your trip.

Hospitals

Hospital Clínic
Carrer de Villaroel, 170
Tel: 93-227 5400
Hospital de Nens (children)
Carrer de Consell de Cent, 437
Tel: 93-231 0512
Hospital del Mar
Passeig Marítim, 25–29
Tel: 93-248 30 00

Emergency Numbers

Emergencies (police, fire, ambulance), tel: 112
Fire Brigade, tel: 080
Ambulance service, tel: 061
Policia Municipal, tel: 092
Mossos d'Esquadra, tel: 088
Road accidents, tel: 088

Gay & Lesbian Travellers

There is a thriving gay and lesbian scene in Barcelona, and the city is considered one of the gay capitals of Europe. This is a far cry from the not-too-distant past when homosexuals suffered repression under Franco. Spain was the third country in Europe to legalise gay marriage in 2005, and in the first six months following the law's approval there was a gay wedding every day in Catalonia.

A whole area of the elegant Eixample district, known as the Gayxample, has fashion shops, bars, clubs, hairdressers and so on particularly focused on the gay community. In the midst of it is Europe's first gay hotel, also 'hetero-friendly', the Axel (see page 255), in a stunning *modernista* building with a designer interior.

In addition there is an annual gay film festival, the International Gay and Lesbian Film Festival of Barcelona (www.cinema lambda.com).

Nearby Sitges (just half an hour south of the city on the coast) is a real mecca for gays, particularly in summer. The drag parade during Carnival in February is renowned.

For advice and information on the latest venues, the lesbian and gay hotline is **Telèfon Rosa**, tel: 900-601 601; www.cogailes.org.

A general guide is www.gaybar-celona.net. (See also page 265.)

Other useful addresses are:
Casal Lambda
Verdaguer i Callís, 10
Tel: 93-319 5550
From 5pm onwards. An information centre campaigning for gay and lesbian rights, offering help and advice.
Col·lectiu Gai de BCN
Ptge Valeri Serra, 23
Tel: 93-453 4125
Sextienda
Rauric, 11
Tel: 93-318 8676

Guides and Tours

If you want to recruit a professional tourist guide or interpreter,

TRANSPORT

ACCOMMODATION

ACTIVITIES

A – Z

LANGUAGE

you should contact:
Barcelona Guide Bureau
Tel: 93-268 2422
City Guides
Tel: 93-412 0674
Professional Association of Barcelona Tour Guides
Tel: 93-319 8416
Context Travel
For more exclusive tours with smaller groups and specialised docents, check out Context Travel (www.contexttravel.com/city/barcelona).

H

Health and Medical Care

There are no special health risks to be aware of in Barcelona. You should take the usual travel precautions and break yourself into the climate and the food gently. Between June and September you should wear a hat and suncream when out during the day.

Food and Drink

In most areas of Barcelona tap water can be drunk without fear,

but it is often dosed with purifying salts which make the taste unpleasant. Mineral water is easily available, and Vichy Catalan is soothing for queasy stomachs.

Catalan cooking is healthy and nutritious, but a change of diet can affect some digestive systems. Avoid excessively oily food.

Another danger area can be tapas, which in hot weather can be a source of infection if they have been left standing on a counter for too long. Most notorious is anything mayonnaise-based, such as the ubiquitous *ensaladilla rusa* (Russian salad), a potential source of salmonella; in some parts of Spain home-made mayonnaise is banned.

With common sense it is easy to spot the 'tired' tapas in greasy bars, which should be avoided.

Treatment

Residents of EEA (European Economic Area) countries, which means EU countries plus Switzerland, Lichtenstein, Iceland and Norway, are entitled to receive state medical treatment in Spain if they have a European Health Insurance Card (EHIC),

which must be obtained in their own country. In the UK this can be done online, by phone or by post (tel: 0845 606 2030; www.ehic.org.uk).

For greater peace of mind, take out private insurance, which is best organised before setting off but can be arranged on arrival in Barcelona through any travel agency.

If you are insured privately or prepared to pay for private health care, Barcelona Centre Mèdic (Avinguda Diagonal, 612; tel: 93-414 0643) is a coordination centre for different specialists and offers an information service for consultations (www.bcm.es). Before undergoing private treatment, check your insurer will foot the bill.

Buying Medicines

Pharmacies *(farmacias)* have a red or green flashing neon cross outside. When closed, *farmacias* post a list of other *farmacias* in the window, indicating the nearest one on duty. Pharmacies stock prescription and non-prescription medications, toiletries, baby food and supplies. Many *farmacias* also stock homeopathic remedies, or will be able to obtain them for you within a day. The following is an English-speaking chemist:
Farmacia Josep Clapés
La Rambla, 98
Tel: 93-301 2843

Alternative Medicine

The Old Town still has many charming herbalist shops, with shelves crammed with alternative health care and people queuing for advice. One of the finest, where they individually mix you a brew according to your ailments, is:
Manantial de Salud
Xuclà, 23
Tel: 93-319 1965

Dentists

Dentists in Spain are not covered by any of the reciprocal agreements between countries, so be prepared to pay for treatment.

Much of the city was built on a grid system which aids navigation.

TRANSPORT

La Rambla is still a popular meeting place for older people.

Even with insurance you may have to pay first and then make a claim on return.

The following clinics offer an emergency service:

Clínica Dental Barcelona
Pau Claris, 194–196
Tel: 93-487 8329
Emergency service daily from 9am–midnight. English-speaking dentists.

Clínica Janos
Muntaner 338, Entlo. 1a
Tel: 93-200 2333
Open Mon–Sat 9.30am–8pm, Sun 10am–2pm.

L

Left Luggage

A left-luggage service *(consigna)* is available in Sants railway station 5.30am–11pm. There are also lockers at Barcelona Nord bus station, and a left-luggage office is open 8am–1am at the sea terminal on Moll Barcelona. Locker Barcelona is a great left-luggage service in the centre, near Plaça de Catalunya (Estruc, 36; tel: 93-302 8796; www.lockerbarcelona.com; daily 8.30am–9pm).

Lost Property

If you lose something on the metro or a bus, go to the TMB office (Metro Diagonal, Mon–Fri 8am–8pm); if you leave something in a taxi, tel: 902-101 564. The municipal lost-property office (Oficina de Troballes) is in Plaça Carles Pi i Sunyer, 8–10 (tel: 010; phone between 8am–10pm, visit 9am–2pm). Lost or stolen passports retrieved by the police are sent to the relevant consulate.

M

Maps

The tourist board issues a good general map of the city *(plano de la ciudad/plànol de la ciutat)*. A transport map is also available from metro stations. The city council online map is excellent for finding streets, metros, services, etc, and has an English version (http://w20.bcn.cat/Guiamap).

Media

Newspapers

The main daily newspapers are:

El País
Based in Madrid but with a Catalan edition, *El País* is the most internationally respected Spanish paper. An English version is published by the *International Herald Tribune*.

El Periódico
This is the more popular Barcelona newspaper, but it is limited on international news. In both Castilian and Catalan.

El Punt Avui
The original Catalan paper *Avui*, founded in 1976 less than a year after Franco's death, was bought by its rival *El Punt*. Staunchly nationalist.

La Vanguardia
The traditional (and moderately Conservative) newspaper of Barcelona has good coverage of local news and events, especially its informative 'What's On' section on Friday.

A weekly paper in English, Catalonia Today, covers international, national and local news in brief and has useful listings and features on Barcelona.

International newspapers can be found on the newsstands on La Rambla and Passeig de Gràcia, and also in several international bookshops, such as FNAC (Plaça de Catalunya).

Magazines

A wealth of magazines cover every interest and indulgence. The main fashion magazines, such as *Vogue*, *Marie Claire* and *Elle*, publish a Spanish edition. Most notable national magazines are:

¡Hola!
The most famous Spanish magazine, with illustrated scandal and gossip on the rich and the royal.

Guía del Ocio
A useful weekly listings magazine for Barcelona. Visit their website www.guiadelociobcn.es.

English Publications

Several freebies with information on the city and listings, such as **Barcelona Connect** (www. barcelonaconnect.com) and

ACCOMMODATION

ACTIVITIES

A – Z

LANGUAGE

Miniguide (www.bcn-inside.com), are distributed to hotels, bars and bookshops. However, the most established is:

Metropolitan

Barcelona's first monthly magazine in English is targeted at residents; it makes interesting reading and carries useful listings. It is distributed free at key points in the city (and around, e.g. Sitges), such as bookshops, bars and cinemas. Check out their website www.barcelona-metropolitan.com.

Television

The principal channels are TVE1 and La2 (state-owned), TV3, and Canal 33, the autonomous Catalan channels. The local channel is BTV. Commercial channels include Antena 3 (general programming), Tele 5 (directed at people at home during the day) and Canal Plus (mainly films, for subscribers only). Satellite programmes are obtainable in many of the larger hotels.

Money

The currency is the euro (€). Bank notes are issued in denominations of 5, 10, 20, 50, 100, 200 and 500; coins in denominations of 1, 2, 5, 10, 20 and 50 *centimos*, and €1 and 2.

Most banks have cashpoints (ATMs), operating 24 hours a day, where money can be withdrawn using most credit and debit cards.

Keep (separately) a record of the individual numbers of your traveller's cheques, so they can be replaced quickly if they are lost or stolen.

Tax

Tax (IVA) on services and goods is 21 percent, and for restaurants and hotels, 10 percent. Visitors from non-EU countries are entitled to tax reclaims on their return home at a Global Refund Office. Look out for 'Tax Free' signs in shop windows. When you leave the EU, Barcelona Cus-

toms must confirm the purchase and stamp the tax-free cheque; you can then take it to the airport branch of Banco Exterior de España and cash the cheque into the currency required. Alternatively, take the tax-free cheque to Turisme de Barcelona in Plaça de Catalunya or Passatge de la Concepció, 7 to cash it in before leaving.

Banks

Bank opening hours vary, but as a general rule they are open all year Mon–Fri 8.30am–2pm, and also Sat 8am–2pm Oct–May. The *cajas* or, in Catalan, *caixes* (savings banks) offer the same service, but are open on Thursday afternoon instead of Saturday morning Oct–May.

There are numerous currency-exchange offices in the city centre, including in La Rambla and in the Plaça de Catalunya Tourist Information Centre. The larger hotels will also exchange money, although often at a less favourable rate.

Foreign banks in the city:

Barclays Bank
Passeig de Gràcia, 45
Tel: 93-481 2020

Lloyds Bank
Avinguda Diagonal, 550
Tel: 902-024 365

Credit Cards

Major international credit cards, such as Visa, Eurocard and MasterCard, can be used, although you will be required to show some form of identity or enter your PIN.

In the case of loss:
American Express
Tel: 902-375 637
Diner's
Tel: 901-101 011
Eurocard, **MasterCard**, **Mastercharge**, **Servired** and **Visa**
Tel: 91-519 2100/900-971 231
Visa International
Tel: 900-991 124

Tipping

There are no golden rules about this. If you feel the need to leave a tip, make it a token rather than an extravagant one. Some restaurants automatically add a service charge to the total, in which case nothing extra is needed. As a yardstick, in restaurants where a charge is not added, it should be around 5–10 percent and about the same in a taxi. In a bar or café, 80 *centimos* – €1.50 is

Classical post office building near the Columbus Monument.

enough, depending on the size of the bill.

Churches are usually open to the worshipper and the visitor.

Opening Hours

In general, offices are open 9am–2pm and 4–8pm, although some open earlier, close later and have shorter lunch breaks. Most official authorities are open 8am–2pm and close to the public in the afternoon. Companies in the outer industrial zones tend to close at 6pm. From mid-June to mid-September, many businesses practise *horas intensivas* from 8am–3pm.

Postal Services

Stamps for letters, postcards and small packets can be bought very conveniently in the many *estancs* to be found in every district. These are state-owned establishments licensed to sell stamps, cigarettes and tobacco, and are easily recognisable by their orange and brown logo, **Tabacs SA**. Opening hours are loosely 9am–1.30pm and 4.30–8pm. Postboxes are yellow.

The main post office is at the bottom of Via Laietana near the port, in Plaça Antoni López. It has collections every hour and is open Mon–Fri 9am–9.30pm, Sat 9am–2pm. Other post offices close at 2pm, apart from the one in Carrer d'Aragó, 282 (near Passeig de Gràcia), which is open until 8.30pm, but with limited services.

Poste Restante letters can be sent to the main post office addressed to the Lista de Correos, 08080 Barcelona. Take ID with you (preferably your passport) when claiming letters.

Public Holidays

Many bars, restaurants and museums close in the afternoon and evening on public holidays and Sundays. If a holiday falls on a Tuesday or a Thursday it is common to take a *pont* or *puente* (bridge) to link the interim day with the weekend. Roads out of the city are extremely busy on the afternoon/evening before a holiday. August is the annual holiday month and many businesses, including restaurants, close down for three or four weeks, although this is happening less in central Barcelona.

The following are the public holidays (national and Catalan):
1 January – New Year's Day
6 January – Reis Mags: Epiphany
Late March/April – Good Friday (variable)
Late March/April – Easter Monday (variable)
1 May – Festa del Treball: Labour Day
Late May – Whitsun: Pentecost (variable)
24 June – Sant Joan: Midsummer's Night
15 August – Assumpció: Assumption
11 September – Diada: Catalan national holiday
24 September – La Mercè: the patroness of Barcelona. This is the city's main fiesta
12 October – Hispanitat/Pilar: Spanish national day
1 November – Tots Sants: All Saints' Day
6 December – Día de la Constitució: Constitution Day
8 December – Immaculada Concepció: Immaculate Conception
25–6 December – Christmas

Public Toilets

There is a notorious dearth of public toilets in Barcelona, but finally the municipal authorities are remedying the situation: public urinals have been installed at strategic points in the city. A few coin-operated cabins exist, although it is usually easier to find a bar. The beaches are well equipped with toilets, many of which are adapted for wheelchair-users, and others can be found in public centres like the airport, the railway and bus stations, shopping centres and museums. Bars and cafés are usually willing to let their services be used, especially if it is for a child.

Religious Services

Mass is usually said between 7am and 2pm on Sunday and feast days. Evening Mass is held between 7 and 9pm on Saturday, Sunday and feast days.
Catholic
Parroquia María Reina
Carretera d'Esplugues, 103

TRANSPORT

ACCOMMODATION

ACTIVITIES

A – Z

LANGUAGE

Tel: 93-203 4115
Sundays 10.30am (in English)
Anglican
St George's Church
Sant Joan de la Salle, 41
Tel: 93-417 8867
Sunday 11am (services in English). This is off the beaten track
above Passeig de la Bonanova
(FGC Av. Tibidabo).
Jewish
The Synagogue
Avenir, 24
Tel: 93-209 3147
Muslim
Centro Islàmico Mosque
Avinguda Meridiana, 326
Tel: 93-351 4901
Toarek Ben Ziad
Hospital, 91
Tel: 93-441 9149
Multicultural, multi-denominational
International Church of Barcelona
Urgell, 133
Tel: 93-894 8084

Student Travellers

For holders of an international
student card (ISIC), or the Euro26
card for people under the age of
30, there are many discounts on
offer: reduced-price tickets at
museums and other cultural centres, and discounts on railways
and other public transport, hostels and shops. The ISIC card for
students is available via www.isic.
org and the European Youth card,
for people under 30 whether a
student or not, is available at
www.euro26.org.

There is a youth hostel in the
Gothic Quarter, **Gothic Point** at
Vigatans, 5, with another, also in
the Old Town, **Center-Rambles**,
at Hospital, 63 (just off La Rambla). Both offer internet access
and security lockers, and can
arrange bike hire and other activities. For other youth hostels in the
city visit www.youth-hostels-in.
com/barcelona.

Telecommunications

Telephone booths are well distributed throughout the city, and are
easy to use and efficient, especially for international calls. Public
telephones take all euro coins
and most accept credit cards. The
minimum charge for a local call is
20 *centimos*. Telephone cards are
available in *estancs* (tobacconists) and post offices. International reverse-charge (call-collect)
calls cannot be made from a
phone box.

There are also privately run
exchanges *(locutoris)*, located
mainly in the Old Town, where you
talk first and pay afterwards.
These are useful for making international calls, or if you are planning on having a long
conversation.

Principal walk-in telephone
exchanges are situated in Sants
railway station and Barcelona
Nord bus station (see page 245).
US access codes are as follows:
AT&T: 900-99 0011
MCI: 900-99 0014
Sprint: 900-99 0013

Useful Numbers

Information: 1004
Directory enquiries: 11818
International directory enquiries:
11825
International operator: 11822
International code: 00
Australia: 61
Canada: 1
Ireland: 353
United Kingdom: 44
United States: 1

The Internet

There are plenty of internet cafés,
and lounges or cafés with Wi-fi in
the city, and many of the *locutori*
(telephone exchanges) now offer
internet service. There is even
Wi-fi in some parks and other
public spaces, indicated with a
blue sign. A couple of options are:

Sports Bar
La Rambla, 31
Bornet
Barra de Ferro, 3
A smaller, attractive option in the
Born.

Time Zone

Spain is one hour ahead of GMT
in winter, two hours in summer
(when UK clocks are also
advanced by an hour for summer
time, so the time difference is still
only one hour), and six hours
ahead of Eastern Seaboard Time.

Tour Operators and Travel Agents

There are plenty of travel agents
in the centre, though many are
going out of business. El Corte
Inglés offers a good service in its
Plaça de Catalunya branch.
Viajes Ecuador
Pau Claris, 75
Tel: 93-301 3966
To find a long list of tour agencies operating from the UK, a
helpful website is www.abta.com/
destinations/barcelona.

Tourist Information

For general tourist information
about the city, call 010.

Information Offices

The main tourist offices are listed
below. In addition, there are stands
in La Rambla, Plaça d'Espanya,
Colon and Barceloneta. Tourist
cards can be bought at all of these.

Barcelona
Plaça de Catalunya
The main city tourist information
centre. Well-equipped and good
for hotel and theatre bookings.
Tel: 93-285 3834
Open daily 9am–9pm
El Prat Airport
In both terminals
Tel: 93-478 4704
Open daily 9am–9pm
City Hall
Plaça Sant Jaume
Open Mon–Fri 8.30am–8pm, Sat

9am–7pm, Sun and public holidays 9am–2pm

Sants Station
Open summer daily 8am–8pm, winter Mon–Fri 8am–8pm, weekends/holidays 8am–2pm

Catalonia
Tourist Information Centre for Catalonia
Palau Robert
Passeig de Gràcia, 107
Tel: 93-238 8091/92/93
www.gencat.net/probert
Mon–Sat 10am–7pm, Sun and public holidays 10am–2.30pm
Information on the rest of Catalonia is available here, along with reading rooms and internet connections, a garden and gift shop.

Alternatively you can phone on 012 or 902-400 012. For information on the area around Barcelona, visit www.diba.cat/turisme.

Tourist Offices Abroad

If you would like information about Barcelona before leaving home, contact your nearest Spanish Tourist Office:

Canada
2 Bloor Street West, 34th Floor, Toronto, Ontario M4W 3E2
Tel: 416-961 3131

UK
6th floor, 64 North Row, London W1K 7DE
Tel: 020 7317 2011 (to book a visit) or 00 800 1010 5050 (freephone for information)
Email: info.londres@tourspain.es

MACBA is a major tourist attraction.

www.spain.info
Note that this office is not open to the public except by appointment.

US
666 Fifth Avenue, 35th floor, New York, NY 10103
Tel: 212-265 8822

V

Visas and Passports

Passports are required for people of all nationalities entering Spain. Carry a photocopy of the identification page for everyday use so that the original document can be left for safety in a secure place (such as a hotel safe). If your passport is lost or stolen, you should report the fact immediately to the police (Mossos d'Esquadra; see page 270).

Visas are needed by non-EU nationals, unless their country has a reciprocal arrangement with Spain.

Travelling with pets. There are no quarantine regulations in Spain, but you will need a pet passport before you take your own animal into the country; the regulations vary according to its country of origin. The requirements are quite complex, so make sure you organise this well in advance of your trip. In the UK visit the websites www.direct.gov.

uk or www.defra.gov.uk for detailed information.

Once in Spain, animals are not permitted in restaurants, cafés and food shops. If you are travelling with a pet, check with your hotel before departure that pets are allowed. On-the-spot fines can be given for not carrying an animal's papers, or not having it on a lead.

W

Websites

A few useful sites are:
Barcelona on the web:
www.barcelonaturisme.cat
www.bcn.cat
www.barcelona-metropolitan.com
www.forfree.cat – a brilliant website that issues information daily on what's on that is free.
Catalonia on the web:
www.gencat.cat
www.gencat.net/turistex
Spain on the web:
www.spaintour.com
www.spain.info

Weights and Measures

Spain follows the metric system. As an approximate guide, 1 kilometre is five-eighths of a mile, 1 metre is roughly 3 feet/1 yard, 1 kilogram is just over 2lbs, 1 litre is just under 2 pints, or one-fifth of a gallon, and 1 hectare is around 2.5 acres.

In many of the larger stores and international chains, labels on clothing show European, UK and US sizes.

Women Travellers

A good source of information on issues that are of particular interest to women is the **Libreria Pròleg**, Sant Pere Més Alt, 46. This is the city's specialist bookshop for feminist subjects and women writers. It is also an exhibition space and occasionally holds talks.

TRANSPORT · ACCOMMODATION · ACTIVITIES · A – Z · LANGUAGE

LANGUAGE

UNDERSTANDING THE LANGUAGE

Catalan

Castilian (Spanish) and Catalan are both official languages in Catalonia. In the wake of the repression of Catalan language and culture under Franco, when its use in public was forbidden, it underwent a resurgence, encouraged by the administration, with the aim of fully implementing it in every aspect of daily life. It is often the only language used in public signs, street names, maps, leaflets and cultural information.

Catalan is a Romance language; with a knowledge of French and Spanish you should find it possible to read a little.

In the rural regions outside Barcelona you may come across people who cannot speak Castilian, but in the city even the most ardent Catalanista should respond if you communicate in Castilian, knowing you are a foreigner. Also, many people who live in the city will be from other parts of Spain and so will be primarily Castilian-speakers.

However, any attempt to speak the simplest phrases in Catalan will be rewarded with appreciation, as it shows you are recognising it as the language of their region.

English is widely spoken in most tourist areas, but even if you speak no Spanish or Catalan at all, it is worth trying to master a few simple words and phrases.

Spanish

Spanish is also a Romance language, derived from the Latin spoken by the Romans who conquered the Iberian peninsula more than 2,000 years ago. Following the discovery of America, Spaniards took their language with them to the four corners of the globe. Today, Spanish is spoken by 495 million people in North, South and Central America and parts of Africa.

Spanish is a phonetic language: words are pronounced as they are spelt, which is why it is somewhat harder for Spaniards to learn English than vice versa (although Spanish distinguishes between the two genders, masculine and feminine, and the subjunctive is an endless source of headaches).

As a general rule, the accent falls on the last syllable, unless it is otherwise marked with an accent (´) or the word ends in s, n or a vowel.

Vowels in Spanish are always pronounced the same way. The double ll is pronounced like the y in 'yes', the double rr is rolled. The h is silent in Spanish, whereas j (and g when it precedes an e or i) is pronounced like a guttural h (as if you were clearing your throat).

Spanish Words and Phrases

Although it is worth trying to speak Catalan first, if you have a knowledge of Castilian it will be totally acceptable, and better than English. Here are some useful expressions:

Yes *Sí*
No *No*
Please *Por favor*
Thank you (very much) *(muchas) gracias*
You're welcome *de nada*
Excuse me *perdóneme*
OK *bién/vale*
Hello *Hola*
How are you? *¿Cómo está usted?*
How much is it? *¿Cuánto es?*
What is your name? *¿Cómo se llama usted?*
My name is ... *Me llamo ...*
Do you speak English? *¿Habla inglés?*
I am British/American *Soy británico(a)/norteamericano(a) (a – for women)*
I don't understand *No entiendo*
Please speak more slowly *Hable más despacio, por favor*
Can you help me? *¿Me puede ayudar?*

I am looking for ... *Estoy buscando ...*
Where is ...? *¿Dónde está ...?*
I'm sorry *Lo siento*
I don't know *No lo sé*
No problem *No hay problema*
Have a good day *Que tenga un buen día*
That's it *Así es*
Here it is *Aquí está*
There it is *Allí está*
Let's go *Vámonos*
See you tomorrow *Hasta mañana*
See you soon *Hasta pronto*
goodbye *adiós*
Show me the word in the book *Muéstreme la palabra en el libro*
At what time? *¿A qué hora?*
When? *¿Cuándo?*
What time is it? *¿Qué hora es?*

Catalan

Good morning *Bon dia*
Good afternoon/evening *Bona tarda*
Good night *Bona nit*
How are you? *Com està vostè?*
Very well thank you, and you? *Molt bé gràcies, i vostè?*
Goodbye, see you again *Adéu, a reveure*
See you later *Fins després*
See you tomorrow *Fins demà*
What's your name? *Com es diu?*
My name is ... *Em dic ...*
Pleased to meet you *Molt de gust*
Where is...? *On és...?*
I'm sorry *Ho sento*
I don't know *No ho sé*
When? *Quan?*
What time is it? *Quina hora és?*
Left *esquerra*
Right *dreta*
Straight on *tot recte*
Opposite *al davant*
Do you have any rooms? *Tenen habitacions lliures si us plau?*
I'd like an external/internal/double room *Voldria una habitació exterior/interior/doble*
... for one/two persons ... *per a una persona/dues persones*

I want a room with a bath *Vull una habitació amb bany*
I have a room reserved in the name of ... *Tinc reservada una habitació a nom de ...*
How much is it? *Quin és el preu?*
It's expensive *És car*
Could I see the room? *Podria veure l'habitació?*
How do you say that in Catalan? *Com es diu això en català?*
Speak a little more slowly, please *Parleu una mica més lent, si us plau*
How do I get to ...? *Per a anar a ...?*
Is it very far/close? *Es lluny/a prop?*
Where's the nearest mechanic? *On és el pròxim taller de reparació?*
Can I change this traveller's cheque? *Pot canviar-me aquest xec de viatge?*
Where can I find a dentist? *On puc trobar un dentista?*
This tooth is hurting *Em fa mal aquesta dent*
Don't take it out. If possible give me something for it until I get home *No me'l extregui. Si és possible doni'm un remei fins que torni a casa*
Please call a doctor *Truqui un metge, si us plau*
Where does it hurt? *On li fa mal?*
I have a bad cold *Estic molt refredat*
I want to make a phone call to ... *Vull trucar a ...*
It's engaged *La línea està ocupada*
I am ... I'd like to speak to Mr ... *Sóc ... voldria parlar amb el senyor ...*
What time will he be back? *A quina hora tornarà?*
Tell him to call me at this number *Digui-li que truqui al número ...*
I'll be in town until Saturday *Seré a la ciutat fins dissabte*

Eating Out

Breakfast/lunch/dinner *Esmorzar/dinar/sopar*

At what time do you serve breakfast? *A quina hora es pot esmorzar?*
Set menu *El menu*
Menu *La carta*
We'd like a table for four *Una taula per a quatre si us plau*
First course *Primer plat*
May we have some water? *Porti'ns aigua mineral*
red wine/white wine? *vi negre/vi blanc*
The bill, please *El compte, si us plau*

Some Typical Dishes

Albergínies fregides *Fried aubergines (eggplant)*
Amanida *Salad*
Amanida catalana *Salad with hard-boiled egg and cold meats*
Arròs a la marinera *Seafood paella*
Arròs negre *Rice cooked in squid ink*
Carxofes *Artichokes*
Canelons *Cannelloni*
Escalivada *Salad of roasted aubergines/peppers*
Escudella *Thick soup with meat, vegetables and noodles*
Espinacs a la catalana *Spinach with garlic, pine nuts and raisins*
Esqueixada *Salt-cod salad*
Faves a la catalana *Broad beans stewed with sausage*
Bacallà a la llauna *Salt cod baked in the oven*
Botifarra amb mongetes *Sausage with haricot beans*
Estofat de conill *Rabbit stew*
de vedella *Veal stew*
de xai *Lamb stew*
Fricandó *Braised veal*
Gambes a la planxa *Grilled prawns*
Pollastre al ajillo *Chicken fried with garlic*
Sipia amb mandonguilles *Cuttlefish with meatballs*
Suquet de peix *Rich fish stew*
Postres *Desserts*
Crema catalana *Custard with caramelised topping*
Formatge *Cheese*
Gelat *Ice cream*
Pastís de poma *Apple tart*
Postre de músics *Mixed nuts and dried fruits*

FURTHER READING

Good Companions

English translations of Catalan works of literature are few, and are difficult to find in Barcelona.

The Angel's Game, by Carlos Ruiz Zafón. Set in 1920s Barcelona, this thriller will please Zafón's many fans.

Barcelona, by Robert Hughes. Describes the city's development in relation to the rest of Catalonia, Spain and Europe. Good on Gaudí and modernisme.

Barcelona: A Guide to Recent Architecture, by Suzanna Strum. A look at some of the city's stunning buildings.

Barcelona the Great Enchantress, by Robert Hughes. A shorter version of his earlier work (see above); particularly good on architecture.

Barcelonas, by Manuel Vázquez Montalbán. Chatty book covering culture, design, history and some of the city's personalities.

Catalan Cuisine, by Colman Andrews. Describes the unique aspects of Catalan cooking; good recipes.

The Cathedral of the Sea, by Ildefonso Falcones. A novel woven around the construction of Santa Maria del Mar in medieval Barcelona.

The City of Marvels (La Ciudad de los Prodigios), by Eduardo Mendoza. Novel about an unscrupulous young man determined to succeed in Barcelona.

Forbidden Territory, by Juan Goytisolo. Autobiography by one of Spain's most important writers.

Gaudí: A Biography, by Gijs van Hensbergen. For anyone who wants to delve deeper into the life of Barcelona's extraordinary architect, written by a Gaudí expert.

Homage to Barcelona, by Colm Toíbìn. An interesting, personal view from this Irish novelist who once lived in Barcelona.

Homage to Catalonia, by George Orwell. Famous account of the author's experiences in the Spanish Civil War.

No Word from Gurb, by Eduardo Mendoza. Entertaining novel by one of Spain's best contemporary writers about an extraterrestrial who has disappeared in the backstreets of Barcelona.

Saving Picasso, by Mark Skeet. A pacey spy novel set in a fictional 1940s Barcelona where the Communists won the Civil War and Franco is dead.

The Shadow of the Wind, by Carlos Ruiz Zafón; translation by Lucia Graves. Read the novel set in Barcelona then discover its places in a walking tour.

The Time of the Doves, by Mercè Rodoreda. Translation of the classic Catalan novel La Plaça del Diamant set in the Spanish Civil War. Visit the eponymous square in Gràcia where the novel took place.

Teach Yourself Catalan, Hodder Arnold. Classic series of language learning books.

Other Insight Guides

The Insight Guides series includes several books on Spain and its islands, all combining the exciting pictures and incisive text associated with this series.

Insight Guides

Insight Guide: Spain contains top photography and complete background reading. The smaller format *Insight Regional Guide: Southern Spain* provides comprehensive coverage of the Costa del Sol and Andalucía, from the white towns of the sierras to vibrant Seville.

Insight Fleximaps

Insight Fleximap: Barcelona is a durable laminated map, with a list of recommended sights.

Insight Guides: Explore

Barcelona is one of the titles in Insight's brand new Explore series. These books provide a series of themed and timed routes, with recommended stops for lunch. The routes are plotted on an accompanying pull-out map.

BARCELONA STREET ATLAS

The key map shows the area of Barcelona covered by the
atlas section. An index of street names and places of interest
shown on the maps can be found on the following pages.
For each entry there is a page number and grid reference

Map Legend

▭═▭	Autopista with Junction
‑‑‑‑	Autopista (under construction)
═══	Dual Carriageway
═══	Main Road
═══	Secondary Road
═══	Minor Road
───	Track
▬ ▪▪	International Boundary
‑ ‑ ‑	Province Boundary
•───•	National Park/Reserve
✚ ✦	Airport
✝ ✝ ✝	Church (ruins)/ Monastery
⌂ ⌂	Castle (ruins)
∴	Archaeological Site
∩	Cave
★	Place of Interest
🏛	Mansion/Stately Home
☀	Viewpoint
⚑	Beach
══	Autopista
══	Dual Carriageway
══ }	Main Roads
── }	Minor Roads
────	Footpath
▬ ▬	Railway
▭	Pedestrian Area
▭	Important Building
▭	Park
Ⓜ	Metro
renfe	RENFE
▨	Tram
▨	Funicular
🚌	Bus Station
❶	Tourist Information
✉	Post Office
✝	Cathedral/Church
☾	Mosque
✡	Synagogue
⚲	Statue/Monument
⚱	Tower

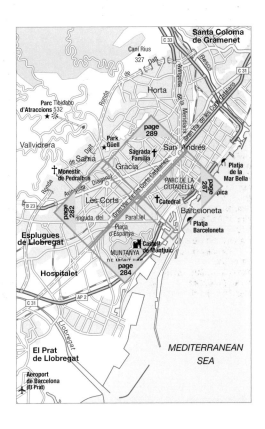

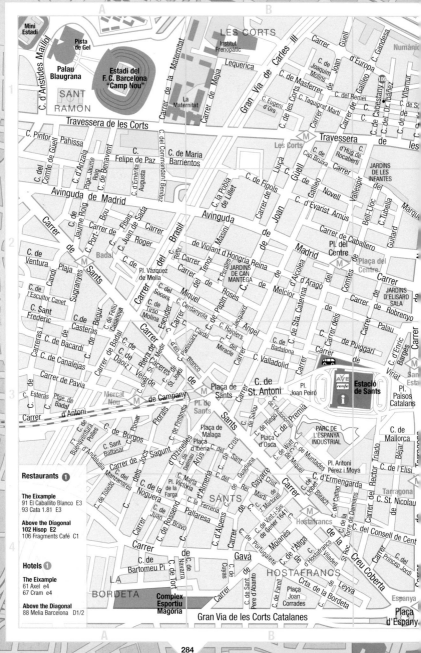

Mini
Estadi

Pista
de Gel

Palau
Blaugrana

Estadi del
F. C. Barcelona
"Camp Nou"

SANT
RAMON

LES CORTS

Institut
Frenopàtic

Travessera de les Corts

La
Maternitat

C. Pintor Pahissa

Avinguda de Madrid

Avinguda de Madrid

C. de Maria
Barrientos

Travessera

Les Corts

JARDINS
DE LES
INFANTES

Avinguda

de

Madrid

Pl. del
Centre

Plaça del
Centre

JARDINS
D'ELISARD
SALA

Carrer de Caballero

JARDINS
DE CAN
MANTEGA

Pl. Vázquez
de Mella

Mercat
Nou

Plaça de
Sants

Pl.
de
Sants

C. de
St. Antoni

Pl.
Joan Peiró

AVE
renfe

Estació
de Sants

Pl.
Països
Catalans

PARC DE
L'ESPANYA
INDUSTRIAL

Plaça de
Malaga

Plaça
d'Osca

Pl. Antoni
Pérez i Moya

C. de
Mallorca

C. de l'Elisi

SANTS

Hostafrancs

Tarragona

C. St. Nicolau

Plaça
de la
Farga

HOSTAFRANCS

Complex
Esportiu
Magòria

LA
BORDETA

Plaça
Joan
Corrades

Espanya

Plaça
d'Espanya

Gran Via de les Corts Catalanes

Restaurants ❶

The Eixample
91 El Caballito Blanco E3
93 Cata 1.81 E3

Above the Diagonal
102 Hisop E2
106 Fragments Café C1

Hotels ❶

The Eixample
61 Axel e4
67 Cram e4

Above the Diagonal
88 Melia Barcelona D1/2

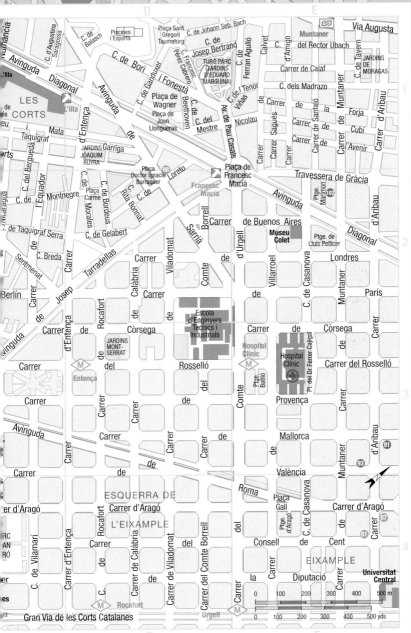

282

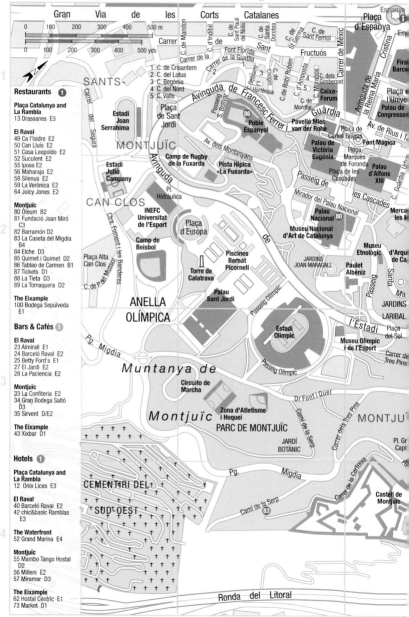

Gran Via de les Corts Catalanes

SANTS-

Restaurants ❶

**Plaça Catalunya and
La Rambla**
13 Drassanes E3

El Raval
49 Ca l'Isidre E2
50 Can Lluís E2
51 Casa Leopoldo E2
52 Suculent E2
55 Iposa E2
56 Maharaja E2
58 Silenus E2
59 La Verònica E2
64 Juicy Jones E2

Montjuïc
80 Oleum B2
81 Fundació Joan Miró
   C3
82 Barramón D2
83 La Caseta del Migdia
   B4
84 Elche D3
85 Quimet i Quimet D2
86 Tablao de Carmen B1
87 Tickets D1
88 La Tieta D3
89 La Tomaquera D2

The Eixample
100 Bodega Sepúlveda
    E1

Bars & Cafés ❶

El Raval
23 Almirall E1
24 Barceló Raval E2
25 Betty Ford's E1
27 El Jardí E2
28 La Paciencia E2

Montjuïc
33 La Confiteria E2
34 Gran Bodega Saltó
   D3
35 Sirvent D/E2

The Eixample
43 Xixbar D1

Hotels ❶

**Plaça Catalunya and
La Rambla**
12 Onix Lices E3

El Raval
40 Barceló Raval E2
42 chic&basic Ramblas
   E3

The Waterfront
52 Grand Marina E4

Montjuïc
55 Mambo Tango Hostal
   D2
56 Milleni E2
57 Miramar D3

The Eixample
62 Hostal Cèntric E1
73 Market D1

MONTJUÏC

CAN CLOS

Plaça Alta
Can Clos

ANELLA
OLÍMPICA

Montjuïc

Muntanya de

Montjuïc

PARC DE MONTJUÏC

CEMENTIRI DEL

SUD-OEST

Ronda del Litoral

Plaça
d'Espanya

1 C. de Crisantem
2 C. del Lotus
3 C. Begònia
4 C. del Nord
5 C. Valls

Estadi
Joan
Serrahima

Plaça
de Sant
Jordi

Avinguda de Francesc Ferrer i

Poble
Espanyol

Pavelló Mies
van der Rohe

Camp de Rugby
de la Fuxarda

Palau de
Victòria
Eugènia

Pista Hípica
«La Fuxarda»

Estadi
Julià
Campany

Pl.
Hidraulica

INEFC
Universitat
de l'Esport

Plaça
d'Europa

Camp de
Beisbol

Torre de
Calatrava

Piscines
Bernat
Picornell

Palau
Sant Jordi

Estadi
Olímpic

Circuito de
Marcha

Zona d'Atletisme
i Hoquei

JARDÍ
BOTÀNIC

Caixa-
Forum

Palau
Nacional

Museu Nacional
d'Art de Catalunya

JARDINS
JOAN MARAGALL

Paulet
Albèniz

Museu Olímpic
i de l'Esport

Dr Font i Quer

Camí de la Serp

Pg. Migdia

Castell de
Montjuïc

Av dels Montanyans

Guàrdia

Font Màgica

Palau
d'Alfons
XIII

les Cascades

Mirador del Palau Nacional

Museu
Etnològic

d'Arqu
de Ca

JARDINS

LARIBAL

l'Estadi

Passeig

Santa

Ma

MONTJU

Pl. Gr
Capi

86

80

83

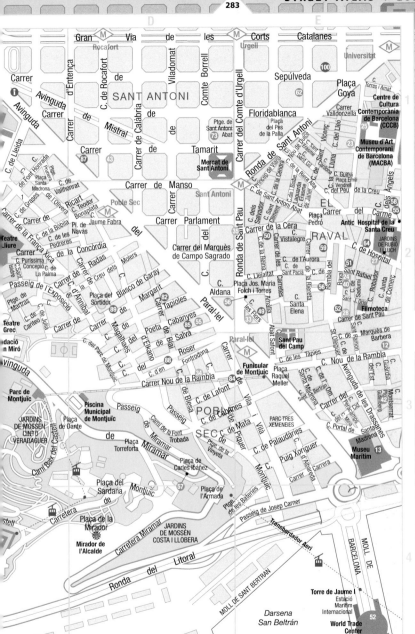

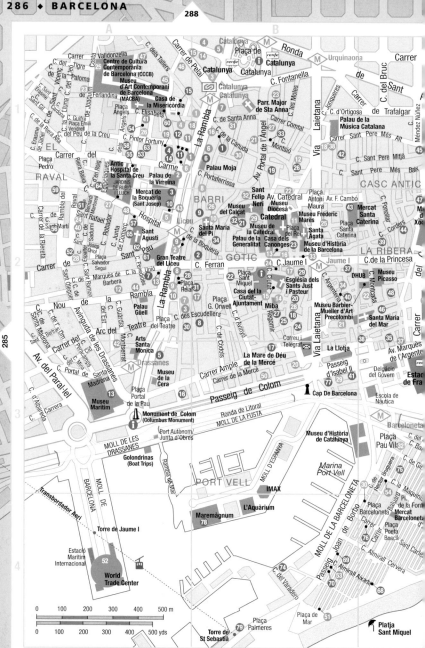

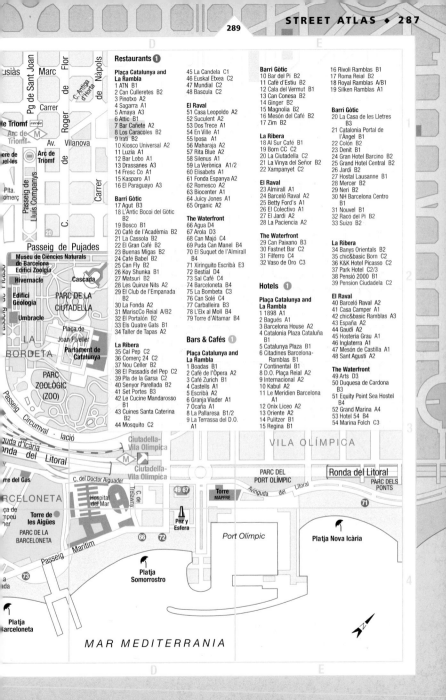

Restaurants ❶

Plaça Catalunya and La Rambla
1 ATN B1
3 Pinotxo A2
4 Sagarra A1
5 Amaya A3
6 Attic B1
7 Bar Cañete A2
8 Los Caracoles B2
9 Irati A2
10 Kiosco Universal A2
11 Luzia A1
12 Bar Lobo A1
13 Drassanes A3
14 Fresc Co A1
15 Kasparo A1
16 El Paraguayo A3

Barri Gòtic
17 Agut B3
18 L'Antic Bocoi del Gòtic B2
19 Bosco B1
20 Cafè de l'Acadèmia B2
21 La Cassola B2
22 El Gran Café B2
23 Buenas Migas B2
24 Café Babel B2
25 Can Fly B2
26 Koy Shunka B1
27 Matsuri B2
28 Les Quinze Nits A2
29 El Club de l'Empanada B2
30 La Fonda A2
31 MariscCo Reial A/B2
32 El Portalón B2
33 Els Quatre Gats B1
34 Taller de Tapas A2

La Ribera
35 Cal Pep C2
36 Comerç 24 C2
37 Nou Celler B2
38 El Passadis del Pep C2
39 Pla de la Garsa C2
40 Senyor Parellada B2
41 Set Portes B3
42 Le Cucine Mandarosso B1
43 Cuines Santa Caterina B2
44 Mosquito C2

45 La Candela C1
46 Euskal Etxea C2
47 Mundial C2
48 Bascula C2

El Raval
51 Casa Leopoldo A2
52 Suculent A2
53 Dos Trece A1
54 En Ville A1
55 Iposa A1
56 Maharaja A2
57 Rita Blue A2
58 Silenus A1
59 La Verònica A1/2
60 Elisabets A1
61 Fonda Espanya A2
62 Romesco A2
63 Biocenter A1
64 Juicy Jones A1
65 Organic A2

The Waterfront
66 Agua D4
67 Arola D3
68 Can Majó C4
69 Puda Can Manel B4
70 El Suquet de l'Almirall B4
71 Xiringuito Escribà E3
72 Bestial D4
73 Sal Café C4
74 Barceloneta B4
75 La Bombeta C3
76 Can Solé C4
77 Carballeira B3
78 L'Eix al Moll B4
79 Torre d'Altamar A4

Bars & Cafés ❶

Plaça Catalunya and La Rambla
1 Boadas B1
2 Cafè de l'Òpera A2
3 Café Zurich B1
4 Castells A2
5 Escribà A2
6 Granja Viader A1
7 Ocaña A2
8 La Pallaresa B1/2
9 La Terrassa del D.O. A1

Barri Gòtic
10 Bar del Pi B2
11 Cafè d'Estiu B2
12 Cala del Vermut B1
13 Can Conesa B2
14 Ginger B2
15 Magnolia B2
16 Mesón del Café A2
17 Zim B2

La Ribera
18 Al Sur Café A1
19 Born CC C2
20 La Ciutadella C2
21 La Vinya del Senyor B2
22 Xampanyet C2

El Raval
23 Almirall A1
24 Barceló Raval A2
25 Betty Ford's A1
26 El Colectivo A1
27 El Jardí A2
28 La Paciencia A2

The Waterfront
29 Can Paixano B3
30 Fastnet Bar C2
31 Filferro C4
32 Vaso de Oro C3

Hotels ❶

Plaça Catalunya and La Rambla
1 1898 A1
2 Bagués A1
3 Barcelona House A2
4 Catalonia Plaza Cataluña B1
5 Catalunya Plaza B1
6 Citadines Barcelona-Ramblas B1
7 Continental B1
8 D.O. Plaça Reial A2
9 Internacional A2
10 Kabul A2
11 Le Meridien Barcelona A1
12 Onix Liceo A2
13 Oriente A2
14 Pulitzer B1
15 Regina B1

16 Rivoli Ramblas B1
17 Roma Reial B2
18 Royal Ramblas A/B1
19 Silken Ramblas A1

Barri Gòtic
20 La Casa de les Lletres B3
21 Catalonia Portal de l'Àngel B1
22 Colón B2
23 Denit B1
24 Gran Hotel Barcino B2
25 Grand Hotel Central B2
26 Jardí B2
27 Hostal Lausanne B1
28 Mercer B2
29 Neri B2
30 NH Barcelona Centro B1
31 Nouvel B1
32 Racó del Pi B2
33 Suizo B2

La Ribera
34 Banys Orientals B2
35 chic&basic Born C2
36 K&K Hotel Picasso C2
37 Park Hotel C2/3
38 Pensió 2000 B1
39 Pension Ciudadela C2

El Raval
40 Barceló Raval A2
41 Casa Camper A1
42 chic&basic Ramblas A3
43 España A2
44 Gaudí A2
45 Hosteria Grau A1
46 Inglaterra A1
47 Mesón de Castilla A1
48 Sant Agustí A2

The Waterfront
49 Arts D3
50 Duquesa de Cardona B3
51 Equity Point Sea Hostel B4
52 Grand Marina A4
53 Hotel 54 B4
54 Marina Folch C3

Passeig de Pujades

Museu de Ciències Naturals de Barcelona
Edifici Zoologia
Hivernacle
Cascada
Edifici Geologia
Umbracle
PARC DE LA CIUTADELLA

Plaça de Joan Fiveller
Parlament de Catalunya

LA BORDETA

PARC ZOOLÒGIC (ZOO)

Passeig de Lluís Companys

Pg. de Sant Joan
Marc
Flor
C. Antiga d'Horta
de Napols
Carrer
de
Roger
de
Vilanova
Carrer
Av.
Arc de Triomf
rusiàs
M
renfe
Arc de Triomf
el·les
Plta. omerç
C.

Passeig Circumval·lació

uda d'Icària
onda del Litoral

CELONETA
mpeu
her
Torre de les Aigües
ça de
PARC DE LA BARCELONETA

Platja Barceloneta
Platja Somorrostro

C. del Doctor Aiguader
C. de Trelawny
Hospital del Mar

Ciutadella-Vila Olímpica
M
Ciutadella-Vila Olímpica

VILA OLÍMPICA

PARC DEL PORT OLÍMPIC

Ronda del Litoral
Avinguda del Litoral
PARC DELS PONTS

49 67
Torre MAPFRE
66 72
73
71

Pez y Esfera

Port Olímpic

Platja Nova Icària

MAR MEDITERRANIA

D
E
1
4

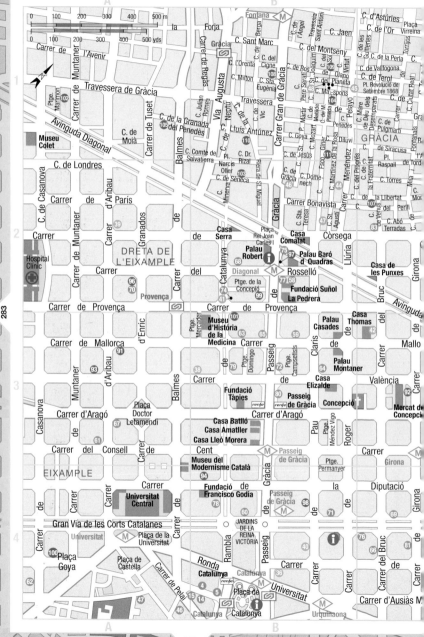

Restaurants ❶

The Eixample
90 Alkimia D2
91 El Caballito Blanco A3
92 Casa Amalia C3
93 Cata 1.81 A3
94 Fastvinic B4
95 Ferrum C2
96 Ponsa A2
97 Roca Moo B2
98 Au Port de la Lune B4
99 Tragaluz B2
101 La Bodegueta B3

Above the Diagonal
102 Hisop A1
103 Roig Robí B2
104 Amir de Nit B1
105 Flash-Flash A1
107 Bilbao C2
108 Botafumeiro B1
109 Envalira B1
110 Roure B1
111 La Singular B1

The Eixample
100 Bodega Sepúlveda E1

Bars & Cafés ❶

The Eixample
36 Bracafé B4
37 Café Adonis C2
38 Cornelia & Co B3
39 Dry Martini A2
40 Laie Libreria Café B4
41 Mauri B2
42 Primavera Café C3

Above the Diagonal
44 L'Astrolabi B1
45 Café del Sol B1
46 Café Vienés B2
47 La Cervesera Artesana B2
48 Sol Soler B1

Hotels ❶

Plaça Catalunya and La Rambla
4 Catalonia Plaza Cataluña B4
5 Catalunya Plaza B4
14 Pulitzer B4
15 Regina B4

El Raval
46 Inglaterra A4
47 Mesón de Castilla A4

The Eixample
58 Actual B2
59 Alma B3
60 Avenida Palace B4
61 Axel A1
62 Hostal Cèntric A4
63 Hostal Ciudad Condal B3
64 Claris B3
65 Condes de Barcelona B3
66 Constanza C4
67 Cram A3
68 Gallery B2
69 Gran Hotel Havana C4
70 Granados 83 A2
71 Indigo B2
72 Majestic B3
74 Murmuri B2
75 Omm B2
76 Palace C4
77 Paseo de Gràcia B2
78 Praktik Rambla B2
79 Regente B3
80 Sixty Two B3
81 Violeta Hostel C4

Above the Diagonal
82 Casa Dover C2
83 Generator C2

STREET INDEX

ART AND PHOTO CREDITS

Aisa 39
akg-images 32
Alamy 115, 183T
Arts Santa Mònica 102T
Bigstock 6B, 10T, 28TL, 52T, 54T, 54/55M, 54/55T, 111, 180, 204T, 204/205T
Carolina García y Eduardo Armentia/Fundació Suñol 199TL
Centre de Cultura Contemporània de Barcelona 145T
Corbis 43
Corrie Wingate/Apa Publications 4/5, 6ML, 6MR, 7MR, 7MR, 6/7T, 7B, 7TR, 8B, 8T, 9BR, 9TR, 8/9M, 10B, 12/13, 14/15, 16, 18, 19, 20, 20/21, 22B, 22T, 22/23T, 23B, 24, 24/25, 28ML, 44/45, 46, 48/49, 50/51B, 55TC, 56/57T, 58, 59, 61R, 60/61, 62, 68/69T, 72B, 80/81, 82/83, 84, 85T, 84/85B, 89, 90, 90/91, 92T, 92B, 92/93B, 97B, 98, 100, 100/101, 102B, 103T, 102/103B, 104, 108, 109, 112, 112/113, 114T, 114B, 116, 117, 118T, 118B, 118/119, 124, 125, 126/127T, 127B, 130, 132B, 132/133, 134B, 134/135, 136T, 140, 141, 142T, 142B, 143, 144B, 144T, 144/145B, 150, 151, 154T, 155, 156B, 156T, 156/157T, 157B, 158, 159T, 158/159B, 160, 161B, 161T, 162, 162/163B, 164/165, 166, 168, 170T, 171BR, 170/171T, 175T, 178T, 184ML, 184BR, 184/185, 186T, 191, 192, 194B, 194TL, 194/195, 196, 196/197, 198L, 199T, 204B, 204/205M, 205TC, 206, 207, 209B, 212, 214,

215B, 216/217, 219, 220T, 220B, 220/221B, 222/223, 224, 225, 226/227B, 228B, 228T, 228/229T, 234T, 234B, 235, 236T, 236/237, 238, 242, 244, 247, 259, 265, 266, 271, 273, 275, 277, 278
CosmoCaixa 215T
David Ruano/El Molino 186B
Dreamstime 26R, 26L, 26/27T, 26/27B, 30/31B, 36, 69BR, 196/197, 240/241T
Fotolia 1, 6/7B, 121B, 131, 205BR, 232/233B
Fototeca9x12 188/189, 216
Getty Images 31T, 34, 37B, 37T, 40, 44, 188T, 241BL
Grand Hotel Central 251
Greg Gladman/Apa Publications 51T, 53, 62/63, 68ML, 70, 72/73, 78/79, 94B, 94/95B, 98/99B, 126, 138, 139, 146, 146/147B, 147T, 149, 168/169, 170B, 193, 213TR, 213BR, 212/213T, 218, 261, 262, 264, 268
Gregory Wrona/Apa Publications 6/7M, 11T, 10/11B, 17T, 16/17B, 27BR, 27TC, 33, 47, 48B, 48T, 50, 55BR, 56TL, 56MR, 56BL, 57MR, 56/57M, 57TR, 60, 64, 66R, 66L, 66/67M, 67BR, 66/67T, 67TC, 66/67B, 68BR, 68MR, 69TR, 72T, 74R, 74/75, 76, 76/77T, 77B, 78, 93T, 94T, 95T, 99T, 106, 120, 120/121T, 128/129, 132T, 134T, 136B, 152, 153T, 154B, 163T, 170/171M, 170/171B, 172, 174, 176B, 178B, 179T, 178/179B, 182, 184TL, 188B, 194TR, 199B, 200, 208/209T, 210T, 210B,

210/211, 221BR, 221TR, 227T, 228/229B, 230T, 230/231T, 231B, 232T, 236B, 240B, 246, 269, 272, 274
Hisop 74L
Hotel Omm 256
iStockphoto 26/27M, 54B, 54/55B, 88, 97T, 110, 152/153B, 174/175B, 180/181, 220/221T, 245, 280
Leonardo 257
Majestic Hotel & Spa 249
Mary Evans Picture Library 41, 96, 241TR
Meliá Hotels International 52B
Ming Tang-Evans/Apa Publications 68/69M
MNAC 189ML, 189BL, 189TR
Museu Blau 169R
North Wind Picture Archives 35
Núñez i Navarro Hotels 250
Olga Planas/Grupo Tragaluz 65, 71, 202
Palau Sant Jordi 183B
Poble Espanyol 173, 176T, 177B, 177T
PortAventura 267
Public domain 28TR, 29, 30T, 30B, 38, 42T, 42B
Ronald Stallard/Museu Picasso 128
Scala Archives 241BR
Starwood Hotels & Resorts 171TR
SuperStock 190
The Art Archive 201, 240T
Vinseum 230B

Cover Credits

Front cover: Casa Batllo, *Getty Images*
Back cover: (top) Parc Guell, *Corrie Wingate/Apa Publications*; (middle) Living statues, La Ramblas *Corrie*

Wingate/Apa Publications; Torre Agbar, *Corrie Wingate/Apa Publications*
Front flap: (from top) Torre Marenostrum; Boat lake, Parc de la

Ciutadella ; La Pedrera chimney; Platja Nova beaches, *All Corrie Wingate/Apa.*
Spine: Palau Guell rooftop chimney *Corrie Wingate/Apa Publications*

INDEX

RESTAURANTS

BARS AND CAFÉS

INSIGHT GUIDES

BARCELONA

Project Editor
Sarah Clark
Series Manager
Tom Stainer
Art Editor
Ian Spick
Map Production
**original cartography Berndtson
& Berndtson, updated by Apa
Cartography Department**
Production
Tynan Dean and Rebeka Davies

Distribution
UK
Dorling Kindersley Ltd
A Penguin Group company
80 Strand, London, WC2R 0RL
sales@uk.dk.com

United States
Ingram Publisher Services
1 Ingram Boulevard, PO Box 3006,
La Vergne, TN 37086-1986
ips@ingramcontent.com

Australia
Universal Publishers
PO Box 307
St Leonards NSW 1590
sales@universalpublishers.com.au

New Zealand
Brown Knows Publications
11 Artesia Close, Shamrock Park
Auckland, New Zealand 2016
sales@brownknows.co.nz

Worldwide
**Apa Publications GmbH & Co.
Verlag KG (Singapore branch)**
7030 Ang Mo Kio Avenue 5
08-65 Northstar @ AMK
Singapore 569880
apasin@singnet.com.sg

Printing
CTPS-China

© 2014 Apa Publications (UK) Ltd
All Rights Reserved

First Edition 1990
Eighth Edition 2014

ABOUT THIS BOOK

What makes an Insight Guide different? Since our first book pioneered the use of creative full-colour photography in travel guides in 1970, we have aimed to provide not only reliable information but also the key to a real understanding of a destination and its people. To achieve this, our books rely on the authority of locally based writers and photographers.

This book turns the spotlight on a city that is forever reinventing itself. The heart and legs of Catalonia, Spain's leading economic region, Barcelona is one of Europe's most vibrant cities with a huge amount to offer visitors.

The contributors

This eighth edition of *City Guide: Barcelona* was commissioned by City Guides series editor **Tom Stainer** and managed by Senior Commissioning Editor **Sarah Clark**. It has been thoroughly updated by **Judy Thomson**, a writer and translator living just off La Rambla, Barcelona's most famous thoroughfare. A long-time contributor to Insight Guides, Thomson built on work she did on previous editions of the book, including writing the photo features on festivals, shopping and the city's best beaches, as well as the features on Catalan food and wine, the city's design aesthetic and 21st Century Barcelona. Other photo features – on markets, Montserrat and Park Güell – were originally written by long-term devotee of the city **Roger Williams**.

This new edition makes use of a stunning new shoot by photographer **Corrie Wingate**, a regular contributor to Insight Guides.

This edition of *City Guide: Barcelona* draws on earlier versions edited by **Catherine Dreghorn**, **Dorothy Stannard**, **Pam Barrett** and **Andrew Eames**. Contributors included **Marcelo Aparicio**, **Xavier Martí**, George Semler, the historian **Dr Felipe Fernández-Armesto**, **Valerie Collins**, **Anne Michie** and architect **Jane Opher**.

The book was copyedited by **Kathryn Glendenning** and indexed by **Penny Phenix**.

SEND US YOUR THOUGHTS

We do our best to ensure the information in our books is as accurate and up-to-date as possible. The books are updated on a regular basis using local contacts, who painstakingly add, amend, and correct as required. However, some details (such as telephone numbers and opening times) are liable to change, and we are ultimately reliant on our readers to put us in the picture.

We welcome your feedback, especially your experience of using the book "on the road". Maybe we recommended a hotel that you liked (or another that you didn't), or you came across a great bar or new attraction that we missed.

We will acknowledge all contributions, and we'll offer an Insight Guide to the best letters received.

Please write to us at:
Insight Guides
PO Box 7910, London SE1 1WE
Or email us at:
insight@apaguide.co.uk

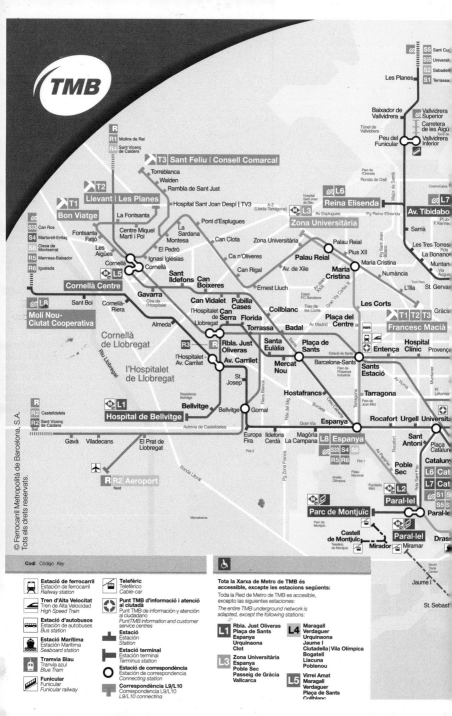